Roadside

of

CALIFORNIA

Ruth Pittman

1995
Mountain Press Publishing Company
Missoula, MT

Copyright © 1995 Ruth Pittman

Roadside History™ is a registered trademark
of Mountain Press Publishing Company

Maps by Carla Majernik

On the cover: *Yosemite Valley* by Albert Bierstadt
Yale University Art Gallery, Gift of Mrs. Vincenzo Ardenghi

Library of Congress Cataloging-in-Publication Data

Pittman, Ruth.
    Roadside history of California / Ruth Pittman.
        p.   cm.
    Includes bibliographical references (p.   ) and index.
    ISBN 0-87842-317-6 (cloth : alk. paper). — ISBN 0-87842-318-4
(pbk. : alk. paper)
    1. California—History.   2. Automobile travel—California—Guide-
books.   3. California—Guidebooks.   I. Title.
F861.P55   1995   95-2918
917.9404'53—dc20   CIP

PRINTED IN THE U.S.A.

Mountain Press Publishing Company
P.O. Box 2399 • Missoula, MT 59806
406-728-1900 • FAX 406-728-1635

*For Frank, who did most of the driving,
and our children, who took over when
he had to let go of the wheel.*

Contents

Acknowledgments

A book of this type could never be written without the help of scores of knowledgeable and patient people. This book is certainly no exception. I am indebted to many librarians, park rangers, museum curators, historical society directors, and so many others of that splendid ilk that a detailed listing of their names would fill a volume the size of a Manhattan phone directory. However, there are some whose help went beyond what any writer could expect, and to them I offer thanks.

To all employees of California's Department of Parks and Recreation: Without fail they were courteous, helpful, and enthusiastic whenever and wherever I sought their help. Some of the many who assisted me (in no particular order) include Jimmy Phillips, Gene Cone, L. Scott Pace, Joseph A. Scott, Douglas H. Meyers, Robin E. Ettinger, Ronald P. Schafer, Gail M. Shoop-Lamy, Joe Martinez, and Gudrun Baxter. It is no wonder California's park system is so splendid when it has employees such as these.

Librarians the length and breadth of the state have given me outstanding advice and help, and none more than Barbara Boyd, Special Collection Librarian of Glendale Public Library. I am also particularly grateful to Patricia Orr of the California Institute of Technology, Office of Public Relations, and to Tracey Vaughan of the Monterey Peninsula Chamber of Commerce and Visitors and Convention Bureau.

Sue Elarth of the Clear Lake Chamber of Commerce earns my special gratitude because she entrusted to me the only existing copy of a book about that exciting area. Others who contributed to making this book colorful and accurate include Bonnie G. Vistica, of the San Joaquin Convention and Visitors Bureau in Stockton; Nancy J. Weisinger, of the Hotel del Coronado; Shirley Newton, of the International Church of the Foursquare Gospel; Claudia Holloway, of the Crystal Cathedral Ministries; and Mable Carlson, Curator of the Julian Pioneer Museum.

Finally, I extend deepest thanks to members of my family—Patti, Don, Bob, Frances, Terri, Laura, and Gale—who served in a hundred ways. They drove when I was too tired, combed dusty files when my eyes gave out, took pictures, and—most of all—enthusiastically supported every phase of the creation of the *Roadside History of California*.

Chronology of California's Main Historic Events

8000 B.C. Pomos inhabit Clear Lake area

2000 B.C. Coast Miwoks live at Olompali

1542   Juan Cabrillo discovers Cape Mendocino

1579   Sir Francis Drake reaches New Albion

1584   Francisco Gali explores California coast

1595   Sebastián Cermeño explores California coast

1602   Sebastián Vizcaíno charts California coast

1734   Russians explore Alaska

1769   Expeditions set out from New Spain to colonize Alta California

1770   Monterey Bay mission and presidio sites dedicated

1772   Sacramento Delta discovered

1776   Pedro Fages and Juan Crespí see Sierra Madre; San Francisco mission and presidio founded; Pobladores reach San Gabriel

1777   San Jose founded

1781   Los Angeles founded

1812   Russians establish Fort Ross

1821   Mexico attains independence from Spain

1823   First land grant made

1824   Quicksilver found in Alameda

1826   Jedediah Smith explores California

1831   Manuel Victoria takes office as governor

1833   Joseph Walker discovers Yosemite Valley

1834   First oranges planted in Los Angeles

1836   Juan Bautista Alvarado proclaims California a free state, names himself governor

1839   John A. Sutter arrives in California

1841   Bidwell-Bartleson party arrives at Sutter's Fort; Sutter buys Fort Ross

1842   Alvarado and Mariano G. Vallejo fall out, turn government over to Manuel Micheltorena

1844   John C. Frémont discovers Lake Tahoe

1846	Bear Flag Revolt; United States declares war on Mexico; Battle at San Pasqual; Sam Brannan arrives in San Francisco; Donner Party trapped in Sierra Nevada
1847	Capitulation treaty signed at Campo de Cahuenga; Stockton takes Los Angeles; Mormon Battalion arrives in San Diego
1848	James Marshall finds gold at Sutter's mill; Treaty of Guadalupe Hidalgo ends war with Mexico
1849	Gold rush populates California; State constitution crafted in Monterey
1850	California admitted to Union; Agoston Haraszthy starts producing wine; Massacre at Bloody Island in Clear Lake; David Jacks arrives in Monterey
1851	First Committee of Vigilance formed at San Francisco
1852	San Quentin Prison opens
1856	Territory of Nataqua founded
1857	Community of Anaheim founded; Earthquakes rock Central Valley
1858	First wine produced in Napa Valley; First Butterfield stage arrives from Missouri
1859	Citadel of Alcatraz completed
1860	First Pony Express rider goes through Gold Country
1865	First producing oil well drilled on Mattole River
1867	First Folsom Dam begun on American River
1868	University of California chartered
1869	First battles of Modoc War fought; Transcontinental railroad completed
1870	Foreign miners' license tax on Chinese declared unconstitutional
1873	Modoc War ends
1874	Central Pacific Railroad built
1875	Bank of California collapses
1879	New constitution adopted in Sacramento
1880	Battle of Mussel Slough
1884	Pollution regulations make hydraulic mining illegal
1885	Santa Fe Railroad reaches Southern California; Stanford University founded
1887	Wright Irrigation Act passed
1892	Edward L. Doheny discovers oil near Los Angeles
1895	Electricity from Folsom Dam reaches Sacramento; Gold found in Rand District

1897	Sierra Railroad built
1901	Pacific Electric Railway Company formed in Los Angeles; Colorado River water reaches Imperial Valley
1905	Salton Sea formed; Yosemite named a national park
1906	Great San Francisco earthquake; First movie studio opens at L.A.
1907	Redlands University opens
1908	Owens Valley water project begins
1913	Water from Owens Valley reaches San Fernando Valley
1915	Panama-Pacific Exposition in San Diego celebrates completion of Panama Canal
1923	Elk Hills oil reserve scandal; President Harding dies at Palace Hotel
1928	Saint Francis Dam disaster
1934	General strike called by Longshoremen in San Francisco
1936	San Francisco-Oakland Bay Bridge opens to traffic
1937	Golden Gate Bridge opens; Central Valley Project started
1942	Executive Order 9066 signed
1944	Port Chicago disaster
1945	Shasta Dam completed
1963	Pacific Gas & Electric opens state's first nuclear power plant at Humboldt Bay
1965	Watts riots in Los Angeles
1978	Proposition 13 (Jarvis-Gann constitutional amendment) passes
1990	National recession reaches California
1994	Orange County declares bankruptcy

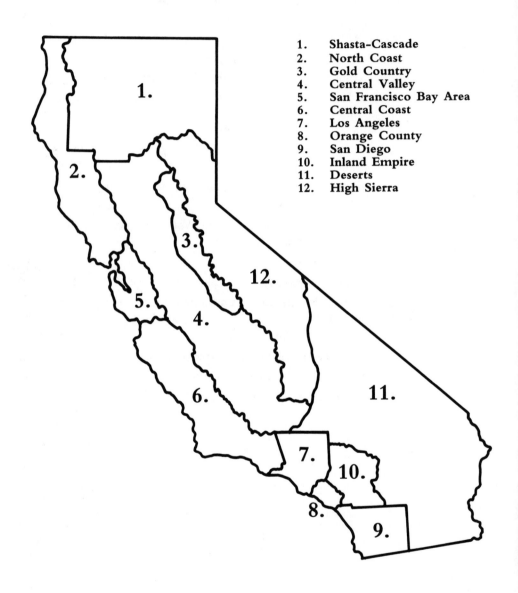

1. Shasta–Cascade
2. North Coast
3. Gold Country
4. Central Valley
5. San Francisco Bay Area
6. Central Coast
7. Los Angeles
8. Orange County
9. San Diego
10. Inland Empire
11. Deserts
12. High Sierra

Introduction
California: A State of Superlatives

According to Irving Stone, writing in *Men to Match My Mountains*, even the name of California is an exaggeration. Stone cites a fiction writer, Garcí Ordóñez de Montalvo, as having written, around 1510, "At the right hand of the Indies there is an island called California, very close to Terrestrial Paradise." Many have accused California boosters of singing the state's praises in exaggerated tones. But to do it justice the tale of California must be told in superlatives: "best," certainly, but also "worst," "first," and even, on occasion, "last."

If a single thread winds through the state's history, or a single tie binds its residents, it is disagreement. Indeed, the entire California story is interwoven with battles of one kind and another. From the time of earliest contact between natives and Spaniards until this very moment, some serious argument has been going on. North debates against south, for example, principally over water; regional rivalries also crop up from time to time concerning culture, good restaurants, museums, and so on. Every few years one faction or another stumps to divide the state into two or more entities.

One colorful battle in all this warring was the Sagebrush War, a disagreement over the boundary between California and Nevada and the property rights of a man named Isaac Roop, who called his cabin Fort Defiance. Tales of the Owens Valley water wars in the south and the Hetch Hetchy Reservoir arguments in the north show how controversy can forge a state. Arguments over transportation of every kind have erupted since the earliest days. Little of any significance has been accomplished in California that wasn't preceded by some kind of battle. Prominent state figures have fought with the federal government over offshore oil and over water from the Colorado River. Indeed, the state's very beginnings sprang from battles with the Indians, who sought to hold the land they had lived on so long and peacefully before intruders came from other lands.

CALIFORNIA'S FIRST RESIDENTS

Many historians treat the saga of California as if it began with the arrival in 1542 of Juan Rodríguez Cabrillo, a Portuguese seaman in the service of Spain. Those chroniclers forget that Cabrillo and the scores who followed in his wake were greeted—that isn't to say welcomed—by the real first residents of California: Indians, Native Americans.

Dolan H. Eargle Jr., an authority on indigenous peoples, writing in *The Earth Is Our Mother*, says many parts of the state had residents twelve thousand years ago and possibly before that. "Apparently," he writes, "these people came directly to California [presumably over the land bridge from Asia] for the same reason that people come here today: the good weather and bountiful food supply."

California's lakes added to the area's early appeal. Lake Mojave covered most of what is now the Mojave Desert; Lake Cahuilla lapped shores near Calexico and Palm Springs. China Lake was filled with water, not bitter alkali dust as it is today, while Mono and Searles Lakes were huge freshwater bodies.

Anthropologists disagree as to how many Native Americans were living in California at the time of its "discovery," but estimates range from 133,000 to 275,000 or even more. According to the Federal Writers' Project book, *California: Guide to the Golden State*, the estimated density of the Indian population at the time of Sir Francis Drake's arrival in 1579 was one inhabitant to each square mile. At that time, the Central Valley was probably more densely populated than any other part of North America.

No matter what their number, these early residents of the Golden State lived well by the standards of their time. They were not nomadic and often stayed in one region for their lifetimes. They were, for the most part, hunter-gatherers.

In many areas dense groves of oak trees provided abundant harvests of acorns, the single most important plant food for the majority of California Indians. Native women dried the fruit of the ubiquitous oaks, ground it with pestles in stone or wooden mortars, and leached out toxic tannic acid with repeated washings, then cooked it into a bland but filling mush. It was usually eaten with meat, fish, or other dishes, when they were available. In the southwestern deserts, mesquite beans provided provender, and on the eastern slopes of the Sierra, piñon nuts. In all areas, native tubers, grasses, flowers, and the like supplemented the acorns. Only natives living near the Colorado River cultivated food crops.

Most tribes hunted small game with snares, sticks, and nets; they also captured grasshoppers and caterpillars that abounded in some areas and seasons. From streams they took fish, including salmon in the north, and those who lived near the sea gathered clams and mussels. The Chumash of the central coast used hook, net, and spear to harvest bonita, yellowtail, shark, halibut, and sardines.

According to Eargle, several tribes and peoples used an elaborate money system to trade among themselves. Neighboring villages socialized, too, exchanging ornaments, ideas, and women. For the most part, however, the various peoples—as distinguished from the smaller units, tribes—were isolated from each other, cut off by mountains, deserts, and distance.

Local tribes occasionally disagreed over rights to use certain oak groves or hunting grounds, but the Indians generally lived in harmony with one another. The exceptions were the Mojaves and Yumas in the far southeast; they exhibited aggressive tribal unity against outsiders.

THE INTRUDERS

Into this not-quite-Eden came the Spaniards, seeking Cíbola—the seven cities of gold—and new territories to colonize. Calling the natives "diggers" because they dug up roots and plants, the new arrivals accused them of being lazy, dirty, and of lax morals. In truth, the Indians had no cultural concept similar to the Europeans' work ethic; they performed the labor necessary to survive. They were far cleaner than their conquerors, whose baggage included death from diseases, such as smallpox and tuberculosis, spread by unsanitary practices. Bathing, for example, was almost unknown at the missions. As for morals, it was the Spaniards who introduced liquor and prostitution into the region.

The Spanish also contemptuously accused the Indians of cowardice because the indigenous West Coast residents lived in peace, unlike the chronically warring natives of other parts of North America. Once the native Californians were introduced to battle, however, they became quite skilled at it.

The Spanish intrusion was delayed for some time because Cabrillo's account of his voyage contained only reports of finding San Diego, "a good closed port," the Santa Monica Bay, islands of the Santa Barbara group, and a headland that was probably Cape Mendocino. Spanish officials were disappointed. Convinced that neither the Strait of Anián—the legendary passageway from Atlantic to Pacific—was to be found in this area, nor the gold and pearls they sought, the Spanish looked away. Hence, during the years between Cabrillo's visit to California and Sir Francis Drake's in 1579, Spain's interest in the territory slept.

Word of Drake's visit to the bay he named in honor of himself (now part of Point Reyes National Seashore) and the area he had christened

Sir Francis Drake, whose visit to New Albion reawakened Spain's interest in Alta California.
—The Bancroft Library

New Albion awakened Spain's interest, however. In 1584 Francisco Gali explored the California coast much more thoroughly than Cabrillo and reported finding a fair land with no snow and many rivers. Eleven years later he was followed by Sebastián Rodríguez Cermeño, a Portuguese who, during his return voyage from Manila to Acapulco, searched for harbors in which Spanish galleons might seek refuge. Even though he lost his ship, Cermeño managed to sight Monterey Bay, which he dubbed San Pedro Bay.

Of far more historical significance, however, was the exploration of Sebastián Vizcaíno, who had bargained for permission to exploit the pearl beds of Baja California with his promise to chart the Alta California coast. Vizcaíno probably hoped primarily to find wealth, but he convinced the reluctant Spanish crown that he would find the Strait of Anián, secure Alta California against future enemies, and bring the gospel to the poor savages who lived there. Thus it was that he left Acapulco on May 5, 1602.

Vizcaíno proceeded up the coast, visiting places mentioned by Cabrillo and renaming everything he saw, in spite of orders to the contrary. It is he, for example, who is responsible for such place names as San Diego, Santa Catalina, Santa Barbara, Point Conception, Monterey, and Buena Ventura, among others. Some accounts say that his ships reached as far north as the forty-third parallel, but the forty-first (near Cape Mendocino) was probably his northern stopping point. What is certain, however, is that he overlooked San Francisco Bay.

Many historians think it was Vizcaíno's fault that Monterey Bay was so difficult for subsequent explorers to identify. His overblown recital of the virtues of that often fog-shrouded harbor made it difficult for others to recognize.

In spite of the avowed success of Vizcaíno's voyage, well over a hundred years would pass before Spain, beset by domestic troubles and problems with international rivals, would finally take steps to colonize California. It was almost too late.

SPANISH COLONIZATION

By 1734 Britain had removed France from contention for the new territory, but Russia was exploring Alaska and looking southward. To protect her interests, Spain would have to start colonizing Alta California. The thriving Philippine trade, too, spurred the less-than-enthusiastic Spaniards; harbors for the Spanish galleons must be found.

Given the assignment to start the colonization were Capt. Gaspar de Portolá, governor of Baja California, and José de Gálvez, visitor-general of New Spain. The latter never saw Alta California, but he developed intricate plans for four colonizing expeditions that set forth in 1769. His plan included eventually establishing missions at San Diego, Monterey, and an intermediate point, plus two presidios, or military forts.

Two of those expeditions went by sea and suffered fearfully. Many died from scurvy and most of the survivors were weakened by the illness when they reached San Diego, almost two months after setting sail. Portolá led the overland party that included Father Junípero Serra, who had been named president of missions in California. Capt. Fernando Rivera y Moncada, who became a military commandant of Alta California, led the second land expedition, which included Father Juan Crespí. Both land parties underwent dreadful trials during their journey and only about half their original number reached San Diego. Most of the missing men had died, but undoubtedly some had deserted because of the incredible hardships.

Illness aside, the colonizers wasted no time, dedicating Mission San Diego de Alcala on July 16, 1769, a little more than two weeks after Portolá and his party arrived. But Portolá missed the ceremony, having set off north on foot with Father Crespí and a band of men to find Monterey. They reached that fabled bay on October 2, but failed to recognize it, because they were looking for the "fine harbor sheltered from all winds" described by Vizcaíno. They pushed on, hungry and exhausted, until they reached what Father Crespí described in his journal as "some immense arms of the sea which penetrate into the mainland"—the outer reaches of San Francisco Bay.

Driven to eating their pack mules, the company struggled back to San Diego, where they found illness and starvation rampant. Legend has it that Portolá vowed to return to Baja California, aborting the expedition, if help didn't arrive from Gálvez. The night before he planned to leave, the story goes, a ship bearing supplies appeared on the horizon. Within a month Portolá was back on the ocean, once again seeking Monterey Bay. This time he succeeded, and on June 3, 1770, Father Crespí dedicated the sites of the mission and presidio. During the next fifty years, the Spaniards completed the chain of twenty-one missions, founding the northernmost—San Francisco Solano—on July 4, 1823.

THE MISSION ERA

The mission system of Alta California has stirred up a great deal of controversy since its inception. Charges of inhumane treatment and exploitation of the natives have been leveled against the padres for years. Eargle writes:

> Suddenly, these natives, who were accustomed to their own independent society, found themselves herded together, fed strange food, deprived of their religion, restrained from their own specific sexual customs, and then treated roughly by padre or soldier when they deviated from the Church's prescribed norm.

In addition, alien living conditions exposed the natives to measles, smallpox, cholera, pneumonia, diphtheria, scarlet fever, syphilis, dysentery, tuberculosis, and typhoid, killing them by the thousands. Eargle estimates the native population diminished by two-thirds during the sixty-seven years from the founding of the first mission to secularization in 1834. Under the direction of the padres, the Indians built sophisticated irrigation systems and learned to weave and spin, to make candles and bread, and to cure hides. They did not learn, however, to be self-sufficient, and when secularization came, they were thrown out into what had become a cold world.

A booklet on Fort Ross, the major Russian settlement in California, edited by Bickford O'Brien, reveals a telling contrast to the Spanish and their mission system. "Over many generations the Kashaya [natives of the far north coast] have experienced fewer acculturation pressures than other California Indians and greater freedom from forced removals to missions and reservations." It points out that, unlike other native groups, these peoples' first encounters with Europeans were with Russians who wanted to acquire sea otter pelts and establish a food base, rather than with Spaniards or Anglo-Americans who sought to change the Indians' way of life.

The Russians treated the Indians fairly, allowing them to pursue their own interests while working for the newcomers. According to O'Brien's booklet, Capt. Otto von Kotzebue, a Russian navigator born in Germany, reported in his journal, "The inhabitants of Ross live in the greatest concord with the Indians, who repair in considerable numbers to the fortress, and work as day laborers for wages. At night they usually remain outside the palisades." He added that the Russians often visited overnight with the Indians and even married them.

Whether the mission system was good for the Indians or not, it was good for developing the economy of the region. The missions formed a chain of settlement extending from San Diego to Sonoma, north of San Francisco Bay—almost two-thirds the length of the modern state. Each mission had its own gardens and herds, which were tended by the Indian neophytes.

The missions assumed a most important role in the prosperity of Alta California. With their increasingly skilled farming and irrigation methods and their herds that multiplied rapidly enough to stock private ranchos, the padres and their converts became an important factor in the agricultural economy of the area. They developed a thriving trade, too, sending blankets to Alaska, otter skins to China, and lumber from the redwood forests to Peru.

The Spaniards established presidios at San Diego, Santa Barbara, Monterey, and San Francisco. They were meant to intimidate the Indian residents, discourage incursions by hostile tribes, fend off foreign intruders, and generally strengthen Spain's hold on California. Pueblos, or towns, gradually grew up around the forts. They were an important part of Spain's long-range colonization plans.

Colonization did not go smoothly. The towns were laid out carefully enough, with land allocated for a plaza, town hall, church, and other important buildings, as well as residences and agriculture. The Spanish government promised colonists land for their homes and crops plus a small cash subsidy. The colonists were to be screened carefully to assure that those responding to government advertisements were seasoned farmers, free of vices and criminal records and able to set a good example for the Indians. As it turned out, however, it was largely the dregs of New Spain's society who came to Alta California.

Mexican residents regarded Alta California as the end of the earth and so resisted all blandishments to relocate there. To obtain colonists, therefore, the jails of Sinaloa and Sonora were emptied of both convicted criminals and political prisoners. Second- and third-generation Californians greeted these new arrivals not with open arms, but with open hostility. In spite of all the planning and government support, the pueblos never really flourished.

Private ranchos were not what the government of Spain had in mind for Alta California because they were hard to defend and control. In spite of government intentions, ranchos cropped up from the practice of granting land for political purposes, as rewards for service to the government, and, in some cases, for money. About twenty-five huge ranchos developed and with them a small land-rich elite population.

Then followed the era of California history that has been romanticized in song and cinema: the easy life replete with great barbecues, singing vaqueros, and starry nights. The ranchos were largely self-sufficient, providing their residents with food, clothing, and housing of their own production. Rancho recipients (generally using Indian laborers) built comfortable adobe homes and oversaw huge cattle herds that supported their way of life. Their generous hospitality accounted for much of the color of that period. Fiestas were held at the drop of a sombrero, with everyone dancing to the music of violin and guitar, clarinet and harp.

Like most legends, that of Alta California under the Spanish is only partly true. There's no question that the landholders and their retinues lived well and were content, but the easy life included neither the mission Indians nor the lower classes. The latter lived in squalid huts in towns or on the edges of the ranchos scrounging for the leavings of the elite. The end of that fabled era began with Mexican independence in 1821, even though its passing wasn't immediately obvious to the Californios.

SECULARIZATION

The first decrees of secularization—removing the missions from the control of Franciscan clergy and turning them over to parish priests—were issued in Spain in 1813 and 1820. Those edicts were heeded in Mexico, but they had little immediate effect in Alta California.

Governor José María Echeandía issued the first California secularization order. He arrived in Alta California in 1825 to enforce the edict, but found it more easily published than accomplished. The idea was to release the Indians from mission jurisdiction, give them a little land and some livestock, and thus allow the missions to become Indian ranchos. The secularization order also granted the padres some land so they could continue living in the style to which they had grown accustomed. Neither natives nor padres, however, seemed eager to change.

The Mexican government, in a state of almost perpetual civil war, was unable to protect the rights of the Indians. After Mexico won its independence from Spain in 1821, the unrest that beset the government in Baja California had boiled up in Alta California as well. Much of the trouble was fomented by Californios, Mexicans born in Alta California, who felt little allegiance to Mexico and protested against officials sent from Mexico to rule the province.

The matter first came to a head soon after Manuel Victoria took office as governor of Alta California in 1831. Victoria opposed secularization, imposed the death penalty for minor infractions, and refused to give the Californios more voice in their affairs. A group of Californios, led by Juan Bandini and José Carrillo, seized the presidio at San Diego and moved on Los Angeles. The only battle of this uprising was fought near Cahuenga Pass. While that engagement resulted in only one or two fatalities (historians disagree) and the wounding of Victoria, it convinced the governor that these independent spirits would probably never be subdued, so he gave up and fled home.

Nonetheless, in 1834, the new governor, José Figueroa, issued a proclamation stating that ten missions would be secularized that year, six in 1835, and the rest in 1836. As with earlier edicts, Figueroa ordered lay administrators to oversee half of mission property and give half to the neophytes, who were forbidden to dispose of it. The padres would continue to oversee the religious aspects of the missions until parish priests became available.

The mission system, however, had not trained the Indians to survive independently; it made them totally dependent on strict rules devised by both priest and soldier. At none of the twenty-one missions were the Indians ready to shift for themselves. That being the case, lands that should have belonged to the Native Americans were quickly grabbed up by greedy rancheros. By 1845 the number of land grants in Alta California had grown from about twenty (in 1823) to nearly eight hundred. Only a few of those were held by Indians. So it was that the natives who had lost the survival skills of their ancestors became peons of the great ranchos.

THE UNITED STATES MOVES IN

The rise and fall of the missions didn't take place in a vacuum. While the Californios were establishing their rich lives, Yankees had discovered the region, too. Traders from New England developed a thriving business, buying pelts of sea otters and fur seals from trappers and missions. Whalers followed, often putting in at California ports to rest and resupply. Even though the Mexican government ruled that no trading be carried on between foreigners and residents of Alta California, these merchant traders—and their wares—were welcomed at ranchos and missions. Before long a thriving trade in hides and tallow developed between New England and California.

And it wasn't only seamen who discovered the area's riches. Fur traders in search of new trapping grounds entered the region. Led by the likes of Jedediah Smith, the traders established overland routes to the West and carried the news of California's appeal back to the United States and its territories. Point man for the emigrant invasion that soon swelled to a flood was John Bidwell, who, with John Bartleson, in 1841 led a group of settlers on a twenty-four-week trek from Missouri to Sutter's Fort. Even reports of the incredible hardships that group experienced couldn't stem the tide of those seeking the pleasant climate and bountiful land of the region.

Officials in the United States, seeing both the hegira from east to west and Russian and British activity on the coast, began to consider Alta California as part of the Manifest Destiny of the United States. Those same officials recognized that Mexico, embroiled in the war for Texan independence, was in no position to defend the area against eastern invaders.

For almost a decade Californios had wrangled over control of the province and its wealth like a gang of kids over a bag of candy. On November 7, 1836, Juan Bautista Alvarado proclaimed Alta California a free and sovereign state until Mexico should repudiate centralism and restore principles of federalism. He made himself provisional governor and appointed Mariano Guadalupe Vallejo military commander of the new state.

Alvarado and Vallejo fell to quarreling with each other, and by 1842 they were so disillusioned that they turned the messy affairs of the state over to the final governor from Mexico, Brig. Gen. Manuel Micheltorena. His administration was no better than his predecessors'. In fact, it was during his term that mission lands were not returned as promised, several unwise land grants were made, and a second battle was fought at Cahuenga Pass. The Californios expelled Micheltorena in 1845.

Micheltoreno's departure effectively ended any Mexican control over Alta California. Newspapers in the East began to clamor for the United States to acquire the territory. President James K. Polk favored such an acquisition, which he thought might be accomplished through a purchase. That didn't prove to be the case, however.

Much of the political maneuvering that went on during this tumultuous time had all the earmarks of a comic opera. The arrival in California of Capt. John C. Frémont, a U.S. topographical engineer and master of derring-do, marked the beginning of the skirmishing that eventually led to the Bear Flag Revolt on June 14, 1846. That engagement, celebrated in songs and tall tales, took place in the little pueblo of Sonoma when a small band of Yankees led by William B. Ide surrounded the home of Gen. Mariano G. Vallejo, seizing him and other Mexican officers. The undefended presidio was taken without a shot. The rebels hauled down the Mexican flag and ran up their own, fashioned—according to legend—of homespun and a strip of red flannel, decorated with a star and a grizzly bear, and displaying the words "California Republic."

Unbeknownst to the 150 or so dauntless rebels, President Polk had signed a declaration of war between Mexico and the United States on May 13, 1846. Fewer than half a dozen engagements made up California's part in that war, which ended on January 13, 1847. On that day Andrés Pico, leader of the last of the Californios, entered into an agreement with Frémont to acknowledge the sovereignty of the United States. Formal transfer of the territory of California didn't take place, however, until the Treaty of Guadalupe Hidalgo was signed on February 2, 1848.

Ironically, with that signing Mexicans ceded all claim to what the earliest explorers had sought: gold. Just nine days before the signers met at that little town in central Mexico, James Marshall found gold in the millrace of John Sutter's new mill. When word of that discovery leaked out, the largest migration in American history began, changing the course of development in California, the United States, and, yes, the world.

THE GOLD RUSH

The discovery was not an unalloyed blessing for the state. Walton Bean, for example, in *California: An Interpretive History*, writes:

> It can be cogently argued . . . that in the long run the state would have been better off if it had contained no gold at all, that because of its other advantages it would eventually have become just as populous and prosperous, and that in the meantime its social evolution would have been not only more gradual but also far more orderly and civilized.

It's easy to take Bean's meaning. The gold rush brought to the state, according to renowned historian Hubert Howe Bancroft, "the toiling farmer, whose mortgage loomed above the growing family, the briefless lawyer, the starving student, the quack, the idler, the harlot, the gambler, the hen-pecked husband." In other words, gold drew persons from all levels of society. Most of those who made the incredibly hard journey came to get their share of the riches, with little thought of social welfare. Most of those who struck it rich simply took their wealth and went home. Those who stayed behind had failed, at least at finding gold. Cynical and embittered, they lingered to look for pickings they had missed. Perhaps the attitude of that early population accounts for the flamboyant politics, unfettered industry, and unusual lifestyles of California through the years.

For the first several months after the initial gold strike, chaos ruled in mines and cities alike. Many towns looked deserted; businesses folded because employees and owners dropped their tools and headed for the goldfields. Despite that chaos and the wrangling in Congress over the question of slavery, California was admitted to the Union in 1850. A regular state government began to function, replacing on-the-spot justice exercised at the mines.

Soon ladies of the evening and mountebanks descended on the state to mine the pockets of successful miners. That influx settled largely in San Francisco, the city that provided support for the diggings. Most miners who sailed around the Horn landed at the bay city, and most entrepreneurs who stocked picks, pans, overalls, and other mining supplies set up shop there.

The less-than-lawful element settled there, too. In the absence of city government, so-called vigilance committees bloomed in San Francisco. Although some people commended these groups for their "law-and-order" attitude, the committees really took the law into their own hands and were little better than lynch mobs.

Thanks to gold, California grew rich early; San Francisco's per capita wealth suddenly became the highest in the nation. Many residents could afford the finer things of life, both material and cultural, but most of them lacked taste and true refinement. The new Californians were largely young—half of the forty-niners were between twenty and thirty—and boisterous; they lacked the civilizing presence of virtuous women. The society that developed on the heels of the gold rush did not resemble that of Boston and New York.

In spite of that lack of old culture, however, the demand for news-papers grew wildly and was satisfied. The papers attracted writers of note, including Mark Twain and Bret Harte. Poets, too, found California engaging. Churches of every denomination flourished, but public schools lagged behind, with early spending for public education being about $9 per child. Only about a quarter of school-age youngsters attended public school, and then for fewer than six months a year. That trend began to change late in the nineteenth century—for white children, at least. With the growth of mining, other industries also got underway, including agriculture (especially cattle ranching), manufacturing, and lumbering.

One of the principal hurdles would-be farmers faced was the question of who owned California's land. Most settlers who flowed in after the mines began to play out sought to homestead on land they presumed belonged to the United States under the treaty of Hidalgo. Spanish land-grant recipients and their heirs, however, had a different understanding. They had been given the land in perpetuity, they asserted, and a political change didn't void the grants. It took an act of Congress and more than four years of commission hearings to get the matter of land ownership even partly sorted out. The congressional act required land claimants to prove the validity of their claims to a board of commissioners; claimants or the federal government could appeal the board's decisions through the court system.

Squatters clouded the situation even more. The "squatter riot" at Sacramento in the summer of 1850, in which several persons were killed, drew the federal government into the fracas. Critics of the 1851 law—Hubert Howe Bancroft among them—asserted that it would have been impossible to have devised a worse plan for unscrambling the state's land-ownership tangle. Indeed, final confirmation of land grants took an average of seventeen years, and many of the grantees were bankrupt by the time they were given clear title. But, even with the advantage of hindsight, no one has ever come up with a better solution.

These land-ownership problems set back California's agriculture industry because many settlers refused to come to a state that, unlike Oregon, didn't grant them a generous portion of land just for taking up residence. But the land was too fertile and the climate too favorable for the industry not to bear rich fruit in time.

Cattle raising, a legacy from the missions, flourished until the drought of 1862–64 nearly wiped out the herds. Wheat then replaced grazing stock as the state's most important agricultural product. Wheat production was largely concentrated in the Sacramento Valley, where John Sutter first raised it.

Lumbering became a booming industry, thanks to the needs of miners for great quantities of milled boards. Moreover, towns were generally constructed of wood, as was fencing in those days before the invention of barbed wire.

Steamships and overland stages provided early transportation, for the most part. In the 1850s John Butterfield's Overland Mail Company won the challenge to carry the mail between San Francisco and the Mississippi. It was a major operation, with 800 people handling 100 coaches and 1,500 horses and mules. Stage stations approximately ten miles apart provided a measure of safety as well as fresh horses. The Butterfield stages brought the southern and northern parts of the state closer together, uniting California probably as much as it ever would be. But Northerners resented the stage company and accused Southerners of dictating its routes for the betterment of their region, to the detriment of the north. The much faster but never profitable Pony Express took over mail delivery in 1860; it ceased operations the following year.

The State Matures

With the completion of the first transcontinental railroad in 1869, new hordes of settlers rushed to California only to find their promised land rife with poverty and unrest. Low wages, widespread unemployment, scarce capital, exorbitant interest rates, and uncertain land titles dampened their enthusiasm. And to top it all off, railroad interests had corrupted the state government with discriminatory freight rates. The railroad owners rewarded their friends, punished their enemies, and made it impossible for some farmers to move their produce to market.

Then, in 1875, the state was shaken by a tragedy of mammoth proportions: the collapse of the Bank of California. Both farms and cities suffered. Wages fell and bread lines grew. Farmers, still reeling from the effects of the drought of the 1860s, couldn't bear responsibility for their mortgages and taxes. At last the politicians reaped the harvest of their appallingly unfair land-distribution tactics, which created vast estates under the rule of owners who controlled water distribution and who set rates that discriminated against small farmers and ranchers.

The hardships created by the economic downturn led to the formation of a new political faction: the Workingmen's Party of California. It agitated for the employment of whites, not Chinese, on the railroad and opposed the economic power of banks, railroads, and large land owners. Headed by Denis Kearney, the proprietor of a small business in San Francisco, the party demanded a new constitution.

In 1878 a constitutional convention convened in Sacramento. After nearly six months it produced a wordy, detailed document several times longer than the constitution of the United States but remarkably little improved over the 1849 version crafted in Monterey. Within a year after the constitutional convention ended, the Workingmen's Party faded away.

The constitution of 1879, much amended, remains in force today. One end it successfully accomplished at the outset was focusing enmity against Chinese laborers. Ever since the first Chinese arrived in California, certain groups agitated against them. The long and elaborate anti-Chinese article of the new constitution blamed them for the job shortage and low wages, and it authorized the legislature to protect the state from "aliens" by halting all immigration from China. It forbade the employment of Chinese by corporations or on public works. The U.S. Supreme Court struck down some sections of the article only to have the U.S. Congress pass laws that accomplished almost the same ends.

California's durable prosperity has long been based largely on its agriculture, which began to diversify soon after the mining boom started to abate in the 1850s. Wheat, the first crop raised in large quantities, was by the end of the century replaced by orchard products. Vineyards also began to affect the state's economy. Some Riverside County efforts to raise mulberry bushes to feed silkworms failed. In spite of the huge demand for cotton created by the Civil War, water shortages delayed its production. Today cotton is one of the state's premier crops.

Distributing water throughout the state has been a problem ever since the period (1853–84) of the hydraulic miners, who often built flumes to transport water thousands of feet so they could wash entire hillsides into streams and expose the gold they sought. Even before that time, many of the missions developed surprisingly sophisticated systems of water distribution. But large-scale agricultural development required more than flumes and pipes that carried water only a few thousand feet.

In the 1870s the gospel of irrigation became widespread. Among the first to irrigate for agricultural purposes were one group of German settlers at Anaheim and another, of Mormons, in San Bernardino. The Wright Irrigation Act of 1887 authorized the establishment of water districts, special units of local government. These entities were granted power of eminent domain—the right to construct dams, canals, and other irrigation devices—and the right to sell bonds to finance such activities.

By 1890 one-quarter of all the state's farms received irrigation water. The rapid increase in the availability of water led to a change in the type of crops California produced. By the end of the century 64 percent of the value of all California crops came from apples, apricots, cherries, peaches, plums, and other water-intensive fruits. But the value of products from vineyards and citrus orchards entitles them to their own places in the annals of the state.

The padres had cultivated vineyards on mission lands and produced wine for sacramental and personal use. Their wine was of poor quality, however, because of inferior grapes and crude production methods. In 1850 Agoston Haraszthy began the work in Northern California that made him the father of the California wine industry. A group of German settlers formed the Los Angeles Vineyard Society in 1857 and established the community of Anaheim. They planted grapes and produced quality wines until the 1870s, when disease destroyed the grape vines. The colony converted to growing oranges.

Citrus fruits of all kinds have been living gold for Californians with a talent for hard work and the patience to wait for trees to mature. While the propagation of grapes and the production of wine over the years became concentrated largely in the north, raising citrus grew to be a function of the southern part of the state. The area around Riverside is still one of the top-producing orange centers of the state. Grapefruit are raised extensively in the Imperial and Coachella Valleys, thanks to irrigation.

Nowadays, kiwi fruit, artichokes, broccoli, almonds, and walnuts also contribute to the wealth of the state. Dates and olives, too, are grown in commercial quantities.

Mining continued to play a significant role in the state's economy, even when gold and silver mines began to play out. Borax compounds scooped from the earth not only contributed substantially to the state's economy but also added to the lore of the state. Every schoolchild is familiar with the saga of the 20-mule team wagons that hauled borax ore from Death Valley to Mojave, the railway terminus.

Less glamorous materials such as gypsum, potash, cement, sand, and gravel are still profitably mined all over the state. In all, according to James D. Hart, some 600 varieties of minerals—45 of which are not found elsewhere—are taken from the earth in California.

Far and away the most precious of all stuffs extracted below ground in the state is oil. Even before the invaders arrived, Native Americans relied on petroleum products for a variety of purposes. The famous La Brea pits in Los Angeles provided tar for sealing roofs, caulking boats, and waterproofing baskets. The Indians called on lighter oils to treat burns and cuts.

According to Walton Bean, the state's first oil well was drilled in 1861, a few miles south of Eureka on the Mattole River. Although that well produced no oil, there were forty others in Humboldt County by 1865, mostly in that same region. Wells in the Ventura region, and even a refinery in Ojai, soon poked up across the landscape. Oil wells were soon pumping in the San Joaquin Valley near Maricopa and McKittrick.

Farther south, Edward L. Doheny discovered oil near Los Angeles in 1892, setting off the city's first boom. By 1900 a thousand wells were operating in the northwest part of the city. Black gold was subsequently discovered in Kern, Santa Barbara, Ventura, and Kings Counties. New fields throughout the state soon flooded the state with oil, so much that uses for it had to be devised. Factories that previously operated on coal switched to oil, and the ever-growing use of automobiles helped to sop up some of the excess. Despite such efforts, exporting oil from Los Angeles harbor in the 1920s made it the largest oil port in the world.

As cities began to grow across the state, the need for urban transportation became obvious and the development of electric railways further spurred the growth of cities. The cable car, invented by Andrew S. Hallidie in San Francisco, enabled residents of that hilly city to get around. Everywhere but in the City by the Bay, electric trolleys soon replaced cable cars.

In 1901 Henry Huntington, nephew of Collis Huntington of railroad fame, sold his inherited controlling interest in the Southern Pacific Railroad, to move from San Francisco to Los Angeles. There he created the Pacific Electric Railway Company, known to fans and detractors alike as the red cars. It was those big, lumbering cars that made it possible for Los Angeles to become the far-flung metropolis that it is. The cars would end up being undermined by automobile and oil industries, and others with special axes to grind, creating all kinds of problems for Angelenos, not the least of which have been freeways and traffic jams. While they lasted, the cars were a colorful part of Southern California.

Over the years the demise of the red cars has provided fodder for dinner table discussion, movie scripts, and legislative argument. In the 1980s and early 1990s, Los Angeles spent astronomical sums to build the first legs of a subway system and light rail lines to supplement the underground routes with above-ground transport from suburbs all around the greater metropolitan area. Old-timers commented that the city was creating the modern equivalent of a red car system.

In spite of the monopolistic practices of Southern Pacific Railroad and its high freight rates, railroads played a large role in the economic boom that increased the population of Los Angeles after the Civil War. At first newcomers to the south arrived by steamer or stagecoach from San Francisco. When the Central Pacific Railroad, in 1876, and the Santa Fe Railroad, in 1885, reached the southern part of the state, that mode of transportation began to contribute to the development of California as residents had long hoped it would.

Competition between the lines triggered a new wave of migration, boosted by colorful promotional campaigns and vastly reduced fares. Newspapers and magazine articles fueled the flood. Not since Vizcaíno's description of Monterey Bay had such (sometimes) unwarranted praise been broadcast about the state. Charles Nordhoff's *California: For Health, Pleasure, and Residence* was said to have had a more far-reaching effect on the fortunes of Southern California than anything else ever written. Many of those lured to the state found that its advantages had been highly overstated. It was neither the place to cure all ills nor the rich land where oranges grew on Joshua trees, as one promoter depicted in his advertising. Nor was it the home of young women who were taller, more attractive, and superior in all ways to college girls of Massachusetts, as was claimed by David Starr Jordan, who became the first president of Stanford University.

It would have been hard for even the most avid promoters to wax too enthusiastic about California's various climates, however. The entire state embraces every climatological zone except tropical. In *Southern California Country*, Carey McWilliams wrote, "The climate of Southern California is . . . the most consistent, the least paradoxical factor in the environment . . . . [I]t is predictable to the point of monotony."

The major drawback, obviously, is the uncertainty of rainfall, even in the northern and wetter parts of the state. Droughts are common, with all their attendant problems. Perhaps that's why a person like Charles Hatfield, who operated as a rainmaker—even though he spurned the title—was able to build up a considerable following in the early years of the twentieth century.

1906, A WATERSHED YEAR

Two events that loom large in the history of California took place at opposite ends of the state in 1906: San Francisco's great earthquake shook the Bay Area almost literally to pieces; and the first movie studio opened in Los Angeles.

Actually, it wasn't the earthquake alone that destroyed San Francisco; it was the fifty or more fires that flamed up within minutes of the early-morning shaking. Gas connections broke, chimneys fell, and stoves tipped over. Unfortunately, most of the flimsy water mains in the city broke, too, and firefighters could only watch helplessly as the city went up in flames. Before the cinders cooled, San Franciscans had resolved to develop a water delivery system that wouldn't fail them again. Those same residents, as they struggled to rebuild, became less indulgent of corruption in a city government that had tolerated the inferior water system, and reformers pushed ahead with plans for an investigation that had taken shape even before the tragedy.

The second event of 1906 that shook up California was the arrival in Los Angeles of a movie studio started by George Van Guysling and Otis M. Gove. The first film they produced was shot on a ranch in what is now Hollywood. Hard on the heels of Van Guysling and Gove came the likes of William Selig—who set up shop on Main Street in downtown Los Angles—D. W. Griffith, Thomas Ince, and Mack Sennett.

In its earliest days, movie-making was controlled by a monopolist trust, headed by Thomas Edison and several others. Independent filmmakers fled from New York and New Jersey to California to escape the restrictions of the trust. After bitter controversy, it was disbanded—in 1915—and the movie industry was free to grow without the controversy the trust had engendered.

And grow it did, creating the star system whereby the faces of certain actors became as familiar as family to moviegoers all over the nation. Much of the nation's population studied the stars' lifestyles and made them models to be emulated. Movie magazines pried into the stars' private lives and reported to avid shop girls across the land. Elaborate movie palaces were built, none more fanciful than the Egyptian Theater in Hollywood, called by the Federal Writers' Project "the Taj Mahal of movie houses."

Whether the movie industry was a blessing or a scourge to society as a whole, it was a tremendous boon to California's economy. Movie-making became big business and continued to prosper, even during the Great Depression, until the advent of television.

BOOM AND GROWTH

Movies made Americans curious about how folks lived in other parts of the nation and the automobile helped them satisfy their curiosity. Thus the automobile created another of the state's prosperous industries: tourism, today second only to agriculture in producing state income. Until the onset of World War II, auto courts and tourist camps blossomed all across the land, particularly along roads that led to California.

Los Angeles became the first major U.S. city whose far-flung growth was attributable to the automobile and electric trolley. The size of the city sparked a building boom in the 1920s that saw the development of colorful communities like Venice, with its canals and bridges; Beverly Hills, with movie stars' mansions; and Santa Monica, first a bay-side resort and then the home of the aerospace industry. From 1920 to 1930 the population of Los Angeles swelled from fewer than a million to well over two million; one-third of these residents owned cars. Cars and trucks made possible the phenomena of the supermarket and outlying shopping centers, ended the isolation of rural areas, and provided a better means of distributing goods from seaports and railheads to consumer outlets.

Although transportation of all kinds was a key to the growth of the state, none was more important than the airplane. Getting from the northwest corner to the southeast, for example, a distance of well over 800 miles, was a daunting journey in the days of stagecoaches and coastwise packets. It's still no drive in the park if undertaken by any transport other than airplane. Thus, it's not surprising that many of the "firsts" of the industry were noted in California and that much of the innovation in air and space travel has its beginnings in California.

Before the stock market crash that introduced the Great Depression, California was booming, particularly in the south. That very boom, however, had pointed up the disparity that existed between the north, where populations were thinner and water plentiful, and the south, where the population was growing exponentially and natural sources of water were almost nonexistent. Los Angeles cast about for sources of water and found one in the Colorado River and another in the Owens Valley. Although both projects stirred up bitter controversy, they also provided abundant water to Los Angeles, for a time. Today, after incredible population growth, dry years leave the entire Los Angeles basin panting and thirsty, once again looking for more water. Santa Barbara and Catalina Island have developed desalination plants, but such a remedy is too costly to be of much help to a large city.

Those who opposed the Boulder Canyon Project that dammed the Colorado and sent its water tumbling toward Angelenos' faucets, did so in part because of the electric power the plant would generate. Although that abundance of electricity would reduce the price of power in the Southwest, the municipally owned electric power company of Los Angeles would control the sale of that power. Thus the project abetted the growth of the public power movement. City-owned power had become reality with the completion in 1913 of the Owens Valley Water Project, which was financed in part by the sale of the electricity it generated. In other words, the money earned by selling power paid for delivering water that the thirsty city needed.

Irrigation for the great Central Valley was made possible by the Central Valley Project, authorized in 1930 and finally started in 1937. It began operation in the 1950s. The project included three dams, five canals, and two power transmission lines. The most impressive of these features are Shasta Dam and Lake Shasta, impounding waters collected from the Sacramento, McCloud, and Pit Rivers.

The Pacific Gas & Electric Company (PG&E) captured the power that resulted from all this trapping and releasing of water in the Central Valley Project. PG&E managed to undercut any legislation that proposed giving that electricity to the public, thereby assuring the company would control this additional power. So it was, and still is, that water and power distribution became the function of the private sector in Northern California and of local government in much of the southern part of the state.

THE GREAT DEPRESSION

Even California's rosy promise couldn't stop the Great Depression from rolling over the state. Unemployment soared as the financial crisis threw residents out of work even while others came to the Golden State fleeing from the dust bowl and deprivations of eastern cities. By the middle of 1934, more than three hundred thousand workers were idle in Los Angeles County. Across the state, about one person in every five depended on public relief. In the cities hunger was rampant while crops were rotting in the fields and orchards of farmers who couldn't afford to harvest the food because its sale wouldn't even cover expenses.

Farm workers were among the hardest hit of the state's laborers and they were increasingly unhappy. Many were migrants, long exploited by growers. A great union movement sprang up and seemed to get off the ground, only to subside in 1934. Growers, on the other hand, banded together in the Associated Farmers, setting the stage for labor strife that has wracked the state right up to the present, even though the farm workers at last have gained union representation with the United Farm Workers (UFW). Table grape boycotts continue sporadically as the UFW fights for better working and living conditions for field workers.

John Steinbeck, a California native born in Salinas, slid under the lens of his writer's microscope the plight of migrant farm workers and dust bowl fugitives, ranch hands, and other common folks of the state. His voice probably drew more attention to the evils of the state's agricultural system than any other, even though he had passed from the scene by the time some improvements were apparent.

In San Francisco, meanwhile, dockworkers tried to improve their lot with the help of labor organizer Harry Bridges from Australia. They formed a new union, the International Longshoremen's Association, and presented demands for a one-dollar-per-hour wage, a six-hour day, and a thirty-hour week. Waterfront employers refused to negotiate and on May 9, 1934, the union called a strike. When Governor Frank Merriam called out the National Guard, a general strike ensued, which, although short-lived, proved to have tremendous effect on the future of labor in California.

Onto the pages of the state's history during the depression stepped the likes of Governor James Rolph, who, with his successor Frank Merriam, provided little in the way of leadership, and Upton Sinclair, the author who sought and failed to replace Merriam. Others prominent at the time included Aimee Semple McPherson; Reverend Robert P. Shuler; Howard Scott, with his Utopian Society; and Dr. Francis Townsend, with his plan for making the lives of older residents more secure.

Even the specter of hunger couldn't pale the colorful lives of Californians. But make no mistake, the state suffered. Hard hit because its economy was so shallowly based on tourism and real estate, California seemed unable to cope with its residents' misery.

War Brings Recovery

It took another world war to finally raise the nation and California from the abysmal depression. The state's population had grown during the '30s by 20 percent; economic and social changes had taken place, too. Great segments of industry had been unionized, and streets and highways had been improved to make the state's almost seven million residents more mobile. But the wartime '40s brought still more changes, some even more dramatic than the gold rush a century earlier.

Even before the United States became directly embroiled in World War II, the war in Europe affected California. The aircraft industry struggled during the depression as Lockheed went into bankruptcy and Douglas, faced with not a single order in four months, kept employees on by having them garden and perform plant maintenance. In May of 1940 President Roosevelt called for an output of sixty thousand airplanes a year and the upturn began. Aircraft accounted for almost 60 percent of the money paid to California prime contractors during the war, but the profits were small. The federal government financed the tremendous expansions needed to meet production goals through "cost plus" contracts, whereby the government agreed to pay all actual aircraft construction costs plus a flat fee.

Douglas, Lockheed, North American, and Northrop primary plants operated in Los Angeles, while Consolidated Vultee (or Convair) and Ryan were in San Diego. The gigantic Douglas plant at Santa Monica was camouflaged by dummy houses, streets, and trees so that from the air it was all but invisible.

The wartime paranoia of the American people was nowhere more in evidence than in California, where every practiced blackout was a bombing run and every person of Asian background a spy. Since its earliest days the state had practiced discrimination, first against the Chinese who came to find gold and stayed to help build the railroads and the Sacramento Delta, then against the Japanese.

Few Japanese had joined the gold rush because leaving Japan was illegal until 1868. In 1869 a small group came under terms of labor contracted for ahead of time and another twenty-six persons settled at Gold Hill in El Dorado County, forming the Wakamatsu Colony. They brought with them sapling mulberry trees, grape cuttings, and other plants, and tried to establish silk and tea plantations, which failed. Over the years a handful of Japanese trickled onto California's shores, but it was only in the 1890s that the flow increased to as many as a thousand a year. The state's Alien Land Law and federal discriminatory practices kept the Japanese population in California to fewer than one hundred thousand persons.

The bombing of Pearl Harbor and the shelling of an oil tank near Santa Barbara roused the state to hysterical hatred. Few will admit even today that the dispossession and internment of Japanese residents—even those who were citizens, born in the United States—were fueled as much by jealousy and greed as by genuine concern for the country's security. It's true, nonetheless, that some Californians resented Japanese success with growing crops that demand intense labor, such as strawberries. Japanese gardeners, with their frugal ways and experience in making small plots profitable, had succeeded in growing lush crops on acreages where less-skilled growers failed. Stripping these citizens of their rights was one way to strip them of the fields they had brought to life. It would take almost fifty years for Congress to authorize reparation payments to all those who demonstrated their loyalty by submitting with dignity to such treatment.

THE POSTWAR YEARS

After the war's end, California's population took another leap, boosted by enthusiastic reports of GIs who had passed through the state on their way to or from the Pacific theater. By 1950 more than 10.5 million persons lived in California, nearly one-fifth of them concentrated in Los Angeles. San Francisco's population stood at about 750,000.

During the decades after World War II, the state's economy was so diverse that, for the most part, it withstood the ravages of recessions that rocked the rest of the country. Of course, some individual industries suffered, but the general economic health of the state remained fair. Food prices soared even as federal subsidies for farmers grew. Wages rose sharply in most industries. Military actions in Korea and Viet Nam generated Department of Defense contracts that employed thousands all over the state. NASA, too, employed California firms to supply many of its needs, and tourism grew to be the second largest industry in the state, trailing only agriculture.

The movie industry, confronted with the popularity of television, fell on hard times. Commercial television broadcasting contracted somewhat with the advent of cable TV. But, by and large, all segments of the entertainment industry kept their heads above water, managing to distract many of California's residents from what was happening to the Golden State.

Such economic well-being didn't stop residents of the state from rising up in protest against taxes, most notably in 1978, with the Jarvis-Gann constitutional amendment, popularly called Proposition 13. As California prospered and its population grew, housing prices—particularly in metropolitan areas—rose to frightening levels. A house costing one-quarter million dollars in 1978, for instance, was not a mansion but a modest middle-class three-bedroom home. As property values rose, so did property taxes. The result was that many folks could no longer afford to keep the homes they had bought years earlier, even though many of them were mortgage-free, or nearly so.

Proposition 13 was a complex piece of legislation, but, simply put, it rolled back all property taxes to 1975–76 levels and allowed them to rise only one percent each year, unless ownership changed hands. The amendment also required a two-thirds approval by voters of any legislation proposing to increase other taxes. The immediate effect of the drastic ceiling was a reduction in such services as libraries, parks, and street cleaning and repairs, many of the very attractions that drew new residents to the state each year. Long-term consequences, however, wouldn't become apparent until the 1990s and the end of the cold war.

By 1990 the state's population had grown to almost thirty million, nearly three times the figure recorded by the census of 1950. Many of these new residents were children who needed to be educated; many others were old or poor and required public assistance to meet the daily challenges of living. Thus, public expenses grew exponentially, but revenue raising was hamstrung by Proposition 13 and subsequently passed, poorly thought-out legislation. Schools at all educational levels suffered deep budget cuts; libraries couldn't afford to buy books; parks had to scale back programs that kept kids off the streets. Health programs for the indigent were curtailed; serious illnesses, once thought conquered, made a comeback.

The Watts riots of 1965 in Los Angeles were a sign of distress that the state's leaders largely ignored. True, politicians from all levels poured into the city immediately after the unrest, but few of the promises they extended ever bore fruit. The McCone Commission, appointed by Governor Pat Brown to investigate causes of the trouble, reported that the city needed more jobs for blacks and Latinos, better housing and schools, and new recreational facilities. For the most part, the commission's recommendations were notable more for what was not accomplished than for what was.

One of the important consequences of those failures was the rise of gangs in Los Angeles. According to Leon Bing, in *Do or Die*, her remarkable book about gangs in Los Angeles, gangs got their start when teenagers from the Watts neighborhoods banded together to protect themselves from other teens, from the police, and from hunger and want. Most social theorists agree that had those young people been given work and effective schooling, the curse of gangs might never have fallen on the state's largest city.

Subsidized housing for low-income families provided the arena for early gang confrontations. In Watts, the earliest Crips formed up among the Mexican-American youths living in Jordan Downs. From another project, Nickerson Gardens, came a bunch of youngsters who called themselves Bloods, and they declared war on the Crips. To protect themselves, other youths collected themselves into still more gangs until, by 1990, Los Angeles had some one hundred gangs with memberships varying from twenty or fewer kids to more than a thousand in a single unit. Gangs became a genuine problem for the city, the state, and the country.

As long as it was possible, the movers and shakers of California— politicians, lobbyists, and the like—ignored the problems besetting the state. Few noticed, or admitted noticing, that the luster was fading from the Golden State.

The recession of 1990 hit California particularly hard. Land values fell and suddenly banks that had loaned money based on super-inflated appraisals found themselves with a bunch of worthless paper and a shortage of solid assets. The end of the cold war brought a drastic reduction in military spending and layoffs in the defense industry. The retail trade, weak for some years, faltered badly; big department stores and boutiques closed. Unemployment grew. The auto industry, hard pressed by recession all over the country, shut down its California plants, throwing thousands out of work. The ranks of the homeless and hungry grew.

People desperate for means to climb out of the recession added to the strife that has plagued California throughout its history. No one doubted that California would survive or questioned that it would regain its gilded promise. The weather hadn't changed; oranges still ripened in thousands of orchards; the demand for lettuce, artichokes, tomatoes, and hundreds of other field crops had not dried up. In the waning years of the twentieth century no one doubted that California would rise again, but many disagreed over what the rosy future would look like and how long it would take to arrive.

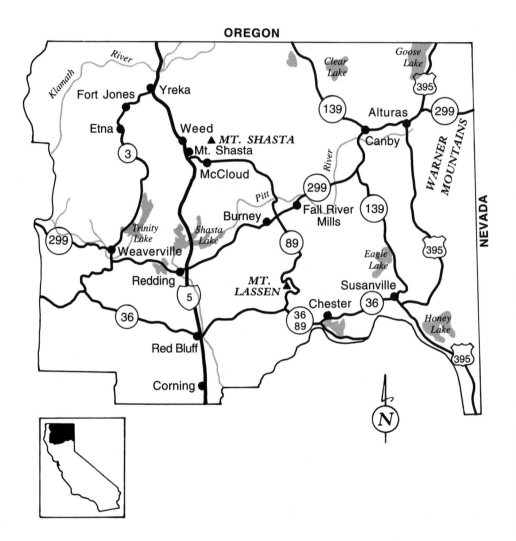

OREGON

Klamath *River*

Fort Jones Yreka

Etna Weed ▲ *MT. SHASTA*
Mt. Shasta

(3) McCloud

Clear
Lake

Goose
Lake

(395)

(139) Alturas (299)

Canby

River

(299)

Pitt

Burney Fall River (139)
Mills

*Trinity
Lake* *Shasta
Lake* (89)

(299) Weaverville

Eagle
Lake

(395)

Redding *MT.
LASSEN* ▲ Susanville

(5) Chester (36)

(36) 36
89 *Honey
Lake*

Red Bluff (395)

Corning

N

NEVADA

WARNER
MOUNTAINS

Part 1

Shasta–Cascade:
The Magnificent Wilderness

The history of the northeastern section of California is rife with quarrels and strife, written in blood—mostly the blood of natives. Warren Beck and David Williams write, "The mountain men who traveled through this region and those who came in their footsteps antagonized the Indians." Friction between natives and newcomers to this territory was to be expected. These Indians had lived in contentment for many centuries, and they resented the invaders who arrived in the middle of the nineteenth century and disrupted their way of life. When settlers usurped a choice oak grove or lush field, the Indians resented it, reasoning—not illogically—that they had been there first. Indians fought to hang on to their ancestral lands; settlers retaliated. Simply put, that is the story behind the troubles between all nonmission Indians and newcomers to California.

A notorious case in point is the Modoc Wars of the Shasta–Cascade region, which started in 1852 when Indians wiped out an emigrant train en route to California from Oregon. Retaliation was swift and brutal— some forty Modoc braves were slaughtered. Such thrusts and parries continued until most of the natives of the area had been either relocated or killed.

These battles came late in the history of emigrants versus natives and were the final stand of the California Indians. As Hubert Howe Bancroft writes in volume seven of his *History of California*, "Thus it is that the California valley cannot grace her annals with a single Indian war bordering on respectability. It can boast, however, a hundred or two of as brutal butcherings, on the part of our honest miners and brave pioneers, as any area of equal extent in the republic. The poor natives of California had neither the strength nor the intelligence to unite in any formidable numbers; hence, when now and then one of them plucked up courage to defend his wife and little ones, or to retaliate on one of the many outrages that were constantly being perpetrated upon them by white persons, sufficient excuse was offered for the miners and settlers to band and shoot down any Indians they met, old or young, innocent or guilty, friendly or hostile, until their appetite for blood was appeased." The old saying, "The only good Indian is a dead Indian," was widely honored in those days and parts.

Notwithstanding their treatment of the natives, many of the historic characters who populated the Shasta-Cascade section of the state were admirable as pioneers in the truest sense of the word, settlers who braved incredible hardships to reach California, even then deemed the Golden State, and to survive after they arrived. The area owes much to the likes of William Cressler, John Bonner, and James Dorris. The determined residents of Shasta, who three times rebuilt their fire-ravaged town, paint a picture of fortitude not often seen, even in the annals of California.

Equally valiant and important to the development of the state were the Chinese, who came first in a trickle and then a rush. James D. Hart writes, "Travel was easy [for Chinese leaving their homeland], for passage costs were repaid by the garnisheeing of future California earnings, but for that reason most of the 25,000 who arrived by 1852 were in virtual bondage to their employers." Hated and reviled, still they came. In the Shasta-Cascade region they reworked old gold mines. Elsewhere they served in San Francisco as domestics, and on the Central Pacific Railroad and the Sacramento Delta. No matter how well they worked and how silently they suffered, their white neighbors found ways to make their lives ever more uncomfortable.

Californians have been accused of being more urgent, noisier, more demanding, and quicker to fight than residents of other states. If, indeed, that claim contains even a germ of truth, Californians' continuing water disputes support it. Contention arises, in part, because 70 percent of the state's water flows in the north and 80 percent of it is used in the south. For much of the state's existence, the north has been battling the south over the movement of water from the former to the latter.

Conceived in 1919, the Central Valley Project languished until 1933, when the legislature got around to adopting the legislation to make it possible. Since the state at that time was in the grip of the Great Depression, federal government picked up the tab. In 1935 the necessary legislation was passed in Washington and construction began in 1937. A linchpin of the project, Shasta Dam impounds the waters of the Sacramento, McCloud, and Pit Rivers in Shasta Lake, north of Redding. It's only the first step in a colossal system that each year moves about 2.3 million acre-feet of water four hundred miles south to provide irrigation for the crops of the Central Valley.

It's fitting that a historical exploration of California start in its remote northeast corner. Here we meet trailblazers, scouts, and settlers, hardy souls who often lived for months without human interaction. As you will see, Shasta-Cascade is still, today, a sparsely settled, magnificent portion of California.

US 395
Oregon Border–Susanville
148 miles

While much of the Shasta-Cascade section of California is heavily forested and steeply graded, this portion of US 395 runs atop a high plateau through desertlike flatland studded with sagebrush. Goose Lake, shriveled to less than half its ancient size, lies to the west and the rugged Warner Mountains soar on the east. There rise peaks that are often snowclad the year round. In some places the road is flanked on both sides by pines and firs of the Modoc National Forest; in others the trees recede, leaving the road hot, dusty, and uninviting to all but those in search of stories of the past.

FANDANGO PASS

Five miles outside of Pine Creek, the first tiny community south of the Oregon border, travelers in search of a colorful chapter in the history of California will take off on one of the many side trips that are essential for seeing some of the most fascinating parts of the state. This one heads southeast on Fandango Pass Road to its junction with Surprise Valley Road, a distance of fourteen miles. Fandango Pass was so named, according to Hart, because a group of forty-niners who camped there got so cold they had to dance to keep from freezing. Mildred Hoover and the Rensches tell a far more romantic tale. They report that emigrants traveling Lassen's Trail sighted Goose Lake from the sixty-one-hundred-foot summit of the pass and believed it to be the Pacific. So relieved were they to have safely reached journey's end that they made camp and rejoiced by dancing a fandango. Midstep, so to speak, the dancers were set upon by a band of Indians and slain to the last infant. More pragmatically, the historical marker near the pass labels it the convergence of the Applegate Trail and the Lassen Cutoff, famous emigrant trails, without mentioning any massacre.

FORT BIDWELL

At the northern end of dry Upper Alkali Lake, 5.5 miles north of Fandango Pass Road on Surprise Valley Road, a monument marks the site of Fort Bidwell, a military post established in 1865 to protect pioneer settlers in the area from marauding Indians. The fort was named for John Bidwell, a significant character in California's story. Abandoned as a military outpost in 1892, it was used as a school for Indians until 1930.

CEDARVILLE

Heading south from the fort, Surprise Valley Road crosses CA 299 at Cedarville, about twenty-five miles from the fort. In the center of town stands a marker denoting the site of the Cressler and Bonner Trading Post, built in 1865 by a man whose last name only survives: Townsend. He lost not only his first name over the years, but also his life soon after he hewed the logs and raised this first mercantile establishment in Modoc County. The widow Townsend sold the tiny cabin to William T. Cressler and John H. Bonner, who carried on a thriving trade there, supplying emigrants who intended to brave Cedar Pass on their way to Alturas and points west.

Beyond the 6,350-foot pass and eighteen miles west of Cedarville, CA 299 briefly joins US 395 just six miles northeast of Alturas. This side trip adds about sixty miles to the trek between Pine Creek and Susanville.

ALTURAS

Alturas, located on the Pit River and once called Dorris Bridge, is the county seat and principal city of Modoc County. It got its original name from its founder, Presley Dorris, the area's first white settler. His house and the wooden bridge he built across a creek at the east end of town still stand.

Infernal Caverns

South of Alturas, US 395 follows the south fork of the Pit River to a little town called Likely. Just north of that curiously named community, sixteen and a half miles south of Alturas and about four miles west of the highway on Westside Road, is the site of one of the most famous battles of the many fought between natives and pioneers: Infernal Caverns. It was there, on September 26–27 in 1867, that a band of Shoshonis and Paiutes, supplemented by a few Pit River Indians—about a hundred in all—faced off against Gen. George Crook and sixty-five troops. The army forces, ordered to subdue the Indians who had been terrorizing colonists of the area, had driven them into this fortress of caves and rocks. In the pitched battle that followed, many of the Indians were killed, as were eight of Crook's men.

THE HONEY LAKE VALLEY

South of Likely, US 395 meanders through a desolate area of sage-brush and little else. The Honey Lake Valley comes into view as a pleasant relief. About forty miles long and twenty wide, it was for some time the only section of Lassen County that boasted settlers. The valley was named, according to Hart, for the aphids' deposits that covered the wild oats growing there. The Federal Writers' Project guide, *California: A Guide to the Golden State*, however, calls the substance that glistened on trees and shrubs "honeydew." From that sticky, sweet material the Indians made a kind of molasses.

Isaac Roop and His Town

The earliest residents of Honey Lake Valley were the Washo and Paiute, but the newcomer who made the biggest splash in the area was Isaac Roop, the valley's first white settler. Roop traveled on horseback from Shasta, about one hundred miles to the west, to establish a hotel on the Noble Emigrant Trail, which had been created to bypass the rigors of the Lassen Trail. He staked a claim in 1853, built a cabin in what is now Susanville, overlooking the long stretch of Honey Lake Valley, and struggled along with only Indians for neighbors until the next year, when Peter Lassen arrived on the scene.

State historical marker number 675 stands in a city park, indicating the spot where the Noble Trail passed through Susanville, which Isaac Roop named for his daughter. The meadow was a welcome haven for weary emigrants en route to Northern California, who rested their stock here and replenished their supplies at Roop's store.

It was in 1855 that Lassen and a handful of prospectors struck gold in the valley. When news of the find got out, a group of miners from the Feather River mining area arrived to stake out claims near Susanville. The area was so remote that the Honey Lake Valley settlers met at the Roop cabin on April 26, 1856, to form their own government. Christening the land the Territory of Nataqua, they declared it to be inde-pendent of California. Roop was elected secretary of the group of about twenty, according to Hoover, and Lassen its surveyor. With boundary lines not yet clearly established, they managed to include in the new territory much land that was actually part of Nevada Territory.

Nataqua was short-lived because the U.S. Congress refused to rec-ognize it, wanting to include the area in Nevada Territory, if California would cede it. California refused. Roop insisted that his area was in-dependent and defied all governments, including those of Plumas County, Nevada, and the United States. He set up headquarters in his cabin, calling it Fort Defiance, and waged what was called The Sagebrush War.

Only a few shots were exchanged between Roop and the sheriff of Plumas County before an armistice resulted in the redrawing of the Nevada-California boundary. Roop's territory was included in Lassen County with Susanville as its seat.

CA 299
Alturas–Weaverville
188 miles

West of Alturas, CA 299 travels through high-desert plateau. At Canby, nineteen miles west of Alturas, another side trip starts.

LAVA BEDS NATIONAL MONUMENT

CA 139 slices northwest from Canby through the Modoc National Forest. Twenty-five miles after leaving Canby, CA 139 crosses the Lava Beds National Monument Road, which loops through the entire park and rejoins CA 139 seven miles south of Tulelake.

Lava beds formed caves where Kientepoos and his band took shelter during the Modoc War. —National Park Service

Centuries ago, a group of volcanoes erupted in what is now called the Klamath Basin, a rugged area straddling the Oregon-California border. That volcanic activity left behind an area of almost 50,000 acres honeycombed with lava tubes, cinder cones, and lava flows that formed some two hundred caves of different sizes and features. Some are filled with dripping ice, others with moss and lichens. Some are huge, others narrow and cramped. Those are the caves that sheltered the Modoc Indians during their last attempt to save their homeland from invaders from the East.

Captain Jack and the Modoc Wars

When settlement got under way along the Lost River, which flows south from Oregon and crosses the California border near CA 139, settlers demanded that the Modocs be removed from the sagebrush-covered plateaus and wooded mountains that had been their home for centuries. Their domed dwellings were scattered along the shores of Tule Lake and the Lost River, where they fished and trapped and gathered seeds and bulbs from the countryside. Nonetheless, settlers insisted the federal government should move them to the Klamath Reservation along with the Klamath and Snake tribes, their traditional enemies.

Modocs moved to the reservation in the late 1850s, but they could tolerate their new living conditions for only a time. Led by Kientepoos—called "Captain Jack" by the settlers—many of the younger Modocs left the Klamath reservation, and returned to the Lost River, demanding a reservation of their own in their traditional homeland. Their presence in that area unnerved the pioneers who had usurped the land. Oregon Indian Superintendent Alfred Meacham prevailed upon Kientepoos and his tribesmen to return to the reservation once again. The Klamaths, however, made life miserable for the Modocs, who fled once more in April of 1869. Kientepoos and his followers settled again on their Lost River land.

Since negotiating had failed, troops from Fort Klamath were ordered to round up the rebels and return them, by force if necessary, to the reservation. The troops were surprised by the number of Modocs they had to cope with; fighting broke out and the Modoc War was on.

The Modoc band included three groups that somewhat casually followed the leadership of Kientepoos. One group, under Hooker Jim, traveled east around Tule Lake, killing fourteen male settlers to retaliate for the attack by the troops. Meanwhile, Kientepoos and the rest of the Lost River Modocs crossed the lake by boat and entered the lava beds. Some time later, Hooker Jim's band joined them, to Kientepoos's displeasure. He was reluctant to be associated with those who had murdered settlers, but he had little choice. The third band, the Hot Creeks,

*Ranger lights stairway in Skull Cave at Lava Beds
National Monument.* —Fred Mang Jr., National Park Service

eventually joined them, after being tricked by settlers into thinking they would be hanged simply because they were Modoc.

The settlers organized more than 300 troops and volunteers to rout that group, which numbered about fifty Modoc men along with women and children, from an area of caves and lava trenches known as Captain Jack's Stronghold. On the fog-shrouded morning of January 16, 1873, the troops entered the area, which they believed to be flatland, sure they would be able to dislodge the Modocs. Instead, the Modocs inflicted heavy casualties and drove the troops in confusion back through the fog. Exhausted and cold, the soldiers fled over the rugged terrain, leaving behind their weapons, ammunition, and wounded. The Modocs were now in a bargaining position.

Kientepoos insisted that he and his people be given a reservation on the Lost River. To avert further bloodshed, President Grant set up a peace commission to meet, unarmed, with the Modoc leaders. Kientepoos was willing to negotiate for a peaceful settlement, but Hooker Jim, under indictment for murdering the settlers and with nothing to lose, convinced Kientepoos and several others that they should kill the commissioners.

On the morning of April 11, 1873, Gen. E. R. S. Canby, Reverend Eleazar Thomas, Alfred Meacham, and Indian Agent Leroy Dyer gathered at the peace tent. There they found not the agreed-upon five unarmed Modocs, but eight, two of whom were obviously armed. Once again, Kientepoos demanded a reservation on Lost River land. When the commissioners refused his demand, he pulled out a revolver and killed General Canby. Thomas was killed by another Modoc, Meacham was wounded, and Dyer escaped unharmed.

The soldiers hurriedly sent for reinforcements and launched a second attack on Captain Jack's Stronghold just four days later. When they took the stronghold on April 17, the troops found it empty. Kientepoos and the others had slipped away through a trench to the Schonchin Lava Flow to the south. There they found in ice caves the water they desperately needed for their 160 or so men, women, and children.

On the morning of May 10, the Modocs were defeated when they launched a surprise attack on the troop encampment at Dry Lake. It was a devastating setback for the Modocs, who then fell to fighting among themselves and soon dissolved into small bands. All were eventually captured and tried. President Grant granted amnesty to some, but Kientepoos, Boston Charlie, Black Jim, and Schonchin John were hanged on the morning of October 3, 1873. The surviving Modocs were shipped to the Quapaw Agency in Oklahoma, where disease accomplished what force had been unable to, and the Modocs soon were a vanished people.

The Modoc War was the only Indian war in California in which a general officer was killed. It was also one of the most costly in the nation's history, considering how few people were involved, and all so that a few settlers could graze their cattle.

The Lava Beds National Monument Road, in looping north and east, passes the Schonchin Lava Flow, many of the caves and craters that gave shelter to the Modocs, Gillem's Camp, army headquarters during the Modoc War, and Captain Jack's Stronghold. The road exits the park at its northeast entrance near Newell.

Rock Art

Besides the volcanic constructions that provided shelter for the embattled Modocs, Lava Beds National Monument is home to some of the most impressive examples of Indian rock art in the nation, both pictographs and petroglyphs. Pictographs are figures painted on rock surfaces and are usually found on boulders inside caves and at cave entrances. Symbol Bridge and Big Painted Cave hold two outstanding examples. Petroglyphs, on the other hand, are figures carved or pecked into the rock. With few exceptions, petroglyphs within the monument are found on cliff faces or boulders along the ancient shorelines of Tule Lake. At the park entrance, eighteen miles east of Captain Jack's Stronghold, rises a high bluff of smooth sandstone into which have been inscribed remarkable petroglyphs.

While experts understand little about why and when this rock art was created, most agree that the symbols are indeed works of art and not writing or messages. Robert F. Heizer and C. W. Clewlow Jr., experts on the topic, say the pictographs were done between 380 and 1,400 years ago; petroglyphs, they suggest, are of somewhat more recent creation.

TULELAKE RELOCATION CENTER

The park road reaches CA 139 once again just east of the petroglyphs and near the town of Newell, where stands California historical marker number 850.2. The plaque on that marker reads, in part, "Tulelake Relocation Center. Tulelake was one of ten concentration camps established during World War II to incarcerate 110,000 persons of Japanese ancestry, of whom the majority were American citizens, behind barbed wire and guard towers without charge or trial."

Leaving that sad spot, CA 139 heads southeast to rejoin CA 299 at Canby, once again. This fascinating side trip adds about 150 miles to the distance between Alturas and Weaverville.

Continuing southwest, CA 299 enters Shasta County, skirts the southern border of Shasta-Trinity National Forest, passes a handful of tiny communities of no great historical interest, and finally, 122 miles from Canby, reaches the city of Redding on I-5.

QUEEN CITY, SHASTA

Six miles west of Redding on CA 299 is Old Shasta, a state historical park. About all that remains of the once-lusty Queen City of the state's northern mining district is a cluster of brick ruins on the south side of what was Main Street and a pair of very old structures still standing on the north. Those refurbished buildings are the courthouse and the Masonic Hall.

Pierson B. Reading discovered gold here in 1848, after working for some time for John Sutter at New Helvetia. Because fine springs flow year-round out of the steep hill above the site, a town called Reading Springs grew up to serve the miners of the area. By September 1849, more than 500 people were living in tents and shanties in the area, enduring the all but intolerable conditions that most prospectors knew. The town's first permanent structure, a log cabin, was raised on High Street late in 1849. During the spring of 1850 a whipsaw mill began operating nearby, supplying boards for the many buildings that then erupted along Main Street. Within two years Reading Springs was a substantial town, indeed, with one- and two-story frame hotels and mercantile establishments lining Main Street. Deciding that their town needed a better name, a group of miners gathered in June 1850 to select one. After a lot of discussion and some ludicrous suggestions (Fountania, for one), the group decided to call the town Shasta City. A few months later it was chosen county seat of the newly defined Shasta County.

Because it was at the end of all roads from San Francisco, Sacramento, and other southerly points, Shasta grew lustily. It served as a staging area for both hopeful prospectors and successful miners and was soon known as Queen City of the North. Beyond Shasta, folks heading for the mines had to transport supplies on mule trains, some up to two hundred animals long. Gold had to be shipped out from Shasta, too. Nearly $100,000 a week left the city in 1852; total for that year was almost $2.5 million.

On December 1, 1852, disaster struck: Fire leveled about one-third of the structures in town. Viewing the fire as a temporary setback, residents quickly rebuilt their town. A few months later, on the afternoon of June 14, 1853, an even more destructive blaze destroyed—in just 33 minutes—the entire commercial center of Shasta. Even though the damage was estimated at half a million dollars, a considerable sum in those days, residents set about rebuilding once again. This time, however, they required that all buildings on Main Street be fireproof. Within two years, twenty-eight new brick-walled and iron-shuttered structures lined Main Street.

By 1855 Shasta boasted five hotels and five stage companies, plus a horse market, a livery stable, a blacksmith shop, and two drugstores. Serving residents and transients were three doctors, four attorneys, one public bathhouse, three bookstores, and a number of other businesses, including restaurants, a jeweler, and a bowling alley—in short, everything a sophisticated population needed.

In 1857, when a wagon road to Weaverville was hewed over Buckhorn Pass, sixteen miles to the west, the decline of Shasta began. No longer was Shasta the only place to store and transship supplies and materials. More roads were constructed in ensuing years and Shasta's downfall gathered momentum. The California-Oregon stage was rerouted, in 1868, to follow the Sacramento River, thereby missing Shasta altogether. In 1872 officials of the Central Pacific Railroad decided to establish their railhead six miles to the east and close to the Sacramento, at an area called Poverty Flat. In July of that year, the beneficiary of that railroad largess was renamed Redding.

Shasta continued to struggle along, in spite of another disastrous fire in 1878, and retained its position as county seat. Even that honor was stripped from the Queen City in 1888, after a hot political battle, when the title of county seat was conferred on Redding.

WEAVERVILLE

West of Shasta, CA 299 passes through the northern edge of the Whiskeytown Unit of a national recreation area and skirts the northern edge of Whiskeytown Lake, beneath whose waters lies the rowdy old town of Whiskeytown. The road crosses Buckhorn Summit on its way to Weaverville, the seat of Trinity County, forty-five miles west of Redding. Weaverville was named in 1850 for John Weaver, an early prospector in the area who built the town's first cabin.

Weaverville has been on the National Register of Historic Places since 1974, and many buildings from its past still stand; eighteen are fashioned from bricks made in nearby kilns. One such is the Pacific Brewery Building, built in 1854–56 and in continuous use ever since. The Weaverville Drug Store building also has seen continuous use since it was constructed in 1855. The store opened in 1862 and has been operating ever since, making it the longest continuously operating drugstore in the state.

Asylum for the Chinese

The frantic rush into the area after the discovery of gold caused Weaverville to mushroom. More than 2,000 Chinese, mostly men, followed the horde of white men to local mines, where they often reworked claims abandoned by white miners, patiently washing old placers for the riches they sought.

As Douglas and Gina McDonald tell us in their booklet about the history of Chinese in the Weaverville area, most of these immigrants had been driven from their homeland by political turmoil and a disastrous flood. They wanted nothing more than to dig fortunes out of the ground and return home. Some of the Chinese men who came to California took their profit from Gum Shun—Gold Mountain, their name for California—and left as planned; others, like their counterparts from European nations, found no gold but found other ways of making the money they needed to send to families waiting hungrily back home.

Throughout the state the Chinese were discriminated against and exploited. Americans were largely responsible for the discrimination, according to Hart, but fellow countrymen joined in the exploitation. Chinese subcontractors sold the labor of Chinese miners to Chinese mining companies that paid very low wages, making it almost impos-

*Chinese teacher
and student.*
—CHS/TICOR,
USC Special
Collections

sible for the miners to work off their passage from China to California. Their situation was not unlike that of thousands of Europeans who came to colonial shores as indentured servants and worked for years to gain their independence.

Harassed by Americans and struggling under the repressive foot of greedy Chinese, this new group of exploited found it all but impossible to rise out of the miserable poverty that debt bondage created. In addition, the state levied a revised form of the foreign miners' license tax, an unjust law initially aimed at Mexicans and revised to target Chinese. Much to the irritation of white miners, who had expected the levy to drive the foreigners off, the Chinese paid the unjust fee, hoping to win favor with other miners. Until 1870, when the state supreme court declared it unconstitutional, the tax accounted for nearly one-quarter of the state's entire revenue. And that was true in spite of thieving tax collectors who often convinced the Chinese miners not to ask for a receipt so the collectors could pocket the money without reporting it. Many Chinese also were victimized by Americans falsely representing themselves as tax collectors.

Even though the first census of Weaverville, taken in 1852, listed only a small number of Chinese, the McDonalds say that as many as

2,500 Chinese men probably lived and worked in and around the city. While they worked their claims, according to a broadside distributed by the Trinity County Chamber of Commerce, the miners lived in Chinatown, which included all the necessary commercial establishments, even brothels, opium dens, and gambling houses.

They were a patient, peaceful lot, generally speaking, but most of the Chinese population of Weaverville belonged to one of two rival homeland associations—tongs—and the tension between the groups was marked. In April 1854 a squabble erupted in a gambling house, ostensibly over a paltry bet. Members of opposing tongs scuffled and then the matter was allowed to drop, but animosity between the two groups continued to grow.

Before long, the McDonalds write, weapons—wicked three-pronged spears that the feuders mounted on long poles—were ordered from local blacksmiths. The tongs were arming for battle. It all came to a head on Saturday, July 15, 1854, when about 700 Chinese clashed in a brief war. "The 'war' would have been a ceremonious contest of show and some skill, with fewer casualties, if some of the nearly 2,000 or so onlookers had not taken a hand," the McDonalds report. White spectators goaded both sides, throwing rocks and even firing a pistol. Thus egged on, the men fell to, and 26 or 27 of the combatants were killed and 60 wounded. A marker commemorating the battle stands today on CA 3, Trinity Lakes Boulevard, just north of CA 299.

Weaverville Joss House in Trinity County. —Trinity County Historical Society

Fully operable stamp mill from Paymaster Gold Mine in Eastman Gulch near Lewiston. Now in Weaverville. —Trinity County Historical Society

Another marker on CA 299 highlights the location of the Weaverville Joss House, a place of worship for the many Chinese who have lived in the area since 1852. Historians believe the original temple was built about that time, even though no mention of it appears in the local press until 1855. Rita Hanover, local historian, believes that first joss house was destroyed by fire in the 1860s. Another was built near the site of the present structure, but its date of construction is unclear. In June 1873 the temple was again ravaged by fire, in spite of the frantic efforts of bucket brigades. Members of the Chinese community rallied and bought a lot adjacent to the destroyed temple on which to build a larger one. Construction was begun on February 7, 1874, and the temple was completed two months later. Dedicated on April 18, that structure stands today.

Now a state historic park, the Weaverville Joss House sits amid a grove of pine and native locust trees and at least one locust imported from China. A picket fence surrounds the temple, which is approached by means of a Chinese bridge across shallow Weaver Creek. Most importantly, two Chow Win dragon fish, believed by some to ward off fire, sit atop the temple.

La Grange Hydraulic Gold Mine

Four miles west of Weaverville, CA 299 passes historical marker number 778, which denotes the vicinity of La Grange Hydraulic Gold Mine, first operated in 1862. It was the largest hydraulic mine in the world until it closed before the First World War.

On leaving the historical marker, CA 299 continues winding through spectacular national forests until at last, one hundred miles west of Weaverville, it reaches the Pacific.

I-5
Oregon Border–Orland
175 miles

YREKA

As the Oregon-California border, I-5 roughly parallels the old Oregon-California trail. Following the eastern edge of the Klamath National Forest, the highway enters Yreka, the seat of Siskiyou County, twenty-five miles south of the border. The town's name is thought to be a corruption of Wai-ri-ki, the natives' name for Mount Shasta. Established in 1851 as an encampment for gold seekers, Yreka suffered through the difficulties of the time—lawlessness, tong wars, and fire—but buildings from the 1850s survive and now house modern businesses.

MT. SHASTA

As I-5 continues southward, the Marble Mountains rise on the west and Shasta Valley sweeps off to the east. It passes through Weed, twenty-five miles south of Yreka, and then reaches the tiny community of Mt. Shasta, eleven miles below Weed. Mt. Shasta is a quaint community in the shadow of the 14,164-foot mountain for which it is named, one of

Main Street, Yreka, California. —CHS/TICOR, USC Special Collections

Passenger train stopped at Shasta Springs, early 1900s.
—CHS/TICOR, USC Special Collections

the great peaks of the nation. Five glaciers glide on the mountain's snow-covered slopes and hot springs bubble at the summit where, according to Indian legend, the Great Spirit dwells.

Mt. Shasta, the town, is home to the Sisson Hatchery, built in 1888 and until 1979 the largest hatchery in the world. Over the years this facility has spawned millions of rainbow trout that have been shipped all around the world. The original hatchery building is now a museum that chronicles the history of fishermen all over the world. The new hatchery sits behind the museum.

CASTLE CRAGS STATE PARK

Continuing south, I-5 passes Dunsmuir, a historic railroad town, and then, about six miles farther along, reaches Castle Crags State Park. Here ancient granite spires as high as 6,000 feet tower above the upper Sacramento River canyon. These dramatic formations were tossed up by volcanoes millions of years ago and are far older than Mt. Shasta, which looms off to the east.

The area around the Crags was the setting for a battle between local Modocs and white settlers. Much as they did in the Lost River region, settlers here drove the natives from their lands. One of the first settlers in the region, "Mountain Joe" Doblondy, frontiersman and scout for John C. Frémont, was responsible for attracting many settlers and thus, to some extent, for causing the strife. While it isn't known exactly when

45

he made the area his home, it is known that he farmed, kept a hotel of sorts, and guided travelers from a spot close to the Crags called Lower Soda Springs Ranch.

Mountain Joe also told tall tales about the wealth to be had for the taking from river bars around the area, thereby luring hundreds of miners to the banks of Soda Creek in 1855. According to Mildred Hoover, "The little valley was soon 'a white sea of tents. Every bar on the Sacramento was the scene of excitement.'" The army of miners, finding little gold, soon left in disgust, but not before they had killed off or driven out the fish and game on which the natives depended. Furious, the Modocs plundered and burned the settlement at Lower Soda Springs, carrying away the foodstuffs they needed to save them from starvation.

Settlers retaliated at Battle Rock, the highest of the Crags, where a band led by Reuben P. Gibson that included Mountain Joe, recruits from neighboring settlements, and a handful of Shastas faced off against the Modocs, who were armed only with bows and arrows. Historical marker number 116, near the head of the foot trail, explains: "Directly under the highest crag in the northwest corner the group of settlers . . . fought with the Modoc Indians. Many on both sides were killed or wounded. This battle was one of a long series of conflicts between the Indians and the whites that culminated in the Modoc War." Poet of the High Sierra, Joaquin Miller, recited a highly exaggerated version of this battle in his *Life among the Modocs*.

SHASTA DAM

As I-5 plunges through the Shasta National Forest and the heart of Shasta County, forty-five miles south of Castle Crags it reaches Project City and the junction with Shasta Dam Boulevard. About seven miles west on that boulevard is the Bureau of Reclamation headquarters and visitors' center, where information aplenty about the dam and its great lake is available.

Shasta Dam is the main unit of the Central Valley Project, which collects the bountiful water of Northern California and distributes it to the thirsty south. Completed in 1945, it is the second highest and second largest dam in mass content in the United States. It is 602 feet tall, 3,500 feet long. Its reservoir, Shasta Lake, covers 29,500 acres; the dam and spillway drop water 480 feet.

After leaving the visitors' center the boulevard loops around and becomes County Road A18, which soon rejoins I-5. The little side trip to the big dam adds about fifteen miles to the journey between Orland and the Oregon border.

REDDING AND ANDERSON

Just two miles farther south I-5 enters Redding, seat of Shasta County. It was laid out in 1872 and named for B. B. Redding, a land agent of the Central Pacific Railroad who planned the town.

West of I-5 and ten miles south of Redding lies the town of Anderson, which, according to Hoover, was once part of the American Ranch owned by Elias Anderson, one of Shasta County's first settlers. Just north of Anderson stands California historical marker number 58, which reads, "Old California-Oregon Road. This marks the location of the main artery of travel used by pioneers between the Trinity River and the northern mines of California and Oregon." Beaten into a hard-packed trail by scouts and prospectors, this historic route was traveled by mule trains, covered wagons, and stagecoaches.

William B. Ide

Thirty miles south of Redding, I-5 reaches Red Bluff, Tehama County seat since 1857. Red Bluff's location near the California-Oregon Road made it a center for miners en route to the Trinity diggings and, later, a shipping point for locally raised wheat, grapes, and lumber. Its greatest claim to fame, however, is the William B. Ide Adobe, a state historic park and former home of one of the leaders of the legendary Bear Flag Revolt.

"The Bear Flag Revolt," writes Kevin Starr, "which history saw so glorious, was, in fact, unspeakably ridiculous, as well as a little tragical, and for the country disastrous." Starr regards the revolt's leaders, Ide and Robert B. Semple, as "a liquor-inflamed frontier orator and a nasal Yankee crank." Other historians see them somewhat differently.

Literature available at the state historic park in Red Bluff takes a far more favorable view of Ide. Born in 1796 at Rutland, Massachusetts, the park brochure tells us, Ide joined a wagon train headed west in the spring of 1845. With his wife and nine children he left Independence, Missouri, in the company of a large wagon train bound for Oregon. Near Fort Hall (Idaho) the family changed direction, joining a party headed for California. They reached Sutter's Fort in late October and subsequently settled in a log cabin on the Sacramento River.

In 1846, hearing rumors that Mexican authorities were going to drive all U.S. citizens out of California, Ide agreed to lead a war party to the pueblo of Sonoma, north of San Francisco. There the Americans slapped Gen. Mariano G. Vallejo and his brother Salvadore into jail and, running up a hastily fashioned Bear Flag over the town plaza, proclaimed California an independent republic. The park literature continues, "These bold moves on the part of the settlers paved the way to occupation of California by armed forces of the United States. The Bear Flag, after flying for a few weeks, was replaced by the Stars and Stripes, July 9, 1846." Ide and most of the other Bear Flag band joined Frémont's forces for the campaign in central California.

When the question of Californian independence from Mexico was settled, Ide returned to his family. With the discovery of gold, in 1848, he and his sons dug some $25,000 from the fields, with which he bought a portion of a Mexican land grant called the Red Bluff Ranch. There Ide built an adobe house overlooking the Sacramento River and established the Adobe Ferry where the California-Oregon Road crossed the river, thus linking the various mining areas of the state. The restored adobe house still stands about one and one-half miles north of Red Bluff on Adobe Road.

When the future of California was assured, Ide settled to serving as a justice of the peace, Roy Bean style, often filling many positions at once. One account reports that during the trial of a horse thief, Ide acted as judge, court clerk, prosecutor, and defense attorney, raising points for both sides and keeping a record of the proceedings. When the jury found the defendant guilty, Ide sentenced him to hang.

I-5 continues south through Corning and on to Orland in Glenn County, the northern end of the great Central Valley.

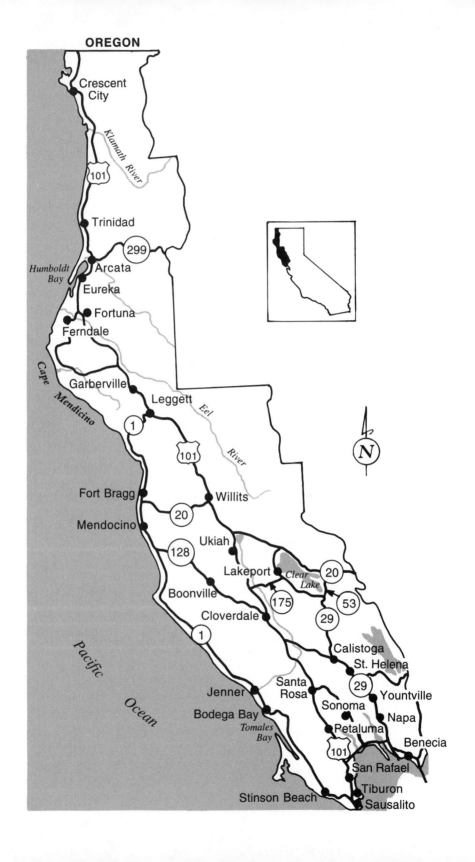

Part 2

The Wild North Coast

The wild north coast of California extends more than four hundred miles from the Oregon border south to the beautiful San Francisco Bay, and about fifty miles inland. Seven counties are within this area defined for the most part by US 101 on the eastern edge and CA 1 on the west. It's a region of rugged shores and pounding surf, of towering redwoods, verdant hills, and bountiful vineyards. The Humboldt County Convention and Visitors Bureau describes this region as "a land of visual splendor," marked by "the tallest trees in the world, rolling lush farm lands, towering mountain tops, and silent peaceful valleys." It's an area of incredible variety both scenically and historically.

The rugged coast, sun-bathed hills, dense forests, and fertile valleys of the region were home to Tolowas and Chumash, to Pomo and Hupa, and to scores of other peoples and tribes for many centuries before European explorers first visited the area. For the most part the native inhabitants lived in peace until the colonial ambitions of Spain, Russia, and the United States converged on California in the nineteenth century.

The mild climate and luxuriant grasslands of the eastern edge of this region made cattle raising easy and profitable for early settlers. Cattle hides became such a common item of barter that they were often referred to as "California bank notes." Rancheros all over the state used the animals' hides and the tallow that they rendered from slaughtered cattle to trade with English, American, and other foreign merchants who shopped up and down the coast. Such trading made it possible for the Californios to obtain manufactured goods from all over the world.

Exploring and mapping the area was a matter of necessity, not adventure, for the workers at the remote gold diggings to the east needed food and equipment, supplies that had to be brought all the way from Sacramento. In 1849, for example, to facilitate transport of those goods, a party from Rich Bar (near Weaverville) set out to carve a trail through the mountains and establish a supply base on the coast. They found Humboldt Bay, an ideal site that was soon abustle with settlers.

Redwood National Park. —Fred Mang Jr., National Park Service

Local natives were eager to trade at first, but the newcomers took over Indian village sites and hunting grounds, killing those natives who tried to defend their homes. It's not surprising that the Indians retaliated, slaughtering families, burning buildings, and scattering farm animals. The natives, however, were outnumbered and outdone in savagery by the settlers. Natives died by the thousands, from disease as well as genocide.

The story of natives in conflict with aggressive newcomers might be compared with modern attacks on the habitats of smaller and even more helpless creatures. Logging has become one of the most important industries of California's northwest, but it has all but destroyed the natural environment of forest denizens, many of which are well on the way to becoming extinct. According to an article in the winter 1989–90 issue of *California Parklands*, "Before European settlement, as recently as one hundred and fifty years ago, two-thirds of the landscape of the Pacific Northwest was covered by a continuous, ancient forest—a 'climax community.' The remaining one-third was in varying stages of natural succession, undergoing the slow process of regeneration." The forest waxed and waned in a continuous cycle of death and rebirth, maintaining a stable habitat for its residents. In the past century and a half, we have managed to destroy almost 90 percent of that virgin forest, leaving no home for the spotted owl and other threatened species.

Loggers are, not unreasonably, concerned about their livelihoods, but destroying forests by overcutting only postpones the ultimate lay-off. When the time comes that there are too few trees left to cut, there will be neither jobs nor spotted owls. As recently as 1984, ancient forests covered more than 51,000 acres of private land in California. By 1992, according to a report from the California Department of Forestry, only 5,000 of those acres remained. This seems to be a case of killing the goose that lays the golden eggs.

California's north coast still has, however, vast areas of undeveloped space, rolling hills, even awe-inspiring forests. They all reveal bits of the state's history to those who will look.

US 101
Oregon Border–Calpella
317 miles

US 101 enters California at Pelican State Beach along, appropriately enough, Pelican Bay. The road climbs from surf-edged meadows, skirts high crags overlooking the sea, and cuts inland a few miles to swoop around Lakes Talawa and Earl. This latter lake was discovered by members of Jedediah Smith's trailblazing party on June 18, 1828. The next day, Smith himself discovered the nearby river that would one day bear his name.

Fifteen miles south of the border, the road passes Point St. George and St. George Reef, where the Pacific Mail side-wheeler *Brother Jonathan* wrecked during a terrible storm in 1865. The boat ran onto a reef hidden just below the turbulent water, consigning 215 passengers and a large gold shipment to the icy sea.

CRESCENT CITY

Battery Point lighthouse, at the end of A Street in Crescent City, is the northernmost of the state's twenty-eight lighthouse stations and the oldest one surviving on the north coast. It stands guard at the northern end of the town, which is the seat of Del Norte County. The first light placed on Battery Point was simply a lantern slung from the top of a sturdy pole following the June 1855 crash of the steamer *America* on the rocks below. The lighthouse, built by the federal government in 1856, is accessible by foot at low tide and houses a museum of maritime lore.

The Lost Cabin

Crescent City sits twenty miles south of the Oregon border at the northern end of a long, shallow bay. It was founded, some historians say, because of the Lost Cabin Legend. Indeed, according to Mildred Hoover, that legend provided much of the impetus to explore this entire section of the state. According to Hoover's version of the tale, soon after gold was discovered on the Trinity River in 1850, an adventurous miner set out across the Coast Range, armed with his rifle and mining gear, to prospect the gulches and ravines of the foothills near the sea. After making a rich find, he built a cabin to shelter him while he piled up wealth. For months he toiled, hiding his gold—a fabulous amount, according to the legend—somewhere near his cabin. Local Indians eventually discovered his retreat and set upon him in overwhelming numbers. Beating him senseless, they left him for dead and then, frustrated because they were unable to find his cache, they put the torch to his cabin before leaving.

The miner wasn't dead, after all, but only stunned. When he regained his senses he managed to stagger back through the mountains to his home, where he eventually died. With his last breath he told friends gathered at his bedside about his hidden fortune, describing its location in exquisite detail. The setting he described obviously had to be somewhere along the north coast.

They came by the score, all those prospectors who hoped to find the Lost Cabin; so far as we know, no one ever located it. Perhaps the old miner wasn't as sane as his friends thought and was relating a fevered dream. Perhaps he was perpetrating one final hoax on his cronies. Perhaps the gold still lies buried somewhere along the wild north coast.

In any event, Crescent City was founded in 1853 by one of those parties of gold seekers. The town flourished, especially when rich new diggings were uncovered in the nearby hills. With the end of the gold frenzy, the town became a lumbering center, which it still is, and—more recently—a popular tourist center.

Many of those tourists make a point of visiting Front and H Streets, where stands state historical marker number 497. The legend on the marker reads, "Beneath this marker are portions of the hull of the 10,745-ton General Petroleum Corporation tanker SS *Emidio*, which on December 20, 1941, became the first ship to be torpedoed and shelled by a Japanese submarine off the Pacific Coast; the *Emidio* was attacked some 200 miles north of San Francisco and five men were killed.

Abandoned, the disabled vessel drifted north and broke in two on the rocks off Crescent City. The bow drifted into the harbor, where it lay southeast of this marker until salvaged in 1950 and 1951."

REQUA

Leaving Crescent City, US 101 cuts through Del Norte Coast Redwoods State Park and reaches Requa, fifteen miles below Crescent City at the mouth of the Klamath River. The town is named for the Rek-woi, who are still prominent in the area. It was here that natives saved Jedediah Smith and his party by feeding fish and berries to the starving explorers, who had killed and eaten their last dog and horse several days earlier.

Requa sits at the northern end of the Hoopa Valley Indian Reservation, largest in the state at 93,000 acres, with a population of about 2,500 persons. The reservation follows both sides of the Klamath River deep into Humboldt County.

TRINIDAD

A little more than seven miles farther along, the road skirts Trinidad Head, where Bruno de Heceta took possession of the bay and headland for Spain on June 11, 1775. The headland was once a whaling station and the nearby town of Trinidad was the first on the north coast. Now a tiny town, Trinidad offers little evidence of the past when, in 1851 and 1852, it was the distribution point for miners in Trinity County to the east. At Ocean and Edwards Streets in Trinidad stands a state historical marker designating the Old Indian Village of Tsurai. The legend reads, "Directly below was located the Yurok village of Tsurai. A prehistoric permanent Indian community, it was first located and described by Captains Bodega and Heceta, June 9–19, 1775. The houses were of hand-split redwood planks, designed for defense and protection. The village was occupied until 1916."

LITTLE RIVER STATE BEACH

Just south of Trinidad, US 101 passes Little River State Beach, where an exploration party headed by Dr. Josiah Gregg reached the coast in December 1849. They had left Weaverville—about one hundred miles inland on today's CA 299—in November and suffered incredible hardships as they searched for what the Indians described as "a large bay with fertile land and tall trees." Their supplies had given out and they were near starvation when, at last, they reached the bay. On his way back to announce his discovery of the bay from the landward side, Gregg, who was possibly lost, died of starvation in Lake County.

ARCATA

Soon after it passes the junction with CA 299, about ten miles south of Trinidad, US 101 enters Arcata, at the northern end of the bay of the same name. It's a lumber center, the home of Humboldt State University and the town that saw Bret Harte's birth as a writer. When it was founded in 1850 the town was christened Uniontown, but it was soon renamed to prevent confusion with another Uniontown in El Dorado County.

At Eighth and H Streets in Arcata stands the Jacoby Storehouse, a historic landmark. Built in 1857 as a one-story building, it served as a principal supply point for the Klamath-Trinity mining-camp trade and was sometimes used as a place of refuge from Indian troubles. Acquired in 1880 by A. Brizard, it is now three stories high, after being enlarged by the owners of the Brizard Mercantile Store.

Gunther's Island

A short side trip around the bay on CA 255 provides a glimpse of what is today called Gunther's Island. In 1860 the place was known as Indian Island and was the campsite of the survivors of three Eel River

Bret Harte received death threats after writing an article that denounced the slaughter at Gunther's Island. —The Bancroft Library

tribes who had been driven from their homeland by settlers. While the men were away fishing in February of that year, a gang of local scoundrels descended upon the campsite, intent on slaughter. Of the affair, Walton Bean writes, "With hatchets and axes they killed 60 Indians, mostly women and children, for no better reason than that some other tribe a hundred miles back in the mountains had been causing trouble." Bret Harte, who at that time was working in Arcata as a compositor for S. G. Whipple, editor of the *Northern California*, and as an agent for Wells, Fargo, was incensed by the murders and denounced them in an article headed "Indiscriminate Massacre of Indians—Women and Children Butchered." Following publication of the article, threats against Harte's life became so menacing that he left Arcata to settle in San Francisco. According to Dolan H. Eargle Jr., the island was renamed to obscure its past.

Continuing southward past the little community of Samoa, CA 255 soon rejoins US 101 at Eureka. This melancholy side trip adds about ten miles to the distance to Calpella.

EUREKA

Swinging wide around the rim of Arcata Bay, US 101 arrives at Eureka, seat of Humboldt County and the largest California town north of Sacramento. It was founded in 1850 as a port and shipping center for the rich mines on the Klamath and Trinity Rivers and now serves the same function for lumbering operations. It is the principal port between San Francisco and the Columbia River in Oregon.

Near the corner of Broadway and Highland, on a high bluff overlooking Humboldt Bay, is Fort Humboldt, established in 1853 by Bvt. Lt. Col. Robert C. Buchanan, who had been ordered there to keep the peace between natives and settlers. By July of the next year Buchanan's men had built fourteen plank buildings, which served as officers' quarters, barracks, commissary, hospital, powder magazine, laundries, and guardhouse. The buildings flanked a large square parade ground exposed on its west side to the bay. A blacksmith's shop, stable, and bakehouse were added later. Duty at Fort Humboldt was dreary: Supplies, mail, and, often, pay were slow to arrive. There was little to do in the way of recreation, and many of the troops drank too much.

One of these lonely, unhappy soldiers was Ulysses S. Grant, who was stationed on the barren bluff for four months. He had not seen his family for two years and reportedly wrote to his wife, "You do not know how forsaken I feel here! . . . How very much I want to see all of you." Grant was a loner who spent little time with his fellow officers, preferring instead to take long, solitary rides into the surrounding wilds. At last he decided to resign from the army and left Eureka for good in May 1854.

Residents of the area were never satisfied with the peace-keeping efforts of Buchanan and his troops, and they constantly harangued the state government to send more troops. When, at last, Governor Leland Stanford in February 1863 established and sent in the volunteer Mountaineer Battalion, large numbers of natives surrendered and asked for peace. The treaty that gave Hoopa Valley to the Indians was signed August 21, 1864, and the region's Indian wars soon ended.

The fort was abandoned as a military post in August 1870, and the land passed into private hands. Eventually the property was transferred to the state and became a historic park. Reconstruction of the fort's buildings began in 1984. The fort's hospital building has been restored and is now the park visitors center.

Forest products have long been a mainstay of this area's economy because of the moist climate and rich soil that encourage the growth of redwoods and Douglas firs, which grow to timbering size in about forty-five years. A reminder of this vital industry stands at the edge of the road that loops through Fort Humboldt State Historic Park.

Early north coast timber operation. —CHS/TICOR, USC Special Collections

Hikers marvel at trees—some as old as 2,000 years—in Redwood National Park. —Richard Frear, National Park Service

An outdoor display of logging equipment that traces the history of redwood logging from its beginnings in the 1850s to the present, it features an authentic logger's cabin complete with furnishings, several huge redwood stumps and logs, early examples of steam "donkeys" that replaced oxen in hauling logs out of the woods, and a host of tools used by loggers.

Eureka is also the site of the first nuclear power plant in California. Situated at the southern end of Humboldt Bay at Field's Landing on Buhne (pronounced "booner") Point, the plant was opened in 1963 by PG&E. It was closed in 1976 to be checked for possible earthquake damage, and permanently decommissioned in 1983. The plant lies just to the west of the freeway.

FERNDALE

Ten miles farther south, CA 211—Mattole Road—takes off from US 101 in a southwesterly direction to start a fascinating side trip. The first town encountered, about five miles from the highway, is Ferndale, a charming Victorian village with meticulously kept homes and gardens. So historically and architecturally authentic is the town that it has been designated a state historic landmark. Settled in 1852 and long known as Cream City, Ferndale has made lasting contributions to the dairy industry.

CAPE MENDOCINO AND PETROLIA

Fifteen miles farther along, Mattole Road reaches Cape Mendocino, presumably named for Antonio de Mendoza, first viceroy of New Spain (Mexico). Discovered and named by Juan Rodríguez Cabrillo in 1542, it is the westernmost point of the mainland United States. The road follows the edge of the cape for some miles, then turns inland to Petrolia. John McKinney, writing in the *Los Angeles Times* of August 9, 1992, describes the town: "The sleepy, storybook hamlet of Petrolia, near the [Petrolia] river's mouth was the site of the state's first producing oil wells, drilled here in 1865." Leland Stanford's Mattole Petroleum Company brought in the most successful producer, Union Well, which yielded one hundred barrels of oil at a one-barrel-a-day pace.

McKinney writes that at the end of the oil boom, settlers flocked to the area to take advantage of the fertile farmland. It's one of the wettest places on the Pacific Coast (a boon in a state that constantly has to cope with water shortages); the tiny town of Honeydew, south of Petrolia, records an average of about one hundred inches of rain a year.

Mattole Road rejoins US 101 at Dyerville in the northern part of the Humboldt Redwood State Park. This side trip adds about fifty scenic and historic miles to the journey to Calpella.

AVENUE OF THE GIANTS

Paralleling the highway at this point is the Avenue of the Giants, old US 101. As the road twists and turns through groves of huge redwoods, you'll have time to sense both a feeling of awe inspired by the magnificent giants and the scent of the pines that grow alongside them. Twenty miles south of Dyerville, just below Phillipsville, the Avenue of the Giants blends back into US 101, but the highway continues to cut through smaller redwood groves.

RICHARDSON GROVE STATE PARK

Eight miles south of Garberville US 101 passes Richardson Grove State Park, one of the earliest parks dedicated to preserving the coast redwoods, *Sequoia sempervirens*. The trees were named for the Cherokee chief, Sequoyah, who devised a phonetic alphabet of eighty-six symbols for his tribal language. Bigger around, but not as tall, are the *Sequoia gigantea* of the Sierra Nevada.

Black Bart

A little more than twenty-five miles from the sequoia grove, on a slight incline, sits a huge boulder, called Black Bart Rock. It is named for a legendary highwayman who, between 1875 and 1883, held up twenty-seven or twenty-eight (depending on which historian you believe) Wells, Fargo stagecoaches. Bart traveled on foot, Mildred Hoover tells us, and was invariably polite as he commanded the drivers to "hand down the box." Face masked with a flour sack, he wore a spotless linen duster, carried a shotgun, and often left bits of poetry signed "Black Bart P08" in the rifled cash boxes. One of these poems, according to James Hart, said,

> I've labored long and hard for bread
> For honor and for riches
> But on my corns too long you've tred
> You fine-haired sons of bitches.

Black Bart was at last exposed in San Francisco after he dropped a handkerchief near the scene of one of his robberies. A laundry mark on the bit of linen led his pursuers to discover that he was the highly respectable Charles C. Bolton (originally Charles Boles), who claimed to be a mining engineer making frequent trips to the gold fields. Once apprehended, Bolton was tried and sentenced to five years in San Quentin. After his release in January 1888, he disappeared.

The highway now descends to Calpella, five miles from the infamous rock. Laid out in 1858, this town is believed to have been named for an Indian chief whose name meant Shell Bearer.

CA 1
Leggett–Richardson Bay
190 miles

The only way to see some of the beauties of California's splendid coastline is to follow CA 1 for its entire length. This section covers the area from the highway's start at Leggett to the San Francisco Bay. For the most part CA 1 clings to the coast, swinging out to follow headlands and back in to skirt coves. At times it edges along sheer bluffs high above the surf; at others it sweeps over hills that are green only after rainy winters.

FORT BRAGG

Thirty-six miles after branching off US 101 at Leggett, CA 1 arrives at Fort Bragg, named for Gen. Braxton Bragg, who achieved fame in the Mexican War. The fort was established in 1857 and abandoned in 1867, whereupon a lumber town grew up. The town was severely damaged in the 1906 earthquake, but was rebuilt at once and is now home to one of the world's largest sawmills, owned by the Georgia-Pacific Corporation. A state historical marker stands at 321 Main Street, denoting the site of the fort.

One of Fort Bragg's main claims to fame is that it is the western terminus of the California Western (Skunk) Railroad (also owned by Georgia-Pacific) that snakes eastward through the redwoods for forty miles to reach Willits on US 101. Originally a logging railroad, the line dates back to 1885. Steam passenger service began in 1904 and was extended to Willits in 1911. In 1925 little yellow gas-powered engines started providing power, prompting riders to say, "You can smell 'em before you can see 'em," thus giving rise to the name Skunk Railroad. The name clings, even though the cars are now hauled by diesel engines.

MENDOCINO

Ten miles south of Fort Bragg is the small community of Mendocino, often called (by chamber-of-commerce types) the New England of the West Coast because of its Cape Cod–style architecture. Many movies and TV shows have been made in the area to take advantage of the rugged landscape and quaint homes.

Along the forty miles that separate Mendocino from Gualala Point lie the quaint villages of Little River, Albion, Point Arena, and Anchor Bay. At Point Arena stands another of the state's lighthouses, this one built in 1870. The 115-foot-tall structure was damaged in the 1906 San Francisco earthquake and reconstructed soon after. It bears the distinction of being the first steel-reinforced concrete lighthouse in the United States.

GUALALA

The final point of historical interest in Mendocino County is Gualala, a lumbering center, which shares its name with an ocean headland just south of the Sonoma County border. The origin of the name has never been firmly determined, although some suggest that it is the Spanish version of the Pomo word *walali*, "where the waters meet." The river of the same name flows south to north along the San Andreas Fault and empties into the sea at Point Arena.

Fort Ross

A little more than twenty-five miles farther south stands one of the most fascinating attractions of the northern span of CA 1: Fort Ross State Historic Park, site of a large Russian settlement.

The Kashaya, who populated the site of Fort Ross for centuries before the Russians came, had a village nearby. They called it Mettini. Dealings between those natives and the Russians got off to a good start in the early nineteenth century when the Russian-American Fur Company opened negotiations with them for a settlement within their territory. The Russians were drawn to the site by the protected cove, oak and redwood forests, tall bluffs, and potential farmland. By 1812, arrangements had been worked out for the Russians to use a parcel of land about one mile by two on a bluff above the cove.

The new arrivals built a fort resembling those they had built in Alaska and Siberia, hewing massive posts for blockhouses and walls. Within these walls they erected kitchens, warehouses, shops, barracks, and a large home for the commandant. On August 30, 1812, when the Russian-American Fur Company flag was raised, the fort's population numbered about one hundred, including twenty-five Russians and eighty Aleut fur hunters.

Just outside the fort settlers planted orchards of apple, cherry, and pear trees. A few of those trees still survive on a slope north of the walls. The Russians, unable to raise commercial quantities of grain at this site because of the climate, turned to garden vegetables and were moderately successful with cabbage, lettuce, beets, onions, and the like. They raised livestock, as well—cattle, of course, but also horses, sheep, pigs, and fowl—to make the settlement self-sufficient and to help supply the Alaskan colonies. The cattle were the most important, providing beef, butter, tallow, and hides for leather.

The enterprise thrived, and between 1816 and 1823, with the help of the Kashaya, the settlers even built four ships, the first to be constructed on the California coast. They also made skiffs, barges, and longboats. Company employees crafted barrels and weapons, forged iron, cast brass, and repaired guns and other equipment. The settlement became the center of manufacturing in California, with its products and repair services much in demand among the Californios.

The Spanish and United States governments felt threatened by this strong Russian presence in a neighborhood they regarded as theirs, but Californios began trading with the Russian-American Fur Company for manufactured goods as early as 1813. Even though the Spanish government had banned such trade, the Californios were eager to sell their grain, and the Russians were equally eager to buy. In 1833 Mariano G. Vallejo of Sonoma bought boots, saddles, guns, clothing, and cutlasses for his soldiers from the Russians.

None of this industry would have been possible without the natives, with whom the Russians maintained generally good relations. Unlike the Spanish, the Russians didn't tamper with the lifestyles of the natives; instead they developed a policy of cooperation that proved very successful. Diane Spencer-Hancock's text about the park includes an excerpt from the 1828 journal of Capt. Otto von Kotzebue, a Russian navigator: "The inhabitants of Ross live in the greatest concord with the Indians, who repair, in considerable numbers, to the fortress, and work as day laborers for wages." The captain went on to note that the natives usually slept outside the fort each night and that there was a good deal of socialization, even intermarriage, among the Russians, Aleuts, and Kashayas. The history of California might have taken a very different turn if the Spanish had practiced similar policies.

Unfortunately, the monotony of farming did not appeal to the Kashayas, who were accustomed to seasonal gathering and to hunting whenever the need arose. The combination of a cool climate and a shortage of labor made farming so unprofitable that the Russians' only outpost in California became a financial liability. In 1839, after officials of the Russian-American Fur Company decided to abandon the fort, they first tried to sell it to the Hudson's Bay Company, then to the Mexican government through General Vallejo, to no avail. In 1841 they succeeded in selling the buildings, livestock, and equipment to John A. Sutter of New Helvetia, who planned to use them for his own fort. To oversee the stripping of the fort, Sutter sent his foreman, John Bidwell.

After passing through several other hands, the land was taken over in 1873 by George W. Call and his family, who ranched in the area for one hundred years. In 1903 the California Historical Landmark League bought the 2.54 acres on which the fort itself stands and later deeded that property to the state.

On a road leading up a steep hill away from the back of the fort is an employee residence with a mailbox labeled "C. A. Call." A marker identifies the place as The Call Ranch. In addition to being a private home, the building houses the oldest continuously operating weather station on the West Coast. It started functioning on November 11, 1874.

CA 1 continues southward, past the small tourist town of Jenner, twelve miles below Fort Ross at the mouth of the Russian River, to Bodega Bay, a shallow inlet on Point Reyes. Some historians believe that this was the bay in which Sir Francis Drake anchored, even though it is today a shallow, sand-choked inlet. It is likely that Spanish seamen discovered and named this bay and the Tomales just to the south in 1775.

CA 1 (locally called Shoreline Drive) plunges through Marin County, along Stimson Beach, and past Muir Woods National Monument. It loops inland toward Richardson Bay to rejoin US 101.

US 101, CA 20/29
San Rafael–Clearlake
165 miles

SAN RAFAEL

Traveling northward just a few miles north of San Francisco Bay, away from Richardson Bay and toward the state's celebrated wine country, the first city you'll come to is San Rafael, seat of Marin County and site of San Quentin prison; the town also boasts a county civic center designed by Frank Lloyd Wright.

San Quentin State Prison, founded in 1852, is the oldest and largest in the state. It sits on Dolores Way just off Main Street and features a museum containing documents, photographs, and artifacts that depict scenes of life behind bars. Housed in the one-time staff residence and inmate post office, the museum contains old uniforms, antique handcuffs, the mask worn by murderer Barbara Graham at her 1955 execution, and models of the gas chamber and gallows.

Mission San Rafael Arcángel was originally built to serve as a sanitarium, a warm and dry spot for Indians from Mission Dolores in San Francisco who were suffering an extremely high death rate. It was founded in December 1817 as both hospital and *asistencia* (assistant mission) to Dolores. The first building was a simple adobe divided into storehouses, hospital, and monastery, with a corridor running along one side. The church—small and plain, with no tower or decorations—was built at one end of the mission house and at right angles to it. In 1823 it was given full mission status.

When San Rafael was secularized in 1833, and the property was turned over to the Indians, Gen. Mariano Vallejo not only appropriated much of the actual property but also herded many of the Indians onto his own ranchos. There they worked for little more than their board.

After being deserted, the mission buildings fell into disrepair but sufficed as quarters for Captain Frémont and his men in 1846. The

Chinese laborers. —CHS/TICOR, USC Special Collections

church was razed in 1870; the present replica was erected in 1949 on the original Fifth Avenue site.

CHINA CAMP STATE PARK

Just three miles northeast of San Rafael, via US 101 and North San Pedro Road, is China Camp State Park, the last surviving Chinese shrimp-fishing village in California. When the goldfields played out, the Chinese who had failed to make fortunes turned to fishing, their traditional trade, for their livelihoods. The San Pablo Bay provided abundant resources in the way of grass shrimp, a delicacy much enjoyed by their fellows back in Canton. During the 1880s nearly five hundred persons lived in the little village, which once boasted three general stores, a marine supply store, and a barbershop. It is now mostly ruins, but several historic structures have been preserved and museum exhibits tell the story of California's Chinese culture.

OLOMPALI STATE HISTORIC PARK

About three miles up the road from Novato, former site of Hamilton Air Force Base—founded in 1930 and deactivated in 1975—stands

Olompali State Historic Park. It's said to be the only historic site in the state that bears evidence of having been home to every culture that has ever lived in the state. Archaeological excavations have revealed that the earliest residents of the site were the Coast Miwok, who lived at Olompali from 2000 B.C. By 1400 it had become one of the largest Miwok trading villages in the region. Sir Francis Drake's men left signs of their presence, too, in the form of an Elizabethan sixpence dated 1567 that was unearthed during a 1974 dig. The coin suggests that the Miwoks encountered the English sailors when Drake lay to in whichever bay it was that he actually sailed into in 1579.

Miwok names inscribed in the baptismal books of the missions of San Francisco, San Jose, and San Rafael between 1814 and 1824 show that the Miwok fell under the sway of the padres some time prior to that period. Moreover, Rancho Olompali was mentioned often in the writings of the padres who passed that way. In any event, it's widely agreed that in 1834 leadership of Olompali passed into the hands of Camillo Ynitia, a Christianized Native American. Ynitia proved to be of such help to Vallejo in controlling the local natives that he was given the rancho by an 1843 grant.

According to historical marker number 210, the building on the property is the oldest house north of San Francisco. "This house was built in 1776 by the father of Camillo Ynitia or Unitia, the last chief of the Olompali Indians. The Indians were taught to make adobe bricks by Lieutenant Bodega and his party while they were surveying and charting the harbor of San Francisco Bay. The old adobe house is inside the house now on the site."

Hoover tells us that Olompali was the site of the only real battle and the lone fatality of the Bear Flag Revolt. "On June 24, 1846, a surprise skirmish occurred at this point, when Lt. Henry L. Ford, of the Bear Flag movement, unaware of the presence of the enemy, made a charge upon the horse corrals while a force of Californians under Joaquín de la Torre and Juan N. Padilla were at breakfast in the ranch house. The Californians retreated after a few shots had been exchanged, one man being killed and another badly wounded." Hart, on the other hand, asserts that both sides suffered fatalities.

The property eventually came into the hands of Maria Black Burdell and her husband, dentist Galen Burdell. They built a spacious wooden home, encasing the adobe—a structure that is partially standing today in spite of several fires. The Burdells created extensive gardens, complete with exotic trees and shrubs and a rock fountain. Remnants of the gardens remain, as do the rock walls built by Chinese laborers.

In the 1950s a group of Jesuits turned the old rancho into a religious retreat. In the 1960s Olompali became a commune for a group calling itself The Chosen Family, whose members included a number of rock groups and celebrities. The Grateful Dead recorded there and even displayed the Olompali hills on one of their album covers. The commune era ended in 1969 when a fire severely damaged the historic old building. California's poor economic condition has slowed development of the park, but it still has many fascinating features to explore.

RANCHO PETALUMA

Fifteen miles north of Novato sits the city of Petaluma and the start of a side trip through some of the most significant history of early California. The trip starts at CA 116, heading east for seven-tenths of a mile, then two miles north on Casa Grande Road to Petaluma Adobe State Historic Park, known as Rancho Petaluma in its heyday. According to park literature, "The land grant that first established the rancho was made in June 1834 by Governor José Figueroa in behalf of the promising young Mexican army officer, Mariano Guadalupe Vallejo, who was then commandant of the presidio at San Francisco." The grant was made to reward Vallejo for his service and to encourage settlement in the area north of San Francisco Bay. That same year, Vallejo was named military commandant and director of colonization of the northern frontier and directed to move his headquarters to Sonoma. Governor Figueroa, believing that the threat of a Russian takeover of that fertile area was real, wanted to establish a strong Mexican presence in the region.

Soon after he received the original grant in 1834, Vallejo started erecting outbuildings—houses, corrals, and the like. In April 1836 construction of the massive main house was begun. Work continued steadily for ten years, but the house still wasn't finished in 1846 when the Bear Flag Revolt ended the Mexican era so abruptly. Even unfinished, the adobe house was twice the size it is today; the eastern half is completely gone.

The population of the rancho was mainly employed in carrying on the hide and tallow trade that helped make Vallejo one of the richest and most powerful men in California. But the rancho was more than just a cattle station. Vallejo's employees raised fine horses and sheep that yielded great mounds of wool. They reaped huge crops of wheat, barley, and corn for both local use and trading. Kitchen gardens provided beans, peas, lentils, and vegetables of all kinds for the rancho tables. A regular beehive of industry, the rancho also produced carpeting, blankets, and other woven materials. Clothing was made on the site. Blacksmiths turned

Mariano G. Vallejo relaxes (circa 1880) in front of his home in Sonoma after his public days ended. —The Bancroft Library

out spurs, nails, tools, and, of course, horseshoes. A tannery on the property even produced the leather needed for shoes, saddles, bridles, and the like. In charge of all this activity was Miguel Alvarado, major-domo of the rancho.

All this activity was brought to a halt by the events of the Bear Flag Revolt that took place a few miles over the hills to the east, about a twenty-minute drive today, in Sonoma. It was there that Vallejo spent most of his days, visiting the rancho only occasionally, no doubt for holidays and fiestas.

SONOMA

Heading for Sonoma, the side trip returns to CA 116 and continues until it reaches CA 12, ten miles farther. Just a short distance north of that junction, CA 12 enters the old pueblo of Sonoma, one of the few formed in California under Spanish-Mexican rule, now a state historic park.

Here are the Mission Solano, northernmost and last in the mission chain, founded in 1823, and the town's central plaza, the largest of its kind in the state. It was surveyed in 1834 by Vallejo, with the help of Capt. William A. Richardson, who later played an important role in the early development of San Francisco. The plaza is one of the earliest designated of all national historic landmarks. The adobe barracks were completed in 1840 or 1841 to house Mexican army troops under the command of General Vallejo. Following the Bear Flag takeover on June 14, 1846, the barracks housed a number of Bear Flag followers until July 9, when the Stars and Stripes was raised over the plaza. Members of various U.S. military forces used the barracks from that date on, for Camp Sonoma—as it came to be called—continued to be an important army post in the area.

In the 1850s Agoston Haraszthy, a Hungarian emigré, arrived in Sonoma with cuttings of the Muscat Alexandria grape, which he planted at Buena Vista, outside Sonoma, the first large vineyard in California. The wine industry, which had been centered in Southern California, soon was thriving in the north, thanks to the innovation of Haraszthy and the hundreds of cuttings he introduced from Europe.

JACK LONDON STATE HISTORIC PARK

CA 12 continues north to Glen Ellen and Jack London State Historic Park, just one and one-half miles west of the little town on London Ranch Road. London, author of scores of popular novels and short stories, bought a seedy 130-acre ranch—Beauty Ranch, he called it—

Jack and Charmian London enjoy a brisk sail on San Francisco Bay. —The Bancroft Library

in the Sonoma Valley, with the idea of building a retreat for himself and his wife, Charmian. Here is the cottage the couple lived in, where London did much of his later writing while the couple built their dream house. Here, too, is the House of Happy Walls, built by Charmian after London's death to enshrine mementos of his life. Unfortunately, only ruins remain of Wolf House, the Londons' dream. It was reduced to ashes just hours before they were to move in. Visitors to the park can also see the final resting place of both Jack and Charmian London.

CA 12 continues north and west until it rejoins CA 101 at Santa Rosa. This side trip adds about forty miles to the distance between San Rafael and Clearlake.

SANTA ROSA

Santa Rosa is the seat of Sonoma County and an important marketing area for ranches and wineries of the county. It was the home of Luther Burbank, the experimental horticulturist, and the site of his famous gardens, as well as the setting for the spooky Alfred Hitchcock movie *Shadow of a Doubt*.

CLEAR LAKE

Fifty-five miles north of Santa Rosa, CA 101 intersects with CA 175, which heads east. That road leads directly to Clear Lake, the locale of some of the more disturbing history of the area.

Clear Lake, about twenty miles long and six wide at its greatest width, is the largest natural freshwater body lying entirely within the state. Its waters aren't particularly clear, although some historians think they once were. Henry K. Mauldin, for example, writes, "Our lake is not very deep at any point. Unlike other California lakes, particularly Tahoe, it is not located in a deep canyon, but [has] a bed that might readily have become a valley." He goes on to explain that it undoubtedly was clear before white settlers arrived to stir up sediments with runoff from farming. "The nutrients washed into the lake have stimulated growth of microscopic organisms in the water of the lake and [are] now the chief reason for its cloudiness."

For thousands of years the land around the lake was the traditional home of the Pomo (meaning "People"), a group comprised of eighteen subtribes, each with its own dialect and chief. Some of those subtribes are Wappo, Miwok, Lake Miwok, and Wintun. Each subtribe usually understood the others' languages, so that communication and trade were easily accomplished.

The first foreigners to occupy land in the beautiful valley of Clear Lake were Mexicans, who arrived about 1840 in the persons of Salvador Vallejo, brother of the renowned general, and his vaqueros. They had the Pomos build them a corral to enclose the cattle they had brought with them, and a log cabin, near the present town of Kelseyville, on CA 29, about six miles south of its junction with CA 175. In 1847 Vallejo sold his holdings to a group of Americans: brothers Andrew and Ben Kelsey, who had arrived with the Bidwell-Bartleson party in 1841, and Charles Stone. Some historians add a man named Edward Shirland to the group.

The Kelseyville Tragedy

The Americans followed Vallejo's lead in using the Pomo as laborers, but—unlike Vallejo—mistreated them shamefully, according to all reports. Eargle writes, "Two settlers, Charles Stone and Andrew Kelsey, oppressed Clear Lake Pomos on their rancho[;] the ill-treatment included lashing, rape, slavery, and murder." A state historic monument on Kelsey Creek in Kelseyville marks the site of the adobe the two white men forced Pomos to build for them. The noncommittal legend reads, "Site of Stone and Kelsey Home. This home was built by Charles Stone and Andy Kelsey on land purchased from Salvador Vallejo. They forced Indians to do the construction work, causing much resentment. Finally, in the fall of 1849 the Indians murdered both Stone and Kelsey; their remains are buried beneath this monument." Of this tragedy, Thomas Knight wrote in an 1879 essay, "Furthermore, these men had the effrontery to take the wife of the then-young chief, Augustine, and keep her for their own use in the adobe. Augustine was sent to Sonoma to work for Ben Kelsey." It's little wonder that the natives resented such treatment and sought vengeance.

In the spring of 1850, a detachment of soldiers from Benicia under the leadership of Capt. Nathaniel Lyon and a company from Sonoma headed by Lieutenant Davidson were sent to punish the Pomos. They trapped between two hundred and three hundred fleeing natives on Bloody Island (then called simply Old Island), at the north end of Clear Lake. No longer an island, the site of this tragedy can be seen from CA 20 between the towns of Upper Lake and Nice. An account published in the *Alta California* of May 28, 1850, read, in part, "Little or no resistance was encountered [by the troops] and the work of butchery was of short duration. The shrieks of the slaughtered victims died away, the roar of muskets had ceased . . . it was the order of extermination fearfully obeyed." E. A. Sherman, in "Sherman Was There," published in the *California Historical Society Quarterly* in 1945, wrote, "There were not less than four hundred warriors killed and drowned at Clear Lake and as many more of squaws and children who plunged into the lake and drowned, through fear, committing suicide."

About ten miles north of Kelseyville via CA 29 and two miles southeast of Upper Lake on CA 20 at Reclamation Road stands a state historical marker that reads: "One-fourth mile west is Bloody Island, now a hill surrounded by reclaimed land, where, in 1850, U.S. soldiers nearly annihilated the inhabitants for the murder of two white men. Doubt exists of these Indians' guilt. In 1851 a treaty was negotiated between whites and Indians."

Sulfur Bank Mine

The journey of exploration around Clear Lake continues past the northern end of the lake and then south, along CA 20 toward its junction with CA 53. Fourteen miles beyond Upper Lake the road reaches Clearlake Oaks. One and one-half miles past that community, at Sulphur Bank Road, stands state historical marker number 428, the site of the Sulphur Bank Mine, a generous producer of quicksilver (mercury). The legend says, "Sulphur Bank Mine. This sulphur mine also became one of the most noted quicksilver producers in the world. First worked for sulphur in 1865, in four years it produced a total of [two million] pounds; reopened and developed for quicksilver in 1873, it is credited with total output of 92,400 flasks, and was an important producer during World Wars I and II."

Continuing along for about four miles, the road reaches CA 53, which heads south to the town of Clearlake. Just before reaching Lower Lake, the road passes Anderson Marsh State Historic Park, on the right-hand side of the road. It was near here that the troops from Benicia and Sonoma rendezvoused before attacking the island-trapped Pomo.

ANDERSON MARSH

The political and religious center for the Pomos from 8000 B.C. until the historic period, Anderson Marsh State Historic Park consists of forty prehistoric sites that contain petroglyphs and rock alignments. A reconstructed Pomo village is a short distance from the site of the continuing archaeological excavations. Part of the park, also, is an old ranch house separated from the parking area by a white picket fence.

Achilles and Mel Grigsby, brothers who arrived in the area by ox team from Tennessee, built the ranch house about 1855 and settled here to raise livestock and produce. Their lives weren't easy because the Clear Lake Water Works Company built a dam on Cache Creek in 1866, flooding much of the ranch in the winter. According to an account of early days at Anderson Marsh published in the spring 1990 issue of *California Parklands: The State Parks Magazine*, in the spring of 1890,

"Mel Grigsby led a bunch of angry ranchers, about 200 it is said, who tore out the dam.

"The Andersons came on the scene in 1885, when John Anderson, a Scottish immigrant, bought land from the company, including the present ranch house area, and settled down with his wife Sarah and their six children." It was the Andersons who added the two-story west wing to the house in 1886. Members of that family lived and worked here until the 1960s.

CA 29
Clearlake–Benicia
65 miles

CALISTOGA

At Lower Lake, a few miles beyond Anderson Marsh, CA 29 joins CA 53 and continues south, heading for the state's famed Wine Country. Thirty-three miles from Clearlake is the historic town of Calistoga, founded by Sam Brannan. To the west of the highway and slightly north of the town is the Old Faithful Geyser of California, one of only three in the nation, which usually spouts off about every fifty minutes. Recent studies have shown that the geyser, in some way, is an indicator of earthquake activity. A report in the *Glendale News Press* of September 4, 1992, shows that the cycle of eruptions is affected by large quakes within 155 miles of the geyser. Indeed, the three major earthquakes that occurred in the 1980s and 1990s took place within one to three days after the geyser's eruption pattern underwent abrupt and dramatic changes.

Another historic site just north of Calistoga on CA 29 is Robert Louis Stevenson State Park, on the shoulder of Mount St. Helena. The renowned author and his bride honeymooned near here while he gathered notes for his rollicking *Silverado Squatters*, published in 1883. A memorial statue marks the site of the now-abandoned cabin in which the couple lived during the spring of 1880.

Calistoga, northernmost town in the chain along CA 29 that makes up much of the Napa Valley Wine Country, was founded in 1859 by Samuel Brannan to take advantage of the area's famous hot springs. The name, according to Hart, is a combination of California and Saratoga, a famous New York State spa.

Brannan, whom Hart characterizes as a "dynamic opportunist," cut a wide swath through California's history, having been involved in the development and economies of several areas. The store he built in Calistoga still stands, as does one of the twenty cottages he built for his resort. Both have been designated state historic landmarks. Brannan also, according to Hoover, planted wine-grape cuttings on the hillsides around Calistoga, thereby helping along the fledgling wine industry.

Yet another historical landmark stands in Calistoga: the site of the home of Nancy Kelsey, the first woman to cross the plains. Married to Benjamin Kelsey—the brother of Andrew, who was involved in the Indian troubles at Clear Lake—she arrived in California with the Bidwell-Bartleson party in 1841. She is credited with being one of the seamstresses who stitched up the Bear Flag after the uprising in Sonoma. The hearthstone is all that can be seen of her home.

BALE GRIST MILL STATE HISTORIC PARK

Six miles farther south on the west side of CA 29/128 stands the Bale Grist Mill State Historic Park, site of the mill Dr. Edward Bale built in 1846. Bale, an English physician, was one of the few survivors of the wreck of the *Harriett* off the coast of Monterey in 1837. For a time he worked for General Vallejo as the Mexican army's surgeon-in-chief, establishing a reputation as a skilled surgeon who liked both his alcohol and a good scrap. Even though he was often publicly drunk and mischievous, Bale was welcomed into the Vallejo family when he married the general's niece, María Ignacia Soberanes.

After becoming a citizen of Mexico in 1841, Bale received a grant of almost eighteen thousand acres in the Napa Valley. The many new arrivals who had settled in the area and planted wheat and corn created a demand for a mill that would convert their grain into flour. Seeing the demand, Bale contracted to have his enormous mill built. The mill became the social center of the area as farmers gathered there, discussing the topics of the day while they waited for their flour to be milled.

Much of the building that stands today is the original, although a great deal of shoring up and reconstruction were necessary to make it safe for visitors. The huge flume that carries water to the great wheel that turns the grinding stones is a complete reconstruction.

The Wine Country

Nine miles south of Calistoga is St. Helena, home of the Charles Krug Winery, founded in 1861 by that pioneering wine maker of the region. Krug produced the first commercial wine of the Napa Valley in 1858 for a man named Patchett. After establishing his reputation making fine wines for other growers, Krug settled in St. Helena and started building a stone winery at the south end of town. After making several additions over the years, he finally declared the splendid winery completed in 1884.

Twenty miles of travel south on CA 29/128 takes you past most of the famous wineries of the Napa Valley. All have tales to tell of their contributions to the state's wine industry. In Yountville, nine miles from St. Helena, for example, is California Historic Landmark number 693, which marks the grave of George C. Yount. A North Carolina–born trapper, Yount came to California in 1831. He, like Bale, worked for General Vallejo, became a Mexican citizen, and received a large land grant, becoming the first former U.S. citizen to be so honored in the Napa Valley. According to the marker, "Friend to all, this kindly host of Caymus Rancho encouraged sturdy American pioneers to establish ranches in this area, so it was well populated before the gold rush."

Eleven miles south of Yountville is Napa, seat of Napa County and gateway to the famed valley. It is a processing and shipping center for the products of the area.

BENICIA

The final point of historic interest in this section of the state is Benicia, just off I-780, six miles southeast of its junction with CA 29, on the north shore of Carquinez Strait. Founded in 1847 by Thomas Larkin and Robert Semple, one of the leaders of the Bear Flag Revolt, on land deeded by Mariano Vallejo, Benicia was named for the general's wife. Larkin was the U.S. consul in Monterey from 1844 to 1848 and was a delegate to the constitutional convention of 1849.

Benicia Capitol State Historic Park, a one-acre park at First and G Streets, features the splendid building that housed the state government from February 1853 to February 1854. An 1846 ad in the *Californian*, the state's first regularly published newspaper (also founded by Robert Semple), attempting to drum up residents for the aborning town, read, "Great sale of city lots—The streets are 80 feet wide, alleys 20 feet wide. Lots 50 yards front and 40 yards back. The whole city comprises five square miles. In front of the city is a commodious bay, large enough for 200 ships to ride at anchor, safe from any wind."

Another newspaper, the *Placer Times and Transcript*, on December 30, 1852, described the building that would serve as the third capitol of the young state: "This is one of the finest public buildings in the State, and as it stands in commanding position, presents a most imposing appearance from the bays and Straits of Carquines. The ground plan is forty-five feet by eighty-seven feet; the base four feet above ground, is of Benicia free stone." The article went on to say the building had two stories of thick brick walls and featured two fluted columns of solid masonry resting on stone bases. In fact, the columns are intricately fashioned of bricks, cleverly canted to form the fluting, as shown by drawings displayed in the foyer.

During the year that the legislature met at Benicia a host of matters came before the body, though slavery was the matter on everyone's mind. It seemed that most decisions made in Benicia were swayed, to one degree or another, by the question of slavery. However, a flour-grading system was created, a lumber inspection service instituted, and a board of prison commissioners constituted and authorized to contract for the building of a prison at San Quentin (the cost of that institution was not to exceed $153,315.) The most significant piece of legislation, however, was a bill calling for revision of the state constitution. Couched in the most patriotic terms and purporting to serve the general welfare, the bill nonetheless was a blatant attempt by pro-slavery forces to divide the state into two parts, north and south, with the northern one free and the southern slave-holding. After a prolonged struggle, Sen. David C. Broderick managed to introduce an amendment that would require any action taken at the proposed constitutional convention to be approved by California voters. Passage of the amendment effectively killed the attempt to divide the state, a move most legislators knew the people of California would never approve.

All of these complex political maneuverings took place just five years after the momentous events recalled in the next chapter.

Part 3
Gold Country

The ironies of history are seldom more obvious than that of the timing of James Marshall's great discovery on January 24, 1848. John Sutter's superintendent picked those shiny specks of gold out of the tailrace of the mill he was building only nine days before the Treaty of Guadalupe Hidalgo put an end to the Mexican War and to Mexico's official presence in California. Setting the Rio Grande as the new boundary of the United States, the treaty gave the present states of California, Nevada, Utah, New Mexico, and Arizona and portions of Wyoming and Colorado to the United States. The irony lies in that it also gave away what the Mexicans had come to California to find: gold. Mexico had given up its territorial claims to the dreams it and Spain had pursued for centuries.

In their *Historical Atlas of California*, Warren Beck and Ynez Haase write, "The quest for the seven cities of Cíbola, the legend of El Dorado where gold had been gathered for years . . . [was] all part of the European dream that America was the promised land." The hardy souls who braved the difficult trek from civilization to the goldfields came because they, too, saw California as a land where gold flowed in streams down mountain sides. With the gold strike in Northern California in 1848, most folks thought these dreams had at last been borne out.

The people of Mexico, however, hadn't discarded their dreams, and when word reached them of Marshall's find, they flocked to California. Some 5,000 Mexicans settled in the Mother lode region between 1848 and 1850. They established the town of Sonora but faced gross discrimination and antipathy, even there. A variety of means were used to persuade them to go home, including an early form of the foreign miners' license tax, passed by the state legislature in 1850. The original tax was repealed in 1851, but a more moderate one was soon enacted and remained in effect until 1870. The first law was drawn to harass Mexicans, while the later one was leveled at the Chinese.

The setting for all these goings-on is called the Mother lode—a narrow strip just a mile wide and 120 miles long that runs roughly between Mariposa on the south and Auburn on the north along the western edge of the Sierra Nevada. The term, however, is applied to most of the area along the length of CA 49, also called the gold belt.

Gold was wrenched from the earth by several means, the least sophisticated of which was placer mining. A placer is a surface mineral deposit formed by the concentration of small particles of heavy minerals (such as gold or platinum) in gravel or small sands. It is probably so named from the Spanish for "sandbank." To retrieve placer deposits, the miner scooped up a pan full of the sand from the bed of a river or creek, shook and swirled the pan under water to float away the lighter materials, and inspected the pan's heavy remains hoping to find tiny flecks or nuggets of gold. Placer mining has been described as the simple but exhausting task of washing tons of gravel and sand to obtain ounces of gold. The technique evolved, over time, as miners developed contraptions—cradles, long toms, sluices, and the like—to wash more gravel faster, but the basic principle changed little.

Quartz mining, often called lode mining, aims to remove gold from rock. Sometimes veins in the quartz are at or near the surface, but more often they lie deep within the earth, where their removal is a complex and expensive operation. First practiced in Mariposa in 1849, quartz mining didn't become popular in California until 1850, when the placers began to play out. The main problem with quartz mining is that once the ore has been dug out of the rock it has to be crushed, usually by a stamp mill, to a powder for the gold to be separated from the dross.

Another mining method—one that was at last declared illegal in 1884 because it wrought such havoc on the environment—is hydraulic mining, which uses a high-powered stream of water to wash away hillsides to get at the gold buried in them. Developed by Edward E. Matteson of Connecticut in 1853, the method certainly accomplished the end of getting at larger amounts of gold-bearing ore more quickly, but it was complicated and expensive. No longer could a couple of miners pool their resources to establish a dig; hydraulic mining operations called for big corporations with deep pockets to provide the equipment needed to despoil enough of the earth to make a profit.

From 1848 to 1873, more than a billion ounces of gold were taken from California soil, most of it from the streams and hills of the Gold Country, and most of it by a fairly small number of men. Those who were successful either returned to the East or settled in some more civilized part of the state. Some of those who remained in California went on to found towns and universities, build railroads and museums, and become part of the state's fabulous history. Some even increased their wealth through activities largely political and often less than admirable.

Some of the players in this magnificent California drama were something between saints and scoundrels. One, Sam Brannan, arrived at Yerba Buena (San Francisco) in 1846 after a trip around Cape Horn as the head of a group of more than two hundred Mormons who were fleeing the bigotry of Illinois and the East. Walton Bean describes Brannan as "a remarkably vigorous young man of Irish ancestry, articulate, ingenious, and highly opportunistic." He established California's first flour mill, began—on January 9, 1847—San Francisco's first newspaper, the *California Star*, and became involved in a host of other ventures, all the while flagrantly using Mormon funds as his own. He was eventually charged with embezzlement and became the defendant in one of the state's first jury trials. Since the jury couldn't agree on a verdict, Elder Brannan continued his activities, including collecting the tithes of his flock. Brigham Young sent a delegation from Salt Lake City to retrieve "the Lord's money." Brannan refused to relinquish it, saying he would turn it over when he got a receipt signed by the Lord.

At the very northern end of the Mother lode country, on the east fork of the Feather River, is Rich Bar, a mining site made famous by one of the few women ever to live among the miners. Shirley Louise Clappe—an intrepid young woman if ever there was one—in 1849 when she was about thirty years old, came around the Horn to California with her husband, Fayette, a doctor. She stayed in San Francisco until 1851 when she decided to see for herself what all the fuss was about. For two years she lived with her husband among the miners, first at Rich Bar and then at Indian Bar. From those sites she wrote twenty-three letters to her sister back home, letters that were later published as *The Shirley Letters*. Few writers have drawn such vivid pictures of hardships and rewards among the placers. She produced some of her most vivid and perceptive writings when the gold began to play out and violence, especially persecution of Mexicans, overran most camps.

The trip along CA 49, through the Mother lode to explore California's golden history, starts on CA 41 in Oakhurst, one of the gateways to Yosemite National Park. Formerly called Fresno Flats, Oakhurst was one of a group of placer mining sites that sprang up in the area. The others bore such colorful names as Texas Flats, Grub Gulch, Coarse Gold, Fine Gold, and Temperance Flat. Little is left to show that men struggled in those places, enduring hardships all but impossible to comprehend, as they chased dreams of great wealth.

CA 49
Oakhurst–Nevada City
215 miles

Most of the story of the gold rush is inscribed along this strand that binds the Gold Country into a single unit. It winds and twists along the foothills of the Sierra Nevada, through countryside that is, even today, largely remote from the bustle of cities.

In 1939, when the Federal Writers' Project produced *California: A Guide to the Golden State*, the authors wrote of this area, "Along State 49 are strewn the relics of these [mining] labors and of the men who performed them; decaying shanties of the 'pick and pan' men, abandoned hillside shafts of the quartz mines, high-piled debris of the hydraulic workings. Some of the gold rush towns have disappeared completely, others are mere heaps of rubbish." Today, however, those relics are gone. Even the ghost towns have vanished, with a couple of remarkable exceptions. Hills of overburden washed away in hydraulic diggings, if they exist at all now, are so overgrown they seem to be natural geologic phenomena. It's only in the tiny towns and carefully preserved parks that life in that fabulous era can be sampled.

OAKHURST

Oakhurst has survived because it sits on the road to Yosemite. Little is known about the town's past. No one can say, for example, who was the first white man to settle here, but local historians agree that Indians probably had a camp here. It was never a true gold-rush town, either, although it was the site of the Enterprise Mine that some say produced as much as $80,000,000 in a single year.

Actually, the town was a cattle and lumber center, with stock finding summer pasture here, after being driven up from the valley. Flocks of sheep often numbered 10,000 or more. Before too long, probably in the late 1860s, stockmen began to settle in a place they called Fresno Flats, but the country remained open range for many years. In 1873 Fresno Flats became a stop on the Washburn Stage Line that came by way of Raymond, to the southwest, and the now-vanished town of Grub Gulch. In 1912 the thriving town was given its more dignified name of Oakhurst.

WASSAMA ROUNDHOUSE STATE HISTORIC PARK

Seven miles north of Oakhurst sits Wassama Roundhouse State Historic Park, one-half mile northeast of CA 49 at Ahwahnee. It's a partially restored Yokut village featuring an old roundhouse, sweat lodge, burial ground, and grinding rocks. The first roundhouse known to be on this site was built in the 1860s, for ceremonial harvests and mourning dances as well as gambling. Because Yokut tradition dictated that on the death of the chief the roundhouse must be burned, the first one was burned in the 1870s or 1880s and its replacement, in 1893. The third roundhouse was built on the same site in 1903, but, for some unknown reason, it wasn't burned when Chief Peter Westphal died in 1924. The land was sold in the 1950s to people who allowed the local Native Americans to continue to bury their dead there. In 1970 the Yokuts convinced the state to buy the property and preserve it as a sacred Indian site. Ceremonies are still conducted in the roundhouse and in the sweat lodge.

MORMON BAR

Mormon Bar, twenty-five miles northeast of Oakhurst, was first settled by a band of Latter-Day Saints, part of the Mormon Battalion. At its conception that group consisted of about five hundred men who headed west in the summer of 1846 only to be recruited into the U.S. Army at Council Bluffs, Iowa, by order of President Polk, who sought to build up a force with which to wage the Mexican War. Led by Lt. Col. Philip St. George Cooke, the battalion marched from Santa Fe to

Wassama Roundhouse State Historic Park, partially restored village of Yokuts. —Frank Pittman

83

San Diego between October 1846 and January 1847. They went on to Los Angeles, where they built a fort, but were mustered out in July without ever seeing battle. About half of them went to Utah, but others remained in California, some to work for Sutter and others to help rescue the Donner Party.

The Mormons didn't stay long at the placer site named after them but moved on to richer pay dirt, leaving the pickings to newcomers. Later, thousands of Chinese worked this ground one more time, as related by a state historical marker standing beside the highway twenty-three miles northwest of Mariposa.

MARIPOSA

Continuing to wind through grass-covered hills studded with oaks and laced with small streams that are usually dry in the summer, CA 49 reaches Mariposa, seat of Mariposa County since 1851. This is an area that was first explored in 1833 by Joseph Walker's party, a band ostensibly engaged in the fur trade, but probably gathering military intelligence under the direction of Capt. Benjamin Bonneville.

Mariposa is the site of the oldest courthouse in the state, a Greek Revival–style building erected in 1854. It has served without pause as the seat of county government and seen a number of landmark mining cases settled within its walls. Much U.S. mining law is based on decisions reached here, at Tenth and Bullion Streets.

BEAR VALLEY

Bear Valley, Frémont's headquarters after the takeover at Sonoma and the end of the Mexican War, stands eleven miles northwest of Mariposa. After buying for $3,000 a vast "floating" Mexican grant, Frémont floated his grant to include this segment of the Mother lode when gold was discovered in the area. The U.S. Supreme Court confirmed his title in 1859 following much expensive litigation.

Frémont grubstaked Mexican miners to work his rich placers, then opened up quartz mines, all of which produced handsomely for some years. In 1851 Frémont built a two-story hotel and, later, a store and a home for himself, which he called The White House. He always claimed his expenses outran the income of his many enterprises, but in 1863 he sold the grant for $6,000,000.

HORNITOS

Before setting off northward again, history seekers may want to take a side trip to the west on County Route J16. Ten miles along that road is the town of Hornitos, Spanish for "little ovens," so named because of its old Mexican tombs in the shape of square bake ovens set atop the ground.

Some historians say the original residents of this town—the first to be incorporated in Mariposa County—were less than first-rate citizens, driven out of nearby Quartzburg because of their uncivilized ways. When the placers at Quartzburg gave out, however, many of its residents weren't too proud to join the residents of Hornitos. Mildred Hoover wrote that Joaquín Murieta, the possibly fictitious bandit, often visited here, where gamblers and roughnecks of every stripe played cards and danced the fandango and "blood was on nearly every doorstep and the sand was caked with it."

One of those residents of Hornitos was Domingo Ghirardelli, a confectioner from Italy who arrived in California via Peru. Unsuccessful at mining, he ran the general store in Hornitos for a time before moving to San Francisco, where he made himself both rich and famous manufacturing chocolate.

Retracing the miles to CA 49 makes this side trip add twenty miles to the distance to Nevada City.

COULTERVILLE

The approach to Coulterville, seventeen miles from Bear Valley, consists of a number of switchbacks descending past mines both open and closed. The small town once contained fifty bars, but today only some staid historical buildings remain, including the Jeffreys Hotel, an imposing adobe with three-foot-thick walls. Close by are the Magnolia Saloon and the Chinese Sun Store.

CHINESE CAMP

Twenty miles farther along, CA 49 arrives at Chinese Camp. Because so many of the Chinese worked as indentured servants, their participation in the gold rush is largely downplayed, but as many as 5,000 of them may have lived in this town alone. Reportedly founded about 1849 by a group of Englishmen who employed Chinese as miners, the town served as headquarters for stage lines in the early 1850s. It was also the setting for one of the first Chinese tong wars fought in the state. That battle took place in September 1856 when members of the Tan Woo Tong faced off against Sam Yap members. The stone and brick post office built in 1854 is still in use, and the Catholic church originally built in 1855 was restored in 1949. The Wells, Fargo Express Company building, erected by the Walkerly brothers, still stands in Chinese Camp, too. When first built it housed a general store along with the office of the Adams Express Company, predecessor of Wells, Fargo.

JAMESTOWN

Jamestown, about five miles from Chinese Camp, was founded by Col. George James on August 8, 1848. Large quantities of gold were taken from nearby Wood's Creek and Jamestown became known as the gateway to the Mother lode.

James, a dashing, colorful man, used investors' money to set up operations at what had been known as Wood's Creek, paying his miners with scrip. When he realized that the proceeds of the operation wouldn't be enough to repay all his creditors, James and his wife decamped in the middle of the night. Irate investors and miners were left holding an empty poke, so to speak. They lost a vote to change the town's name to American Camp.

A number of original buildings in "Jimtown" tell the tale of the town's past. One of the oldest is the Hadley Building, probably built in the 1850s.

A part of Jamestown's claim to fame is that it contains Railtown 1897 State Historic Park. The park holds some of the old rolling stock of the Sierra Railroad, built by Thomas Bullock in 1897 as a common

Railtown 1897 State Historic Park features rolling stock of the Sierra Railroad, built in 1897 by Thomas Bullock.
—Tuolumne County Visitors Bureau

One of the many engines at Railtown 1897 State Historic Park that have been featured in movies and TV. —Tuolumne County Visitors Bureau

carrier to transport lumber products from the mountains to the main line at Oakdale, a distance of about fifty-seven miles. According to the April–June 1977 issue of *Chispa*, the quarterly of the Historical Society of Tuolumne County, when diesel engines took over in 1955, the railroad kept some of the old steam locomotives and antique passenger and freight cars specifically for use in motion pictures. They have appeared in productions such as *The Virginian* in 1929, *Go West* with the Marx Brothers in 1940 and, more recently, *High Noon, Butch Cassidy and the Sundance Kid*, and the TV series *Little House on the Prairie*. An old roundhouse and shops are also part of the park, which is open only in the summer.

Sonora

Just a couple of miles north of Jamestown, CA 108/49 (labeled Stockton Street) enters Sonora. Named after the Mexican state from which many of the forty-niners came, Sonora in its heyday was one of the richest and wildest towns in Gold Country. The many adobe buildings that dot the city preserve its Mexican past. The town jail, built in 1857, now houses the Tuolumne County Museum, where artifacts from the gold rush are on display. In 1850 the passage of the foreign miners' license tax prompted an uprising of Mexicans in Sonora. So many Frenchmen joined in the uprising that the riot was also called a French Revolution. It led to the expulsion from the community of many foreigners.

In the middle of town, CA 108 heads south before turning east toward the mountains, while CA 49 continues north as Washington Street. A short distance from that junction stands St. James Episcopal Church, the oldest Episcopal church building in the state. On October 4, 1849, William Kip, the first Episcopal bishop of California, celebrated the first services there.

Columbia State Historic Park

Just two miles farther north and four miles off the highway is Columbia State Historic Park. According to an article by Michele

Main Street, Columbia State Historic Park. —Tuolumne County Visitors Bureau

Visitors ride the express stage at Columbia State Historic Park. —Tuolumne County Visitors Bureau

and Tom Grimm, in the *Los Angeles Times*, "Columbia is the gem of California's mother lode country, a town of living history that makes visitors think they've been caught in a time warp." It's a boomtown that never saw the bust, one of the best preserved of the gold-rush towns, where gold was discovered on March 27, 1850. (Historians agree on the date of the discovery, but differ on who did the discovering; several, however, credit Dr. Thaddeus Hildreth and some friends with the rich find.)

Columbia was a rich, noisy, wicked town, according to the Federal Writers' Project guide, where diversions such as cruel bull and bear fights entertained the residents. The Fallon Hotel and Theater once resounded with the voice of Edwin Booth (brother of John Wilkes Booth, Lincoln's assassin) as Richard III. Lola Montez did her renowned tabletop spider dance here, too, for miners who pried $87 million in gold from the earth around Columbia.

CARSON HILL

Fourteen miles from Sonora stands the village of Carson Hill, named for the hill that rises behind it, whose slopes are reputed to have been the richest diggings in the entire Mother lode. In a little creek flowing there, according to the Federal Writers' Project guide, James H. Carson found gold in August 1848. It was such a rich find that in just ten days he panned 180 ounces of the precious dust. The largest nugget ever found in the United States was discovered here, too, in 1854. Weighing 195 pounds troy, the precious find was worth $43,000 at the time.

ANGELS CAMP

Continuing through the foothills of the Sierra Nevada for another four miles, the road reaches Angels Camp, founded in 1848 by George Angel, a member of Stevenson's Regiment. This outfit was a motley group of young men who ventured out from New York under the leadership of a politician, Col. Jonathan D. Stevenson, and a few regular army officers. Arriving in San Francisco too late to take part in the Mexican War, they served garrison duty until the regiment was disbanded in 1848. Many members of the group went off to find wealth in the hills while others stayed to make mischief in San Francisco.

It was Mark Twain, however, who made Angels Camp famous with "The Celebrated Jumping Frog of Calaveras County." That storied event is still saluted each spring during the county fair. Bret Harte also used Angels Camp as the setting for his story "The Luck of Roaring Camp."

SAN ANDREAS

Next along the golden chain is San Andreas, seat of Calaveras County, settled by Mexicans in 1848 and, reputedly, locale of the early activities of the bandit Joaquín Murieta. This romantic figure of the gold-rush days was regarded in these parts as a sort of Robin Hood of the Old West. James Hart recounts the romantic legend that Murieta arrived in the area in search of gold, like so many of his fellow Mexicans. Taking exception to the prejudice he encountered, he swore to wreak vengeance on the hated Yanquis. In truth, while a number of robberies and killings in the mining region were attributed to Murieta, the fanciful stories about him began with publication in 1854 of *The Life and Adventures of Joaquín Murieta* by John R. Ridge. Black Bart lent his fame to San Andreas, too. Here the poetic highwayman was jailed and tried in the courthouse that is now a museum, before he went to San Quentin to serve his time.

MOKELUMNE HILL

Ten miles north of San Andreas is Mokelumne Hill, from 1852 until 1866 the seat of Calaveras County. It was settled in 1848 when gold was discovered in the region by discharged members of Stevenson's

regiment. Still to be seen in Mokelumne Hill is the International Order of Odd Fellows (IOOF) Hall, the first three-story building raised in California outside the coastal towns. The hall was originally only two stories high, but the third floor was added later to meet the needs of the lodge. Another preserved historical structure is the Congregational Church, built in 1856 and now the oldest Congregational Church building in the state. Probably the most interesting old structure is the one on Main Street that served as the courthouse until 1866, when San Andreas was named county seat. At that time, George W. Leger acquired the building and made it a part of his hotel, which has been in operation since early gold-rush days. In 1874, when it was called the Grand Hotel, a fire swept through the building and destroyed its dance hall. Restored in 1879, it has been known ever since as the Leger Hotel.

Leger Hotel on Main Street in Mokelumne Hill. Built in 1851 and destroyed by fire in 1874, it was restored in 1879. —Calaveras County Museum and Archives

Congregational Church. Built in 1856, it is now the oldest Congregational Church building in the state. —Calaveras County Museum and Archives

Calaveras County Courthouse at San Andreas prior to construction of the Hall of Records. —Calaveras County Museum and Archives

Jackson

The next link in the golden chain, beyond seven miles of open rolling hills, is Jackson, seat of Amador County. It was named for Alden M. Jackson (often given the honorary title of Colonel), a New England lawyer widely acclaimed for his ability to settle disputes out of court. From 1848 to 1851 the town was an important stopping point on the Carson Pass Emigrant Trail, which met up here with roads from Sacramento and Stockton. That Jackson was a jolly sort of place is borne out by a tale told by the Federal Writers' Project guide: "At a spring on the banks of Jackson Creek, teamsters hauling freight between Drytown [about seven miles north] and Mokelumne Hill, below, and miners on their way through the mother lode used to break their journeys. So convivial were those overnight stops that piles of bottles collected and gave the town its first name, Bottileas." It was 1850 when the town acquired its more dignified name.

Two nearby quartz mines, Argonaut and Kennedy, played significant roles in the economic development of the state, long after most mines were forgotten. The Kennedy Mine, discovered in 1856, with a vertical shaft of 5,912 feet, was the deepest in the nation and produced gold worth $45 million before it shut down in 1942. The Argonaut, which yielded $25 million, was the setting for the mother lode's worst mine disaster. On August 27, 1922, a fire that blazed at the 3,500-foot level trapped forty-eight miners; few survived. Nonetheless, the mine continued to operate until 1942.

On the Jackson Elementary School grounds, at the intersection of Church and North Streets, is state historical marker number 865, denoting the site of Jackson's Pioneer Jewish Synagogue. The legend on the plaque reads, "On September 18, 1857, Congregation B'nai Israel of Jackson dedicated on this site the first Synagogue in the Mother lode. High holiday worship continued until 1869 when the larger Masonic Hall was used to accommodate the congregation. The wooden structure then served as a schoolhouse until 1888. Relocated onto a nearby lot, it became a private dwelling, and was razed in 1948." Also in Jackson, on Main Street, is the site of Pioneer Hall, which saw within its walls the creation of the Order of Native Daughters of the Golden West on September 11, 1886.

VOLCANO

A short but fascinating side trip starts at Jackson, heading east on CA 88. At Pine Grove, about six miles east of Jackson, a little, squiggly road called Pine Grove-Volcano Road takes off toward the north. Six miles from Pine Grove is the site of what was once one of the richest and most populous towns of Gold Country: Volcano. According to the state historical marker on the spot, it was discovered in 1848 by Colonel Stevenson's men, who mined in the area at places they christened with colorful names. In 1855 hydraulic mining operations got started, bringing thousands of fortune hunters to form a town that in its heyday boasted seventeen hotels, a library, a theater, and quick justice.

A Native Mess Hall

The side trip continues, retracing the route just driven for 4.5 miles to the entrance to Indian Grinding Rock State Historic Park. (In California, state parks are always marked by brown signs, so they're usually easy to find, even in remote areas.) Called Chaw-Se by the Miwoks who lived here, this park's main feature is the "community kitchen," a spectacular slab of limestone—173 feet by 82 feet—indented with more than a thousand mortar holes, evidence of a million meals prepared by the Indians who lived in the area centuries ago. The slab provided an ideal spot for the natives to pound acorns for soups, mush, or patties that they baked on hot rocks and ate like slices of bread or tortillas. Almost four hundred petroglyphs are visible on the rock, too, many quite distinct in spite of centuries of exposure to weather. In addition to the grinding rock, the park features a ceremonial roundhouse, the largest in California, built in 1974. The 135-acre park is dotted with oak trees heavy with acorns that no doubt account for the presence of the grinding rock.

The side trip now returns west on CA 88 to CA 49, having added about twenty-two miles to the distance to Nevada City.

SUTTER CREEK, AMADOR CITY, AND DRYTOWN

Over the next seven miles CA 49 passes Sutter Creek, Amador City, and Drytown. Called the Golden Heart of the Mother lode, this area yielded more than half of the mother lode's gold.

Sutter Creek was named after John A. Sutter, the first white man to come to the area (in 1846) and the first to mine locally (in 1848). Little mining was carried on at Sutter Creek until 1851, when quartz mining got started. Quartz mining was a hazardous business, since the art of shoring up shafts and tunnels was not yet understood by miners. It was an expensive proposition, too; capital outlay often exceeded the value of the gold produced. Alvinza Hayward, however, managed to make a success of it, buying out several mines from which he took millions.

An even more significant player in the goldfields of the area was Leland Stanford, who financed the nearby Lincoln Mine for Robert Downs. Maintaining a controlling interest in that mine until 1872, Stanford reaped returns that made it possible for him to become a co-owner of the Central Pacific Railroad.

EL DORADO

Thirty-two miles north of Sutter Creek is El Dorado, called Mud Flats when it was an important camp on the Carson Emigrant Trail. By 1849–50 it had become the crossroads for freight and stage lines, as well as the busy center of the mining district, with a population of several thousand. Its Nevada House was a trading post and remount station on the Pony Express route.

PLACERVILLE

Just a couple of miles farther along CA 49 is Placerville, the seat of El Dorado County, a town with a lurid past, and one of the most historically significant areas along the golden chain. The town was born, historians say, when latecomers to Coloma found all the likely spots spoken for and began to look about for better pickings. The Argonauts, as some writer dubbed these questers for the golden ore, scrambled up hills, down ravines, and through gulches in search of better diggings. By the summer of 1848 they had shaped a new camp, called Dry Diggins because they had to carry the scooped-up earth down to running water to slosh in their pans. It was backbreaking labor, and some newcomers weren't about to work that hard, even for a share of the abundant riches to be had. Murders and robberies became commonplace in this area along the American River, with many weary miners losing their pokes of gold dust to knife-wielding thugs.

Early in 1849, after one particularly brutal crime, a hastily impaneled citizens' jury met to weigh the fate of the accused. According to a report from the El Dorado County Chamber of Commerce, "When the question was asked, 'What shall be done with them?' someone shouted, 'Hang them!' The majority were in agreement. And so it was that the first known hanging in the Mother lode was carried out." Word of the hanging quickly spread and Dry Diggins was soon known as Hangtown. Today a state historical marker stands at 305 Main Street, the site of Elstner's Hay Yard in which grew the hangman's tree that was used so often during those violent days.

Another state historical marker stands at 543 Main Street, identifying the site of Studebaker's Shop. The legend tells us that John Studebaker rented the back of the blacksmith shop that once stood here, where he worked on wagon wheels and the like. He made wheelbarrows for the miners, too, and ammunition wagons for the Union Army during the Civil War. From this small operation grew a wagon and carriage business that eventually led to his manufacture of Studebaker automobiles.

Yet another historical marker stands at Main and Sacramento Streets to mark the site that was initially a remount station of the Pony Express and then western terminus of the service from July 1, 1861, until the service was discontinued on October 26, 1861. It was here, according to the legend on the marker, that Sam Hamilton, the first eastbound rider from Sacramento, stopped for a fresh mount and added a letter to his pouch on April 4, 1860. He rode off on his way to Sportsman's Hall (Twelve-Mile House), twelve miles east in Cedar Grove.

By 1854 Hangtown had become the third largest city in California, surpassed only by San Francisco and Sacramento. It was time, residents agreed, for a more dignified name for their town, which was incorporated as Placerville. It gained the rank of county seat in 1857.

COLOMA: WHERE IT ALL BEGAN

About seven miles from Placerville is Coloma, the place where all the shouting started. The area was originally the home of the peaceful Maidu, who called it Cullomah, "beautiful valley," from which comes today's name. And beautiful it was, with fine stands of trees and a swiftly flowing river.

John August Sutter,
one of the first settlers
of the Gold Country.
—The Bancroft Library

One of the principal players in the drama that would play out here and engulf the entire world was Capt. John A. Sutter of Switzerland, who ran away from his wife, five children, and a heap of debts in Switzerland, hoping to make his fortune in America. Another was James William Marshall, a bachelor from New Jersey and Missouri.

Arriving in California in 1839, Sutter spent eight years making arrangements for a land grant with the Mexican government, establishing credit in Monterey and Yerba Buena, and obtaining a grant of about 50,000 acres, on which he built a fine fort at the confluence of the Sacramento and American Rivers. With followers he had recruited all along the way, including Kanakas (Hawaiian natives), he managed to make the establishment he called New Helvetia largely self-sustaining. There he welcomed all comers.

One of those who showed up at the gates of the fort was James Marshall, who became one of Sutter's most trusted associates. Marshall worked for Sutter as a carpenter until he joined Frémont's California Volunteers to fight in the Mexican War. Because Marshall was such a

James Marshall, whose discovery of nuggets in the millrace at Sutter's Fort led to California's gold rush.
—The Bancroft Library

good workman, Sutter rehired him at war's end to help lay out a millrace (a ditch supplying water to turn the mill wheel) and diversion dam for a grist mill he planned to build a little way up the American River.

He'd need a sawmill, too, Sutter realized, to supply lumber for the gristmill and other projects he had in mind. For months Sutter studied possible sites for the sawmill. He hoped to produce more of both lumber and flour than his colony would need and export the surplus to San Francisco, but he had to plan carefully in order not to waste the contents of his slim purse.

After a great deal of pondering, Sutter decided to locate his sawmill about forty-five miles east-northeast of New Helvetia on land beside the south fork of the American River. The site consisted of about twelve square miles he bought from the Maidu for some hats, shirts, flour, and trinkets. Construction began on the sawmill late in 1847. The crew, which included a group of recently discharged members of the Mormon Battalion, worked diligently, and the weather cooperated. Progress was good and by January of 1848 the mill foundation was in place, the dam was under way, and the ditch forming the head- and tailraces had been partially dug.

On Monday, January 24, 1848, Marshall—who was overseeing the construction project as Sutter's partner—was inspecting the tailrace, the channel that carries away the water turning the wheel. With the flow of water interrupted, he could see a shiny, pea-sized object in the gravel; he picked it up. Then he picked up several others. He laid the biggest piece on a rock and hammered on it. When it didn't break, but flattened out until it was the size of a small coin, he was pretty sure that what he'd picked up was gold. Filling the crown of his hat with the bits of shiny material, Marshall took them to the carpenter's bench, where he beat on them some more, boiled them in a lye solution, and heated them. They didn't melt or react. Deciding he'd better report his find to Sutter, Marshall set off on the long ride to New Helvetia. He arrived there on Friday in the midst of a driving rainstorm. Sutter would later say, according to information presented at Marshall Gold Discovery State Historic Park, "He drew out a rag from his pocket. Opening it carefully, he held it before me in his hand. It contained what might have been an ounce and a half of gold dust, flakes and grains." Sutter insisted on testing the material all over again, using nitric acid, heating, pounding—

An 1848 photo of Sutter's Mill on the South Fork of the American River. The man in the foreground may be James Marshall. —The Bancroft Library

every test he knew. The shiny bits withstood them all, for they were, indeed, gold.

Marshall and Sutter agreed to keep the discovery secret so they could finish the mill construction and to protect their rights. But it was too late; too many people already shared the secret. Sutter himself let the cat out of the bag when he couldn't resist boasting. Before long, Sam Brannan, who owned a general store at the fort, heard the news.

Brannan was a shrewd businessman who could spot a fortune in the making when he saw it. He rode over to the mill site to talk with the workmen, many of whom were members of the Mormon Church, of which he was an elder. Each church member gave Brannan one-tenth of the gold he'd found so far, as his tithe for the church. Brannan put it all into a quinine bottle, then headed for San Francisco, after first stocking his store with all the miners' necessities—picks, shovels, pans, blankets, and the like—he could lay hands on.

Once in San Francisco, Brannan paraded through the streets, waving the full quinine bottle and shouting, "Gold, gold, gold from the American River!" Rumors about a gold strike had been floating around for some weeks, but here was proof. The word spread, and all over California sailors deserted ships in harbors, ranchers left their herds untended, soldiers abandoned their posts, and farmers left their fields half plowed. The California gold rush was on. Brannan had made sure that a steady stream of customers would need the supplies he had stockpiled at his store in New Helvetia.

When eastern newspapers got the word, they played it up sensationally. People came by land and by sea. Many came on the famous Yankee clippers, others by train across the Isthmus of Panama—a dismal journey, by all accounts. The greatest mass migration in human history was under way, with California as its destination.

Marshall Gold Discovery State Historic Park

Marshall Gold Discovery State Historic Park preserves the evidence of this upheaval. Here you can see the spot where Marshall picked up the nuggets and an exact replica of the mill, relocated because the river has changed course. Marshall's grave site is here, too, as is the monument erected in his honor in 1890. What once was the business district of Coloma is now the site of an exhibit of equipment used in all three kinds of gold mining. A model of a gold-miner's cabin stands nearby, too, as do two Chinese stores—the actual buildings, not replicas.

Built by one Jonas Wilder before 1860 and leased to Chinese merchants, the stores stood at the edge of a large Chinese community. They sold traditional foods, clothing, and the like. It was in such places that Chinese could receive news from home and socialize. A plaque in one of the stores says, in part, "Following the California gold rush of '49, swarms of Chinese miners came to make their mark on the diggings in the mother lode, including the Coloma Valley. They were industrious and self-contained and mostly content to thoroughly comb the old diggings, thus they reclaimed much gold that would have been overlooked." The Wah Hop Store and Bank is still furnished with dishes and bowls, an abacus, a safe, and other typical Chinese items.

No Fortunes for Them

Like many other forty-niners, neither Sutter nor Marshall got rich in the gold rush. Sutter never had any luck prospecting after that first find. Gold seekers and squatters overran his lands. Having finally brought his wife and children from Europe, he retired to a farm on the Feather River. When a fire of suspicious origin destroyed his home there, Sutter packed up and with his family went to Pennsylvania, where he spent his remaining years trying, unsuccessfully, to get the U.S. Congress to reimburse him for the property he lost at the start of the gold rush.

Marshall didn't fare any better. For a time prospectors who thought he had some magic ability to locate gold would hire him as a guide. When he was unable to spot rich veins any better than the next man, he was accused of being a charlatan. He found some gold, of course, but never the great wealth he dreamed of. He collected a small state pension for a time, gave lectures, and performed odd jobs. He died in 1885 in Kelsey, a small town a few miles east of Coloma.

AUBURN

Auburn, seat of Placer County, is twenty miles north of Coloma. It was one of the earliest mining camps in the state and became a cultural center, as well, during the 1860s and 1870s.

At the foot of the slope leading up to the Southern Pacific train depot stands a historical marker showing where construction of the transcontinental railroad got underway once again after having been delayed for months by political opposition and lack of funds. The railroad was being constructed from west to east, roughly along the route of I-80. Before reaching Auburn, it passed through Roseville, about eighteen miles from Sacramento, where track arrived on April 25, 1864; Rocklin, four miles farther east, a major locomotive center where trains were generally broken in two in order to climb the steep grade ahead; and Newcastle, where construction was halted on June 10, 1864. It was here that stagecoaches transferred passengers from the Dutch Flat wagon road. At Colfax, seventeen miles northeast of Auburn on I-80, the real assault on the

Sierra began. For ten months that town was a vital supply depot for the construction and a junction point for stage lines. The marker in Auburn, however, points out that this is where the Central Pacific, resupplied with money, for the first time augmented its forces with Chinese laborers.

GRASS VALLEY AND THE EMPIRE MINE

Continuing northward for twenty-four miles, CA 49 reaches the Empire Mine, one of the state's deepest, richest, and most famous gold-quartz mines. On Empire Street in Grass Valley, just east of CA 49, it is today a state historic park.

Like so many of the Gold Country's rich discoveries, this one was made by accident. George Roberts, a lumberman, stumbled onto the yellow flecks while surveying trees in the area of today's Empire Mine parking lot. It was the fall of 1850. Word of his find got out and soon the place was overrun with prospectors who were disheartened to find that the gold lay, not on top of the earth in placers, but deep beneath it in quartz veins. The solution was obvious: dig. And dig they did. When the mine finally closed in 1956, the granite bedrock was honeycombed with 367 miles of tunnels, some of them more than a mile deep. Roberts sold his rights to the mine in 1851 for a mere $350, considering himself ahead in the deal. He couldn't have known that by 1864 the mine would have produced gold worth more more than a million dollars. In 1975 the state acquired the property for a park.

Grass Valley grew up to serve the miners, many of them from Cornwall, England. They were experienced hard-rock miners who knew how to tear the most from the earth. They carried down the shafts with them their famous meat-and-potato pies called pasties, which they ate for lunch. They saved scraps, however, to feed to the rats, for those greedy rodents were important indicators of air quality in the mine: If methane, for example, started building up, the rats would start to die, alerting the miners.

Gold Hill, the site of the first discovery of gold-bearing quartz in the area, is marked today by a tablet that stands on Jenkins Street between Hocking and French Avenues in Grass Valley. It memorializes the beginning of quartz mining in California.

Also in Grass Valley, on Mill Street, are the homes of Lola Montez, the famous Irish dancer, and Lotta Crabtree, an English actress, dancer, and singer. Montez is credited with teaching the young Crabtree to sing and dance. Both women were much in demand to entertain miners throughout the Gold Country.

On Main Street is the Holbrooke Hotel, built in 1862 around the Golden Gate Saloon. The saloon, opened in 1852, is the oldest continuously operating saloon in the Gold Country. The hotel's brick and fieldstone construction is an outstanding example of the type of buildings erected during the gold-rush years.

Nevada City, just four miles farther along, brings us to the end of our exploration on CA 49, the golden chain. It is the beginning, however, of the final side trip of this segment of the historical tour of California.

The Scourge of Hydraulic Mining

Fifteen miles northeast of Nevada City on North Bloomfield Road is Malakoff Diggins State Historic Park, where gold was discovered in 1851. The park's terrain ranges in elevation from twenty-two hundred to forty-two hundred feet and varies from open meadow to forest- and chaparral-covered slopes and deep canyons. Hydraulic mining was employed there for several years, only to be outlawed in 1884. By that time, however, Malakoff Diggins was the largest and richest hydraulic gold mine in the world, having produced millions of dollars worth of gold and having left a gaping hole in the earth.

The story of Malakoff Diggins begins with three miners from what is now Nevada City, who set out to find less crowded conditions in which to seek their fortunes. To the northeast, in a beautiful little valley with a promising stream, they found gold. The word of their find leaked out, of course, and scores of other hopefuls joined them. When the newcomers weren't as lucky as the original trio, they pronounced the whole place a humbug, labeling the stream Humbug Creek. During the next couple of years some settlers came to raise cattle and crops; they found new gold deposits and a settlement sprouted up. It was named

Holbrooke Hotel in Grass Valley was built in 1862 around the Golden Gate Saloon, the oldest continuously operating saloon in Gold Country. —Grass Valley and Nevada County Chamber of Commerce

Humbug after the creek, and it flourished. By 1857 the town had grown big enough to boast a post office and school as well as several businesses. Now residents wanted a more sedate name for their town, so they changed it to North Bloomfield. When surface claims played out, many settlers sold their rights to a man named Julius Poquillon, who amassed more than fifteen hundred acres by the mid-1860s. He and a group of San Francisco investors then formed the North Bloomfield Gravel Mining Company.

Since the ore in this area was extremely low grade, hydraulic mining was the only method that might yield a profit. Some three hundred Chinese who lived in the town's two Chinese settlements built the dams and ditches needed to bring in the enormous flow of water the process required. By 1876 the mine was in full operation, with seven giant water cannons, called monitors, gushing around the clock to destroy the once-beautiful valley. Huge streams of water under high pressure washed away entire hillsides to get at small traces of gold. Richard A. Lovett, writing in *California Parklands*, says, "It was so destructive, however, that it eroded millions of tons of debris down the Yuba and Feather rivers, threatening to drown the valley below in mud, and raising the bed of the Yuba River high enough that at one time it was above street level in Marysville. The silt traveled all the way to the Golden Gate and interfered with navigation in the Carquinez Strait."

Farmers and ranchers who lived downstream were continually bringing legal action against the mining company. At last, in January 1884, a federal judge, Lorenzo Sawyer, handed down his momentous decision favoring the valley farmers. He declared that hydraulic miners could no longer dispose of their runoff in public waterways, effectively making the process illegal. It was probably the first environmental ruling issued in the United States, if not the world. The company was ordered to curtail its activities, to clean up its act. By the early 1900s, the new controls had made hydraulic mining unprofitable and the world's largest hydraulic mine was silenced forever.

Today, some of the original buildings still stand, and some have been restored to their original condition. But the most telling evidence of the past of Malakoff Diggins is the mine pit with its colorful cliffs, nearly 7,000 feet long, as much as 3,000 feet wide, and nearly 600 feet deep in places.

The trip through the Mother lode country may be at an end, but there are other gold discoveries to explore. Some are in the southern part of the state and at least one is on the eastern side of the Sierra Nevada. They lie along other highways.

A carriage transports visitors along Broad Street in Nevada City at the end of the golden chain. —Grass Valley and Nevada County Chamber of Commerce

Part 4

The Fertile Central Valley

California's lush Central Valley consists of 18,000 square miles of smaller valleys that lie between the coastal hills and the Sierra Nevada. Larger than Vermont and New Hampshire combined, it is, acre for acre, the richest agricultural region in the world. Some five hundred miles long, it is threaded by I-5 and CA 99, both running the entire length of the great valley and slicing through sixteen counties. CA 99 was once the major north-to-south roadway in the state, but it was superseded in the 1960s by I-5, a high-speed, and for the most part boring, multilane freeway.

Also slicing through the great Central Valley is the famed San Andreas Fault. According to Robert Cleland, in *California in Our Time, 1900–1940*, the fault leaves the sea near the mouth of Alder Creek, above Point Arena in Mendocino County, and makes its way toward the Mexican border. For a time it closely parallels the coast, crosses the Golden Gate and extends to Chittenden (near Watsonville) in the Pajaro Valley of Monterey County. From Chittenden the fault follows the axis of the Gabilan Mountains, which define the boundary between Monterey and San Benito Counties, and runs through the so-called Carrizo Plain (between the Panza Range of Los Padres National Forest and the Temblor Range in eastern San Luis Obispo County) on the edge of the San Joaquin Valley. It continues for many miles along the slope of the Sierra Nevada Mountains, and finally curves eastward past the San Bernardino and San Jacinto Mountains to lose itself in the Imperial Valley.

Bounded on the north by the Klamath Mountains and the southern Cascades, the Central Valley's southern boundaries are defined by the Tehachapi Mountains, the Transverse Ranges, and the southern Coast Ranges. To the east lie the Cascade Range and the Sierra Nevada. Its western edge is marked by the Coast Range.

The great valley is really two major valleys, the Sacramento at its northern end, carved by the Sacramento River, which flows out of the northern Sierra, and the San Joaquin Valley, shaped by the San Joaquin River, which rises in the southern Sierra and flows northward. The two rivers merge to form a fan-shaped delta east of San Francisco before emptying into San Francisco Bay.

Jedediah Smith wrote in the journal he kept of his travels, "The Indians [of the Sacramento Valley] are numerous, honest and peaceable in their dispositions. They live in a country where the soil is good and the climate pleasant with the exception of two or three months in the winter when there is too much rain." Smith concluded that the Creator had scattered more than an ordinary share of his bounty among the people of the Sacramento Valley.

Smith may have been first to remark on this partiality on the part of the Creator, but he wasn't the last. Early and often men have noted that the Sacramento Valley contains only one-third of the land, but produces two-thirds of the water of the Central Valley. The San Joaquin Valley, on the other hand, holds most of the land and contributes a much smaller portion of the water. Both valleys were equally dealt with in regard to the scourge of flooding, however. Additionally, in exceptionally dry years, before human intervention, the delta suffered because salt from the sea would rush upstream against the lessening currents of low rivers to damage both farms and municipal water supplies.

As Stephan Birmingham notes, even architecture in the valley had to adapt to the vagaries of nature. "One way to recognize a California house that at least predates the era of air conditioning is to observe whether it is built high off the ground (sometimes even on stilts) and is approached by a long flight of steps—precautions against the seasonal floods that used to occur in Central Valley regions." In Sacramento, Leland Stanford's home, the original governor's mansion, and a dozen other historic houses demonstrate the truth of Birmingham's architectural observation. Most of today's valley homes sit at ground level, testimony to the efficacy of the area's flood-control systems.

With the advent of gasoline- and electric-powered pumps, large farms used more than their share of available water for irrigation. The water table of the valley fell, and many farmers who couldn't afford the new pumps watched their crops shrivel in the burning sun. Shallow lakes, such as Lake Kern and Tulare Lake, once fed by melting snows of the high Sierra flowing in Kings, Kaweah, and Kern Rivers, dried up, leaving marshlands or barren earth.

In 1919, Robert B. Marshall hit on a way to stabilize the Central Valley's water supply: a large dam on the upper Sacramento River, which would feed two aqueducts running down either side of the valley. Under this plan the valley would gain much-needed water, as would San Francisco Bay Area cities. In the south, the project would divert the Kern

River to Los Angeles and the southern coast. Southern California bowed out of the project before the state legislature endorsed it, in 1933, and voters passed a $170-million bond issue. In 1935 the federal government stepped in with more money and took over the project, hoping to provide water for irrigation, impede flooding, improve navigation on the lower Sacramento, create water recreation spots, generate hydroelectric power, and stop the incursion of saltwater into the delta. It was finally completed in 1955, although the first power generated had been delivered in 1944, and the first water had arrived in 1951. Components of this Central Valley Project (CVP) are the Shasta and Keswick Dams on the Sacramento River, Folsom Dam on the American, New Melones Dam on the Stanislaus, and Friant Dam on the San Joaquin. The project also includes a network of canals that delivers water all over the valley.

One of the earliest means of trying to control the shortage or surplus of water was prayer; even today, prayers for rain are offered up at many Catholic masses during times of prolonged drought. Norris Hundley Jr., in *The Great Thirst*, tells of a missionary at San Antonio de Padua mission who drafted an Indian shaman into God's service when he learned the native was considered a rainmaker. "The priest locked up the shaman with the warning that he would remain incarcerated until he ended the drought. The Indian told the priest to put the congregation in the church and to bring him a barrel of water. He then performed a special ritual which . . . was followed by rain." Not all prayers or rainmakers have been so successful, but both have been called upon in various parts of California.

Just as rainmakers have been featured in several parts of the state, other characters who played important roles in the development of California often didn't confine their activities to a single area. In spite of the difficulties of travel of the times, a few men—and a woman or two—starred in several settings, including the Central Valley. John Sutter is a case in point, as are Sam Brannan and Nancy Kelsey.

Generally speaking, urbane San Franciscans scorn the people of the Central Valley, regarding them as crude and uncouth. Valley dwellers, however, know their place in history. Writes Birmingham, "There is a sense here in the Valley of the continuation of history—of the gold rush, of the opening up of the West by the railroads, of the growth of California from the earliest days to where it is now, the most populous state in the Union." Birmingham cites C. K. McClatchy, fourth-generation editor of the valley's chain of *Bee* newspapers, as having said, "This valley is one of the most thrilling places to be alive that I know." Its history would suggest that McClatchy is right.

CA 99
Red Bluff–Bakersfield
403 miles

CHICO

The first community of any significance on this leg of the historical exploration of California is Chico, which sits where CA 99 meets CA 32, forty-one miles southeast of Red Bluff. The site of a campus of the state university system, it is one of the more dynamic towns in Butte County.

Chico is also the town founded and shaped by John Bidwell, one of the first overland travelers to California. Inspired by letters from John Marsh singing the praises of California, Bidwell left Missouri for the West, in 1841, in a party that included John Bartleson, Josiah Belden, Joseph Chiles, and Nicholas Dawson. One other member of the group who is seldom mentioned in accounts of the difficult trek was Nancy Kelsey, the lone woman in the party, who bore in her arms an infant daughter, Ann. The twenty-four-week journey was a terrible one during which all the travelers suffered greatly, even having to eat their mules to avert starvation. Reaching the ranch of John Sutter in late November, Bidwell went right to work for the proprietor of New Helvetia (New Switzerland)—now known as Sutter's Fort.

Bidwell became a naturalized citizen of Mexico in order to receive a large land grant, then helped to defend Governor Manuel Micheltorena in the revolt of 1844. He wrote the 1846 resolution of independence from Mexico and joined Frémont's California Battalion, a contingent of about 230 American settlers who served in the Bear Flag Revolt and subsequent actions until mustered out in 1847. Returning to New Helvetia and Sutter's service, Bidwell worked as the Swiss's principal bookkeeper and general assistant. One of the chores he performed was to draw up Sutter's contract with James Marshall for the construction of a sawmill on the American River. In January 1848 he helped Sutter confirm the nature of the small nuggets Marshall carried in his famous dash through the rain from Coloma to Sutter's Fort. He made a rich strike on the Feather River, but in 1849 decided he'd rather farm than muck about in the goldfields. Disposing of most of his Mexican land grant, he invested part of his goldfield earnings in a huge ranch that he named Rancho del Arroyo Chico.

In 1860 Bidwell laid out the town of Chico: sixty blocks, including a plaza. He gave land for public buildings to the city and a lot to anyone

110

who would build a permanent home on it. He also donated land for each church denomination and sites for cemeteries and schools. In 1877, when the state decided to build a normal school in Northern California, Bidwell donated his cherry orchard for its site, thereby saving the town from being just another farm town in the Sacramento Valley. In 1921 the school became Chico State Teachers' College and subsequently a part of the state university system.

Except for his years in Washington, D.C., as a congressman (1865–67), Bidwell spent the rest of his life in his town. It was in Washington that he met his future wife, Annie Kennedy. As a congressman he enthusiastically supported a number of controversial causes, including women's suffrage, secret ballots, the temperance movement, and public regulation of utilities. Some historians say his uncompromising stands on such issues led directly to his political downfall.

Bidwell became a leader in California agriculture, eager to take advantage of new technology, new watering methods, and better equipment. He continually experimented with different varieties of fruit, vegetables, and grain, growing some four hundred varieties of fruit trees in his experimental orchard. With regard to his grain, an item in the *Daily Alta Californian* reported, "Bidwell's mill . . . produces an excellent article of flour. So well is it known to the public that its brand is a vouch of excellence and consequently it sells at an advance over other brands. We have been informed that the general [an honorary title] says the mill is the most profitable of all his industries." In 1878 at the Paris International Exposition, wheat from Bidwell's mill won the gold medal as the finest wheat in the world.

Before he met Annie in Washington, Bidwell lived in an adobe near a stream that ran through the rancho. That building was razed on completion of the mansion he and Annie lived in from 1868 until their deaths. There they entertained the likes of John Muir, founder of the Sierra Club, Asa Gray, leading American botanist of the day, and Susan B. Anthony. Today their three-story, twenty-six-room home is a state historic park on the Esplanade in central Chico. It has served as the setting for many movies.

OROVILLE

Twenty-one miles south of Chico, CA 162 crosses CA 99, and there begins a side trip to the east to Oroville, the seat of Butte County, located on CA 70. Founded in 1850 as Ophir and renamed a few years later, Oroville became a trade center because of its location at the confluence of the North and Middle Forks of the Feather River.

During mining days Oroville had a huge Chinatown, second in size only to the one in San Francisco; a fine temple remains at 1500 Broderick Street. It was dedicated in 1863 after being built by local Chinese laborers, with funds for construction materials and furnishings donated by the emperor and empress of China. In 1935 Chinese residents deeded the temple to the city. It is today a state historical landmark.

Oroville is also the site of an important, though little-celebrated, moment in the state annals. California Historic Landmark number 809 stands on the Oroville-Quincy Highway at Oak Avenue, noting the spot at which an era ended. It was there, in a corral belonging to a group of butchers, that a Yahi man was found, hungry and scrabbling for food. According to Walton Bean, "The gold seekers of the 1850s had hunted the Yahi as if they were wild animals, and by 1870 it was supposed that they were extinct." One still survived, however, and he was called Ishi, the Yahi word for "man," after he was captured in that corral on August 29, 1911. Taken to the University of California in San Francisco by some anthropologists, Ishi adapted remarkably well to his new environment, even learning about five hundred words of English. He taught the professors about his people and their way of life before he caught a cold and died, the last survivor of pre-contact California civilization.

THE SUTTER BUTTES

Twenty-five miles south of Oroville, on CA 70, the Sutter Buttes come into view, ten miles or so west of the highway. They rise unexpectedly from the valley floor, three volcanic hills that reach as high as two thousand feet and in the spring are covered with wildflowers. Utilized as a lookout point by both natives and newcomers, the buttes were first noted by Spaniards, then by Jedediah Smith in 1828. John C. Frémont camped amid the buttes from May 30 to June 8, 1846, just before he took part in the Bear Flag Revolt in Sonoma.

MARYSVILLE

Six miles farther along on CA 70 is Marysville, seat of Yuba County, where the Feather and Yuba Rivers merge. Marysville was founded in 1850 and named for Mary Murphy Covillaud, a survivor of the Donner Party and the wife of one of the founders. Because of its location, Marysville became a primary trading center for the northern mines, controlling traffic of men and goods from the Central Valley to diggings in Yuba, Nevada, Butte, and Placer Counties.

Hydraulic mining operations to the north choked the Yuba River and made its bed rise at such an alarming rate that earthen levees had to be constructed to protect the city from flooding. Also built to ward off flooding was the Chinese temple that sits on the levee at the foot of D Street, honoring the river god Bok-Kai. It is the only joss house in the nation to honor that deity and is the setting for the town's annual Bomb Day celebration.

WHEATLAND, A MONUMENT TO MIGRANT WORKERS

One more spot of special historical interest remains to be explored on this side trip: Wheatland, eleven miles south of Marysville on CA 65. In the days of the Argonauts the place was known as Johnson's Ranch and was the first California settlement reached by wagon trains using the emigrant trail over the Sierra through what is now known as Donner Pass. It was here that seven members of the tragic Donner group sought help in 1846 for their still-trapped fellows.

The area's other claim to fame arose more than sixty years later, on August 13, 1913, at the hops fields of Ralph Durst, one of the state's largest employers of migrant workers. Employing a tactic that would be used again and again over the years, Durst ran alluring ads in newspapers all over California and Oregon saying that he was looking for twenty-seven hundred pickers for his harvest; twenty-eight hundred, mostly aliens, showed up. Durst really intended to hire only about fifteen hundred, but knew he could pay much lower wages if he had a surplus of applicants. The pickers who did get on earned ninety cents for each sack picked, and even the best couldn't work fast enough to harvest two sacks a day.

Walton Bean sets the stage for the tragedy to follow: "Conditions in his work camp were barbaric. As housing, a few tents were available for rental, but most of the workers built their own rude shelters of gunnysacks and poles, or slept in the open. For 2,800 men, women, and children there were eight outdoor toilets, which also had to serve as the only garbage disposal facilities." It isn't unusual for August temperatures in the Central Valley to soar, and soar they did that summer. In spite of readings well above one hundred degrees in the shade (of which there was little), Durst refused to provide drinking water in the fields. Nor would he permit workers to rent a water wagon and pull it onto the field themselves. Instead, he allowed a cousin to sell the thirsty pickers lemonade made with citric acid.

News of the workers' plight brought to the scene one Richard "Blackie" Ford, a member of the radical IWW (Industrial Workers of the World). Holding a mass meeting of workers, Ford faced off with Durst, who slapped the organizer. The following day, when Ford was speaking to another mass meeting, a sheriff's posse from Marysville arrived to arrest agitators. One of the deputies fired a shot into the air, causing a general melee in which the district attorney, a deputy sheriff, and two workers were killed and many others injured. Governor Hiram Johnson dispatched the National Guard and several workers, along with Ford, were taken into custody. In a trial held early in 1914, Ford and another IWW member were found guilty of second-degree murder for having fomented the unrest. Durst received no punishment. The governor did, however, appoint a commission to investigate conditions under which migratory workers had to work.

Another outcome of the riot was the formation of Kelley's Army, a force of about fifteen hundred unemployed migratory and unskilled workers. Recruited by Charles T. Kelley, the group marched to Sacramento to petition for legislative aid. Some eight hundred deputized citizens armed with pick handles met them there and drove them from the city. It would be many years before the plight of migrant workers was seriously addressed by state government.

The side trip now retraces the eleven miles of CA 65 to Marysville. It adds only about twenty-five miles to the distance to Bakersfield, because its route roughly parallels that of CA 99.

SUTTER COUNTY

Crossing the Twin Cities Bridge from Marysville to Yuba City, the historical trek goes as well from Yuba County to Sutter, from CA 70 back to CA 99, and from the east bank of the Yuba River to the west. Sam Brannan, with Pierson B. Reading and Henry Cheever, laid out Yuba City in July 1849 as a gold-rush development. Today it is the seat of Sutter County, an agricultural marketing center, and home to a number of fruit-packing plants.

Sutter County was named for John Sutter, who was granted most of the land that the county now comprises. It was in this area that Sutter had his Hock Farm, to which he retreated when the gold-rush activity drove him from New Helvetia. The plaque commemorating that site sits alongside CA 99 at Messick Road, south of Yuba City. The actual farm buildings stood on the banks of the Feather River opposite the plaque.

To the west about eight miles, on CA 20 near the town of Sutter, stands a monument marking where William Thompson, an Englishman, settled with his family in 1863. In 1872 Thompson imported from New York three grape cuttings, only one of which survived. That one cutting—a seedless variety—thrived to produce the beginnings of California's huge raisin and table-grape industry that in 1988 brought more than three million tons of grapes to market.

ALL ROADS LEAD TO SACRAMENTO

Forty-two miles south of Yuba City, CA 99, I-5, I-80, and CA 50 all converge at Sacramento, capital of California, seat of the county of the same name and—as might be expected—a city rife with historical interest.

Sutter's Fort

The first white man to settle in the area was John Sutter, who called himself "Captain," claiming to have been an officer in the Swiss Army. Sutter arrived in California at Yerba Buena (later called San Francisco) by way of Oregon Territory, the Sandwich Islands (later called Hawaii), and Sitka, Alaska. During his travels he acquired a cortege that included five white men and eight Kanakas (Hawaiians) and an assortment of tools, provisions, and weapons, including a cannon or two. With these goods and some false credentials he approached Governor Alvarado to ask for a grant of land.

Alvarado made Sutter a Mexican citizen and gave him permission to explore the rivers and take possession of any piece of unoccupied land he fancied. With his retinue and gear in three boats, Sutter set off to find the mouth of the Sacramento River. During the eight days of his search, Sutter made friends with a band of Indians in war paint, learned a great deal about the surrounding countryside, and eventually sailed

Restored Sutter's Fort in the heart of Sacramento is now a state historic park. This view shows Sutter's holdings prior to the gold rush. —Sacramento Convention and Visitors Bureau

Old Sacramento National Historic Landmark features preserved and restored buildings from the capital's early days. —Sacramento Convention and Visitors Bureau

up the American River. On August 12, 1839, he landed on that river's banks near its confluence with the Sacramento River.

By winter Sutter and his men had managed to build a forty-foot-long adobe building that would become the nucleus of his fort. With the help of local Indians and a passing American or two, he soon had an establishment with eighteen-foot walls, a headquarters building, and a line of workshops. He laid down a rough road to the river so he could ship goods to San Francisco, planted crops the following summer, and acquired cattle and horses to graze on his seventy-six-square-mile holding.

For a time, all went well for Sutter and his fort, which became known as the end of the California Trail. Wagon-weary emigrants stopped there for rest and resupply. He enjoyed welcoming these visitors to his establishment and counted John Bidwell and John Frémont among his guests. In 1841 Sutter bought all that wasn't nailed down of the Russians' Fort Ross and hauled it to New Helvetia, as he called his ranch. He was planning to create a city called Sutterville nearby, but history overwhelmed him.

In 1846 California became part of the United States and Sutter's Mexican land grant was largely dissolved, although he did manage to hold on to some land and his cattle. Sutter determined to try one more gambit: a sawmill on the American River from which he could float

116

milled lumber to the Central Valley to sell for premium prices. James Marshall's discovery of gold put an end to that plan. As the Federal Writers' Project guide tells, "Trampling hordes from the East overran his hospitable fort, stole his cattle, drove off his Indians, disputed his rights to the land. His white retainers deserted for the mines." In short, the gold his partner found proved to be Sutter's undoing.

Today, Sutter's Fort has been reconstructed and is a state historic park at 28th and L Streets in Sacramento. The two-story central building made of adobe and oak is all that remains of the original fort.

According to Faren Maree Bachelis, in *The Pelican Guide to Sacramento and the Gold Country*, the city of Sacramento was the creation of John Sutter Jr. and Sam Brannan, the wily entrepreneur who played such a large role in the onset of the rush for gold. Phyllis Zauner says, "To escape his creditors, Sutter put everything he owned . . . in his son's name and hightailed it out of town." To pay off his father's debts, the twenty-two-year-old Sutter struck up a deal with Sam Brannan and sold lots on the waterfront for $500 each.

With the discovery of gold, the flow of newcomers to Sacramento became a flood. On June 16, 1849, the *Placer Times* reported that one hundred houses and twenty-five stores had been built and that Sam Brannan had a magnificent hotel under way. Anyone with anything to sell could make a fortune. Gambling houses flourished, and by the end

Restored riverboat Delta King, *permanently anchored at the wharf on Old Sacramento's waterfront, now serves as a hotel and restaurant.* —Sacramento Convention and Visitors Bureau

117

of 1849 Sacramento was a well-defined city, its streets lined with hotels, stores, saloons, and a theater.

Much of the original city has been preserved or reconstructed and is now Old Sacramento, a state historic park bounded by the river and Second Street, I and L Streets. In spite of its very commercial aspect, it is genuinely illustrative of the early days of California's capital.

Adjacent to Old Sacramento is the Railroad Museum, a collection of western railroading history, which includes famous steam locomotives and the spot where Governor Leland Stanford, on January 8, 1863, turned the first earth to begin construction of the Central Pacific Railroad. More than six years later, on May 10, 1869, the line that began here met up with the Union Pacific Railroad at Promontory, Utah.

At the northwest corner of Front and K Streets in Old Sacramento is the site of the stagecoach terminal of the 1850s and of the Sacramento Valley Railroad, the first railroad west of the Rockies. The original plan called for the line to connect Sacramento to Marysville, but a shortage of funds shortened the tracks and ended them in Folsom.

Birth of the Big Four

Short though it was, the twenty-two-mile railroad line gave a cachet to its builder, Theodore Judah, described by Phyllis Zauner as "a brilliant young engineer with an obsession to build a transcontinental railroad." It was Judah's plan that made the Central Pacific Railroad a reality, one of the engineering marvels of the time, crossing the Sierras over grades believed to be impossible to surmount. At the outset he tried to solicit funds for his project from San Francisco and Sacramento businessmen. San Franciscans turned him away. In Sacramento, however, he found a hardware dealer named Collis Huntington who could see the import of his plan.

Huntington persuaded his partner, Mark Hopkins, to go along with the scheme, and together they convinced grocer Leland Stanford and Charles Crocker to invest. These men became known as the Big Four and were inextricably linked to the grandest railroad monopoly of all time, a monopoly that directed the course of California's history for decades. Judah, who not only originated the idea and planned the route but also lobbied Congress for a contract, died in October of 1863, the year construction of the railroad began.

The other men in the venture took over completely. Stanford became president of the Central Pacific Railroad Company and handler of political matters in California. Hopkins served as treasurer. Crocker oversaw the actual construction, while Huntington took charge of eastern business arrangements and federal financing. All four made immense fortunes

*Collis P. Huntington, one
of the men known as the
Big Four.* —The Bancroft Library

from the railroad and even more from building a line from San Francisco through the San Joaquin Valley to Los Angeles and east to New Orleans, the Southern Pacific.

Huntington took over as president of the Southern Pacific Railroad in 1890, after a falling-out with Stanford over business policy. After Huntington's death it was revealed that he had bribed public officials and used his power ruthlessly to make money.

Mark Hopkins was the oldest of the Big Four and the most modest. He was also the first to die. His widow finished building the huge mansion the couple had planned together, an edifice that after her death became the first home of the forerunner of the San Francisco Art Institute. Later still, the grounds became the setting for the posh Mark Hopkins Hotel on Nob Hill in San Francisco.

Overseeing construction, Charles Crocker drove the work gangs to get the line completed, then went on to become president of the Southern Pacific Railroad after it was completed in 1877. He invested

Leland Stanford, another member of the Big Four. He was elected state senator after serving a term as governor.
—The Bancroft Library

in other land holdings, including the Del Monte Hotel, an elegant resort near Monterey.

Leland Stanford made the biggest political splash of the four, as founder of the Republican Party in California. He was elected eighth governor of the state in 1861. It's not surprising that during his two-year term he was a strong advocate of railroad interests. California's legislature elected him to the U.S. Senate in 1885 and reelected him in 1891, even though he contributed little to legislative affairs. His impressive home in Sacramento is today a state historic park at 802 N Street.

It wasn't only the transcontinental railroad that ended in Sacramento; the legendary Pony Express had its western terminus there, too, from the inception of the service until July 1861. A monument at Second and J Streets honors the incredibly brave young men who carried the mail from St. Joseph, Missouri, to Sacramento, a distance of 1,980 miles. Zauner writes that the Pony Express set up two hundred relay stations and employed five hundred horses and eighty riders under age twenty-one, who could weigh no more than 125 pounds, and were "brave beyond belief." They changed horses every half hour, leaping off one saddle and onto the other with the mail in hand, spending two minutes or less in the exchange.

The first mail pouch to be so carried reached Sacramento on April 13, 1860. It had been ten days in transit and held eighty letters destined

*Charles Crocker,
another of the Big
Four. He actually
supervised the laying
of the tracks for the
Central Pacific
Railroad.*
—The Bancroft Library

for Sacramento and San Francisco. The cost of sending those letters was five dollars per half ounce.

Riders were paid about $100 a month, plus bonuses for speed, but were out of work eighteen months after the service started. The need for the Pony Express ended with the completion of the Overland Telegraph Line, which reached Sacramento on October 4, 1861.

California's Capitol

Several years before the Pony Express began its service, the state legislature agreed that a state as wealthy as California should have a capitol building, a showplace. In 1856 legislators authorized an expenditure of $300,000 to build a capitol on the plaza square that John Sutter Jr. had donated to the city. Unfortunately, times were tough and even that meager sum wasn't available. The legislature continued to meet in the borrowed county courthouse until county officials donated land for the capitol, a four-block plot from L to N Streets between Tenth and Eleventh. By 1860 a half-million dollars had been raised for construction and work began. It was 1874 before the building—the western half of today's edifice—was truly complete, at a cost of $2.6 million, but impatient residents of the city staged a ball in the unfinished capitol in 1869. It was the social event of the decade, according to newspaper accounts of the affair.

In 1906 elevators, modern plumbing, and wiring were installed to update the building, all at the expense of its original elegance. Over the

121

years further remodeling was done and by 1972 the entire structure was seedy-looking, a poor advertisement for the Golden State, and potentially dangerous in the event of an earthquake. Rather than raze the building, legislators decided to restore it. The capitol was closed and cloaked with scaffolding, and reconstruction began. For eight years carpenters and artisans labored to restore it to its former elegance, at a cost of $70 million. In 1982 state senators and assemblymen returned to their chambers, which now sit amid museum rooms open to the public through free tours.

An Assembly Center

Historical marker number 937, in Walerga Park at the northwest corner of Palm Avenue and College Oak Drive, marks yet another spot that demands attention in Sacramento. Its plaque reads, "The temporary detention camps (also known as 'assembly centers') represent the first phase of the mass incarceration of 97,785 Californians of Japanese ancestry during World War II. Pursuant to Executive Order 9066 signed by President Franklin D. Roosevelt on February 19, 1942, thirteen makeshift detention facilities were constructed at various California racetracks, fairgrounds, and labor camps. These facilities were intended to confine Japanese Americans until more permanent concentration camps, such as those at Manzanar and Tule Lake in California, could be built in isolated areas of the country. Beginning on March 30, 1942, all native-born Americans and longtime legal residents of Japanese ancestry living in California were ordered to surrender themselves for detention." One of those assembly centers stood here.

FOLSOM, A SITE OF POWER

A little more than twenty miles northeast of downtown Sacramento on US 50 is Folsom, into which the first train to operate west of the Rockies steamed on February 22, 1856, ending a run from Sacramento. The line linked mining camps in the hills with riverboats in the capital city and ignited the gold-mining boom in Folsom.

The town was a dream of Joseph L. Folsom, a West Point graduate and member of Stevenson's Battalion. He hired Theodore Judah to lay out the town and sell lots, a chore Judah completed the year after Folsom died. Originally planned as Granite City, the town was renamed to honor its founder.

Horatio Putnam Livermore, a man important to Folsom, is one of the least-honored contributors to California's success, no doubt because his activities have been confused with those of Robert Livermore, who was not related to Horatio. Horatio came to California from Maine in

1849 with his father, Horatio Gates Livermore, while Robert Livermore jumped ship in California a quarter century earlier in 1822, was naturalized as a Mexican citizen in 1844, and settled and grew wealthy in the valley that came to bear his name. Elected a state senator in 1854, the elder Horatio Livermore was intrigued by the possibilities of the American River and of a company organized to divert its water to diggings in the foothills. By 1862 he and his sons had acquired control of the Natoma Water and Mining Company.

In 1861 the younger Horatio Livermore conceived of a dam across the American River that would provide water power for an industrial city near Folsom. It wasn't until 1867, however, that construction of that dam began, and then it proceeded by fits and starts. The Natoma Company expended almost $120,000 to lay a railroad from Folsom to the dam site and to build a foundation for the dam at Stony Bar Gorge. The following year the Livermores entered into a contract with the state prison board for convict labor to complete the dam. In return for that labor, the Livermores donated 350 acres of land on the eastern bank of the river as a site for the proposed Folsom Prison. They also turned over to the prison board the railroad and the rights to some of the waterpower. Unfortunately, no convicts would be available to provide labor to build the dam until the prison was built, so completion of the dam had to wait.

Overcrowding at San Quentin Prison had made Folsom Prison a pressing necessity. One hundred of San Quentin's most unruly residents were sent to occupy Folsom's first cell block. Those first inmates built accommodations for 140 more convicts in the form of eight dungeons and seventy cells, cells that records say had cast-iron doors, straw pallets for beds, and buckets for plumbing.

In 1881 the stockholders of the Natoma Water and Mining Company formed the Folsom Water and Power Company, taking over all Natoma's properties and rights concerning waterpower. The new company insisted that the state follow through on the original labor agreement.

In 1882 construction began again on the dam, after another round of negotiations over the amount of convict labor to be provided. During the next six years, prisoners provided more than 500,000 man-days of labor. The prison quarry, opened that same year, provided stone for the dam. At the same time, prison inmates were working on the prison powerhouse, which was completed in 1891. Electricity lit the prison starting in 1893, when the dam was at last completed, one year after the death of Horatio Gates Livermore.

During those years of haggling, Horatio P. Livermore realized that his dream of moving logs and turning machinery by direct waterpower was an impractical one. Not so impractical, he was sure, was the idea that turbines turned by water flowing from the Folsom Dam could generate electricity for the city of Sacramento, twenty-two miles to the west. He incorporated the Sacramento Electric Power & Light Company to build the powerhouse and construct the long-distance power line to carry the electricity. He was joined in this venture by his brother Charles; Albert Gallatin, of Huntington and Hopkins Hardware; and the General Electric Company.

Five miles was about the farthest electricity had ever been transmitted up to that time, but Livermore persuaded manufacturers to design a workable system to carry the output of a power plant at Folsom to Sacramento. Two years later the power-producing plant was completed. After extensive testing, the Folsom Powerhouse generated 11,000 volts of electricity and, on July 13, 1895, transmitted it to the Sacramento

William C. Ralston, founder of the Bank of California and one of the state's leading boosters until his mysterious death.
—The Bancroft Library

substation, where it was greeted by a one-hundred-gun salute. By September of that same year, Sacramento glowed with 25,000 incandescent lamps and 600 arc lights.

The original generating plant, which operated continuously until 1952, has been preserved at Folsom Powerhouse State Park on Greenback Lane. The substation that received the electricity stands today at the northeast corner of Sixth and H Streets in Sacramento. It is still in use, an electrical substation of the city's utility district. Today the modern Folsom Dam, dedicated in 1956, tames the turbulent American River and generates up to 162,000 kilowatts of electric power. Seven years in the making, Folsom Dam towers 350 feet above the streambed and is operated by the U.S. Bureau of Reclamation as an integral part of the Central Valley Project.

LODI

From Folsom the historical trek retraces the twenty-two miles to Sacramento and regains CA 99. Twenty-nine miles south of Sacramento, where the Mokelumne River crosses CA 99, stands Lodi, a market center particularly known for its Tokay grapes. Since 1907 Lodi has been noted for its Mission Revival–style ceremonial arch, one of the few remaining in the state. Located at the southeast corner of East Pine and South Sacramento Streets, the arch is today a historical landmark. It was built as a monument to the city's first grape festival called the Tokay Carnival, and has presided over similar affairs ever since.

In spite of valley boosters' claims to the contrary, in the thirty-four-mile stretch of CA 99 between Lodi and Modesto, seat of Stanislaus County, there is little that is historically remarkable.

TRIBUTE TO A MODEST MAN

Modesto's main claim to historical fame seems to be that it was originally named after William C. Ralston, banker extraordinaire, who modestly declined the honor; hence the name, Modesto. In his *California: An Interpretive History*, Walton Bean suggests that Ralston declined the honor because he felt the tribute was too humble, not too grand.

Ralston arrived in San Francisco from Ohio in 1854 and promptly made a name for himself in banking circles. Ten years later he was one of the founders of the spectacularly successful Bank of California, for a time one of the most highly regarded banks in the Far West. In spite of his financial success he was blackballed from membership in the exclusive Bohemian Club of San Francisco. He had a finger in a hundred civic pies and financed with his own and the bank's money such enterprises as steamship lines, mines in the Comstock Lode, a theater, and

Castle Air Museum at Atwater, near Merced, contains a fine collection of vintage planes. —Merced Convention and Visitors Bureau

the Palace Hotel. He drowned mysteriously in the San Francisco Bay, where he often swam, after his bank collapsed in 1875.

Modesto was also the childhood home of film director George Lucas, and the town's McHenry Avenue inspired his film *American Graffiti*.

MERCED

The thirty-nine miles that separate Modesto from Merced are typical of the Central Valley: a mostly flat expanse studded with small farming communities, hot and dry much of the year. Soil in the area is incredibly fertile under irrigation.

Merced is the seat of Merced County and a way station on the route to Yosemite National Park. According to the town's Convention and Visitors Bureau, Presidents Taft and Roosevelt rested in Merced, as did movie stars such as Mae West, Mary Pickford, and Buster Keaton.

CHOWCHILLA

Fifteen miles farther south is Chowchilla, a town that was much in the news in 1975 when a busload of schoolchildren was kidnapped and held in a bunker beneath the ground. All the children were safely rescued, largely through their own ingenuity.

Fresno, City of the Ash Trees

Fresno, the largest city between Sacramento and Bakersfield, and the marketing center of the San Joaquin Valley, is just under forty miles from Chowchilla. In *A Companion to California,* James D. Hart points out that Fresno's history is all post–gold rush, without much Spanish or Mexican influence. Notwithstanding that opinion, it must be noted that Fresno is Spanish for "ash tree."

Some 10,000 Yokuts distributed among about fifty separate tribes were the earliest inhabitants of the area; they met Frémont, Kit Carson, Alexis Godey, and "Broken Hand" Fitzpatrick when the white men crossed the San Joaquin Valley. It was the coming of farmers in the 1860s and of the Central Railroad in 1872 that gave the city its life. Seat of Fresno County since 1874, superseding Millerton, Fresno's population in 1989 was well over 300,000.

Contributing to the remarkable growth of the area were Francis Eisen, M. Theo Kearney, and Frank and George Roeding, who were responsible for introducing or expanding production of its principal crops. Eisen is credited by the Fresno Convention and Visitors' Bureau with being the father of the wine industry in the county. That group also relates that Eisen began the raisin industry in 1875 when he accidentally let some of his grapes dry on the vine. That tale may be apocryphal, however; Hart suggests that commercial raisin production began in 1873.

Kingsburg farmer of the 1930s places trays of grapes on the ground to dry in the sun.
—Kingsburg Swedish Village

In any event, the San Joaquin Valley climate is ideal for drying grapes, using mostly muscat and Thompson varieties. Today, raisins annually contribute more than $500 million to the state's economy.

One of the participants in the Mussel Slough affair of 1880, Kearney organized an association of raisin growers that brought him both wealth and a reputation for being ruthless. Kearney's French Renaissance–style mansion on West Kearney Boulevard is today a museum and is on the National Register of Historic Places.

George Roeding, a San Francisco–born horticulturist, started the California Association of Nurserymen and discovered, in 1899, that in order to flourish, Smyrna figs must be pollinated by a certain Middle Eastern wasp. Since that discovery was made, figs have become one of Fresno County's important crops, adding more than $10 million to the economy each year. George Roeding's father, Frederick Christian, was a San Francisco banker with vast land holdings in the San Joaquin Valley. He donated 157 acres to the City of Fresno for a park.

Fresno claims as one of its most famous sons William Saroyan, who was born there on August 31, 1908. His childhood home at 3204 East El Monte Way has been added to the local register of historic places. As a lad Saroyan sold newspapers on street corners; before his death he had become a writer of national repute, noted for his novels *The Human Comedy* and *Adventures of Wesley Jackson*. He was the first American writer to win the Pulitzer Prize and the Drama Critics' Circle Award in the same year, 1940, for his play *The Time of Your Life*.

A COFFEE POT IN THE NIGHT

Thirty miles south of Fresno is the city of Kingsburg, a determinedly ethnic community. Originally it was Kings River Switch, a railroad settlement of the Central Pacific Railroad (now the Southern Pacific), established in 1874. Today the city's water tower is a huge, authentically decorated coffee pot that is lighted at night, clearly marking the town for drivers on CA 99.

The Wagner brothers, Thomas and Louie, the first known white men in the area, began raising sheep around 1857 on a ranch they established three miles south of the present-day city. The Kingsburg Chamber of Commerce reports that another sheep rancher, William T. Cole, emulated local Indians by digging a canal to bring water to his sheep. Other settlers in later years would follow that example to irrigate their crops and start their portion of the valley blooming and producing.

The settlers who gave the town its accent were two contingents of Swedes who arrived in the 1880s, the first led by Frank Rosendahl and

C. A. Johnson. Andrew Ericson later brought a larger group to the area. In 1921, 94 percent of the area's population was Swedish.

The Mussel Slough Affair

At the junction of CA 99 and CA 198 begins a side trip of extreme, if tragic, historic significance. Eleven miles west of that junction is Hanford, seat of Kings County, named for James Hanford, treasurer of the Central Pacific. A little farther along, about five miles, Fourteenth Avenue heads north toward Armona, Grangeville, and Hardwick. About midway between the latter two communities, at 5833 Fourteenth Avenue, stands California Historic Landmark number 245, denoting the site of one of the state's disastrous land wars.

On May 11, 1880, in the so-called battle of Mussel Slough, five men were killed on the spot and two were fatally wounded. The disagreement stemmed from the Central Pacific's practice of inviting settlers to

This Lutheran church at Kingsburg was one of the first to be built in the state.
—Kingsburg
Swedish Village

the area and offering to sell them land to which the railroad didn't yet hold title, at prices vaguely promised to be as low as $2.50 an acre. Improvements the settlers made while waiting for clear title wouldn't add to the cost of the land, railroad officials assured. Between 1872 and 1875 settlers pooled their resources and built an elaborate system of irrigation devices, making the land productive and far more valuable.

In 1878, when the railroad finally got its titles, it notified settlers that land prices would range from $17 to $40 per acre. Settlers charged that the prices included their hard-won improvements, but the courts ruled that there had been no contract between the railroad and settlers. Settlers tried to negotiate lower prices, to no avail, Huntington insisting on getting "what the land was worth," no matter what. Two buyers from other parts of the valley, Walter J. Crow and Mills D. Hart, agreed to pay $25 per acre for the now-irrigated and productive land.

When United States Marshal Alonzo W. Poole arrived with Crow and Hart to put them in possession of the acreage they had bought, a group of more than twenty settlers tried to hold them off and the deadly battle ensued. Five of the settlers were later convicted of resisting a federal officer and sentenced to jail terms, but public opinion viewed all the settlers as heroes for standing up to the widely unpopular railroad. Frank Norris's novel *The Octopus* dramatizes the event.

Returning now to CA 99, this side trip adds about forty miles to the distance to Bakersfield.

ALLENSWORTH

County Road J22, which crosses CA 99 about twenty-two miles south of its junction with CA 198, at Earlimart, marks the start of another rewarding side trip. This one travels seven miles west on County Road J22 and then a couple of miles south on CA 43 to reach Colonel Allensworth State Historic Park.

In its heyday, Allensworth was a thriving community with two general stores, a bakery, barbershop, drugstore, livery stable, hotel, school, and library. Cotton, alfalfa, grains, and sugar beets flourished in the fields. It was a town planned, organized, and governed by blacks, and all at the instigation of Allen Allensworth, born a slave and three times sold down the river for trying to learn to read. Seeing the Civil War as an opportunity, Allensworth joined the Union forces, first the army when it occupied Louisville, Kentucky, and then the navy. At war's end, he figured out how to get an education and went on to become a lieutenant colonel and the ranking chaplain of the U.S. Army by the time he retired in 1906.

On seeing Angel Island, his final army post, Allensworth decided California was the place to retire to, but found Los Angeles too racist and crowded for his taste. Eventually he and a group of friends bought land in the San Joaquin Valley and created a town where blacks could live and work in dignity, without confronting racial prejudice, and attain their full potential. Allen Allensworth was killed by a careless motorcyclist in 1914 and didn't live to see his town shrivel up in the hot sun when big farming interests rescinded the water rights needed to keep Allensworth alive.

The route now returns to CA 99, twenty miles having been added to the journey to Bakersfield.

BAKER'S TOWN

Bakersfield, the seat of Kern County and presently one of the most rapidly growing cities in the state, stands where CA 99 crosses the Kern River and meets CA 58, at the center of the county. With a population of more than 185,000, it covers eighty-six square miles and is the site of a campus of the state university system.

First inhabitants of the area were Yokuts, who are known to have settled there some eight thousand years ago. They were displaced by Spanish explorers, Mexican holders of land grants, and fortune hunters from the East, who sought gold and oil.

The city was named for Col. Thomas Baker, an engineer in the state militia who arrived in 1862 to explore the possibility of creating a navigable waterway from the former Kern Lake to San Francisco Bay. He stayed to receive a land grant on which to grow alfalfa and lay out the townsite in 1869. A memorial plaque honoring Colonel Baker has been placed in the Bakersfield City Hall at Truxton and Chester Avenues.

In 1885 gold was discovered in the bed of the Kern River and Bakersfield took on the aura of a gold-rush town. The Federal Writers' Project guide says the town soon became as rough and tough as any camp in the Mother Lode country had been, with miners swaggering in the streets, gamblers plumbing the miners' pockets in the saloons, and guns blazing away at all hours. Fire destroyed most of the town's original buildings in 1889; the rebuilt city was considerably modernized.

Oil was discovered nearby in 1899, drawing new hordes of wealth seekers to the town. California Historic Landmark number 290, across the river from Hart Memorial Park, seven miles northeast of Bakersfield on Round Mountain Road, marks the site of the discovery well of the Kern River oil field. Agriculture bloomed, too, and sheep ranching. Cotton farming was found to be profitable. The Chinese came to work on the railroad, the Basque to raise sheep, and the Italians to plow the fertile fields, all lending to the town a rich diversity that exists today. The westward migration prompted by the dust bowl of the 1930s swelled the population in the area as well.

The Kern County Museum and Pioneer Village at 3801 Chester Avenue displays an exciting picture of Bakersfield's early days. Its features include an 1899 general store, a one-room schoolhouse, a grand Queen Anne Victorian mansion, a sheepherder's movable hut, and an early dentist's office, all moved from their original locations and restored.

THE TEHACHAPI LOOP

One last side trip remains to visit on this phase of the exploration of California's central valley. Its route follows CA 58 winding southeast through the Tehachapi Mountains, studded with gnarled old oak trees and often snow clad. Forty miles from Bakersfield the route leaves the freeway at the Keene exit and continues east on Old State Highway for about three miles. California Historic Landmark number 508 notes the spot from which can be seen the Tehachapi Loop, an engineering marvel by which railroad tracks of the Southern Pacific spiral around a central hill while gaining elevation to surmount the steep Tehachapi Pass. According to the legend on the plaque, a 4,000-foot train will cross 77 feet above its end cars still in the tunnel at the bottom, looking for all the world like a snake about to swallow its own tail. This feat of engineering ingenuity was completed in 1876 under the direction of William Hood, a Southern Pacific Railroad engineer.

A great deal more of California's past lies to the east of this spot, but it will be explored in the section that probes into the state's deserts. This side trip now returns to CA 99 in Bakersfield, having added some eighty miles to the total trip.

I-5
Gorman–Woodland
335 miles

GORMAN

Gorman, a wide spot in the road at the summit of Tejon Pass, is one of the few places where direction of travel on I-5 can be easily reversed. So the exploration of the western portion of the Central Valley begins there, a good place for a meal or cup of coffee, or even an overnight stay. The brilliant yellow umbrellas of the artist Christo dotted the surrounding hillsides during the fall of 1991. They were prematurely removed after one was toppled by one of the area's common gale-force winds, killing a young woman. In spring seasons following winters of normal rainfall, a riot of wildflowers—blue lupines, orange poppies, yellow desert dandelions, and the like—will blanket these same hills.

BEALE, FORT TEJON, AND CAMELS

Just about three miles north of Gorman, thirty-six miles south of Bakersfield, in Grapevine Canyon, stands Fort Tejon, today a state historic park but originally a military outpost. It was established to protect and control Indians who lived on the nearby Sebastian Reservation and to discourage attacks by more warlike tribes on settlers and reservation Indians alike. Founders hoped the fort's presence would discourage the infamous bandit Joaquín Murieta, too.

Native Americans who lived in the area were Emigdiano, an inland group of the Chumash. Unlike their coast-dwelling relatives, the Emigdiano avoided contact with European explorers and settlers. Indeed, they never joined the Indians who were gathered into the Sebastian Reservation but did work as independent contractors for the army, once the fort was established. One of their villages, Lapau, was situated at the bottom of Grapevine Canyon.

In 1853, President Fillmore named Edward F. Beale, one of the heroes of the battle of San Pasqual, superintendent of Indian Affairs for California and Nevada. After looking over the situation, Beale decided what was needed to deter marauding Miwoks and Yokuts was a large Indian reservation at the southern end of the San Joaquin Valley, with a military fort nearby. Fort Tejon was that fort; its first detachment of dragoons arrived on August 10, 1854. Construction of barracks and the like began immediately and continued off and on for six years.

The men of Fort Tejon didn't have time to be bored. Patrols visited unexplored regions of the Owens Valley, rode the supply route to Los Angeles, chased bandits, and occasionally provided escorts for groups traveling to Salt Lake City. The fort also became the social center of the San Joaquin area and a stop on the Butterfield Overland Mail route. It was deadly boring for officers' wives, however, who found the hot, dry summers difficult.

In 1857 the area around Fort Tejon was rocked by a series of earthquakes, one of which the U.S. Coast and Geodetic Survey has judged to have been as severe as the one that leveled much of San Francisco in 1906. The shaking continued for three days, but the fort wasn't seriously damaged. It remained in use until September 11, 1864, when it was abandoned, its usefulness at an end. Before that date, however, one act of a little-known national drama took place at Fort Tejon.

Part of the great camel experiment of the U.S. Army was played out in these rolling hills. Moving supplies to California across the Mojave Desert from Yuma, Arizona, was a grueling process and, in 1855, Secretary of War Jefferson Davis persuaded Congress that camels would be better suited to the task than horses. In Italy, for example, 250 camels were reputed to be doing the work of 1,000 horses. Harlen D. Fowler in *Camels to California* relates how Davis was laughed out of the hall in 1851 when he first made the suggestion to Congress. A year later, however, lawmakers decided the experiment might be worth a try in view of the vast expanses of land that were becoming part of the United States and needing delivery of mail and supplies.

A herd of seventy-five camels procured from various spots in Africa was subsequently rounded up in Texas; twenty-eight of them were dispatched to Fort Tejon. The expedition set off from San Antonio in early September 1857, headed for California, twelve hundred miles to the west. Killing two birds with one stone, Beale, who was in charge of getting the animals to Fort Tejon, used them to carry forage and supplies for a road-surveying party he had been commissioned to lead from Fort Defiance, New Mexico Territory, to the Colorado River. Forage for the camels was an unnecessary burden, for they considered the desert's ubiquitous greasewood a delicacy. When the party arrived at Fort Tejon four months later, the men reported an uneventful journey, although some did admit that the animals' peculiar gait made them seasick.

Camels were used for a variety of assignments during the next four years. Early in 1861, three of them hauled provisions for the party that was surveying the California-Nevada border. When the surveyors ran into trouble, the camels helped the men escape from their attackers. Nonetheless, the exotic animals were judged to be no faster than horses and not as valuable as their supporters had predicted. Eventually the Fort Tejon camels were sent to Los Angeles, where they were housed in a stable on Main Street. They were used for a time to transport mail and carry harbor baggage up from San Pedro. In 1864 they were auctioned off. Beale bought several for his ranch adjacent to the fort and trained two to pull a sulky in which he would ride to Los Angeles, a hundred miles to the south.

Most of the camels introduced into the country for this experiment, and their offspring, were eventually turned loose in the deserts, where they were sighted as recently as 1907. In April 1934 the *Oakland Tribune* reported that the last member of the camel corps had died at a zoo in Los Angeles, but some desert dwellers insist they still occasionally see camels crossing distant sandy stretches.

Camels weren't the only thing Edward Beale bought up. He also acquired, with some friends, the lands of the Sebastian Indian Reservation, which the government had abandoned. In addition, throughout the 1860s he bought tens of thousands of acres in the Tehachapi Hills, land he called Tejon Ranch. On that land, according to his friend Charles Nordhoff, Beale grazed more than 100,000 sheep, which were herded by local Indians, particularly those from the abandoned reservation. Beale hired hundreds of people to grow crops as well as tend sheep. According to Nordhoff, Beale employed, besides shepherds, a general superintendent, bookkeeper, storekeeper, blacksmith, gardeners, and house servants.

When Beale died in 1893, the vast ranch was taken over by a group of investors led by Harrison Gray Otis, publisher of the *Los Angeles Times*. A corporation still owned, at least in part, by the *Times* runs that ranch today.

Lakeview Number One

The journey now resumes on I-5. A little more than twenty miles north of Fort Tejon the route exits the interstate west onto CA 166 for a looping side trip. At Maricopa, where CA 166 meets CA 33, it turns north for about a mile and a half, to Petroleum Club Road, there to view California Historic Landmark number 485, the site of Lakeview Number One, one of the most spectacular oil gushers the world has ever seen. On March 14, 1910, oil erupted from the newly drilled well at a rate of 18,000 barrels a day; the flow later increased to as much as 68,000 daily barrels, completely destroying the derrick. The owner of this well that produced 9 million barrels in its eighteen-month life was Union Oil Company.

After the well collapsed in on itself, stemming the flow, the surrounding area became an oil empire, according to Bean. The capital of that empire was the nearby town of Taft, named for the incumbent president.

California's Little Teapot Dome

To the north and east of Taft lie the fields of the Elk Hills Naval Petroleum Reserve, where millions of barrels of oil lie beneath the surface, waiting to be pumped out as needed. It is the second largest oil field in the nation, exceeded only by the one on the North Slope of Alaska.

In 1923, according to Bean, Edward L. Doheny and other oilmen persuaded the federal government to extract the oil of Elk Hills and store it in above-ground tanks so that it would be available for immediate use in the event of war. Secretary of the Interior Albert B. Fall, who was a friend of Doheny, agreed to lease the Elk Hills land to Doheny's group for no fee. A large part of the oil was to be stored in tanks that Doheny would build on the West Coast and at Pearl Harbor. The businessmen would retain a portion of all the transferred oil for their own profit.

Before the plan had advanced very far it was learned that Fall had been given $100,000 in return for making the deal. He was convicted of accepting the bribe; Doheny was found innocent of paying it. In spite of that ruling, the government canceled Doheny's leases because they had been granted in return for a bribe.

The exquisite irony of this affair is that the nation tended to view it as picayune when compared to the scandal of similar dealings involving Teapot Dome in Wyoming. In that deal, Fall received $300,000, presumably because it involved a more valuable field. The Wyoming field, however, proved to be a relatively unimportant one, while the value of the Elk Hills reserve was unsurpassed until the Alaskan oil deposits were discovered more than forty years later.

After leaving the Taft area, the route turns northeastward on CA 119 to regain I-5 some fifteen miles later. This side trip adds about twenty-five miles to the distance to Woodland.

For almost two hundred miles I-5 crosses a mostly flat and treeless plain, on which it's easy to believe that the freeway was built for no other reason than to get from Southern California to Northern California in a hurry. There are no state parks or even historic landmarks for thirty or so miles on either side of the road. Far off to the east lie Death Valley National Monument and three national parks: Kings Canyon, Sequoia, and Yosemite. To the west are the incomparable beauties of the coastline, all historically rich. But here there is little of note.

PARKFIELD

About twenty-five miles north of the spot where the historic trail rejoined I-5, it crosses CA 46 near Lost Hills. This is the beginning of a side trip of interest because of its ongoing suspense. Thirty miles or so northwest of the junction of CA 46 and I-5, where CA 46 joins CA 41, a little unnamed road takes off to the north alongside Cholame Creek. Some fifteen miles farther, the road reaches Parkfield, a hamlet much in the news in 1992.

Parkfield happens to be the bit of civilization closest to the San Andreas Fault in this sparsely populated area, and for eight years prior to 1992 had been under the magnifying glass of a U.S. Geological Survey team. During this study, according to an article in the *Los Angeles Times*, federal and state officials developed criteria for issuing earthquake alerts. Late in 1991 such a warning was issued; there was, scientists predicted, a 95 percent likelihood that an earthquake measuring six or more on the Richter scale would rattle central California before the new year. Such quakes have struck the area in 1857, 1881, 1901, 1922, 1934, and 1966. Because the average interval between those quakes is twenty-two years, scientists were pretty confident that another quake would shake Parkfield within four years, either way, of 1988. It didn't happen. Nonetheless, the sophisticated instruments and some of the experts remain in place, trying to learn more about California's biggest mystery: earthquakes.

The historical exploration route now returns to CA 41, then turns northeast for twenty-nine miles to I-5, having added about sixty-five miles to the trip to Woodland.

LOS BANOS

Ninety-three miles farther along I-5 the search for history reaches CA 152, a road of some interest. To the east about seven miles is Los Banos, founded in the early 1860s by Henry Miller as a company town.

The Henry Miller of Merced County fame isn't the famed author who helped to popularize the Big Sur region of California. The Henry Miller here under discussion was a wheeler-dealer of the first water, whose very arrival in the state had shady overtones. In reality Miller was Heinrich Alfred Kreiser, a German native, who arrived in New York in 1847 with no assets except his training as a butcher. By 1849 he had saved enough from his wages to buy from a friend a ticket to California. That the ticket was marked "nontransferable" didn't bother Kreiser; he simply changed his name to that of his friend, Henry Miller. Just a few years later a special act of the California legislature made the name change official.

In the meantime, Miller got his start operating a butcher shop in San Francisco, then joined forces with another German butcher, Charles Lux. The two men soon pooled resources to buy up cattle ranches in the San Joaquin Valley, acquiring ownership of almost a million and a half acres and control of many times that by means not always entirely straightforward. Because they controlled so much land, Miller and Lux gained control of water rights, too. Their disputes with other landowners in the valley eventually led to the 1887 passage of the Wright Act.

Named for a state senator from Modesto, the Wright Act made possible the formation of water districts that would have the power of eminent domain, the right to sell bonds to purchase water rights, and the right to build dams, canals, and other means of irrigation. For the first time riparian rights—the right of owners of lands along a watercourse to control the use of water it contained—were challenged, permitting irrigation districts to divert rivers for flood control and the like.

A historical plaque now marks the spot, at 1460 East Pacheco Boulevard in Los Banos, where the Canal Farm Inn stood. Established in 1873, it was the original San Joaquin Valley headquarters of Henry Miller.

PACHECO PASS

Fifteen miles west of Los Banos, about eight miles west of I-5, the historic Pacheco Pass starts. At 1,386 feet, the pass doesn't represent a formidable climb for today's automobiles, but it was a different story for vehicles of the Butterfield stage line. Discovered in 1805 by Lt. Gabriel Moraga, Pacheco Pass has long been a main route between the Santa Clara and the San Joaquin Valleys. A marker noting that significance stands at the Romero Overlook near San Luis Dam.

The journey now resumes, back on I-5. Seeing both of these historic spots adds about thirty miles to the distance to Woodland.

STOCKTON

Ninety miles after I-5 crosses CA 152, it reaches Stockton, seat of San Joaquin County and entry point to the Sacramento Delta, a deep-water seaport seventy-five miles from the ocean. Founded in 1847 by Capt. Charles M. Weber, it was first called Tuleberg, after the dense stands of tules that bordered every river and creek in the area.

Charles Weber was in the Bidwell-Bartleson emigrant train that arrived in California in November of 1841. He first settled in the San Jose area, where he opened a store, operated a flour mill, and pioneered the manufacture of shoes in the area. After being naturalized as a Mexican citizen in 1844, he received a land grant of almost 50,000 acres in the San Joaquin Valley, where he began to raise cattle. When ordered by General Castro to take up arms against the Americans in 1846, Weber refused and was jailed until after the signing of the treaty at Cahuenga Pass, which ended the war between Mexican and U.S. forces in California.

Soon after his release, Weber and Commo. Robert F. Stockton, one of the principals in the war and the treaty signing, became friends. Stockton promised to send a schooner-load of settlers and supplies to Tuleberg to help the town get started. Even though Stockton never carried out his promise, Weber renamed his town in honor of the commodore.

When the gold rush hit California, Weber found the first gold in Amador County, but decided he could profit more by concentrating on making Stockton a distribution center for the mines. Incorporated on August 15, 1850, the town became the county seat later that year. Thousands who were headed for the mines passed through Stockton. Some came by boat up river; others traveled by land from San Jose, over Livermore Pass. Freighting and staging activities grew enormously, local commerce boomed, and farming in the surrounding area bloomed. Stockton was well on the way to becoming an important city. When Weber died in 1881 his city was one of the most industrialized in California, second only to San Francisco.

The deepening of the Stockton Channel and construction of a new port facility in the 1930s helped Stockton weather the Depression and provided the setting for ten shipyards during World War II. Today agriculture and food processing are the city's main sources of revenue. It is home to University of the Pacific and one of the leading entryways to the recreational aspects of the Sacramento Delta: fishing, sailing, houseboating, and the like.

JOHN MARSH

A fascinating side trip takes off from Stockton via CA 4 at the southern edge of the city. About twenty-six miles to the west is Brentwood, a small town of little notoriety, where the route turns north on Walnut for three or four miles, then back to the east on Marsh Creek Road. Follow the road a mile and a half or so beyond the four-way stop. A sign for Sparrow Ranch marks a spot across the road from the destination of this side trip: the John Marsh home.

John Marsh may have been a scalawag, as some historians think, cruel and dishonest to his employees, but he built a beautiful mansion for the woman he loved. His story starts in Andover, Massachusetts, where he graduated from Phillips Academy and Harvard. In 1823 he went west to Fort Snelling in what is now Minnesota to tutor officers' children and study a little medicine. He then moved to Wisconsin, where he served for a time as an Indian agent and published a Sioux grammar in 1831. Threatened with arrest for selling arms to the Indians for use in the Black Hawk War, he fled to Santa Fe and, eventually, Los Angeles, arriving there in 1836.

Convincing the mayor of Los Angeles that he held a medical degree, Marsh practiced medicine in that city, charging exorbitant fees that enabled him to amass enough money to buy from José Noriega, alcalde of San Jose, a land grant called Los Medanos (sandbanks) ranch. Moving

"Doctor" John Marsh became California's first practicing physician, even though he held no medical degree.
—The Bancroft Library

there, he lived in a small adobe that became the end of the trail for many emigrants, whom he welcomed with open arms, even if he did charge them large sums for aid and supplies. He was one of the state's first extravagant boosters, writing glowing letters of praise to friends back east and offering advice on travel routes, even though he had never used those routes himself.

In 1851 he married Abigail Tuck, a former schoolteacher from the East. Immediately the couple began to plan an elaborate mansion, the finest house in California. It is a yellow brick and fieldstone edifice, three stories high, with three peaked gables and a square crenelated tower, plus four chimneys and a balcony that runs around one and one-half sides of the structure. Unfortunately, Abigail died before the house was completed, so Marsh lived there in a single room, growing ever more cantankerous.

Marsh lived in his magnificent, though unfinished, home only a few weeks. Very soon after he moved into it in 1856, three ranch hands who were angry over being ill-treated and underpaid murdered the tightfisted Marsh. His lovely home today awaits restoration as part of a state historic park.

When Marsh died, the ranch was passed on to Alice, his daughter with Abigail, and Charles, Marsh's son with an Indian woman he had married before moving to California. Apparently Abigail learned of that earlier liaison when Charles showed up at the adobe house looking for his father.

Visiting this setting of a genuine romance story adds about sixty miles to the distance between Gorman and Woodland.

THE CHINESE IN THE DELTA

About twenty-five miles from Stockton, County Road E13 crosses I-5, heading west toward the Sacramento River and the hamlet of Locke, the only rural community in the nation built and settled by Chinese. According to Hal Schell's *Delta Map and Guide*, the town is an anachronism, a tiny chunk of the past sitting in the middle of the present.

The first building in Locke was a saloon erected in 1912 by Tin Sin Chan, who is generally credited as the town's founder. The town's main street is lined with weathered clapboard buildings, two-story for the most part, with the upper story at levee level in the front. Some have overhanging balconies that create welcome shade from the blistering sun. Although most of the signs have faded to illegibility, it's still possible to recognize a former bakery, a gas station, and a school. It looks for all the world like a town from the gold-rush days.

When a 1915 fire destroyed the Chinatown section of nearby Walnut Grove, its residents elected to build a new town on land owned by rancher George Locke. Sympathetic to the plight of Chinese, who were forbidden by the Alien Land Law to own land, he granted them leases. To this day, according to Schell, most of Locke's homeowners don't hold title to the land beneath their houses. One of the town's former gambling halls has been made into the Dai Loy Museum, on Main Street, where tales of the past are told so visitors don't forget the contributions of the Chinese to the delta.

THE DELTA

The Sacramento Delta lies at the confluence of the south-flowing Sacramento River and the north-flowing San Joaquin River. The delta forms a triangle, the points of which are located at Sacramento, Antioch, and Stockton. When Padre Juan Crespí and Pedro Fages first saw it, swollen by winter rains in March 1772, they thought it was a great inland sea. Laced with waterways, marshes, swamps, and boggy peat, the delta has always needed dikes and levees to control the water. The earliest settlers who tried to farm the area built crude levees of peat, which didn't last long.

When construction of the transcontinental railroad was completed in 1869, Chinese laborers who had laid those miles and miles of rails were available for other work. They soon began shaping, with hand shovels and wheelbarrows, the great earthen levees that held back the delta water. It has been said that the Chinese moved soil for the trivial sum of thirteen cents per cubic foot. Able to do the same job for about five cents for each cubic yard scooped from the river bottom, the clamshell dredge soon replaced the human laborers. By 1930 some 700,000 acres of prime land had been reclaimed, creating fifty-five artificial islands.

Today, asparagus, tomatoes, pears, field corn, sugar beets, and alfalfa grow on that land. Oceangoing vessels glide up the dredged channels and call at Stockton to take on cotton for Taiwan, coal for Japan, sulfur for India, dried milk for Brazil, and copper for Germany and Korea.

Returning to I-5, this side trip adds only about ten miles to the journey to Woodland.

WOODLAND

The route continues now, bypassing Sacramento on I-5 and continuing to the junction with CA 113. Just off that road stands Woodland, the seat of Yolo County, established in 1853 as Yolo City and renamed in 1859 for its location amid a fine stand of oak trees.

At the corner of Second Street and Dead Cat Alley stands the Woodland Opera House, a spacious, simple, two-story red brick structure. Built in 1895–96 with a plain exterior and an interior that is an exquisite example of nineteenth-century theaters, it features a dress circle, a horseshoe balcony, and a large orchestra seating area. The first production presented in the opera house was Bronson Howard's *Saratoga*, staged on June 15, 1896.

During the next seventeen years the opera house was seldom dark, as more than three hundred touring companies crossed its boards. Such presentations as *Uncle Tom's Cabin, Shore Acres, The Runaways*, and many other productions, including minstrel shows, melodramas, and plays by Shakespeare, kept the rafters ringing with applause. The advent of moving pictures caused business to fall off, and a lawsuit by a woman who fell when leaving the theater in 1912 ended the opera house's long run. It closed in 1913, never to be reopened. While standing empty the beautiful facility deteriorated and suffered severe fire damage in 1937. In 1973 it was entered on the National Register of Historic Places and was subsequently deeded to the state to be restored, largely by local efforts, and named a state historic park.

The search for roadside history continues in and around San Francisco.

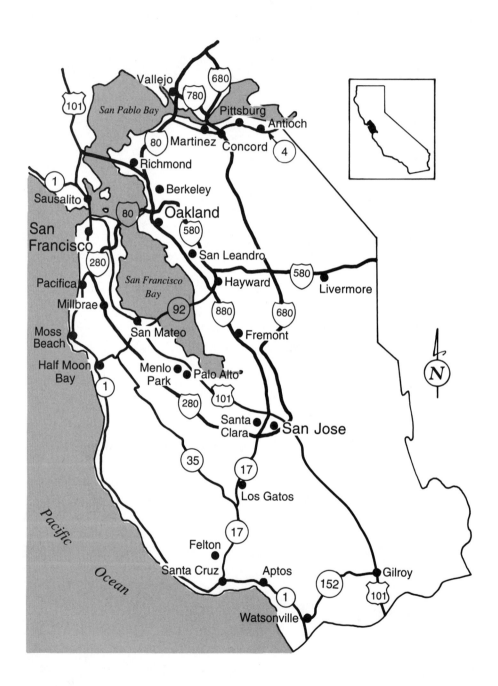

Part 5
The Golden Bay Area

Originally inhabited by coast-dwelling Indians, the area around the San Francisco Bay wasn't settled by Europeans until 1776, when Spaniards established a military post at what is now the Presidio, and Franciscan monks founded Mission San Francisco de Asís, called Mission Dolores, in today's Mission District of San Francisco.

San Francisco was an almost overnight phenomenon, rushing to big-city status while upstarts like Los Angeles were still adobe pueblos. In 1849 it boasted few comforts, according to JoAnn Levy in *They Saw the Elephant*. Not only were the streets not paved with gold, they weren't paved at all; they were calf deep in mud in winter and ankle deep in dust in summer. Hotels were expensive makeshifts constructed of canvas and planks. Rooms with canvas and paper walls cost from $25 to $250 a week. It was a far cry from the city it would become.

"The City," as it has been known throughout its existence, got rich too fast; its first families got rich too fast and were too rough. What the City lacked, according to Stephan Birmingham, was tradition, a sense of how the upper crust did things. In the early days even the upper crust didn't know how to do much besides make money and squabble.

The Vigilance Committees

The vigilance committees of the 1850s, parodies of due process, were in large part a result of the rawness of the city's residents. Anger and haste ruled the streets, with little regard for the rights of defendants or witnesses. Many historians have upheld, even praised, the work of the vigilantes of San Francisco, but there's no escaping the truth: These self-righteous bullies were criminals.

Samuel Brannan, a man who raised the business of "looking out for number one" to a fine art, did more than anyone to instigate vigilantism in San Francisco, all the while building the first great fortune in California with money he stole from the Mormon Church. On June 8, 1851, in his newspaper the *Alta California*, Brannan called for the formation of a Committee of Vigilance. That group's first official act was to summarily hang a man accused of a rather petty robbery.

The City's example led to a series of citizen-decreed lynchings in other towns and in mining communities. In Downieville, for example, a Mexican woman was lynched for defending herself against a drunk who broke into her cabin in the middle of the night. In the dusty village of Los Angeles there were even more hangings than there were in San Francisco.

The vigilante movement in the City fell silent for a while, only to be reactivated in 1856 over the shootings of James King of William, a newspaper editor, and Gen. William H. Richardson, a United States marshall. The leader of the reborn group was William Tell Coleman, a successful merchant in mining towns and in San Francisco, who would go on to even greater notoriety in the northern desert. This time the vigilantes were opposed by the Law and Order Committee, a group of prominent citizens who denounced them. Leaders of this group were Mayor James Van Ness and Gen. William T. Sherman, at that time commander of the San Francisco district of the California militia.

When James King of William died, vigilantes hanged, with great public ceremony, the two who had shot him. Law and Order leaders hoped that the vigilantes, having tasted blood, would now disband. On the contrary, they expanded their activities, making several arrests and fortifying their headquarters building, called Fort Gunnybags, on Sacramento Street between Davis and Front Streets. Governor John Johnson called out the militia, but couldn't get the federal government to arm them. Justice David S. Terry became the Law and Order faction's chief adviser and convinced Gen. John E. Wool to provide some guns for the defense of the city. Vigilantes intercepted the shipment and chaos reigned. At last, after a great deal of legal and illegal maneuvering, the Committee of Vigilance disbanded. Its headquarters was preserved for a time as a museum.

The leaders of the vigilante movement formed the People's Party and won most of the City's elections for the next ten years. They left to the state a tradition of contempt for the law that has colored much of life in California ever since.

By 1900, San Francisco had become one of the most corrupt cities on earth. Bribery was taken for granted; no business was carried on without payment of bribes to the proper parties, which often included lawyer Abraham Ruef. This City native had, through bribery, graft, and patronage, become virtual boss of San Francisco. Birmingham cites the *San Francisco Chronicle* as having said, in 1901, "If you wish to construct a building in defiance of the fire ordinances you must see Ruef. . . . Ruef is by all odds the most dangerous boss this city has hitherto endured." Finally, a group of citizens including Francis J. Heney, Fremont Older, Rudolph Spreckels, and James D. Phelan exposed the mayor and Ruef. Both Mayor Schmitz and Abe Ruef were tried and convicted of criminal behavior. Ruef was pardoned after serving just five years. An appellate court overturned the conviction of Schmitz, who later was elected to the City's board of supervisors.

Through the years, controversy has raged about what makes San Francisco special. Even the City's famous sourdough bread is different from that baked anyplace else in the world. (Just watch a planeload of passengers debark from a flight from San Francisco. Almost half of them will be carrying shopping bags crammed with the long, crusty loaves.) No one factor can account for San Francisco's uniqueness, but there's no doubt its geography plays a part.

The earthquake of April 18, 1906, helped to shape the City's character and destiny. Estimated to have been of magnitude 8.6 on the Richter scale, the shaker, and the fire it set off, leveled 28,000 buildings. The shock lasted only twenty-eight seconds, but its reverberations have never stopped. Few brick buildings are built in California, for example, and until very recently high-rise buildings were banned in most cities.

Its location gets a lot of credit for making San Francisco what it was and has become. First, proximity to the goldfields inspired its incredible growth. Next, its magnificent bay, so alluring to shippers and tourists alike, helped to shape its destiny. A third influential factor has been water. The City is all but surrounded by water, and the state's largest rivers empty into its bay, yet, in spite of all this water, the City is still water poor, receiving only about twenty inches of precipitation in the average year. It's not surprising, then, that residents of the City fretted about a water shortage early on and started casting about for a solution to the problem. In 1900 a new city charter authorized a municipal water system to replace the Spring Valley Water Company, a monopoly controlled by William Ralston that had been delivering water to the thirsty city since 1862. In 1934 the Hetch Hetchy Valley in the High Sierra would provide a solution that satisfied only those who profited from it.

To the lack of potable water add the fog that shrouds the area around the San Francisco Bay throughout the summer season. It was almost certainly the fog that helped create the cities of the peninsula and across the bay. When newcomers could no longer stand the cold, dreary, and gray days, they would move just a few miles to where the sun was hot and bright most of the time, giving rise to the likes of San Mateo,

Redwood City, even Richmond and Berkeley. Admittedly, the earthquake of 1906 contributed to that urge to migrate, too.

CA 113, I-80, I-780, and I-680
Woodland–San Jose
120 miles

Eleven miles from Woodland on CA 113 is the bustling city of Davis, home of a campus of the University of California. It was named for Jerome C. Davis, a rancher of the 1850s, but it wasn't until 1905 that its fate started to take shape. In that year, according to Mildred Hoover, an act of the state legislature created the University Farm at Davis, whose first buildings rose in 1907. Fifteen years later that school became an offshoot of Berkeley's College of Agriculture. In 1959 it was named a general university with its own graduate studies programs. As the university grew, so did the town, whose population multiplied fourfold between 1960 and 1983.

VALLEJO

Leaving Davis, the route to San Jose meets I-80 and proceeds southwest some forty miles to Vallejo, where the Napa River flows into San Pablo Bay. Mariano Vallejo founded the city on his rancho and in 1852 offered it to the state for a capital. It enjoyed that prestige for just one week, January 5 to 12, before the legislators complained about the skimpy, unfinished facilities and moved to Sacramento. A year later they were flooded out and tried again to make Vallejo their political home, but this try lasted only a month before they moved along the Carquinez Strait to Benicia.

The loss of the capital wasn't a fatal blow to Vallejo, however, because in 1854 Mare Island Naval Shipyard was founded nearby. Mare Island, established by Comdr. David G. Farragut, was the navy's first Pacific installation. It included an ammunition depot, hospital, and Marine barracks, according to the historical plaque at the entrance to the facility on the southwest corner of Tennessee Street and Mare Island Way.

CROCKETT

A short but immensely interesting side trip starts just outside Vallejo, traveling along I-80 for five miles. The route crosses the Carquinez Strait via the bridge named in its honor to come to the little town of Crockett, founded in 1881 by Joseph P. Crockett, Thomas Edwards Sr., and W.

148

C. Ralston. The trio became involved in a series of enterprises, including the town's first industry, a foundry. Their activities also included banking, newspaper publishing, gold mining, and railroading. Joseph Crockett also served as a justice of the California Supreme Court between 1868 and 1873.

Crockett's claim to fame, however, is sweeter than any of those industries. It rests on sugar refining—cane sugar, to be precise. Since a March morning in 1906 the California and Hawaiian Sugar Company has been producing sugar and molasses, refining the entire output of Hawaii. Today the refinery employs more than nine hundred persons to process 750,000 tons of sugar a year. It is the largest sugar refinery in the world.

Returning to the junction of I-80 and I-780, this side trip adds eight miles to the distance to San Jose. At that junction, the route travels slightly eastward for seven miles to the junction of I-780 and I-680 at the entrance to the Benicia-Martinez Bridge spanning Suisun Bay. Suisun Bay is named after a subtribe of the Patwin and is home to a large fleet of vessels "mothballed" since World War II.

PORT CHICAGO

Seven miles south of the bridge entrance the highway crosses CA 4, with side trips in both directions. The first heads east on CA 4 toward the naval installation that extends about six miles southward from Suisun Bay. Today called the Concord Naval Weapons Station, during World War II it was known as Port Chicago, the site of one of the darker moments in California history. Here, beside a pier in Suisun Bay, ships tied up while being loaded with ammunition of all types: small-arms ammunition, artillery projectiles, depth charges, incendiary bombs, fragmentation bombs, blockbusters weighing up to a ton each. Indeed, according to Robert L. Allen's report of the events at Port Chicago, the nuclear bomb that was dropped on Hiroshima was shipped out via Port Chicago.

Three miles off the interstate and a mile or so north on Port Chicago Highway is the tiny community of Clyde, and the entrance gate to the ammunition depot. On July 17, 1944, at a few minutes after 10 P.M., something went terribly wrong. Two ships were moored at the pier. One, the *Quinalt Victory*, was brand new and awaiting its first loading, slated to start at midnight. The other, the *E. A. Bryan*, had been taking on explosives for four days and, by the time of the disaster, had forty-six hundred tons of high explosives and ammunition in its holds. Ninety-eight men were removing materiel from boxcars and stowing it in the

Port Chicago Ammunition Depot as it appeared from the air on November 20, 1942, before the tragedy.
—National Archives

ship's deep holds. Besides the men who were loading, more than a hundred were rigging the new ship for its first voyage. A small collection of officers, an armed guard detail, and sixty-seven crew members of the two ships were also on the pier and ships.

For a reason that has never been determined, two violent explosions rocked the scene and everything—pier, ships, railroad cars, and human beings—was blasted into tiny fragments mostly too small to identify. The small town of Port Chicago, a mile and a half away, was practically razed, and 320 men were wiped from the face of the earth. The disgraceful part of the tragedy was that, as a matter of naval policy, all the seamen who actually handled the ammunition were black; all the officers were white. Of the dead, 202 were black. The enlisted men had received no training in how to handle explosives, the officers very little. Indeed, officers had routinely assured handlers that the bombs couldn't explode because they had no detonators.

A few weeks later, after being denied the thirty-day leave granted to white survivors, black survivors of the disaster were ordered back to work, once again loading ammunition at a port nearby. More than two hundred refused to handle explosive matériel, saying they were afraid. Fifty of that group were singled out, by some arcane criteria never revealed, and tried for mutiny. The trial was held at the Treasure Island Naval Station, where Thurgood Marshall, future U.S. Supreme Court

Justice, was an observer. All fifty were found guilty and all served time in prison at Terminal Island in Los Angeles. The uproar that greeted the verdicts and the resentment engendered by the case are generally seen being instrumental in ending official segregation in the navy. By early 1946, all the mutineers had been released from prison, although their mutiny convictions would stand for years.

The town of Port Chicago no longer exists. Its residents rebuilt, but the navy fought them to buy them out. All that remains today of Port Chicago, besides bad memories, is the outline of its streets amid the grassy buffer that separates the weapons depot from the civilian world.

A small plaque topped by an American flag marked the sorrowful spot until 1994. That year the National Park Service dedicated a one-acre memorial on Suisun Bay within the Concord Naval Weapons Station to all who died on the home front during World War II. It pays special homage to those who died here.

PITTSBURG

Continuing east on CA 4 for nine miles, the side trip passes Pittsburg, near the confluence of the Sacramento and San Joaquin Rivers. In 1849 Jonathan B. Stevenson, of Stevenson's Regiment, bought land in the area and hired William Tecumseh Sherman, at that time an obscure young engineer, to lay out a town that would rival New York City. They called it New York Landing. When coal was discovered on the shoulders of nearby Mount Diablo, residents changed the settlement's name to Black Diamond. It wasn't until 1910, after the Columbia Steel Company built a modern mill in the town, that it was christened Pittsburg.

ANTIOCH

In Antioch, the goal of this side trip, Somersville Road branches southward, and nearly four miles along it is the Black Diamond Mines Regional Preserve. Mine openings, tailings, railroad beds, and a pioneer cemetery preserved in that park show the extent of activity from 1860 to 1914 in the largest coal-mining district in California. The route returns to I-780/680, having added forty miles to the distance to San Jose.

MARTINEZ

Another side trip begins immediately, this one heading west on CA 4 just a few miles to Martinez, seat of Contra Costa County. At the intersection of CA 4 and Alhambra Avenue stands the home of John Muir, the famous naturalist who spearheaded the drive to have Yosemite named a national park. He was also instrumental in the creation of many

Jonathan D. Stevenson, a Democratic ward politician of New York City who recruited and led the Stevenson Regiment.
—The Bancroft Library

forest reservations during the administrations of Presidents Cleveland and Teddy Roosevelt. His name has been given to more sites in California than any other person, including wilderness trails, forests, a redwood grove, and a pass in Kings Canyon National Park.

Right next to the marker for Muir's home is one identifying an adobe Vicente Martínez built in 1849 on land inherited from his father, don Ignacio Martínez. A Spanish officer, the elder Martínez became commandante of the presidio at San Francisco and later an alcalde of that city.

Martinez is also the birthplace of baseball player Joe DiMaggio, although no historical marker identifies that site as yet. This city's final claim to fame stands across the street from 4575 Pacheco Boulevard. There, according to a state historical plaque, Dr. John Marsh met his death, murdered by a group of ruffians on September 24, 1856.

The route now returns to I-780/680, this side trip having added ten miles to the distance to San Jose.

A Devilish Mountain

Thirteen miles from its junction with CA 4, I-680 reaches Danville, after passing through small towns set in rolling hills that are either green or golden, depending on the time of year. This little town stands in the shadow of Mount Diablo, a 3,849-foot peak rising about fourteen miles to the east. The mountain, which sits in the middle of Mount Diablo State Park, was selected in 1851 as the initial point for land surveys of Northern California and Nevada. The Mount Diablo Base and Meridian Lines rise at its peak, according to state historical marker number 905.

Warren A. Beck and Ynez D. Haase in their *Historical Atlas of California* note that the principal meridians and base lines of California were decreed by the Northwest Ordinance of 1785, providing for the orderly surveying and sale of public lands. The ordinance stated that the United States should be divided into six-mile-square townships by lines intersecting true north (from pole to pole) and at right angles. Of the thirty-five meridians in the United States, California is home to three: the Humboldt, Mount Diablo, and San Bernardino.

The marker that stands in Mount Diablo State Park at the summit of the mountain notes that because of its wide variation in wind, rainfall, and temperatures, it also encompasses a preserve for a variety of plant and animal life.

Nine miles south of Danville, I-680 crosses I-580, for another short side trip, this one to Livermore.

Livermore

In 1772, when Capt. Pedro Fages, at that time head of the Spanish garrison at Monterey, was looking for a land route to Drake's Bay, he entered the Livermore Valley and camped there, the first white man to set foot in the area. The next day he and his party proceeded south to the plateau that would become the setting for Mission San José de Guadalupe.

Fifty years later, Robert Livermore, an English sailor, jumped ship at Monterey and began working on ranches in the area. At one of those ranches he met María Josefa Higuera, whom he married in 1838. Taking Mexican citizenship in 1844, Livermore obtained a vast grant in what was then called Valle de San José. His rancho, Las Positas, was the forerunner of today's city of Livermore. After building an adobe home, Livermore began to graze cattle, sheep, and horses, then added orchards of pears, apples, and olives and was one of the first to plant grape vines outside the missions. In 1846 he bought an adjacent rancho. In 1851 he converted his adobe into a hotel for travelers to the goldfields. He started negotiations for a railroad to cross his land but died in 1858, before he could accomplish that dream.

In 1869 the Southern Pacific Railroad completed its line through the Livermore Valley to the San Francisco area; the following year William Mendenhall laid out a town within the boundaries of Livermore's rancho and named it in honor of his friend. The town was incorporated in 1876, just a few years before it was learned that the soil and climate of the area are ideal for raising wine grapes. Today, vineyards owned by Concannon, Wente Brothers, and Retzlaff all flourish in the sun-drenched valley.

In 1952 the tenor of the town changed when the University of California established its Lawrence Livermore Laboratory there. The facility, site of nuclear weapons research, drew electrical engineering and electronic firms, leading to a rapid population growth.

Retracing the way to I-680, the side trip to Livermore has added twenty miles to the distance to San Jose.

Fremont and Mission San José

Twelve miles south of its intersection with I-580, I-680 crosses CA 238, Mission Boulevard in Fremont. On that street to the east of the freeway, at Washington Boulevard, stands Mission San José, the fourteenth in the chain of missions. Founded in 1797 by Father Fermín Lasuén, it was named for Saint Joseph. Through the years, in spite of serving as a base for punitive forays against the Indians, the mission prospered. A destructive earthquake along the nearby Hayward Fault in 1868 laid low most of the buildings, sparing only a portion of the padres' quarters. The following year a wooden Gothic-style church was erected on the foundation of the original mission. It was called St. Joseph and served the faithful of the area for more than a hundred years.

In 1985 an authentic restoration of the original mission was completed, the culmination of years of painstaking work by archaeologists, architects, and fund-raisers. The wooden church was carefully relocated to Burlingame and the replacement constructed with historic tools. It has been called an impressively authentic replica.

Returning to I-680 and continuing for about twenty miles, the route at last reaches San Jose.

San Jose, the First Capital

San Jose, with a population of just under one million, is the third largest city in California (following Los Angeles and San Diego) and the seat of Santa Clara County. It sits ten miles below the southern tip of San Francisco Bay, marking the end of the Bay Area.

154

San Jose's old post office on South Market Street was built in 1892. It now serves as the San Jose Museum of Art. —San Jose Convention and Visitors Bureau

It is a city with a rich history, founded in 1777 by José Joaquín Moraga as El Pueblo de San José de Guadalupe, the first pueblo in the state. The settlement, by a decree of Governor Felipe de Neve, was to raise crops and cattle to feed soldiers encamped at the presidios of Monterey and San Francisco. It grew slowly, in spite of being the major community north of Monterey, and had only seven hundred residents by 1848. However, new residents flocked to the city with the rush to the goldfields, when it became a supply center for miners. By 1850 the town was incorporated and claimed a population of 3,000.

San Jose was the first state capital, from 1849 to 1851, and was the site of the 1849–50 legislature of one thousand drinks. That first legislative assembly of the new state was so called, James Hart relates, because Senator Thomas Jefferson Green repeatedly made motions to adjourn and take one thousand drinks at his expense as part of his campaign to be elected major general of the state militia. The site of that first state legislature meeting is marked in City Plaza Park in the 100 block of South Market Street. The legislature conducted only two sessions in the small adobe that stood here before moving to Benicia.

Plaza Park is part of the original plaza of the 1797 Pueblo de San José where cock fights, horse races, and public hangings were held. About one block north of where the state capitol building stood is the site of the *juzgado* (town hall) of the Pueblo of San José. That structure con-

*Saint Joseph's
Church, San Jose.*
—San Jose Convention
and Visitors Bureau

tained the jail, the court, and officials' offices. Some experts believe the word *juzgado* to be the source of the slang term *hoosegow* for jail.

At 110 South Market Street is the old post office, a Romanesque-style structure designed by Willoughby Edbrooke and built in 1892 of sandstone blocks taken from the Goodrich Quarry in nearby New Almaden. The last structure of its kind on the West Coast, it became the San Jose Museum of Art in 1970.

In the same area, at the southwest corner of First and San Fernando Streets, stood the Garden City Bank Building from which emanated the country's first radio programs of news and music. Starting in 1909, three years before Congress passed the Radio Act of 1912, Charles Herrold, a radio pioneer, broadcast from his College of Engineering and Wireless office in the building. Herrold's wife, Sybil, was the first woman disc jockey in the nation, and together the couple initiated commercial radio advertising, a not-unmitigated blessing.

Up the street a couple of blocks and a bit west, in the 100 block of West Saint James Street, stands Pellier Park, all that remains of the

City Gardens Nursery established by Louis Pellier in 1850. Here Pellier and his brothers, Frenchmen all, grew the first sweet plums that could be dried without spoiling and without seed removal. Voilá! French prunes. For a time the production of prunes was centered in Santa Clara County, but today they're grown in eight California counties, accounting for virtually all the prune production in the nation and adding about $166 million to the state's economy annually.

The Ugly Past

Just to the east of Pellier Park, on St. James Street between First and Third, is St. James Park, the scene of one of the ugliest chapters in San Jose's story. It began one Thursday evening in early November, 1933, when the heir to the Hart Department Store fortune was kidnapped as he left work at the store. In the investigation that followed, it was learned that very soon after the young man was taken from his car, his kidnappers flung him off the San Mateo Bridge into the San Francisco Bay. Knocked unconscious and with concrete blocks tied to his feet, he drowned, but not before he awoke, struggled, and cried out for help.

The bumbling perpetrators of the crime were soon captured and put in the San Jose jail. A mob stormed the building, which was defended only halfheartedly, and dragged the murderers out. Beaten and stripped nearly naked, the two were taunted and subsequently lynched in St. James Park on Sunday, November 26, 1933.

The disgrace of the affair lies not in the kidnapping and murder, tragic though it may have been. Even the actual lynching isn't any more shameful than any other such execrable deed. No, the dishonor for the city of San Jose stems from the fact that the men weren't protected while in custody. Police officials in San Jose failed to marshal full strength in defending the men for whom they were responsible. Sheriff's men lobbed tear gas at the mob, but the only result was that the deputies were unable to identify the vigilantes who manned the battering ram that broke down the jail door. The highway patrol, warned early on that trouble was brewing, was inexplicably slow to respond. Officers from Alameda County and Oakland arrived at the park only in time to cut the bodies down.

California Governor James Rolph canceled a trip to Boise, Idaho, because, he said, "I want to be on the job." It became obvious, however, that he stayed behind to forestall interference by the National Guard, which might have prevented the lynchings. Harry Farrell, in recounting the entire affair, says that immediately after the lynching, Governor Rolph told reporters, "This is a fine lesson to the whole nation. There will be less kidnapping now." The town's newspapers printed editorials prais-

This aerial view of the Winchester Mystery House in San Jose shows how the modest home grew during its owner's lifetime. —San Jose Convention and Visitors Bureau

ing the citizens of San Jose, saying justice had been done. In a final shameful detail, Governor Rolph declared he would pardon any persons found guilty of participating in the lynching. No one was ever even brought to trial.

A Mysterious House

At 525 South Winchester Boulevard, near Stevens Creek Boulevard, stands one of the most bizarre of San Jose's historic attractions: the Winchester Mystery House. Bought as an 8-room farmhouse on 162 acres of land in 1884, it was a 160-room mansion surrounded by lush gardens when its owner, Sarah Winchester, died in 1922. How it got that way isn't really a mystery.

Tiny Sarah Pardee was twenty-two years old in 1862 when she married William Wirt Winchester, son of the inventor of the famous Winchester repeating rifle. The couple had been wed four years when their only child, Annie, was born. She died at one month, of marasmus— malnutrition or failure to thrive. Desolate, Sarah never recovered from the tragedy. In fact, she was still grieving when, fifteen years later, William, too, died. Casting about desperately for solace, Sarah sought help from a spiritualist.

The medium told Sarah that the loss of her loved ones was a curse levied by the spirits of all the people who had been killed by the Winchester rifle. The only way to assuage her grief, the seer said, was for Sarah to move west, buy a house, and build on it continuously. The grieving widow, with a fortune of $20 million and an almost 49 percent share of the rifle manufacturing company, obeyed.

Once settled into the house in San Jose, she hired a large domestic staff and set a team of carpenters and gardeners to work on her property. Within six months, the farmhouse had grown into a 26-room mansion. Sarah found the planning and supervision to be excellent therapy, so she kept her workmen busy building and remodeling twenty-four hours a day until her death.

At that time the house had 160 rooms with priceless crystal chandeliers, rosewood furniture, and floors of the most exotic hardwoods. It also had forty stairways, some of which led nowhere, doors that opened onto blank walls, and a grand ballroom that had been assembled without a single nail to mar its acoustics. A six-foot cypress hedge surrounded the gardens, which included blooming flower beds edged with rare boxwood and shaded by exotic trees. Ornate Victorian fountains tossed bubbles into the air from spouting frogs and life-size statues. A year after Sarah's death, the house was sold and has been open as a tourist attraction ever since.

Beginning of the Beekeeping Industry

The last historic spot to be explored before taking off on a roundabout route to Oakland stands at 1661 Airport Boulevard, where an important industry got its start. The production of honey contributes almost $10 million to the state's economy each year, but that amount is trivial when compared to the value of the honey producers themselves. Called the most economically valuable of all insects, the honeybee's reputation rests on the worth of its beeswax and honey. Actually, however, the value of the honeybee derives from the way it pollinates crops. Without the little buzzer, many of the crops that make California the world's leading producer of foodstuffs wouldn't propagate or bear fruit. For example, more than 100,000 colonies of bees are moved into Kern County each year to pollinate the alfalfa seed crop alone.

It's no wonder, then, that state historical marker number 945 has been placed where the first beehive in the state stood. It was here, in 1853, that Christopher Shelton set up the one hive that had managed to survive the arduous trek from the East. Shelton had bought twelve beehives in New York and transported them by rail, mule pack, and steamship to San Francisco. Most of the insects died, but those that did weather the trip provided the foundation for California's beekeeping industry.

US 101, County Road 152, CA 17, and I-880
San Jose–Oakland
145 miles

THE NEW ALMADEN QUICKSILVER MINE

This segment of the trip to Oakland opens with a side trip to a little-known but historically interesting mine. Instead of departing San Jose via US 101, the side trip travels a couple of miles along old Monterey Road to the Capitol Expressway, County Road G21. Two and one-half miles west County Road G21 meets the Almaden Expressway, County Road G8. A little more than six miles south of that junction, the expressway ends to become Almaden Road. Two miles after that change, the road runs alongside Almaden Quicksilver County Park and enters the community of New Almaden, a charming village containing Victorian homes and some of the original buildings of the New Almaden Quicksilver Mine.

In this area the natives found a plentiful source of the red ore cinnabar, which they used to paint their bodies. Cinnabar is mercuric sulfide, a mineral that is the principal source of mercury for commercial uses. Comparatively rare, in the United Sates it is found only in California and Nevada. One method of extracting gold from ore combines the gold-bearing ore with mercury to form an amalgam, from which the mercury is removed by distillation, leaving behind the gold.

When newcomers discovered the Almaden deposit in 1824, they mistook the quicksilver for silver; even so, mining didn't begin in earnest until 1845, when Alexander Forbes leased the site for his firm, Barron, Forbes & Company. The deposit annually yielded about a million dollars worth of mercury, most of which was used in the gold mining then going on to the north. It was the most productive mercury mine in the nation, according to Hart, and it operated until the 1970s.

The route reverses itself now, to return to CA 82, southbound, having added less than twenty miles to the distance to Oakland. Two and one-half miles from its junction with County Road G21, the highway metamorphoses into the business loop of US 101. It jogs eastward just south of Madrone to join the US 101 freeway for nine miles. Then it exits onto CA 152 heading west. This road wanders through the Santa Cruz Mountains, climbs Hecker Pass, and drops into Watsonville, noted for its apples, all in about eighteen miles.

Aptos and Soquel

One and one-half miles outside Watsonville, the road reaches CA 1, at this point an expressway named Cabrillo Highway that swoops around the northern half of Monterey Bay to serve the many beach communities in the area. It passes Aptos, a resort community that was once the setting for a mansion owned by Claus Spreckels, California's sugar king; and Soquel, where Portolá and his men first remarked on the unusual, big red trees that grew in the area. Pedro Fages wrote, "Here are trees of girth so great that eight men placed side by side with extended arms are unable to embrace them." Such a reaction to one's first glimpse of the coastal redwoods (*Sequoia sempervirens*) isn't all that unusual.

Fifteen miles after entering the expressway, the route departs it on CA 17 heading north, bypassing Santa Cruz, which we'll explore on the trek between Daly City and Watsonville along CA 1.

A Wild Coach Driver

CA 17 parallels part of Old Santa Cruz Highway, where Cockeyed Charlie Parkhurst used to cuss and whip the horses pulling the mail coach through the Santa Cruz Mountains on the road from Santa Cruz to San Jose. Parkhurst was a driver of the post–gold-rush era, famous for a rough tongue and a black eye patch, who, after her death, was discovered to have been a woman. Because her name (in its masculine form) was found on the Santa Cruz voters' register of 1866, she was almost certainly the first woman to vote in California.

Los Gatos

A little more than halfway through the thirty-one miles that separate Santa Cruz and Santa Clara, CA 17 reaches Los Gatos, named for the wildcats that once roamed there. At 75 Church Street stands a historical marker designating the site of Forbes Flour Mill, a four-story stone mill built in 1854 by James Alexander Forbes. The town that grew up around the mill was at first called Forbes Mill, then Forbestown, and finally Los Gatos.

Santa Clara

Continuing for three miles, CA 17 arrives at County Road G4 (the San Tomas Expressway). After a brief jaunt (about six miles), that road reaches Santa Clara and crosses El Camino Real, the King's Highway, a route that loosely defines the path traveled by the padres as they founded the state's chain of missions. Only a few crooklike standards holding replicas of mission bells today mark the highway, roughly old US 101, most of them having disappeared over the years. They were placed to remind travelers of the original purpose of the road, bits of which can still be seen.

In Santa Clara, on the Alameda at Lexington Street, stands Mission Santa Clara de Asís, founded in 1777 by Father Junípero Serra and named to honor Saint Claire of Assisi, who founded the order of Poor Clares. The mission was eighth in the chain and was established to help stabilize the area around San Francisco. The present structure is a 1929 interpretation in stucco and concrete of designs that were only painted on the original structure built here in 1825. This is the fifth building erected, the first four having been destroyed by earthquake, flood, and fire. The University of Santa Clara stands on the original mission's site. The mission was once connected to the pueblo San Jose by a tree-lined road, the Alameda. Today the towns merge, one into the other.

The U.S. occupation of California brought about one of the most turbulent times in the state's history. During that period, Mexican leaders at both ends of the state attempted to stem the tide of U.S. conquest. Most of the so-called battles that marked the war were little more than skirmishes with few casualties. The one that was fought in Santa Clara about four miles north of the mission on January 2, 1847, resulted in the death of four Mexicans and the wounding of two Americans. After an armistice of five days, Marine Capt. Ward Marston, leader of the U.S. force, and Francisco Sanchez, who headed the Mexican-Californian ranchers, signed a peace treaty. A state historical plaque at the northeast corner of El Camino Real and Lincoln Street in Civic Center Park marks the site of that signing.

At 981 Fremont Street stands a Queen Anne–style mansion, built in 1892, that was once the home of C. C. Morse of the Ferry Morse Seed Company. Morse was a pioneer in California's seed industry, today a major contributor to the state's economy.

Exploration of this dense area continues along US 101, the Bayshore Freeway, to pass Moffett Field, about four miles north of the San Tomas Expressway (County Road G4).

HOME OF DIRIGIBLES

Moffett Field is a U.S. Naval air station at the eastern edge of the residential community of Mountain View, remarkable for its vast hangar, almost a quarter of a mile long. Opened in 1933 as a base for dirigibles, the installation was named for Rear Adm. William A. Moffett, who died that year in the crash of the *Akron*, the navy's first dirigible. It was also home to the *Macon*, sister ship of the *Akron*, which crashed in 1935. The USS *Macon* was the largest aircraft in the world, according to an article by Gordon Vaeth in *National Geographic*. She was longer than two football fields, an airborne aircraft carrier that cradled five Sparrowhawk fighter biplanes in her belly. When she crashed off Point Sur, condemning two of her eighty-three crew members to death, the navy's dirigible program died, too. When the navy abandoned its lighter-than-air program, Moffett Field became a center for aeronautical research. According to James Hart, it has the world's largest wind tunnel for testing aircraft.

PALO ALTO

Just off the freeway, five miles farther along, is Palo Alto, known primarily as the home of Stanford University and its research organizations. Leland Stanford and his wife, Jane, founded the university in 1885 to honor their only son, who died at 15. It is the site of a linear accelerator two miles long, the largest in the world. The school's first class, enrolled in 1891 and numbering 559 students—some of whom were women—included Herbert Hoover.

On the campus grounds, at 623 Mirada Road, is the 1919 Lou Henry Hoover House, designed in an innovative architectural style and maintained as the Hoover family home from 1920 to 1944. Herbert Hoover was here when he learned he had been elected president of the United States in 1928. The house was given to the university when Mrs. Hoover died.

Also on the school's grounds, on Campus Drive West, is a marker denoting the spot where Eadweard Muybridge, an English photographer and one-time employee of the U.S. Coast and Geodetic Survey, first experimented with moving pictures. Hired by Leland Stanford, he triggered a series of twenty-four cameras to show horses and cattle in motion, thereby proving that for an instant running horses have all four feet off the ground.

Meet Julia Morgan

Nearby, on Mitchell Lane near University Avenue and El Camino Real, stands a building designed by Julia Morgan for the YWCA. Built to be a meeting place at Camp Fremont for servicemen and visitors, it was dedicated in 1919 to those who died in World War I. It was moved to Palo Alto to become the first municipally sponsored community center in the nation, and is the only structure remaining from the state's World War I training camps.

Julia Morgan, born in San Francisco in 1872, was the first woman to graduate from the state university with a degree in mechanical engineering. She was also the first woman to be a graduate in architecture from the École des Beaux-Arts. Her first major work was reconstructing the Fairmont Hotel after the earthquake and fire of 1906. The culmination of her career was her creation of William Randolph Hearst's estate at San Simeon, today a tourist mecca called Hearst Castle.

The Start of Silicon Valley

Palo Alto is the northern end of that area called the Silicon Valley, a hotbed of electronics research and development that extends southward to San Jose. It was here, at the southeast corner of Channing Avenue and Emerson Street, that the industry was born, in the laboratory and factory of the Federal Telegraph Company. On this site Dr. Lee de Forest, inventor of the triode—the prototype of electronic amplifiers—worked from 1910 to 1913 developing long-distance telephone capability. He is called the Father of the Radio.

THE SAN MATEO BRIDGE

After covering another fourteen miles, the Bayshore Freeway reaches CA 92 and the entrance to the San Mateo toll bridge, a span almost thirteen miles long built in 1929. From the eastern end of the bridge, it is only fifteen miles along I-880 to Oakland, the largest city of Alameda County.

OAKLAND, THE OTHER CITY ON THE BAY

Oakland is the city that Herb Caen, columnist for the *San Francisco Chronicle*, said exists only because the Bay Bridge had to end somewhere. And Gertrude Stein, the sharp-penned writer who lived in the other city on the bay for twelve years, said of Oakland, "There's no there there."

Warmer and sunnier than its competitor across the bay, Oakland's climate is nonetheless tempered in summer by cooling breezes and fog from the ocean. Even before the famous bridge was built, many who worked in the City (San Francisco) commuted from Oakland to enjoy its brighter days, flower-covered hillsides in spring (most of which are now beneath housing developments), and semitropical trees.

Oakland is also the city that suffered the destructive shaking of the San Francisco-Oakland Bay Bridge during the 1989 Loma Prieta earthquake. That magnitude 7.5 shaker also collapsed a portion of the Nimitz Freeway, I-880, which was a two-level structure in Oakland. Almost fifty persons lost their lives in that disaster.

Oakland is the hub of the Bay Area Rapid Transit system (BART), which extends its four legs some seventy-one miles to Richmond, Daly City, Concord, and Fremont. Part of the high-speed system is elevated, part beneath the ground, and part tunnels beneath the San Francisco Bay from Oakland to the City. A subway was hotly contested for years in the Bay Area before being finally approved. Construction began in 1962, and the first passengers boarded in 1972. Today more than a quarter-million passengers ride each week.

Acceptance of the system was rather slow in coming, but the 1989 earthquake made BART. According to a 1993 article in the *Los Angeles Times*, "With the Bay Bridge down and crucial sections of other freeways closed for repairs, BART was unscarred and bore a crushing load of commuters in the days after the quake—and bore it well." The article goes on to say that many of those temporary riders became permanent converts to the subway.

Horace W. Carpentier and his associates (who were actually squatters) in 1852 laid out the town of Oakland on a land grant owned by the four sons of Luís María Peralta, a land-grant holder. Caught in the chaos that followed passage of the congressional land grant act of 1852, which forced land-grant holders to prove the validity of their claims, the Peraltas trusted Carpentier, who tricked them into giving him all their valuable waterfront property. In exchange, Carpentier promised to build three wharves and a school on what had been their land. He incorporated the city of Oakland on part of this property, and named himself mayor. In 1868 Carpentier offered the Central Pacific Railroad a controlling interest in all the waterfront land if it would make Oakland the end of the line for the new railroad. Carpentier and Leland Stanford became principal stockholders in a corporation formed to control that land, creating a monopoly on the waterfront that would persist well into the twentieth century.

Another of the city's early developers—and one of a somewhat different stripe—was Samuel Merritt, who became mayor in 1867. During his term he dammed a muddy slough to create the saltwater lake bearing his name that is today a centerpiece of downtown Oakland. It is the only natural body of saltwater in the nation to be located in the heart of a city.

For five years, from its March 23, 1868, charter date until 1873, when it moved to Berkeley, the University of California occupied buildings between Franklin and Harrison Streets, from 12th to 14th in Oakland. A historical marker notes the spot at the northeast corner of 13th and Franklin Streets.

By 1870 Oakland boasted two banks, three newspapers, and a city directory. Bear fights had been banned, baseball games had replaced bullfights, and church parties took the place of fiestas. Gaslights brightened lower Broadway, and a seminary for young ladies—the forerunner of Mills College, first college for women west of the Rockies—was about to open. The city was growing in sophistication as well as population.

Regarded as a suburb of the city across the bay, Oakland nonetheless was home to some of the famous writers of the time. Jack London prowled its streets, using its tough waterfront as background for later books. Edwin Markham was teaching school in Oakland when he wrote his *Man with the Hoe*, protesting the brutalization of labor. Joaquin Miller lived for a long time on his estate in the hills that he called "The Hights." According to Hart, Miller was variously regarded as an eccentric, bard, advocate of free love, and a last remnant of the Old West. His property was purchased by the city in 1919 and is now Joaquin Miller Park on Sanborn Drive.

The phenomenal growth of Oakland shortly before the turn of the century is attributed largely to F. M. "Borax" Smith, of Death Valley fame. Using the profits from his borax mines, Smith invested heavily in Oakland, tying together all the street railway systems of the East Bay in founding the Key Route Ferry System. With Lloyd Tevis and R. G. Hanford, Smith in 1910 formed the United Properties Company, pooling the real estate the three had previously acquired individually. This corporation was arguably the largest in California history, according to the Federal Writers' Project's *San Francisco: The Bay and Its Cities*, except for the Southern Pacific Railroad, which was controlled by Easterners. United Properties absorbed and developed railways, a ferry system, public utilities, and real estate in the East Bay. It expanded too rapidly, however, practiced unsound financial tactics, and collapsed in 1913, taking with it the fortunes of the three men. It was Smith who suffered most; he lost more than $24 million. The city of Oakland, on the other hand, profited from the trouble, because it got to keep the developments owned by the corporation.

BERKELEY

A little more than five miles up the road—either I-80 or San Pablo Avenue—is Berkeley, home of the University of California. Berkeley was founded, a little more traditionally than Oakland, in 1866 on another part of the same Peralta land grant. Although it has gained its international reputation because of the university, it boasts a good deal of light industry along the bay.

The university campus, first opened in 1873, embraces a host of historic landmarks, including Founders' Rock, University House, the Faculty Club and Glade, Hearst Greek Theater, Hearst Memorial Mining

Building, Doe Library, Sather Tower and Esplanade, Sather Gate and Bridge, Hearst Gymnasium, and halls named to honor benefactors Durant, Wellman, Hilgard, Giannini, and Wheeler. One of California's noted architects created a work that stands at 2315 Durant Avenue. It is Julia Morgan's outstanding example of California design, the Berkeley City Club, which combines with great effect Moorish and Gothic elements. It dates from 1929.

The first class to graduate from the University of California, twelve men, did so in 1873, after the school moved from Oakland. The university faced financial, administrative, and policy problems at the outset and didn't manage to enroll a thousand students until 1895. Private gifts were, nonetheless, forthcoming: James Lick donated an observatory on Mount Hamilton in 1888; Dr. H. H. Toland contributed the forerunner of the university's medical school in San Francisco in 1873; and the state's first chief justice, Judge Hastings, provided funds to establish the law school.

During the tenure of its eighth president, Benjamin Ide Wheeler, the school expanded in both size and scholarship. In the two decades from 1899 to 1919, summer sessions were held to train teachers, a number of distinguished buildings went up, the student body grew to 7,000—about half women—and the University Extension was created for general adult education. The University Farm School at Davis was born

Sather Gate at the University of California, Berkeley, was the scene of students' free speech demonstrations during the 1960s. —Jean Doris Kahn

167

*Campanile at the University
of California, Berkeley.*
—Jean Doris Kahn

during Wheeler's administration, as were the Citrus Experiment Station at Riverside and the Scripps Institution for Biological Research at La Jolla.

The school continued to grow and thrive until the unrest of the sixties that began with the 1964 Free Speech Movement. In the fall of that year students undertook a program of civil disobedience against the university when it tried to enforce its rules against student political activity, rules that were clearly unconstitutional. The United States Supreme Court, Walton Bean points out, had ruled in 1963 that student speakers could even advocate violations of the law, provided their words didn't constitute a clear and present danger.

In spite of dramatic expansion that created many campuses around the state, the university went on to become overcrowded and underfunded. Part-time teachers were paid abysmally low wages and the quality of education fell off; tuition soared. The luster was dimmed on the state's plans to educate all its children. By the 1990s, even community colleges were beyond the means of many of the children of the poor, no matter how deserving.

The last item of historic interest to be explored before crossing the bay is Piedmont Way, fashioned in 1865 by Frederick Law Olmsted, the nation's foremost landscape architect. Designed to be a roadway following the natural contours of the land and shaded by overhanging trees, it was Olmsted's first residential street design. Similar parkways across the country have been modeled on this one. The marker describing the street stands on Piedmont Avenue between Gayley Road and Dwight Road.

I-80, US 101, and I-280
San Francisco–Daly City
15 miles

The Bay Bridge
Returning to I-80, the route itself becomes of historic interest as it crosses the bay via the San Francisco-Oakland Bay Bridge. Designed by C. H. Purcell, an employee of the California Department of Public Works, the renowned double-deck bridge was begun in 1933 and completed in 1936. It is, according to Hart, the world's longest steel bridge, at four

Oakland Bay Bridge on November 11, 1943, linked a nearly clear Oakland with fog-shrouded San Francisco. —National Archives

Goat Island Naval Training Station as it appeared in 1918. —National Archives

1921 view of Naval Training Station at Goat Island, renamed Yerba Buena in 1931. —National Archives

and one-half miles. From the toll plaza in Oakland to the Rincon Hill end in San Francisco it is eight and one-quarter miles long and accommodates motor vehicles only. Originally built to carry trains on the lower level, it was reconstructed in 1964–65 and the tracks were eliminated. At night it is festooned with sodium vapor lights that penetrate even the worst fogs.

The eastern approach starts at a toll plaza near the northeastern end of the Oakland Army Base, with westbound traffic traveling on the upper deck only. The eastern segment of the bridge is a cantilevered span of 1,400 feet. The bridge's center rests on Yerba Buena Island, where it passes through a double-tiered tunnel to reach the twin suspension bridges linked together by a concrete pier to form a single smooth arc that makes up the western portion.

YERBA BUENA ISLAND

Yerba Buena (Spanish for "good herb") Island is connected by a causeway to the artificial Treasure Island created for the Golden Gate International Exposition of 1939. Today Treasure Island is the home of a U.S. Naval station. In September 1944 it was the site of the mutiny trial of the Port Chicago Fifty.

SAN FRANCISCO

Planned by Spanish authorities as an adjunct to the Presidio, which had been established in 1776 to protect Mission Dolores, the pueblo of San Francisco wasn't established until 1834. Even then, it wasn't nearly as successful as San Jose.

The actual city we know today got its start at what is now 823–27 Grant Avenue between Clay and Washington Streets, far from both presidio and mission. William A. Richardson, appointed captain of the port by General Vallejo, built an adobe there in 1836 to replace the tent he had put up in 1835. The settlement, called Yerba Buena, was on a little cove, for the water reached that point in those days. Portsmouth Square, on Kearney between Washington and Clay in the financial district, was originally the town plaza for the new colony and was the site of a Mexican customs house. Comdr. John B. Montgomery anchored the USS *Portsmouth* near there when he took possession of the settlement for the United States on July 9, 1846.

By 1850, following the gold rush, San Francisco was a bustling city of 25,000 residents. Few towns in history have had more diverse populations: Yankees and Californios rubbed elbows with Chinese and Chileans, Frenchmen and Spaniards. From all over the world men

Oakland City Hall overlooks Lake Merritt. —Jean Doris Kahn

Bay Area Rapid Transit (BART) trains run under the bay between San Francisco and Oakland. —Jean Doris Kahn

answered the call of "Gold!" and most of them had to go through San Francisco to find it. Ducks from Australia, Kanakas from Hawaii, good burghers from Switzerland, vaqueros from Baja California—all had come to find wealth. Few did.

Possibly the most important event ever to occur in San Francisco took place on April 25, 1945, in the Civic Center. There the representatives of fifty nations convened to plan a world society that would be free from war. For more than two months they deliberated and at last came up with the United Nations Charter, which was unanimously adopted and signed by all participants on June 26 in the War Memorial Veterans Building. State historical marker 964 notes that significant time and place.

Market Street

Visitors exiting the Bay Bridge at the San Francisco end will do well to leave the freeway as quickly as possible if they want to see the city. About half a mile to the northwest is Market Street, the best-known thoroughfare in town. It was laid out by Jasper O'Farrell in his 1847 mapping of the part of San Francisco bounded by Post, Leavenworth, and Francisco Streets and the bay. The subway now runs under Market Street from the bay to Van Ness Avenue, with stations less than one-half mile apart. About midway in that length, at Powell and Market Streets, is the cable car turntable that stars in films and commercials featuring the City.

The Cable Cars

The cable car is San Francisco's trademark, invented by Andrew S. Hallidie to negotiate the city's steep hills. The first car to be drawn up a moving endless cable ran on August 2, 1873, along Clay Street from Kearney to Leavenworth, and was an instant hit. Residents and tourists alike have made the clangy open cars an integral part of the City by the Bay. Some years ago, serious consideration was given to getting rid of the drafty vehicles, but the outcry was so great that the proposal was scuttled. Today twenty-six cars ply the two Powell Street routes and eleven swoop along the California Street line. Cars of the Powell routes ascend Nob and Russian Hills to terminals at either Beach Street at Hyde or Bay Street near Columbus. Much of what history buffs want to see is along cable car lines.

The Beach Street end of the Powell-Hyde line is close to Fisherman's Wharf, Ghirardelli Square, the Maritime National Historical Park, and the pier at the western end of the Embarcadero from which ferries depart for Tiburon, Alcatraz, and Angel Island. This route passes Union

Cable car clangs through San Francisco's Chinatown. —Jean Doris Kahn

Square and the San Francisco Art Institute. The Powell-Mason branch that ends at Columbus Avenue runs within a few blocks of Telegraph Hill and Coit Tower.

Cars on the California Street line run west from California and Market, not far from the Ferry Building, climb Nob Hill, and clang down again. They racket through the heart of Chinatown, passing Old Saint Mary's Church and the Fairmont Hotel, and end up at Van Ness Avenue.

The Scenic Drive

San Francisco, with its forty hills—the important ones being Nob, Russian, Telegraph, Rincon, Twin Peaks, Lone Mountain, and Mount Davidson—isn't really a town for walking. In recognition of that truth, planners of the 1939–40 Golden Gate International Exposition devised a forty-nine-mile scenic drive as the best way to see the city. It opened the year before the exposition and Franklin D. Roosevelt was one of the first motorists to try it.

Marked by blue-and-white seagull signs, the drive covers the most important scenic and historic points of San Francisco as it zigs and zags through the Civic Center, Japantown, Union Square, Chinatown, Nob Hill, North Beach, and Telegraph Hill. It passes Fisherman's Wharf, the Marina, and the Palace of Fine Arts. Passing the southern approach to

174

the Golden Gate Bridge, it winds through the Presidio and beside the Palace of the Legion of Honor, then doubles back to wind through Golden Gate Park. Down past the zoo it goes, past Lake Merced, through the Sunset District. It swings over to the neighborhood known as the Mission District, past the mission called Dolores, over to Potrero Hill, and around to the Embarcadero.

The Ferry Building

At the foot of Market Street on the Embarcadero is the Ferry Building, built in 1898 of gray sandstone from Colusa and designed by A. Page Brown. Remarkable for its 235-foot clock tower, it withstood the 1906 quake to serve for years as the major entry point for visitors to San Francisco. The Embarcadero Freeway cutting across its face diminished the building's beauty and importance until the freeway was damaged in the 1989 earthquake and was subsequently torn down.

The Magnificent Palace

About six blocks along Market Street from the Ferry Building, at Montgomery, stands the Palace Hotel, an elegant inn of eight hundred rooms dating back to 1875. It was one of the civic projects of William C. Ralston, who was born in Ohio, moved to San Francisco in 1854, and gained a reputation as a financier in short order. Just ten years after his arrival, Ralston and D. O. Mills, a banker from New York, founded the Bank of California.

Following his successful establishment in 1859 of a Sacramento bank named for himself, Mills was inspired to invest, with Ralston and other capitalists, in another bank, this one in San Francisco. Mills went on to become a regent of the University of California and the owner of a great estate in the peninsula town of Millbrae. When he died in New York, he left an estate of $60 million.

Ralston, on the other hand, remained a Californian all his days and was elected president of the Bank of California in 1872. A genuine California booster, he financed, both on his own and with bank money, a wide range of ventures: steamship lines, railroads, a theater, woolen and silk mills, mines in Nevada, and the Palace Hotel. Directing his empire from an estate in Belmont, he cut quite a swath both politically and socially, but eventually overextended himself. In August 1875, when a run on the Bank of California made it close its doors, Ralston went for a swim in the bay, as he often did, but this time he drowned. When it was found that he had been insolvent and deep in debt, many of his holdings, including the Palace Hotel, were taken over by William Sharon, whom Ralston had made his representative in Nevada.

*Coit Tower stands
watch from
Telegraph Hill.*
—San Francisco Convention
and Visitors Bureau

Famous for its six-story Palm Court with a glass roof, the Palace Hotel had five hydraulic elevators, luxurious furnishings, good service, and great food. It was destroyed by the earthquake and fire of 1906 but was replaced by an elegant new building designed by George W. Kelham that featured a glass-roofed Garden Court dining room. It was in the Palace that Warren G. Harding, twenty-ninth president of the United States, died, on August 2, 1923. The hotel was owned by William Sharon's heirs until 1954, when it became part of the Sheraton chain. In 1990–91 the Garden Court underwent extensive restoration that required two years of work by preservation architects. Today it reflects much of its original flavor.

Telegraph Hill and Coit Tower

Traveling northwest along the Embarcadero, the forty-nine-mile drive passes Telegraph Hill, named for the semaphore placed at its crest in 1850 to signal the arrival of ships in the bay. The hill rises 274 feet over the northeast end of the bay and is topped by Coit Tower. The tower was built in 1933 with money left to the city for that purpose by Lillie

Residence of attorney Melvin Belli in San Francisco's Jackson Square is a feature of the old Barbary Coast district. In 1849 the building housed California's first Masonic Lodge.
—Ted Needham, San Francisco Convention and Visitors Bureau

The Garden Court of the Sheraton-Palace Hotel on Market Street is a San Francisco landmark. The court was once a covered carriage entrance. —San Francisco Convention and Visitors Bureau

Eureka, *a 300-foot wooden ferryboat in service until 1957, is a national historic landmark. She is permanently moored at Hyde Street Pier in San Francisco.* —San Francisco Maritime National Historical Park

Balclutha, *a memorial to the grand days of sail, is a square-rigger anchored at San Francisco Maritime National Historical Park at Hyde Street Pier.*
—Steve Danford, San Francisco Maritime National Historical Park

Angel Island

The largest island in San Francisco Bay, Angel Island covers only about one square mile, but it boasts enough history for an area the size of Texas. From 1850 to 1853 the state anchored ships' hulks off the island and housed prisoners in them. Before that it was often used as a pirates' supply station and afterward as an army artillery emplacement and immigrant detention center, sort of the Ellis Island of the West.

The island's first gun batteries were installed in 1863 and the last installation, a Nike missile station, was deactivated in 1964. During periods of war, especially the Spanish-American War, Angel Island was one of the busiest posts in the country. It served as a processing center for men about to debark for the Philippines and as a reception center for those who came back with tropical diseases. From 1910 until 1940 the Hospital Cove facilities were used by the U.S. Public Health Service to intern an estimated 175,000 Chinese immigrants.

Sometimes the stays of those internees were long and they inscribed poetry on the wooden walls of their barracks. Some of their writing expresses the bitterness they felt on learning they had to undergo medical and legal tests not required of immigrants from other nations. Most of it, however, simply tells of their loneliness and longing for their homeland.

Alcatraz

The island of Alcatraz (Spanish for "pelican"), about two miles south of Angel Island and just east of the Golden Gate, won its harsh reputation as a federal penitentiary, which it was for only thirty years, from 1933 to 1963. Few people know that it was an army post for eighty years, first a heavy artillery installation, then a military prison. Indeed, it was the army that constructed the prison buildings that became so famous as the home of notorious criminals.

The Citadel of Alcatraz was a structure unique on many points. Completed in late 1859, it was a three-story structure, built of brick and stone and surrounded by a dry moat. Oddly enough, it was designed to be defended by rifle fire alone and didn't have a single cannon port. Never was a shot fired in anger from the Citadel; nor did the cannons of Alcatraz ever fire on a foe. During the Civil War the Confederate raider *Shenandoah* attacked the Union's whaling fleet in Pacific waters but never attempted to slip past the Golden Gate, probably deterred by the formidable guns of Alcatraz.

The importance of Alcatraz as a prison grew, and in 1908 it was enlarged. The upper two stories of the Citadel were demolished; the basement level and dry moat remained as foundation and basement for a new prison. Roughly one-third of the old structure survives, leading

Bay/Delta Model is a working-scale model of the delta, built in 1956 by the U.S. Army Corps of Engineers. It stands at the northern end of Sausalito, just a short ferry ride from San Francisco. Its depiction of the Golden Gate Bridge is six feet long; the Bay Bridge, in the foreground, is twenty-three feet long. —Army Corps of Engineers

to strange stories of Spanish dungeons beneath the one-time federal penitentiary.

Fort Mason

Fort Mason, lying just west of the Maritime Museum at the end of Franklin Street, was the army's San Francisco port of embarkation from 1909 through 1963. It consisted of piers, storehouses, and retaining walls constructed in 1910. Shipments of troops, weapons, ammunition, and supplies left these facilities to reach the Philippines, Guam, China, Alaska, Hawaii, and the Panama Canal. The installation was enlarged several times to meet the demands of both world wars. Fort Mason supplied the whole Pacific Theater during the Second World War, but it was strained at the seams. The Oakland Army Terminal was built to replace it, although Fort Mason remained a significant facility through the Korean War. Closed down in 1963, it is today part of the Golden Gate National Recreation Area.

The Presidio

When the Spanish term *presidio* is used in connection with California, it is usually the Presidio of San Francisco that comes to mind. That famous old garrison sits immediately west of Fort Mason and extends along the northern end of the city from Lyon Street to 24th Avenue. Established by Spanish troops under Capt. Juan Bautista de Anza in June of 1776, until 1994 it was the country's oldest military post in continuous operation. It is now part of the National Park Service. It was a major command post during the Mexican, Civil, and Spanish-American Wars, as well as both world wars and the Korean War.

Garrisoned by a token detachment of U.S. troops from 1847 to 1862, it was left all but empty when the call of the gold rush lured many of those troops to desert. Those who remained patched up old Spanish adobe buildings and built a few new ones. In 1854 Secretary of War Jefferson Davis ordered the post abandoned for a time, but it was soon remanned and before too long gained its own structures.

The oldest building on base is the Presidio Army Museum, built in 1862 as Wright General Hospital. Also built in 1862 was the complex of wooden Victorian houses that served as officers' quarters.

Gun ports of Old Fort Point once housed 127 muzzle-loading cannons. Built before the outbreak of the Civil War and deactivitated in 1914, the brick-and-granite bastion guarded the Golden Gate for 53 years. —San Francisco Convention and Visitors Bureau

World-famous Golden Gate Bridge as it looked in November 1936, shortly before it opened to traffic. —National Archives

At the southwest end of the Golden Gate Bridge are some of the old artillery gun emplacements that were constructed between 1893 and 1908. They are visible to travelers on US 101 and CA 1 approaching the famous bridge.

The Golden Gate Bridge

The Golden Gate Bridge spans the distance between Fort Point on the San Francisco end and Lime Point at the Marin County end. Construction of this engineering marvel began on January 5, 1933. The bridge opened to traffic on May 28, 1937. Its main center span is 4,200 feet long, and each side span 1,125 feet. The total length of the bridge, including approaches, is 8,940 feet, more than a mile and a half. The towers rise 746 feet above high tide, and the center span swings 220 feet above low water. The towers are as tall as an eighty-five-story building. More than 112,000 automobiles travel its length each day.

San Francisco National Cemetery

The scenic drive continues past the entrance to the famous bridge to see the rest of the Presidio. A number of unusual epitaphs mark

184

headstones in the San Francisco National Cemetery that sits at the heart of the Presidio. One identifies the final resting place of Pvt. John Brown of Fort Yuma, California, buried here on July 23, 1852, the first to lie in this hallowed ground. Another stands guard over the grave of Pauline Cushman Fryer, an actress and Union spy during the Civil War, who was awarded the rank of brevet major for her service to the Union cause. One stone carries the simple inscription, "Two Bits". It marks the grave of an Indian scout who served the U.S. Army.

Two more headstones of note stand in this burial ground: those of Congressman Phil Burton and his wife, Sala. Back in the 1960s, when the first talk of closing the Presidio arose, developers began to talk of someday taking control of the land for a tract of luxury homes. In 1972 that talk prompted Burton to write a law requiring that if the army should ever abandon the post it would be incorporated into the Golden Gate National Recreation Area. The people of California owe Phil Burton more than just a grave site with a view of San Francisco Bay.

Mission Dolores

Weaving in and out, back and forth through the fabled city, the forty-nine-mile exploration trip reaches Dolores Street between 16th and 17th Streets, three blocks south of Market. Here sits Mission Dolores.

The true name of this sixth mission in the chain, founded in 1776 by Father Francisco Palóu, is San Francisco de Asís, in honor of St. Francis of Assisi. Chosen by Juan Bautista de Anza, the site of the original mission was on the bank of a little creek that he named Arroyo de Los Dolores, and it was by that name the mission came to be known. At the same time he was picking the spot for the mission, Anza chose the location for the presidio. Construction of both facilities proceeded apace and by October 9, 1776, a wooden church plastered with mud and roofed with tules stood ready to welcome celebrants.

Mission life was uncomfortable for the Indians of the area. Chilling fogs and blustery winds off the ocean made the miseries of measles and other European diseases even harder to bear, so for much of its life the mission was plagued with the problem of runaways. Feeling they owed no allegiance to Dolores, the neophytes often sought the opposite shore, where the sun shone and friends welcomed.

When the neighborhood began to decline, becoming a center for gambling, horse racing, and tavern life, Father Palóu decided to move his church to a better site. The mission that stands today was dedicated in 1791. Spared by the earthquake and fire, a large part of its quadrangle just disappeared with time. But the church itself endured, untouched, one of the few without elaborate columns, arches, or buttresses,

Filofi Gardens at Woodside, the 1916 country estate of William Bourn, founder of an early Napa Valley winery. The gardens were donated by subsequent owners to the National Foundation for Historic Preservation. —Jean Doris Kahn

a marvel of simple beauty. Even well-meaning restorers haven't spoiled it and the City's Mission Dolores looks much as it did in the 1790s.

DALY CITY

Leaving San Francisco, the exploratory route follows US 101 to its junction with I-280, then proceeds about five miles to Daly City and CA 1, near the Pacific side of the peninsula.

After the earthquake and fire of 1906, residents of San Francisco sought refuge at John Daly's dairy ranch south of the City. Thus it was that Daly City came into being, to remain a sleepy town until the end of World War II, when it mushroomed as a bedroom community for San Francisco. It now claims a population of more than 90,000.

186

HALF MOON BAY

After running past one spectacular beach after another for eighteen miles, the route arrives at Half Moon Bay, the oldest town in San Mateo County. Famous as the locale of confrontations between rumrunners and the Coast Guard during prohibition days, Half Moon Bay is today a quiet town, noted mainly for artichokes and tourists.

The town boasts forty-eight structures of historical or architectural interest, some dating back as far as 1855. One of them, the James Johnston house, called the White House of Half Moon Bay, is of saltbox design built with mortise-and-tenon construction and wooden pegs. Such construction is an unusual sight on the Pacific Coast and some experts believe its plan was copied from the original owner's Ohio home. It includes, however, Spanish touches such as a second-floor chapel and an enclosed patio and is regarded as a significant example of cultural transfer. As such, it is listed on the National Register of Historic Places and is being reconstructed.

PESCADERO

Continuing to skirt the coast for about fifteen miles, CA 1 reaches Pescadero. When the SS *Colombia* ran ashore here and was battered to pieces, residents of the town—at that time mostly former New Englanders—waded into the surf to rescue the ship's cargo: white lead. Within a matter of days every house in town had been painted gleaming white, earning the town the name Spotless Town.

PIGEON POINT

Pigeon Point, named for the clipper ship *Carrier Pigeon* that wrecked here in 1853, sits about halfway between Half Moon Bay and Santa Cruz. On a cliff high above the sea stands the Pigeon Point Light, a brick lighthouse more than 120 years old. Since 1872 this light has been flashing over the Pacific, its 900,000-candlepower light visible for eighteen miles. Its first-order Fresnel lens, originally installed at Cape Hatteras, North Carolina, is no longer in use but can be seen in the lantern room.

SANTA CRUZ

Running now between the Santa Cruz Mountains on the one hand and the sea on the other, CA 1 passes side roads leading to the likes of Ben Lomond, Bonny Doon, and Felton, all mountain resorts. About thirty miles from Pigeon Point is Santa Cruz, on the northern cusp of Monterey Bay.

Santa Cruz is a beach resort and seat of the county of that name, a town with a rich history. Portolá stopped here in 1769, a mission was founded in 1791, and the pueblo of Branciforte was established in 1797 by Diego de Borica, governor of the Californias from 1794 to 1800.

With Father Fermín Lasuén, Borica founded six missions in addition to this pueblo. He worked to improve the lot of the Indians, teaching them farming and trades and abolishing the death penalty for them. As an enlightened governor, he tried to institute compulsory primary education and worked to separate Alta and Baja California, even drawing the dividing line that was eventually settled upon.

Branciforte was conceived as a place of settlement for retired soldiers and their families, providing cheap colonization and a ready militia in the event of threats from foreign powers. In that guise it was a dismal failure, so Spanish authorities populated it with a boatload of men convicted of minor crimes. Even the promise of an adobe house, a musket, a plow, and a few animals wasn't enough to inspire the motley crew to turn their hands to farming. In 1802 a new viceroy suspended support for the pueblo and its population dwindled away. The present county of Santa Cruz was named Branciforte from February 18 to April 5, 1850. A historical plaque at the southwest corner of Water Street and Branciforte Avenue says the settlement existed as a separate township until 1905, when it was annexed to the city of Santa Cruz.

Santa Cruz, the mission that inspired the ill-fated pueblo, itself had an unhappy fate. Its beginning, though, was auspicious. When it was founded in 1791, the mission named for the holy cross stood on a commanding site—at what is now the northeast corner of Mission and Emmet Streets—with a good climate and fertile soil. Indians of the area seemed willing to accept the Spaniards' God and way of life. Within six years workshops and a two-story granary filled out the mission quadrangle.

Then a series of misfortunes struck. The first was the founding of Branciforte just across the river; the ruffians who settled there took over the Indians' pastureland. The death of a padre under suspicious circumstances contributed to the mission's downfall, as did the arrival in 1818 of the pirate Hyppolyte de Bouchard, who scared the padres into abandoning their property. The scoundrels of Branciforte plundered the mission while it was abandoned, taking tools, foodstuffs, and wine, leaving it destitute. The mission never regained its vigor, declining even more as the community across the river grew more unruly. In 1840, after secularization, the church tower fell; the church itself followed suit after an earthquake in 1857. A frame church was built on the site and stood until 1889, when it was replaced by the structure now standing. In 1931 a small replica of the original mission was built at Emmet and School Streets, two hundred feet from the original site.

For a little less than fifteen miles, CA 1—now the Cabrillo Highway—swoops just inland of Monterey Bay to reach Watsonville and the end of the historical journey through California's fabled Bay Area. The search for the past continues southward.

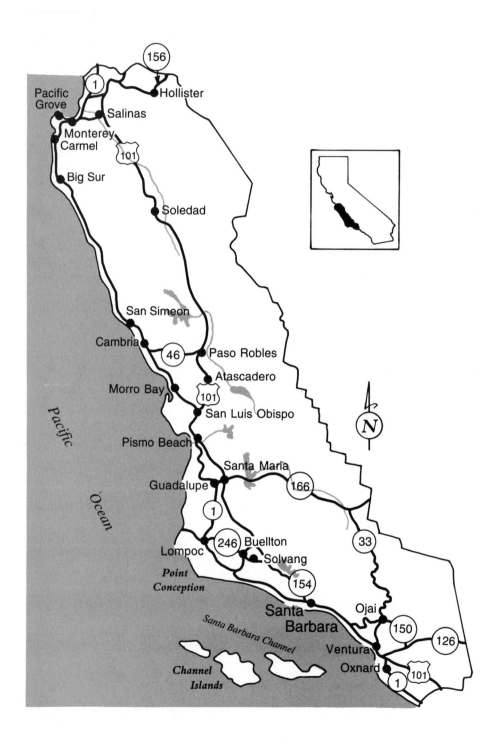

Part 6
The Captivating Central Coast

In the area loosely defined as the Central Coast of California are ten missions, almost half of the twenty-one that run much of the length of the state. The missions fascinate most who see them, even those who aren't of religious bent. The work of unskilled hands is evident in every one, but in some more than others. Some were restored without benefit of research and so reflect the romanticized picture that has been painted of the missions over the years. The fortunate ones regained their original appearance after years of study and through the work of skillful artisans. Undoubtedly, part of the missions' appeal is that they are the oldest historic relics on the Pacific coast.

In spite of their air of permanence, the missions were intended to be temporary establishments that would become parish churches ten years after their founding. Secularization was supposed to bring about what the padres resisted: the independence of the Indians. Indeed, it appeared that the padres were right in their insistence that the mission Indians were not prepared to direct their own lives; most fell into the hands of unscrupulous settlers and commissioners appointed to oversee the secularization process, who took the Indians' lands and exploited their labor. Thus, most of the missions fell into disrepair or vanished altogether. A few managed to survive almost intact in spite of earthquakes, fires, and the depredation of man, and others have been faithfully restored. Whatever shape they're in, the missions are a legacy handed down directly from the past to today's California.

The genius behind the missions was Junípero Serra, missionary and padre, born on the island of Majorca. In 1749, with his friend Francisco Palóu, he was sent to Mexico, where almost immediately after his arrival he was lamed by the bite of a snake or insect. In 1769 he was appointed president of the missions in Baja California. That same year he accompanied Portolá on the Sacred Expedition to Alta California to found at San Diego the first of nine missions he would establish in his lifetime. The Catholic Church is considering sainthood for Father Serra, a move that isn't totally popular in California.

The outlaw Tiburcio Vasquez was hanged in March 1875.
—CHS/TICOR,
USC Special Collections

Fermín Francisco de Lasuén, another Spanish-born padre, picked up the burden of father-president of California's missions when Serra died in 1785. Lasuén, in his eighteen-year tenure, built many fine structures to replace the crude churches he found, established nine additional missions, and more than doubled the system's Indian population. James Hart says Lasuén was noted as a determined, pious, and gentle man and a good administrator. He has, however, been all but ignored by history, overshadowed by Serra's charisma. Even though their goal was to convert the native population to Christianity, these two men influenced California's history more than they could possibly know. Much of what is known about California's Spanish and Mexican settlement eras is told through the missions.

Although no marker stands to commemorate his presence, the outrageous stagecoach robber and cattle thief Tiburcio Vasquez had at least a temporary influence on the state; he operated in areas of the Central Coast for much of his criminal career. He lived in San Juan Bautista for a time, and perpetrated a particularly vicious murder in the tiny town that is now known as Paicines, near Hollister. A handsome rogue, he was often popular with residents of areas he victimized and was able to persuade them to help him outwit posses on his trail. He was finally captured outside Los Angeles, and was tried and hanged in San Jose, where he is buried.

Another scoundrel who plundered the ranchos of the Central Coast was David Jacks, a Scot who showed up in Monterey in 1850 with $4,000 he was eager to invest. He loaned his money to ranch owners at usurious rates, then took over the properties when the owners couldn't repay the loans. According to Anne B. Fisher, he also paid delinquent taxes on huge tracts of land without informing the owners, then appropriated the land when he wasn't reimbursed. In that fashion he acquired great real estate holdings, a reputation as a tightfisted bully, and the hatred of much of the population of the Central Coast. He even managed to acquire control of the state's only native cheese, first made in 1892, and to this day known as Monterey jack or jack cheese. David Jacks provides ample evidence that all the thieves in the Central Coast weren't highwaymen.

CA 152/25/156/68 and US 101
Watsonville–Monterey
78 miles

Because of the mountains that lie between the coast and US 101, few roads connect the two, and those that do aren't always the most enjoyable to drive. Hence, explorers of the state sometimes have to retrace their steps to see the best of the state's historic landmarks. Case in point is the first segment of this journey through the Central Coast. The route leaves Watsonville via CA 152, climbs Hecker Pass, and arrives at Gilroy, on US 101.

GILROY, GARLIC CAPITAL OF THE WORLD

Gilroy bills itself as Garlic Capital of the World and at harvest time needs no introduction, for the pungent odor of the bulbous root fills the air. It is the scene of a garlic festival each fall.

The city was founded in 1870 and named for John Gilroy, whose real name was John Cameron, who had died the year before. He changed his name, Hubert Howe Bancroft says, because he had run away from his home in England as a minor and wanted to avoid being caught and jailed. Having fallen ill aboard the *Isaac Todd*, according to Bancroft, Gilroy was left behind at Monterey in 1814 when the ship sailed. Both Hart and Bancroft say he was the first white non-Hispanic settler in

California. He was naturalized as a citizen of Mexico in 1833, married a Mexican woman, and became part owner of a land grant covering the area. Bancroft describes Gilroy as an honest, good-natured man, beloved by all, but one too fond of cards and grog, who lost all his cattle and lands and died in poverty.

SAN JUAN BAUTISTA

Two miles south of Gilroy the route leaves US 101 to turn southeast toward San Juan Bautista. Traveling four miles along CA 156 it reaches the town, mission, and state historic park all at the same name, where several phases of California's past are represented.

Before the Spaniards came, the little San Juan Valley was home to the Mutsun, who lived in beehive-shaped huts fashioned of willows and coarse grass. The men hunted, using spear points and arrowheads of chert and obsidian; the women gathered acorns, berries, and seeds. The women also made baskets used for storing food, trapping fish, leaching acorns, even boiling, so tightly were they woven. The Mutsun played a variety of games, sang and danced, and made music with whistles, flutes, and rattles constructed of birds' bones. The last full-blooded Mutsun Indian died in 1930 and is buried in the cemetery beside the mission. At one time some 1,200 Mutsun lived at the mission and more than 4,000 of them are buried in the adjacent cemetery.

Beside an old stone wall that stands below the cemetery runs a short fragment of the original El Camino Real, the King's Highway. This is the roadway that connected all of California's missions and went on to serve as the state's main stage and wagon road. Some historians say the padres marked their way by sprinkling mustard seed as they walked from one mission to the next, accounting for the yellow plant that once bloomed along so many miles of El Camino Real. The section visible here leaves the broad plain below and climbs the hill to enter the central plaza of the mission.

Mission San Juan Bautista

Mission San Juan Bautista was founded June 24, 1797, by Father Fermín de Lasuén. The fifteenth mission in the chain, it was the largest of them all. The building that stands today is the second church to have been built, started in 1803 and dedicated in 1812. It withstood the devastating quakes of 1812, which occurred on a fault somewhat removed from San Juan, but the 1906 shaker damaged it badly. The padres had unwittingly sited the church right on the edge of the San Andreas Fault. After the 1906 temblor, Mission San Juan Bautista was reinforced with steel, concrete, and heavy cross-bracing, according to *The California Missions*. It has served as a parish church almost without interruption since its completion.

The reredos—the wall behind the altar—is one of this mission's outstanding features, painted in brilliant colors that have remained bright through all the years. The colorful work was done by Thomas Doak, a sailor on the *Albatross* who jumped ship at Monterey in 1816. Baptized that same year as Felipe Santiago, he married an heiress of the Castro family and became the first U.S. citizen to settle permanently in California.

The mission isn't part of the San Juan Bautista State Historic Park, but most of it is open to visitors. The park comprises the rest of the buildings facing the plaza in front of the church: the Plaza Hotel, Castro House, Plaza Stable, a blacksmith shop, Plaza Hall, and a small cottage.

Soon after the start of the gold rush, San Juan became the marketplace to which ranchers brought their livestock to sell to buyers from San Francisco and San Jose. The Plaza Hotel became their headquarters, as it was for drummers who would hire rigs at the stable to make their sales pitches in surrounding towns. The hotel earned renown for its fine food, prepared by Angelo Zanetta, and for its congenial bar and good beds managed by Zanetta's partner, John Comfort. Gen. William Tecumseh Sherman and banker W. C. Ralston are just two of the many famous persons who stopped at the Plaza.

The two-story Castro House next to the hotel is also known as the Breen Home. The adobe was built about 1838 as an office and home for Don José María Castro, interim governor of California in 1835 and 1836. It has been restored to look much as it did when Castro first built it, although it is furnished as it might have been during the Breens' occupancy.

Patrick and Margaret Breen and their seven children, after surviving the ordeal at Donner Pass, arrived in San Juan Bautista penniless. They were given permission to stay in the mission until one of the sons, John, struck it rich in the earliest days of the gold rush. In December 1848 the Breens bought the Castro house and four hundred prime acres around it. Successive generations of Breens held title to that property and lived in the house until 1933, when the property became part of the state historic park. Breens are still prominent citizens in the area.

The stable was built about 1861 to accommodate the heavy wagon and stage traffic that was San Juan's lifeblood. At one time seven stage lines operated through the town, with up to eleven stages coming and going each day. It was also on the main supply route between quicksilver

John C. Frémont, hero of many of early California's dramas. —The Bancroft Library

mines in the county and Hollister, Watsonville, and Santa Cruz. When the railroad bypassed San Juan Bautista in 1876, the town's boom years ended. The stable has been restored to look much as it did during that heyday and contains an assortment of carriages and wagons as well as harness and tack.

Next to the stable stands the Plaza Hall, built by Zanetta from adobe bricks left on the site after the demolition of what had been a barracks for soldiers or a dormitory for the unmarried Indian women of the mission. Hoping that San Juan would become the seat of the newly formed San Benito County, Zanetta built the two-story building to serve as the county courthouse. When Hollister won that honor, Zanetta remodeled the first floor to house his family and the second for public meetings and celebrations.

FREMONT PEAK

A side trip of some interest takes off from CA 156 along San Juan Canyon Road (County Road G1). Eleven miles south of town stands Fremont Peak State Park, where Bvt. Capt. John Frémont and his men raised the American flag atop the highest peak they could find. When, in March 1846, Frémont had appeared in Monterey, he was ordered by military commander Col. José Castro to leave the state. Ever defiant of authority, Frémont led his men to the top of Gabilan Peak overlooking the San Benito and Salinas Valleys, Monterey Bay, and the Santa Lucia Mountains. There the disobedient soldiers camped for three days before finally deciding—reluctantly—that they'd better comply with Castro's order.

In November of 1846, after the outbreak of war between Mexico and the United States, Frémont returned to San Juan (as a lieutenant colonel in the U.S. Army) and spent almost two weeks gathering horses, mules, and supplies for his little army. Nearly seven weeks after leaving the area, Frémont managed to meet with Andrés Pico at Campo de Cahuenga to sign the treaty that ended hostilities between Mexico and the Californians.

HOLLISTER

This portion of the side trip returns to CA 156, having added twenty-two miles to the distance to Monterey, and continues. Eight miles east of San Juan Bautista on CA 156 sits Hollister, named for Col. William Hollister, the first man to drive sheep across the country. Frank Norris gathered material for his novel *The Octopus* here and Niven Busch wrote *The Hate Merchants* in an office overlooking San Benito Street, the town's main street. One hot Sunday in 1947 a small army of motorcycle riders invaded the little city, inspiring the movie *The Wild Ones,* starring Marlon Brando. Some of the picture was filmed in Hollister.

Hollister's claim to fame, however, isn't literary or cinematic, but geologic, for the town sits at the conjunction of the San Andreas, Calaveras, Hayward, and Tres Pinos Faults. As might be expected, it is the scene of frequent small earthquakes and some rather big ones. Scarcely an unbroken sidewalk exists in the town, and residents used to claim they hardly noticed the shakings until the town suffered extensive damage from the Loma Prieta quake.

To return to US 101, the route retraces itself along CA 156, adding another twenty miles to the distance to Monterey.

SALINAS

Seventeen miles south of its junction with CA 156, US 101 reaches Salinas, at the northern end of the Salinas Valley, between the Gabilan Mountains and the Santa Lucia Range. Salinas was founded in 1856 and incorporated in 1874. The seat of Monterey County, it's best known as the birthplace of Nobelist author John Steinbeck and the home of the Smucker jam and jelly processing facility. The author's boyhood home at 132 Central Avenue is beautifully preserved and is being used as a nonprofit luncheon restaurant. The Salinas Valley is the state's leading producer of lettuce, which adds almost $600 million annually to California's coffers. Strawberries, mushrooms, and asparagus thrive here, too. Every July since 1910, Salinas has been the scene of one of the largest rodeos in the nation.

The grounds on which that lively event takes place each year stir up shameful memories for some Californians. The plaque on the historical marker standing at 940 North Main Street explains: "This monument is dedicated to the 3,586 Monterey Bay area residents of Japanese ancestry, most of whom were American citizens, temporarily confined in the Salinas Rodeo Grounds during World War II, from April to July 1942." Such infamous holding centers were scattered over the state; they now serve as mute reminders of injustices done in the name of national security.

One of the principal players in the history of the Salinas Valley was William Edward Petty Hartnell, who was born in England in 1798 and came to California in 1822 as the agent for a shopkeeper in Lima, Peru. His first deal was a good one, with the padre at Mission San Miguel who agreed to sell all of the mission's output of tallow and hides to Hartnell's principal. Anne Fisher writes that Hartnell became a Catholic, married Maria Teresa de la Guerra, and received a handsome land grant, part of which included a lovely area known as the Alisal. In 1834 Hartnell established there the College of San Jose, which opened with fifteen students.

For years Hartnell was much the man of affairs in the Monterey Bay area. From 1833 to 1836 he served as an agent for the Russians. In 1839 Governor Juan Bautista Alvarado named him inspector of the missions, and in 1849 he was appointed translator to the constitutional convention in Monterey. When he died in 1854 he left his widow in straitened circumstances, and David Jacks took over much of the Alisal. According to Fisher, Doña Teresa somehow managed to regain control of her husband's prime property, failed college and all.

Because of the problem of traveling back and forth between the coastal route, CA 1 and US 101, much of this portion of the state has to be seen in side trips. One of them now leaves Salinas heading southeast on US 101, to see Spreckels and the Missions Soledad and San Antonio.

SPRECKELS

Production of sugar from beets began in the state in the 1870s, but Claus Spreckels was first to do it with real success. In the 1890s the sugar baron founded a community named for himself just south of Salinas after gaining a virtual monopoly on processing sugarcane from Hawaii.

Having succeeded in improving the sugar beet so that it would grow in the Salinas Valley, Spreckels planted thousands of acres of the ugly roots and in 1899 built what Fisher says was at the time the largest sugar processing plant in the world. Japanese laborers who had worked in the barley fields turned their talents to the sugar beet fields and were soon thriving.

Henry T. Oxnard followed Spreckels in the beet sugar business, establishing a processing plant at the town named for him. By 1917, 137,000 acres of sugar beets in California were producing more than 200,000 tons of sugar each year and Spreckels had given up processing cane.

Soledad

Thirty-six miles south of Salinas on US 101 stands Soledad, locale of the correctional facility that was the setting for the 1970 killing of a prison guard that led to political unrest and the taking of hostages. The so-called Soledad Brothers were three unrelated black prisoners who were incarcerated in the Soledad facility. The brother of one of them took hostages at a San Rafael courthouse, demanding the release of the Soledad trio in return for the freedom of his hostages. The melee ended with the death of four persons, including a judge. Angela Davis, a former assistant professor at UCLA, was accused of smuggling a gun to the kidnapper. After a highly publicized trial, she was acquitted of any complicity in the affair.

One and one-half miles south of the city, just off the freeway, stands the Richardson Adobe, a well-preserved house that has seen much of the history of the area. It stands on what was Los Coches Rancho, granted to María Josefa Soberanes de Richardson in 1841. Her husband, William Brunner Richardson (no relation to the man for whom Richardson Bay is named) built the house for her in 1843 and planted the trees in 1846. In 1846 and 1847 it was headquarters for Frémont's encampment. Subsequently used as a stage coach stop and post office, the property was acquired by David Jacks in 1865 for about $3,000, a small fraction of its value. Fifty years later the Jacks Corporation, wanting to sell the property, had to pay an additional $10,000 to the heirs of Doña Soberanes to clear the title. One of Jack's descendants deeded the property to the state in 1958.

Nuestra Señora de la Soledad

About a mile along nearby Fort Romie Road (County Road G17) stands Mission Nuestra Señora de la Soledad, Our Lady of Solitude. Dedicated in 1791 by Father Lasuén, the mission was slow in developing. It was six years before the permanent church was completed, because there were few natives in the isolated area to convert and put to work. Eventually the mission did prosper, however, with crops flourishing and herds multiplying; by 1800 the mission counted five hundred neophytes. It reached its population peak in 1820 when conversions, according to *The California Missions*, totaled more than 2,000. José Joaquín de Arrillaga, twice Spanish governor of Alta California, died while visiting here in 1814 and was buried under the church floor. His grave was obliterated during a flood and was discovered during the most recent reconstruction.

Floods were a common plague; the nearby Salinas River rose to wash away mission buildings and crops in 1824, 1828, and again in 1832. A few years later secularization finished the destruction. By 1843 almost nothing was left of the once-proud mission. The building's decay was hastened when its roof tiles were sold to Governor Alvarado for use on his new summer home, leaving the water-soluble adobe bricks exposed to the elements. Now a mission of the parish church of Soledad, the chapel and the padres' wing have been restored, both under the auspices of the Native Daughters of the Golden West.

MISSION SAN ANTONIO DE PADUA

One more spot of history remains to be explored in this side trip, another mission. Those who believe "when you've seen one mission, you've seen 'em all" might do well to return to the Monterey Road (CA 68) at this point. History buffs who realize that each mission has a different tale to tell will continue on US 101 for twenty miles to County Road G14. Twenty-three miles southwest on that road, in the middle of Hunter Liggett Military Reservation, stands San Antonio de Padua, the third mission established in California.

Most of the story of San Antonio is happy. Founded by Father Serra in 1791 in a pleasant basin studded with oaks, alders, and willows and watered by a fresh stream, it quickly drew the attention of friendly natives. They came in droves with gifts of acorns, pine nuts, and wild seeds, which they presented in return for shiny beads and trinkets handed out by the padres. One of them was Father Buenaventura Sitjar, who labored at San Antonio for thirty-seven years, guiding the neophytes and overseeing the building of a gristmill and a system of dams and aqueducts that delivered water to the fields. He also wrote a grammar of the Mutsun language, spoken by natives of the area.

With secularization the Indians were driven away; without parishioners the mission couldn't survive. Abandoned for forty-six years, it fell into ruins, helped along by plunderers who carried away construction materials of every kind. But the decay of the missions had a bright side, hard as that might be to imagine.

A band of concerned Californians led by Joseph R. Knowland, *Oakland Tribune* publisher and U.S. senator, formed the California Historic Landmarks League, dedicated to the preservation of the missions. After an intense fund-raising effort, the group set to work in 1903 to restore Mission San Antonio de Padua as their first project. Completed in 1907, that restoration remained until the Hearst Foundation and the Franciscans of California in 1948 underwrote another, more extensive one. Thanks to that effort, the mission is now an accurate replica of the original 1813 version, well worth traveling so far to explore.

The route now returns to US 101 and heads back again toward Salinas and Monterey. This long side trip adds 109 miles to the journey to Monterey.

Monterey, California's Political Birthplace

Near the center of Salinas, the route leaves US 101 to swoop in a seventeen-mile arc along scenic CA 68 to the northern edge of the Monterey Peninsula. Through wooded acres it goes, past the golf club and airport, to arrive at one of the most densely historic places in the state—the Plymouth Colony of the Pacific Coast, perhaps, or the Williamsburg of the West. For here the history of California—and much of the United States—got its start. San Francisco may have been home to the gold rush, and Los Angeles to oil wells and movies, but Monterey is the true setting for the state's political birth as part of the United States.

It was here that Vizcaíno landed in 1602 to name the bay and claim the surrounding land for Spain; it was here that both Spanish and Mexican governments tried in vain to direct the course of Alta California. Portolá and Crespí landed here in 1770, followed in short order by Junípero Serra. Almost simultaneously they established the presidio and the mission: San Carlos Borromeo de Carmelo.

The mission joyously founded in 1770 couldn't survive in Monterey. Few Indians were available to convert, the presidio and its bad influences were too close, and crops wouldn't do well in the damp and foggy climate. So Serra moved the mission in 1771 to sunnier, drier Carmel. A storeroom served as chapel for the presidio until a church of stone and adobe could be built in 1775. That building was replaced in 1794 by the Royal Chapel that stands today on Church Street near Figueroa. Civic affairs of the area proceeded rapidly under the direction of don Pedro Fages, Portolá's lieutenant.

Thomas O. Larkin served the United States as consul in Monterey from 1844 to 1848. His home is one of the restored buildings in Monterey State Historic Park.
—The Bancroft Library

Today much of downtown Monterey is a state historic park, filled with reminders of Spanish days, the Mexican period, and the early American era. Almost fifty structures from the past line the streets in the heart of Monterey.

In the plaza between Scott and Decatur Streets stands the old Custom House, the oldest government building on the West Coast, designated California Historic Landmark number 1. Duties collected here were the main source of revenue for the local Mexican government. Here, Commo. John Sloat ran up the American flag to signal that California had become part of the United States.

In Colton Hall on Pacific Street between Jefferson and Madison, forty-eight delegates met on the upper floor from September 1 to October 15, 1849, to draw up the constitution under which California would be admitted to the Union the following year. Built by Rev. Walter Colton, the first U.S. mayor in Monterey, the building served as a public hall and schoolhouse. With Robert Semple, Colton edited the area's first newspaper from 1836 to 1837.

The state's first theater, at Scott and Pacific Streets, was built about 1844 by Jack Swan to be a sailors' lodging. In 1848 a bunch of rowdies from Stevenson's Regiment commandeered the building to put on plays. It subsequently served as a whaling station after a lookout station on the roof was added.

Nearby, at Scott Street and Calle Principal, is the Pacific House, built as a hotel around 1835 by James McKinley. In 1850 it housed a public house and, later, law offices, a newspaper, small stores, and a ballroom. David Jacks bought the property in 1880; in 1954 Miss Margaret Jacks donated it to the state of California.

The homes of Juan Bautista Alvarado, Thomas Oliver Larkin, and Juan Bautista Cooper, Larkin's half brother, are all exquisitely preserved and open to visitors as part of the Monterey State Historic Park.

In the heart of Cannery Row, formerly a stand of eighteen smelly sardine-packing houses, is the Monterey Bay Aquarium, built on the site of the old Hovden Cannery. Largely funded by David Packard, of computer fame, the innovative two-story exhibit was adroitly designed to look almost like the building it replaced. It thus blends right in with the surrounding shops and restaurants.

When Monterey Bay Aquarium opened in October 1984, it was the largest aquarium in the world. —Monterey Bay Aquarium

The architecture of the Monterey Bay Aquarium faithfully reflects that of the site's predecessor, Hovden Cannery, which packed Portola brand sardines until the 1950s. —Monterey Bay Aquarium

A forty-three-foot gray whale replica, complete with calf, welcomes visitors to the Monterey Bay Aquarium. —Monterey Bay Aquarium

*The Kelp Forest presents a diver's
view of the seaweed community
along California's central coast.*
—Monterey Bay Aquarium

CA 1
Monterey–San Luis Obispo
131 miles

What has been called "the slowest way between Carmel and Monterey" is also the most scenic: the Seventeen Mile Drive. In the 1880s, guests of the Hotel Del Monte in Monterey enjoyed driving along the coast, around the Monterey Peninsula to Carmel. They made the day-long excursion in stages drawn by four and six horses, with a stopover for lunch at what is now the eighteenth fairway of Pebble Beach golf course. Today the drive is entirely within Del Monte Forest, a private preserve of more than 5,000 acres with nine miles of spectacular ocean frontage. It is a toll road. The entrance to use is called the Highway 1 Gate; the route bears north from the gate and swings through the heart of the peninsula toward the coast, passing panoramic views of Monterey Bay and the Gabilan Mountains. It reaches the sea at Spanish Bay, where Portolá camped in 1769 when he was searching for the elusive Monterey

Bay. Visible from Point Joe, since earliest days of exploration mistaken for the entrance to Monterey Bay, is one of the few places on earth where ocean currents meet, creating turbulence on even the calmest days. At Cypress Point stands what has been called "the most photographed tree in the world," a lone Monterey cypress that leans into the ocean winds as if posing for pictures.

Carmel-by-the-Sea

The drive continues around the rest of the peninsula and to the Carmel Gate. Here is the artist colony of which Clint Eastwood was once mayor, and where eating ice cream cones in public was banned. David Starr Jordan and Gertrude Atherton praised the area's beauty and tranquility, but it was Lincoln Steffens, Upton Sinclair, Sinclair Lewis, and writers of their class who made the town famous, beyond what its setting had already done.

San Carlos Borromeo de Carmelo

The town's earliest fame, however, rested on being the site of Father Serra's second mission: San Carlos Borromeo de Carmelo. Many authorities say it is the most beautiful of all the missions. The building that stands today at the southwest corner of Lasuen Drive and Del Rio Road in Carmel is the seventh to stand there. The very first, a crude log shelter, was raised in 1771, when Serra moved the mission because he deemed Monterey unsuitable. He searched the hillsides and valleys until he found this spot in Carmel Valley, less than one-half mile from the sea.

Even though he was seldom there, Serra's headquarters were at Borromeo, where he maintained a tiny cell some yards from the church. Restoration of the church building to its present state began in the 1930s; it is today considered one of the most carefully researched and reconstructed of the churches in the mission system. It is classified as a basilica because of its connection with Father Serra.

The route now continues along CA 1, this portion of which was the brainchild of Dr. John Roberts, according to the Federal Writers' Project guide. In 1897, the story goes, Roberts had for patients the residents of isolated ranches south of Monterey. Riding horseback over the mountains of the Santa Lucia Range, he learned every canyon and foothill. Later he hiked along the coast between Monterey and San Luis Obispo, planning the road that he eventually convinced the state legislature to approve in 1919. Work began the following year and hundreds of men labored to complete, by 1937, the section of this most scenic road between Carmel and San Simeon.

POINT LOBOS

Just south of Carmel the road passes Point Lobos, a rocky promontory that landscape artists have described as the greatest meeting of
land and water in the world. Trees and grasses bow deeply before winds
that sweep almost constantly across the point, the northernmost habitat
of the brown pelican and the southernmost of the Monterey cypress.

POINT SUR LIGHT STATION

Nineteen miles south of Monterey, the Point Sur light has withstood
fierce winds for almost one hundred years to warn mariners of the rocky
seas below. A sandbar connects the rocky point to the mainland.

Although the SS *Los Angeles* had wrecked nearby in 1872 and almost
all on board perished, it was the wreck of the *Ventura* in 1879 that
aroused interest in a lighthouse on this point. Other ships that have gone
down on Point Sur's rocks include the *Rhine Maru*, the *Panama*, and
the *S. Catania* in 1930 and, as recently as 1956, the *Howard Olson*.
Shipwrecks weren't unmitigated disasters; they always meant new supplies for the folks on shore. When the ships broke up, their cargoes of
lumber, foodstuffs, trade goods, and the like floated ashore for the local
population to salvage.

Visible from the highway are huge stone buildings that make up the
Point Sur State Historic Park. While the lighthouse itself remains the
property of the Coast Guard, the other buildings belong to the state
parks system. Here are the lighthouse with its forty-foot central lamp
tower and smaller extensions at north and south ends, the head keeper's
dwelling, the blacksmith shop, the barn, and the pump house and cistern.

SAN SIMEON AND HEARST CASTLE

The narrow black ribbon that is CA 1 continues winding along the
exquisite coastline, over deep chasms spanned by bridges that look more
like the work of spiders than structures of concrete and stone. Around
hairpin curves it swoops, climbing to a thousand feet and plunging down
almost within range of the sea spray. Continuing past Big Sur State Park
and the Los Padres National Forest for seventy miles, the road reaches
San Simeon, the setting for the fabulous Hearst Castle, a state historical
monument.

On a hilltop in the Santa Lucia Mountains, overlooking the sea,
stands La Cuesta Encantada, the Enchanted Hill, William Randolph
Hearst's estate of 165 rooms amid 127 acres of gardens. Designed by
Julia Morgan in the Mediterranean style, the estate includes the main
building known as La Casa Grande, three guest houses, and indoor and

La Casa Grande, the main house, at Hearst San Simeon State Historical Monument. The palatial estate was the home of newspaper publisher William Randolph Hearst.
—Ken Raveill, Hearst San Simeon State Historical Monument

outdoor pools, all surrounded by lavish gardens, huge trees, and landscaping that involved moving tons of soil into place on the estate. Workmen labored almost twenty-eight years to create a home for the man who at one time published twenty-six newspapers and sixteen magazines. His California publications included the *Examiner* and *Call-Bulletin* of San Francisco, the *Examiner* and *Herald-Express* of Los Angeles, and the *Oakland Post-Enquirer*. He exerted an immense influence over California journalism, politics, and culture. Walton Bean comments that he wielded an enormous amount of power for a man who never entirely ceased to be a spoiled child.

Hearst's wife, Millicent, never lived in his mansion; he shared it with actress Marion Davies, who appeared in forty-six movies, all of which were produced by Hearst's Cosmopolitan Productions. He was an avid fan of aviation, a pioneer in producing newsreels and movies, and a passionate collector of silver, tapestry, English furniture, and pottery. Hearst and Davies left San Simeon in 1947 because of his ill health. He died in Beverly Hills in 1951.

MISSION SAN MIGUEL ARCÁNGEL

The distance from San Simeon to San Luis Obispo via CA 1 is thirty-seven miles. A side trip to one more mission adds forty-two miles to that distance. The side trip starts at the junction of CA 1 and CA 46, proceeds for twenty-two miles along CA 46, and then turns north on US 101 for ten miles to reach San Miguel.

Mission San Miguel Arcángel was founded on July 25, 1797, by Father Lasuén as the sixteenth in the chain of missions. It was planned to fill in the long gap between San Antonio to the north and San Luis Obispo to the south. The first structure was a mud-roofed affair that lasted about a year; a similar, but slightly larger building replaced it. In 1806 a fire destroyed many of the mission's buildings and their contents. The fire consumed workshops and full granaries, stockpiles of wool and hides, and the church roof. It was a devastating blow, but the nearest missions contributed clothing, grain, and tools to tide the neophytes and padres over. Within a year the mission was once again functioning smoothly. A new church was planned and the Indians were kept busy making adobe bricks for future use. Construction of the new church began in 1816 and proceeded rapidly because of the ready supply of bricks. The mission is austerely simple on the outside, with a unique colonnade of arches in varied sizes and shapes. Spanish artist Estevan Munras with Indian assistants decorated the interior with bright, glowing designs. Simulated balconies, doors, and archways are painted on the walls and the elaborate reredos features a dramatic all-seeing eye above a statue of Saint Michael.

In 1846, just three days before the Stars and Stripes was raised over the customhouse at Monterey, Governor Pío Pico sold all the mission buildings except the church and priests' quarters. One of the buyers was William Reed, an English sailor and one of the many miners who fared only moderately well in the goldfields. Paying only $300 for a portion of the mission, Reed installed his family of three in one wing, while he ran a store in another part. Because he had bragged about the gold he had taken from the diggings, Reed and his family were set upon in 1849 by a band of drunken tramps looking for his hoard. The ruffians killed Reed, his family, and six servants. According to Fisher, one small child eluded the murderers and was found several days later, lost amid the tall mustard plants surrounding the mission. The maniacs who did the horrible deed were overtaken near the coast. One of them was shot on the spot, another leaped into the ocean and drowned, and the rest were taken to Santa Barbara where they were later executed.

*Pio Pico, the last Mexican
governor of California.*
—CHS/TICOR,
USC Special Collections

The side trip now proceeds forty miles south to San Luis Obispo, where US 101 joins CA 1.

CA 1/246 and US 101
San Luis Obispo–I-5
170 miles

SAN LUIS OBISPO AND MISSION SAN LUIS OBISPO DE TOLOSO

Right in the center of town and just a few blocks off CA 1—El Camino Real—stands Mission San Luis Obispo de Tolosa. Named for Saint Louis, Bishop of Toulouse, it was the fifth mission and was founded September 1, 1772, in what soldiers called La Cañada de los Osos, Valley of the Bears. San Luis Obispo, the first mission to boast a tile roof, is unique among California's missions because its belfry and vestibule are a single unit. After selecting the site, on a low hill beside a brisk stream, Father Serra departed, leaving Father José Cavaller to get the mission's business underway.

210

Most Indians of the area were friendly enough but unimpressed by gifts the padres offered. What need had they of beads and gewgaws when they lived in an area so plentifully endowed? To the south of the mission, however, lived natives who were downright hostile. In 1776 they set fire to several buildings in the compound by shooting flaming arrows into their thatched roofs. Two of those responsible were captured and sent to Monterey for punishment, but the raids continued.

The missions were obviously vulnerable to fire because of the dry tule thatch used for roofing. Recalling the tiled roofs of Spanish structures, the padres began to experiment with making tiles to replace the thatch. They found that fermented clay, tromped in pits by animals, patted over curved wooden molds, then dried in the sun, and, finally, baked in kilns, worked well. Before long, all other missions copied those red tiles, which not only protected against fire, but also kept interiors dry during the rainy season.

During the Mexican War, San Luis Obispo was the setting for a farcical skirmish between Frémont and a group of women and children who had taken to living in the mission after secularization. In the dead of night Frémont surrounded the compound with his troops, only to find at daybreak that it was occupied only by noncombatants.

St. Stephens Episcopal Church in San Luis Obispo.
—San Luis Obispo Chamber of Commerce

One of San Luis Obispo's many restored Victorian homes.
—San Luis Obispo Chamber of Commerce

Fog shrouds Morro Rock at Morro Bay. —Don DeBenedictis

After what was left of the mission was returned to the Church, it suffered a remodeling that made it look like an ordinary parish church. It remained that way until 1934, when it was restored to its former elegant simplicity.

The city of San Luis Obispo, seat of the county of the same name, is one of eight cities in the state that grew up around the missions. It is home to California Polytechnic University, established in 1901, and Ah Louis Store, the first Chinese store in the county. The store at Palm and Chorro Streets served as bank, counting house, and post office for the many Chinese laborers who dug the eight tunnels through the Mountains of Cuesta for the Southern Pacific.

Thirteen miles south of San Luis Obispo, at Pismo Beach, CA 1 separates from US 101, with the latter striking off slightly east, while CA 1 continues southward along the coast. The route follows CA 1.

Guadalupe

Guadalupe, a small town on CA 1 twelve miles south of Pismo Beach, is home to colorful fields of flowers grown for their seeds and acres of sugar beets, and sheltered from western sea breezes by great hills. But those hills rising where the Santa Maria River meets the sea aren't mounds covered with grass or chaparral; they are great golden sand dunes that shift and change at the whim of ocean gales. They conceal a treasure long buried.

More than seventy years ago Guadalupe was the location for the filming of Cecil B. DeMille's first version of *The Ten Commandments*. Amid the dunes west of town was assembled a mammoth set that included 35-foot-high statues, five-ton sphinxes, and chariots enough for *Ben Hur*. When he completed filming in 1923, DeMille directed that the entire set be dismantled and buried where it stood. Peter Brosnan, a film historian, has spent ten years locating and mapping the exact site of the relics; now he hopes to conduct a "dig" to recover all 250 tons of them. From time to time pieces of the set become visible as winds shift the sands, but they are almost as quickly covered over again.

Lompoc

CA 1 continues southward toward Point Conception, skirting Vandenberg Air Force Base, which was created to test intercontinental ballistic missiles and to launch satellites. Twenty-four miles from Guadalupe it reaches Lompoc, a city with a Chumash name, known for its fields of flowers. Here, Hart says, more than half of the world's supply of flower seeds is grown.

Segment of the original El Camino Real crosses the pathway leading to restored Mission La Purísima near Lompoc. —La Purísima Mission State Historic Park

MISSION LA PURÍSIMA CONCEPCIÓN

Five miles northeast of Lompoc on CA 246 stands a state historic park that enshrines Mission La Purísima Concepción. Father Lasuén founded this eleventh mission, named for The Immaculate Conception of Mary, on December 8, 1787, at a site in the heart of today's Lompoc. In 1812, a series of violent earthquakes reduced the thriving mission to rubble. After the third quake the hillside behind the mission opened up, and water completed the devastation.

Indomitable Padre Mariano Payeras immediately sought a safer site; he chose the little Valley of the Watercress, on the other side of the Santa Ynez River. The padres' residence was the first permanent structure to rise on the new site. Built with immense buttresses on the southwest end and walls more than four feet thick, it was intended to survive even the worst earthquakes. It couldn't survive neglect, however.

The mission flourished until the death of Father Payeras in 1823, even though the new main church crumbled at its northeast corner because it sat atop a spring. Ever resourceful, the padres raised the roof of their private chapel to permit installation of a choir loft and celebrated public masses there.

La Purísima's real place in history, however, is in the story of its reconstruction. After the missions were secularized, La Purísima suffered one indignity after another: sheep were stabled in its rooms, a blacksmith set up shop there, and it even housed a saloon. After falling almost totally into dust, it was all but forgotten, until a small group of mission lovers rallied to save it. In 1933 the Civilian Conservation Corps

Restored bell tower at Mission La Purísima guards the mission cemetery.
—Frank Pittman

Replica of a Chumash dwelling on the grounds of Mission La Purísima. —La Purísima Mission State Historic Park

(CCC) was put to work restoring the entire compound. In one of the largest historical restoration projects ever undertaken in the United States, hundreds of young men toiled for seven years to set La Purísima to rights. They used hand tools, historic methods, and materials preserved as they were excavated from rubble. They even used the crumbled adobe bricks from the original to make new bricks for the restoration. With its outbuildings and a water-supply system, La Purísima is the state's only complete mission compound.

The missions of California owe a debt of gratitude to the CCC and La Purísima, for it was there that researchers discovered—sometimes by trial and error—how to make reconstructions both faithful to the originals and safe. Lessons learned at La Purísima were put to work in restoring other California missions, and it shows.

POINT ARGUELLO

To the west of Lompoc is Point Arguello, where the coastline of the state takes a sharp turn eastward. Here, just north of Point Conception, lies an area of rocky outcroppings that, according to Glen Cunningham in the *Fedco Reporter*, crews of Spanish galleons called "the Devil's jaw." Sailors of today call it "the graveyard of ships." Shipwrecks were common in this area throughout California's history, and even as recently as 1931 a coastwise steamer, the *Harvard*, met her end on these rocks on a run from Los Angeles to San Francisco. But the tragedy that took place here on September 8, 1923, outstripped all others.

A flotilla of navy destroyers sailing single file down the coast from San Francisco and navigating by dead reckoning met a violent end when officers of the lead ship miscalculated their position. Thinking they were well south of Point Arguello, they gave orders to turn east, as they thought, into the Santa Barbara Channel. That first ship ran into a dense fog and piled up on the rocks; with flashing lights and sirens the crew tried to warn off the other ships. As the ship's generator flooded, however, the signals ceased. The other six ships dutifully followed their leader; in minutes all were grounded. Twenty-three lives and all the ships were lost. If it hadn't been for the generous residents of Lompoc and San Luis Obispo, the human toll might have been greater in what was the U.S. Navy's greatest peacetime disaster.

BUELLTON

Departing Lompoc the route travels eastward on CA 246 for eighteen miles to a wide place in the road made famous by soup. Named for a family of ranchers who settled in the area in the 1870s, the town of Buellton gained an official post office in 1920. In 1924 Anton and Juliette Andersen, once of Denmark, opened a little restaurant they christened Andersen's Electrical Cafe, in honor of their new electric stove. Situated on the state's principal north-south thoroughfare and at an east-west crossroad, the restaurant thrived. The mainstay of the menu was Juliette's family's version of split pea soup. So popular was the hearty potage that in just three years the young couple was processing a ton of peas a year at what is now called Andersen's Pea Soup Restaurant.

SOLVANG

Five miles from the intersection of US 101 and CA 246 is the Danish community of Solvang, whose name means "sunny field." Founded in 1911 by the Danish-American Corporation, it was the site of a college established by professors from Illinois. The college didn't last, but the town, with its windmills and authentic Danish architecture, flourished.

Mission Santa Inés

The area around Solvang is called the Santa Ynez Valley, a variation on the spelling of Santa Inés (Saint Agnes), the name of the nineteenth mission in the chain, which stands at the eastern edge of Solvang. It was founded in 1804 by Father Estevan Tapis and soon became famous for its herds of cattle and rich crops. In 1812, however, the great earthquake destroyed the church and damaged many of the other buildings. Rebuilding commenced almost at once, helped along by Joseph Chapman, who had been a member of the pirate Hyppolyte Bouchard's crew. When the raider left California, Chapman stayed behind, reformed, and became general handyman at Santa Inés.

Prosperity continued at the isolated mission until Mexico's independence from Spain brought on the Indian revolt of 1824. When Mexico stopped sending money to the missions in 1821, the padres were forced to feed their assigned soldiers from their own slim cupboards. It was the Indians, of course, who bore the brunt of the soldiers' discontent. After a guard at Santa Inés flogged a neophyte from Purísima, the Indians rebelled. The ensuing fight—muskets against bows and arrows—resulted in the death of two Indians and in fires that destroyed much of the mission. Having no quarrel with the padres, the Indians helped to quench the flames.

When military reinforcements arrived from Santa Barbara the day after the fight, the Indians fled to La Purísima. A battle that lasted three hours took place near the mission, with the Indians hopelessly outgunned. Sixteen Indians were killed and many wounded; only one soldier died.

The military exacted a severe price for the uprising: seven Indians were executed and eighteen others imprisoned.

Order was eventually restored and reconstruction got underway, only to be overtaken by secularization. Half of Mission Santa Inés became home to a local family while the padres lived in the other half. Then, from 1844 to 1846, the mission served as temporary quarters for The College of Our Lady of Refuge of Sinners, a seminary.

Neglected for years, Santa Inés crumbled, with the pulpit collapsing under an astonished priest one Sunday in the 1860s. In 1904 Father Alexander Buckler, then pastor of the mission, began a long-term program of restoration. Less than a quarter of the original compound was restored, including the campanario with its three bells, rebuilt in 1948. *The California Missions* says the church interior today probably looks much the way it did around 1817.

SAN MARCOS PASS ROAD

From Solvang there are two ways to get to Santa Barbara: by US 101, about fifty miles, mostly along the ocean, or across thirty twisting miles, past Lake Cachuma, and over San Marcos Pass. Since two spots of historical interest lie along the shorter route, it becomes the way for this journey.

San Marcos Pass Road, CA 154, intersects CA 246 just east of the mission. The route travels south along CA 154 past the artificial reservoir named Lake Cachuma and reaches San Marcos Pass, fourteen miles from Santa Ynez. The pass is a moderate one, 2,224 feet, twelve miles northeast of Santa Barbara. It was one of the passes used by early mission padres and explorers to cross from inland to the coast.

On Christmas Eve, 1846, the settler Benjamin Foxen led Frémont over this pass, while to the west, at much-lower Gaviota Pass, a troop of Californios lay in wait. They wanted to prevent Frémont from reaching Los Angeles to reinforce Commodore Stockton and his men. A modest climb for today's automobiles, the San Marcos trail was difficult for men and horses, and it took the Americans the entire day to swing their artillery pieces across one deep chasm after another, on ropes. Once at the summit of the pass, Foxen's eldest son, William, guided them; having successfully eluded the Californios, the Americans occupied Santa Barbara on Christmas Day.

Slightly more than two miles from the foot of the pass (eight miles from US 101), Painted Cave Road exits CA 154 toward the north. It's a small road, poorly marked and easy to miss. Two miles along that road on the left is one of the smallest of all the state's historic sites:

Chumash Painted Cave State Historic Park. There, beside the road, with space for only a single car to park and no room to turn around, is a cave that contains some of the finest examples of native art in the country.

Dolan Eargle says Chumash rock paintings are some of the most imaginative in the United States. Several yellowish sandstone caves containing examples of those works lurk in this small park, but only the one beside the road is accessible to the public. Barred to protect it from vandals and quite dark, its walls still gleam with the vivid reds and yellows, whites and blacks, with which they were decorated two or three hundred years ago. Centipedes are depicted, as are wheels, crosses, and fanciful leaves. Some experts suggest that the artists had to be under the sway of a hallucinogen like jimsonweed to create such images.

This little side trip adds four miles to the distance between Santa Ynez and Santa Barbara.

SANTA BARBARA

Santa Barbara's history begins with the Chumash who inhabited about 7,000 square miles in the central California coastal region. Burton Mound, a historical landmark on Mason Street at Burton Circle, is believed to have been the Chumash village Syujtun (or Syuhtun), the middle of their range. Cabrillo noted the village in 1542, as did Father Crespí and Portolá in 1769. This site has been the source of some of the most important archaeological evidence found in the state. Excavations conducted in 1923 revealed that three distinct native cultures have lived on the site. Many of the relics unearthed, such as sandstone bowls so smooth they might have been turned on a lathe, show unusual beauty and pride in artistic excellence.

Just a few blocks north of the mound, at Santa Barbara and Canyon Perdido Streets, is El Presidio de Santa Barbara State Historic Park. Here only one building and part of another remain of what was military headquarters for all the territory between Los Angeles and San Luis Obispo from 1782 until 1846. It was established so the government could control the natives and protect settlers of this large area. Still standing are the guards' house and an adobe dwelling. The padres' quarters and the chapel are reconstructions on original foundations. Restoration work continues.

Nearby stands the adobe home of the De la Guerra family, begun in 1819 by mission Indians and completed in 1826. The De la Guerras were one of the first families of early Santa Barbara; the daughter, María Teresa, married William Hartnell of Salinas.

Mission Santa Bárbara

Two miles to the northwest, at the end of Laguna Street, is Santa Bárbara, the tenth mission, founded in 1786 by Father Lasuén. It was the second of three that Father Serra had dreamed would bridge the distance from San Gabriel to San Luis Obispo. Because Serra died in 1784, it was left to Lasuén to choose the site and get the mission started. The first buildings were formed of logs and roofed with reeds daubed with mud. Over time the traditional quadrangle was completed with the addition of an adobe dormitory, kitchen, and storeroom. Outbuildings included more than two hundred homes for the Indians, a tannery, pottery, and warehouse. The mission's water system was so remarkable that, according to *The California Missions*, parts of it are still used by Santa Barbara's water company.

As the mission prospered, new and larger churches were built to accommodate all the neophytes. Almost destroyed by the earthquake of 1812, the third church was patched up while another was being built. This church, largely the one that stands today, was dedicated in 1820. In 1925, a severe quake damaged this edifice, but California rallied to the cause, raising nearly $400,000 for repairs. Over the ensuing years, other refurbishing has been required, but the only mission with two grand towers is today called Queen of the Missions.

Santa Barbara, the city we know today, got its start as a winter resort for families enriched by the Civil War, who were looking for ways to spend their spare time and money. According to Stephan Birmingham, settlers from the post-war days included the Mortons of salt fame, the Fleischmanns of yeast, and the Hammonds of organs. In the 1920s architect George Washington Smith employed a Spanish style when rebuilding homes and public buildings damaged by the 1925 earthquake. Birmingham calls Smith's style both extreme and expensive, with vaulted ceilings, bell towers, balconies, and courtyards. Today the city is determinedly Spanish, with shopping districts and a courthouse in that style.

It wouldn't be right to leave Santa Barbara without seeing its famous Moreton Bay fig tree growing at the corner of Montecito and Chapala Streets, close to US 101 Freeway. A young girl in 1877 planted the fig, which *The California Missions* describes as the largest tree of its kind in the United States. Today its 160-foot spread of branches could shelter 10,000 persons.

CARPENTERIA

The journey to Ventura resumes on US 101 heading down the coast toward Los Angeles. Twelve miles from Santa Barbara is Carpenteria, site of a Chumash settlement. According to Hoover, Father Crespí of Portolá's cortege wrote that in 1769 the party discovered springs where Indians caulked their canoes with asphaltum. The padre named the village "Carpenter Shop."

Ventura

A little more than thirteen miles farther along on US 101 is Ventura, seat of the county of that same name. Most historians agree that Cabrillo landed in the neighborhood of Ventura in 1542 and Portolá and Anza camped there in 1769 and 1774. It is also the setting for Mission San Buenaventura, the ninth and last that Padre Serra dedicated.

Mission San Buenaventura

It was planned to be the third member of the mission chain, but local events interfered and San Buenaventura's founding was put off until Easter Sunday, March 31, 1782. Construction of a chapel, dwelling, and stockade began at once, after Father Serra celebrated mass on the site. Local Chumash were happy to help with the building in return for beads and other trifles. But, *The California Missions* tells us, the Chumash were intelligent and wary and thus were slow to give up their freedom for confinement within the mission compound.

The first mission church was destroyed by fire within ten years, and construction of a stone one was begun. That building was completed in 1809, only to be severely damaged by the 1812 earthquake. Within a year, however, repairs were completed and a huge buttress added beside the front entrance. Save for the threat of a visit from the pirate Bouchard in 1818 and a brawl with hostile Mojaves, life at Buenaventura was for the most part filled with prosperity and peace. The gardens, in particular, flourished, blessed with an excellent climate and an ingenious water system designed by the padres. In 1794 Capt. George Vancouver visited the mission and carried away twenty mule-loads of green vegetables and fruits with which to provision his ship anchored at Santa Barbara.

Under secularization the mission was stripped of all its lands, but the church survived to serve the parish. In 1893 the resident priest tore down all the outer buildings and inflicted dubious changes on the church interior itself. He installed stained glass, painted over the original Chumash designs, and removed an exquisite wooden pulpit that hung from one wall. Fortunately, someone hid from this well-intentioned bungler the two bells carved from two-foot blocks of wood that were used during Holy Week when metal bells must be silent. They are now in the mission museum that was built in 1929. The church, too, was saved, undergoing restoration that was completed in 1957.

At the intersection of Poli Street and North California Street stands the Ventura County courthouse, an outstanding example of neoclassic architecture, a style widely popular in the United States at the turn of the century. Designed by Albert C. Martin Sr., the building was dedicated in 1913.

One segment remains to be explored in this look at the Central Coast of California. Several other sites of historical interest are found in the area, but they will be examined in part 7, the section about the greater Los Angeles area. This route travels east on CA 126 (Telegraph Road) for thirty miles, to meet I-5, where the trek through Los Angeles starts.

SANTA PAULA AND PIRU

Santa Paula, twelve miles east of Ventura, was originally the site of Mupu, a village where the Chumash who helped build San Buenaventura lived. Oranges and lemons were introduced into the area in 1875. In 1883, oil exploration began, and the first oil refinery was built here in 1887.

Twenty-two miles east of Santa Paula, near Piru, is Rancho Camulos, a portion of a land grant made to Antonio De Valle by Governor Juan Alvarado. After visiting here, Helen Hunt Jackson made this adobe the setting for her novel *Ramona*, describing the home in great detail. A state historical marker denotes the site.

Santa Paula, Fillmore, and Piru are linked by more than just CA 126. They all suffered a night of terror back in 1928. Since the cause of the terror was located in Los Angeles County, the disaster will be looked at in the next section of this book.

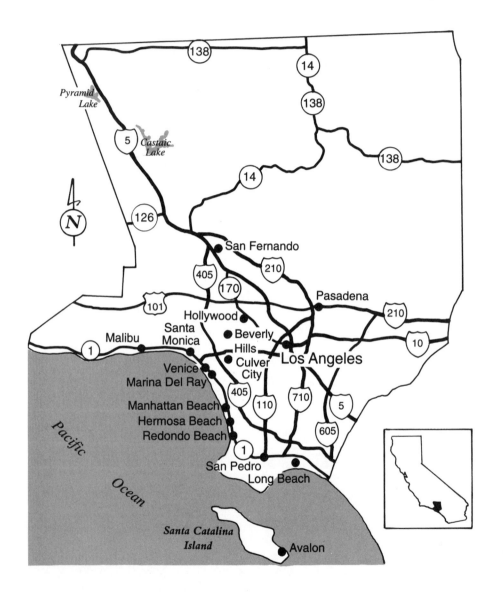

Part 7

Los Angeles, Paradise Plagued

One question that arises when exploring Los Angeles is where does it begin and end? What is L.A. and what is not? When you're in Hollywood, say, or Hyde Park or Venice, you're in Los Angeles; when you're in Santa Monica, Beverly Hills, or El Segundo, you are not. A host of other communities are either part of Los Angeles or simply neighbors. And it really doesn't matter, except on election day. It's all L.A.

The area that is now Los Angeles entered the pages of recorded history in 1542 when Cabrillo named San Pedro Harbor the Bay of Smokes because of the many campfires staining the air over twenty-eight Indian villages in the area. One of those villages, Yang-na, is known to have been at the center of today's downtown.

Herbert Bolton cites missionary Juan Crespí as having told his diary in 1769 of a river Portolá named Porciuncula and a plain generously endowed with cottonwoods and alders. His was the first recorded sighting by a nonnative of the Los Angeles plain. Portolá's party also saw the gooey pits of Rancho La Brea and explored the San Fernando Valley.

Another ten years passed, however, before Felipe de Neve founded a pueblo he named la Reina de los Angeles ("the Queen of the Angels") in 1781, populating it with forty-four settlers from Sinaloa. Even then the population was ethnically diverse, with Indians and blacks well represented among the Spaniards. By the beginning of the nineteenth century, some 315 persons lived in thirty adobes. Although geographically isolated, the settlement was most populous of all the pueblos in California.

Los Angeles was even considered for the honor of being provincial capital in 1816, but Monterey prevailed. Before too long the likes of Joseph Chapman, pirate turned carpenter; John Temple, real estate wizard; and William Wolfskill, who covered the area with orange groves, arrived to help shape Los Angeles. At the outbreak of the Mexican War, U.S. forces seized the city, but it was quickly lost when Angelenos revolted against the harsh rule of Lt. Archibald Gillespie of the marines.

Los Angeles, circa 1873, looking north from the junction of Main and Spring Streets at Ninth Street. —CHS/TICOR, USC Special Collections

When Mexican rule ended, the city was poised for greatness, but the gold rush diverted the world's attention to the north and turned Los Angeles into little more than a ghost town. It grew, though slowly, thanks to the port at Wilmington (courtesy of Phineas Banning) and two railroads: the Southern Pacific and Santa Fe. Stephan Birmingham writes that even after the state was admitted to the Union, Los Angeles was a sluggish, dispirited town where lynch law prevailed.

Controversy has never been foreign to Los Angeles; it seemed to be born with the pueblo. For example, according to John McKinney in a *Los Angeles Times* article, soon after Mission San Fernando was founded in 1799, the padres dammed the Los Angeles River to provide for their water needs. Thirsty settlers downstream took exception, claiming the water was rightfully theirs. So began the first of the many water disputes that continue today.

Today's Los Angeles River is all but a nonentity. Concrete lined for most of its length, it drains the San Fernando Valley and rushes runoff water to the sea. Modern disagreements pit environmentalists pushing to have the river restored to its original state against those favoring a variety of other uses, including at least one assemblyman who sees it as an eight-lane, high-speed motorway.

Over the years water rights have been determined by laissez-faire, localism, and monopolies, making it possible for some entrepreneurs to grow rich—sometimes through scheming and skullduggery—by grabbing control of water rights and then selling them to drought-plagued farmers or thirsty towns. C. C. Wright, a lawyer from Modesto, got himself elected to the state senate so he could push through a bill allowing for the formation of water districts, the Wright Irrigation Act of 1887. That law, in much-amended form, still rules water distribution in California today. It made possible the agriculture industry that created the state's wealth.

The Wright Act provided water principally for farmers, however, so experiments with other methods of water regulation were launched. These included mutual water companies devised by Mormons. They were business ventures owned and controlled by stockholders who held not only the water rights, but also the rights to build dams and distribution canals.

Other communities sought other means of getting water, and few means were more colorful than the rainmakers, of whom Charles Hatfield was the star. Early in the twentieth century this Glendale resident became famous for contracts he signed with several Southern California cities, including San Diego.

Residents of the tiny community of Malibou Lake, in the Santa Monica Mountains above Malibu Creek State Park, made a similar effort in 1961. When the dam that created the lake needed inspection in 1959, state officials drained two-thirds of the lake's water, expecting winter rains to replace it. Little rain fell, so Edmond Jeffery was summoned. He arrived with twenty-five feet of scaffolding and a reputation as a rainmaker who had learned his craft from Hatfield, dead these several years.

Each morning Jeffery climbed to the top of his scaffolding tower and hoisted up chemicals from an aide below. After burning those chemicals for four days, Jeffery had produced little more than some high clouds and reports that it might be drizzling in Agoura, almost five miles away. Air quality officials fretted about the smoke; Jeffery insisted it would keep mosquitoes away and went right on firing up to earn the $250 plus room and board he was being paid. On the eighth day a light drizzle fell, resulting, weather officials said, from a storm front that reached from San Francisco to San Diego. Jeffery claimed credit for the moisture. Lake Malibou officials debated paying him $2,000 more to stay until the lake was full. The motion lost and Jeffery left town. The lake was filled by natural means later that same season.

Jeffery was just performing a somewhat unconventional version of the cloud seeding that captured the fancy of county officials in the 1940s. Seeders put into clouds chemicals of one kind or another that cause moisture to precipitate from the clouds. There has been no consensus

William Mulholland—hero to thirsty residents of Los Angeles, villain to those who lived in the Owens Valley. Long erroneously believed to be responsible for the St. Francis Dam disaster. —The Bancroft Library

on the success of these efforts, but Angelenos were astonished to learn, during the floods of 1993, that Los Angeles County officials were still paying cloud seeders who had been under contract for years. (They were called off that year, when homes started sliding down hillsides because the entire area was saturated.)

One man who promised to deliver water to Los Angeles succeeded. He is today both hailed as a hero and condemned as a villain of, well, the first water. That man is William Mulholland. The system that delivered the promised water wasn't Mulholland's brainchild, however; the man who conceived it was Fred Eaton, a city engineer and mayor of Los Angeles from 1899 to 1901.

James Hart credits Eaton as being a very civic-minded Angeleno, responsible for the city's park system, particularly Pershing Square. Eaton also had a hand in founding Los Angeles's electric railway. His greatest coup, however, was starting the Owens Valley Project.

For years Eaton had spent his vacations scouting around for more water for his thirsty city. At last he saw the answer in the Owens River, which rises on the eastern slope of the Sierra Nevada above Mono Lake. Believing that a large reservoir at the upper end of the supply line would be vital to the success of the project, Eaton bought land and water rights in Long Valley, north of the Owens Valley. His goal was to make the water system a private enterprise that would benefit both himself and Los Angeles when he sold part of the water to irrigate the Owens Valley and the rest to Los Angeles.

In 1904 Los Angeles faced the prospect of an actual water famine. Population had more than doubled to 250,000 in the preceding five years, while rainfall was far below normal. Now William Mulholland pressed Eaton for details of his plan to bring water from the Owens Valley. Agreeing that his friend's scheme would work, Mulholland predicted the solution to the city's chronic water shortage could be had for under $25 million.

Eaton went quietly about the Owens Valley, buying up land and water rights necessary to the plan. In 1905 Los Angeles voters approved it, first authorizing start-up money and then, in 1907, approving a bond issue of more than $23 million to build the system. Construction began in 1908. Residents of the Owens Valley weren't asked for their opinions.

A crew of 5,000 men, working through winters that seemed arctic and summers that rivaled hell, completed in five years a task that even by today's standards would be considered daunting. They built a system of aqueducts 232 miles long, including 142 tunnels that totaled 53 of those miles. The rest of the delivery system consists of three large reservoirs and both open and covered canals that cross the Mojave Desert, climb the San Gabriel Mountains, and drop into the San Fernando Valley. It was November of 1913 when the system was finished, at almost exactly the cost Mulholland had predicted.

Since the Owens River flows several thousand feet above the city, water running to Los Angeles has to drop a great distance, producing a vast amount of hydroelectric energy. Ignoring the protests of private power companies, such as Southern California Edison, the city took charge of all that power, starting in 1916 with a generating plant in San Francisquito Canyon. Los Angeles thus became a principal player in the light and power business.

Everyone except the residents of the Owens Valley deemed the water-delivery system an unqualified success. Almost everyone involved, especially those who had the foresight to buy up San Fernando Valley land, profited enormously. And all that water made the growth and development of the San Fernando Valley a foregone conclusion.

It wasn't only water that accounted for the phenomenal growth of the Los Angeles area. Gold was discovered near the San Fernando Mission in 1842, six years before Marshall's find on the American River. The field quickly played out. The Southern Pacific Railroad arrived in Southern California in 1876, followed in 1885 by the Santa Fe. Seven years

Los Angeles, looking south from Broadway.
—CHS/TICOR,
USC Special Collections

later Edward Doheny discovered oil in the heart of the city, at Second Street and Glendale Boulevard. All these events inspired boom times for Los Angeles—short-lived booms, for the most part.

It was the coming of the moviemakers that really put the city on the map. In 1911 the Nestor Company rented an old tavern and barn at Sunset Boulevard and Gower Street and started to make movies. Even though cynics thought moving pictures were a fad that would soon fade away, movies made Los Angeles. And Los Angeles seemed tailor-made for movie-making. It offered a short rainy season, long days of brilliant sunshine, and settings that cried out to be filmed: deserts, mountain tops, seashore—whatever a producer could dream up, the Los Angeles area could provide.

On the other hand, what made the whole sprawling entity work was transportation. As today's residents of the city and its suburbs fight freeway gridlock each day, they mourn the passing of the big red cars. The Pacific Electric Company extended the area's first electric rail system, started in 1895 by Moses Sherman and Eli Clark. It linked Los Angeles with Pasadena and Santa Monica and was, in large part, responsible for the growth of beach towns. The present subway that day by day inches its way toward the San Fernando Valley isn't expected to ever equal the Pacific Electric system.

230

In 1901 Henry Huntington sold his inherited interest in Southern Pacific to move to Los Angeles. Along with E. H. Harriman and others, Huntington bought out Sherman and Clark's electric line and, in 1901, incorporated it as the Pacific Electric Railway Company. The system grew dramatically, building a spur to Long Beach and acquiring most of the small independent lines in the area. When, in 1910, Huntington controlled most of the trolley service in Southern California, he sold out to Southern Pacific for a substantial profit.

At its peak in the 1920s, the Pacific Electric system carried passengers from the sea to the desert, welding forty-two communities within a thirty-five-mile radius into a single burgeoning body. It consisted of over a thousand miles of track and carried more than a million passengers each year. The lines that ran to Santa Monica and Venice were in large part responsible for the growth of Beverly Hills and Culver City. By 1961, however, the red cars were only a memory, replaced by automobiles on freeways.

Through the years ethnic groups, of which there are many in this culturally diverse city, have battled each other. The days of the Zoot-Suit Riots in 1943 saw clashes between young men of Mexican ancestry and "whites." Even earlier, the Chinese were scapegoats for everything

Santa Monica, 1939. —Dick Whittington, USC Special Collections

that troubled the city. African Americans have long been harassed in Los Angeles, and both the Watts riots of 1965 and the Rodney King affair of 1991 were results of such treatment of blacks. The most recent events were particularly violent because the state was in the grip of a severe recession at the time, creating extreme hardships for residents of the south-central area of the city. Looting and burning seemed to provide a relief valve for some.

The West Coast, and especially Los Angeles, has long been credited, or blamed, for starting most fads that sweep the nation from time to time. It doesn't seem appropriate to say that gangs are an L.A. invention, although they seem to have developed in Los Angeles aspects largely unknown in other cities. Leon Bing, in her outstanding study of gangs in Los Angeles, *Do or Die*, explores how gangs became a big business that influences the course of daily life in all parts of the city.

Carey McWilliams, writer and one-time state commissioner of housing and immigration, as cited by Robert Cleland, claims it is L.A.'s very diversity that makes it the perfect testing ground for every fad and cult that comes along, as well as for new styles and different manners. Cultures and customs of old worlds and new blend to create an entirely new fabric, a tapestry bright and colorful.

No matter what Easterners might say, living in Los Angeles, Southern California, isn't all surfing and skiing and dancing the latest craze all night. It's a matter of learning how to get along with people whose customs, skin colors, eye shapes, and languages are different, but who have all the same human needs. And that is why cults often get started here, but so do scientific discoveries and sociological movements that will eventually make the United States even better and stronger.

I-5, CA 170, and US 101
Santa Clarita Valley–Downtown Los Angeles
40 miles

THE SAINT FRANCIS DAM DISASTER

The darkest chapter in the saga of Los Angeles's quest for water was written near the start of this part of the historical trek through California. When CA 126 reaches I-5, a brief side trip leaves the freeway at the Saugus exit, only two miles from the junction with CA 126. At Saugus it turns north on San Francisquito Canyon Road and travels just over nine miles. There, at San Francisquito Power Plant Number Two stands a marker noting the Saint Francis Dam disaster.

On March 12, 1928, just at dusk, according to an October, 1992, article in the *Los Angeles Times*, a sightseeing family stood at the foot of the two-year-old, two hundred-foot-tall Saint Francis Dam, high in San Francisquito Canyon. The father of the little family noticed water seeping into the sandy soil at the foot of the dam. He told his wife he feared the dam was about to break and they must hurry out of harm's way.

Earlier that day, before noon, dam-keeper Tony Harnischfeger also had noticed water seepage. Charles F. Outland says the dam-keeper reported the leak to his superiors in Los Angeles, noting that the leak was passing muddy water, ominous evidence that material beneath the foot of the dam was eroding. Informed of the problem, William Mulholland and his assistant, Harvey Van Norman, hurried to the dam. The two men, with Harnischfeger, inspected it for over two hours and found no sign of a dangerous leak. Mulholland and Van Norman returned to Los Angeles in time for a late lunch. The dam-keeper went about his usual routine, but he was anxious. The coroner's inquest following the tragedy revealed that Harnischfeger had worried for weeks before March 12 that the dam would break.

And break it did, at three minutes before midnight that very night, carrying to their deaths the dam-keeper and his family, along with at least 450 others. When the dam gave way, twelve billion gallons of water formed a wall as high as a ten-story building and raced down the narrow canyon. In the first hour after the break, that water traveled nine miles, reaming out the canyon like a Roto-Rooter. Down the Santa Clara Valley it went, crushing power stations, homes, and bridges, flattening orchards. It all but erased the towns of Piru, Fillmore, Santa Paula, and Saticoy, with those on the eastern end of the valley suffering the most damage, since the water spread out and slowed as it neared the sea. Almost forty miles of devastation lay in the wake of that monstrous wave.

Within hours survivors were calling for Mulholland's head—or at least his resignation. At the inquest, he accepted full responsibility for the tragedy, and for years he bore that burden. Recent findings have shown, however, that the collapse of Saint Francis Dam was attributable to an old landslide that lay beneath its eastern edge. Geological knowledge at the time the dam site was selected simply wasn't sophisticated enough to recognize that fatal flaw, according to the *Times* article. Thus, more than fifty years after his death, Mulholland was exonerated. However, Owens Valley residents have never forgiven him for the rape of their valley. They, too, were cleared of the charge that the collapse of the dam was caused by dynamite set by disgruntled ranchers to avenge the theft of Owens Valley water.

Opening of the Los Angeles-Owens River Aqueduct on November 5, 1913.
—CHS/TICOR, USC Special Collections

The route now returns to I-5, the side trip having added twenty miles to the distance to downtown Los Angeles.

THE START OF THE PETROLEUM INDUSTRY

Just a couple of miles south of the Saugus exit is Pico Canyon Road, west of the freeway. A little more than three miles along this road stands an oil well, Pico Number Four, the first commercially productive well in the state. It was spudded in early 1876 under the direction of Demetrious G. Scofield. Producing at the rate of 150 barrels a day, it inspired the formation of the Pacific Coast Oil Company, predecessor of Standard Oil of California, and the construction nearby of the state's first refinery. The well stimulated the development of the California petroleum industry.

THE CASCADES

About eight miles south of the Saugus exit, visible from the north-bound freeway, is the Cascades, terminus of the Los Angeles-Owens River Aqueduct. It was here that Mulholland stood on November 5, 1913 and gestured at the first water tumbling down. "There it is. Take it," he is reputed to have said. According to the historical marker that stands one-tenth of a mile north of the intersection of Foothill and Balboa Boulevards, water splashing down this hill has traveled 338 miles from the eastern slopes of the Sierra Nevada.

MISSION SAN FERNANDO REY DE ESPAÑA

A little more than four miles farther along, I-5 reaches the Mission Road exit, the route of an important side trip. Just west of the freeway, one and one-half miles from the city of San Fernando, stands Mission San Fernando Rey de España (Saint Ferdinand, King of Spain). It was seventeenth of the twenty-one missions and was founded by Father Lasuén in 1797.

Lasuén selected this site, according to *The California Missions*, because the local Indians were friendly and the four springs running through it seemed to guarantee ample water for agricultural development. The compound grew steadily, reaping bountiful harvests of converts, as well as olives, fruits, nuts, dates, and field crops. Cattle raising was important, too, with hides and tallow contributing to the well-being of the mission.

But life didn't proceed without problems for the mission and its residents. The earthquakes of 1812 severely damaged so much of the church that it had to be reinforced with new beams and a brick buttress. After secularization, the entire quadrangle fell into disrepair, and even the floor of the church was dug up as a result of rumors that the padres had buried gold there. When the courts returned the buildings to the Church in 1861, little was left, and what did remain fell prey to souvenir hunters. Tiles, beams, even the bells were stolen; nails in the church were pulled out as mementos. The only structure remaining, an outbuilding, was used to house hogs in 1896.

Mission San Fernando Rey de España in the San Fernando Valley. —Anaheim Public Library

235

Charles Lummis in 1902.
—CHS/TICOR, USC Special Collections

The mission's salvation appeared in the unexpected form of a man, Charles Lummis, who walked to California from Ohio in 1884 and 1885. After writing up that experience for the *Los Angeles Times*, Lummis became the paper's city editor. Fascinated by the Indians of the southwest, he founded the Southwest Museum in 1914. He also created the Landmarks Club, which was dedicated to restoring missions and other historic buildings.

One August day that organization held a colorful celebration they called San Fernando Mission Candle Day. About 6,000 persons turned out to buy candles for one dollar each. Lighting their candles after dark, the entire group held high their flickering lights and walked in procession among the crumbling buildings. The money raised was used to put a new roof on the church.

Once started, restoration continued, albeit slowly. The mission was in fair shape, however, when the Sylmar earthquake of 1971 damaged it beyond repair. The building that now stands is an exact replica of the original.

The journey resumes back on I-5, with about five miles added to this segment. Roughly four miles from Mission Road the route turns south onto CA 170, the Hollywood Freeway. Through the San Fernando

Valley it goes, past Pacoima, Mission Hills, Panorama City, Van Nuys, and Sun Valley. All this bustle and development were made possible by water from the Owens Valley.

CAHUENGA PASS

In Studio City, CA 170 merges with US 101 to continue south through Cahuenga Pass and past Universal City. Portolá used this gap when exploring the San Fernando Valley; it was the setting for the 1831 battle in which Governor Manuel Victoria was wounded and put to rout. Near here, in 1845, Castro and Alvarado overthrew Manuel Micheltorena, the final governor sent by Mexico. They took exception to his currying favor with foreigners by giving them huge land grants, they resented his crude and unruly troops, and they disagreed with his centralist Mexican views. During the rebellion in Cahuenga Pass nobody was killed, but Micheltorena was expelled, never to return to Alta California.

The most significant event that took place here was the signing of the Capitulation Treaty on January 13, 1847. Signers were Andrés Pico, commander of the Mexican troops at San Pasqual, and John Charles Frémont for the U.S. Army. This treaty put an end to the Mexican War in California. The historical marker for Campo de Cahuenga stands at 3919 Lankershim Boulevard in North Hollywood.

The famous "HOLLYWOOD" sign in the Hollywood Hills proclaims the location of the once-glamorous city. —Michelle and Tom Grimm, Los Angeles Convention and Visitors Bureau

Vitagraph Studios films a scene in Hollywood's early days.
—CHS/TICOR, USC Special Collections

The Hollywood Bowl, near Cahuenga Pass, is a famous spot for picnics as well as musical events. —Donna Carroll, Los Angeles Convention and Visitors Bureau

*Cement court of
Mann's Chinese Theater
in Hollywood features
the hand- and footprints
of scores of movie stars.*
—Michelle and Tom Grimm,
Los Angeles Convention
and Visitors Bureau

Movie Studios

Nearby and just off the freeway at Lankershim Boulevard is Universal Studios, once the largest motion picture production facility in the world. Now a theme park, it is also used for making films and TV shows.

The route passes the Hollywood Bowl and, on Highland Avenue, the Cecil B. DeMille studio barn. The historical marker—at 2100 North Highland Avenue—identifying this significant structure says it was originally a barn of which DeMille rented half. Here, in 1913, he made *The Squaw Man*, the first feature-length motion picture filmed in Hollywood, and the one that proved longer films could be successful. The company moved to Van Ness Avenue and Marathon Street, to eventually become Paramount Studios. The one-time barn is now a museum dedicated to movies of the silent era.

Other movie studios that gave Hollywood its reputation include Hampton, at 1041 Formosa Avenue, now the site of the Formosa Cafe, a popular watering hole for movie-studio employees. Early on, United Artists productions were filmed at this site and then Samuel Goldwyn Studios took it over. Charlie Chaplin had his own movie studio at 1416

Foursquare Gospel Temple in the Echo Park area of Los Angeles is where Aimee Semple McPherson spread the Word. —International Gospel Church

Aimee Semple McPherson, the colorful founder of the Church of the Foursquare Gospel. —The Bancroft Library

North La Brea. Today the two-block compound houses Polygram's A&M Records. Still another production company, Fiction Pictures, operated at 650 North Bronson Avenue. Paramount still stands at 5451 Marathon Street. Since 1917 the location has housed movie studios where the likes of Mary Pickford, Claudette Colbert, Mae West, Bob Hope, and Bing Crosby crafted their fame.

The Hollywood Bowl lies just off this freeway at Highland Avenue. A natural amphitheater seating 20,000, it boasts acoustic shells designed by Frank Lloyd Wright in 1924 and 1928.

Aimee Semple McPherson and Her Church

Just before reaching downtown, the Hollywood Freeway passes through an area called Echo Park. Historical explorers who are interested in the cults that have begun or flourished in Los Angeles may want to exit the freeway at Alvarado Street and continue east on Temple Street, which lies just south of the freeway. At 1100 Glendale Boulevard, not far from its intersection with Temple and across the street from Echo Park Lake, stands the Angelus Temple. Today that refurbished building houses the headquarters of the International Foursquare Gospel Church. When it was dedicated in 1923 it was the showcase for Aimee Semple McPherson, evangelist and founder of the Church of the Foursquare Gospel.

McPherson arrived in Los Angeles in 1918 and drew attention at once with her combination of good looks and untraditional preaching methods. She promised to heal the sick and make the lame walk, all the while delivering a blend of entertainment and religion. Effective at raising money, she soon extended her reach via radio sermons broadcast during a daily *Sunshine Hour*. In 1926 she became embroiled in a scandal and was accused of conspiring to "commit acts injurious to public morals." In spite of lurid court hearings and whispers of a secret rendezvous with an engineer from her radio station, the charges were eventually dropped. She continued with her ministry, but receipts fell off because of her blemished reputation. In 1944 Aimee Semple McPherson died from an overdose of barbiturates. She is credited with making it possible for women to become ministers as well as with founding a church that today has almost two million members at more than 25,000 churches and meeting sites all over the world.

Downtown L.A.

About six miles after passing the Highland exit, the route reaches downtown Los Angeles. Here are El Pueblo de Los Angeles Historic

The skyline of downtown Los Angeles has appeared in many movies and TV shows. In the center background stands the round 73-story First Interstate World Center.
—Michelle and Tom Grimm, Los Angeles Convention and Visitors Bureau

Bullock's Department Store on Wilshire Boulevard, 1938. —Whittington, USC Special Collections

A view of Los Angeles, looking north from the courthouse, circa 1898.
—CHS/TICOR, USC Special Collections

Park, Times Mirror Square, the Civic Center, the Central Library, and the 73-story First Interstate World Center that looks for all the world like a giant's wedding cake.

El Pueblo de Los Angeles Historic Monument (between Alameda and Hill, Arcadia and Macy, beside I-110) enshrines the beginnings of Los Angeles, founded by Governor Felipe de Neve in 1781. It was the second pueblo in the state, after San Jose. The original town site flooded in 1815 and had to be abandoned in favor of higher ground, on which the historic park stands today. The plaza, much restored, is the very one at which earliest Angelenos congregated two hundred years ago.

More than twenty-five structures from the past still stand in the park. They include the city's first Masonic temple; its first fire station; Pico House, the first luxury hotel in the city; and the Merced Theatre, the first building constructed for theater productions. Another of the park's features is the Avila Adobe, built in 1818, the oldest building in Los Angeles. It served as headquarters for Commo. Robert Stockton in 1847 when he captured Los Angeles. Declaring California to be U.S. territory, he appointed himself governor.

Also to be seen in El Pueblo Park is the Old Plaza Firehouse, the Old Plaza Church, oldest in the city, and Olvera Street. Both John L.

Los Angeles City Hall, once the tallest building in the city, served as the Daily Planet building in the Superman TV series.
—Michelle and Tom Grimm, Los Angeles Convention and Visitors Bureau

Chapman and the Federal Writers' Project guide say the Old Plaza Church was built under the direction of Joseph (rechristened José after his reformation) Chapman, the pirate turned carpenter who also helped out at Santa Inés Mission. Olvera Street is a colorful block-long Mexican marketplace, with mariachi music, traditional foods, candies, and souvenirs of all kinds, many dispensed from open stalls lining the street. The lane was restored in 1929–30 through the almost single-handed efforts of Christine Sterling.

Across Alameda Street from the historic park is Union Station, the last major railroad terminal built in the nation. Completed in 1939, it served the Southern Pacific, Union Pacific, and Santa Fe Railroads, receiving such luxury trains as the Super-Chief. It is today an Amtrak terminal and center point of the many modes of commuter transportation that converge in Los Angeles.

L.A.'s Civic Center, one of the largest government complexes in the country, stands between Temple Street and Beverly Boulevard, Grand Avenue and Hill Street. It includes the city hall, a thirty-two-floor pyramid that was the tallest building in the city when it was built in 1928. It features an observation balcony on the top floor and is finished in granite and glazed terra-cotta. At one time it sported a light, called the Lindberg airplane beacon, at its top, but that was removed years ago.

City hall houses, among other things, the offices of the mayor and city council members. Tom Bradley, who left office in 1993, held his

244

post as mayor for an unprecedented five terms, twenty years. The very first mayor of Los Angeles served only a single year, the legal term when he was elected July 1, 1850. His name was Alpheus Hodges, but little else is recorded about him except that he was "a leading physician." According to an article in the *Los Angeles Times*, Hodges came to L.A. from Virginia and took office when he was only twenty-eight; he was the youngest man ever to hold the post. The little pueblo then boasted fewer than 2,000 residents, who lived in small adobe structures with flat roofs. The streets were narrow and alternated between being muddy sinks and dusty lanes.

In spite of his meager constituency, Mayor Hodges was a busy man, for he was also county coroner. He was a co-owner of the Bella Union Hotel, in the 300 block of North Main, which served as the county courthouse, and is credited with sponsoring construction of a wooden ditch to distribute water through the town.

In the governmental complex with the city hall is the County Hall of Justice at Temple and Broadway, in 1925 the first building to rise in the Civic Center. Once housing all county criminal courts and offices of the sheriff, district attorney, and coroner, it was vacated by Los Angeles County in 1993. The Hall of Justice was the setting for the trial of Sirhan

The famous La Brea tar pits have yielded much information about Los Angeles's prehistory, as well as hundreds of skeletons of animals trapped in the thick goo.
—Frank Pittman

Rodeo Drive in Beverly Hills is a renowned shopping mecca for the wealthy. —Michelle and Tom Grimm, Los Angeles Convention and Visitors Bureau

Sirhan, convicted killer of presidential candidate Robert Kennedy, and of the Manson Family. Members of that group were found guilty of the 1969 murders of seven persons, including actress Sharon Tate.

Just a block or so away, at 202 West First Street, is the home of the *Los Angeles Times*, arguably the largest daily newspaper in the nation. In 1881, just a year after its founding, Harrison Gray Otis bought a quarter interest in the paper. He went on to become the editor and, in 1886, the sole owner.

Otis came to California from his native Ohio in 1876. As owner of the paper, he soon became a force to be reckoned with in Los Angeles. He was a strong supporter of development in the area and a vehement opponent of the union shop. So outspoken was his paper during a strike to unionize the metal trades that the Times Building was bombed on October 1, 1910. Twenty persons died and seventeen were injured in the bombing ostensibly perpetrated by James and John McNamara. Clarence Darrow defended the brothers, who, mid-trial, suddenly admitted their guilt.

Another *Times* employee, Harry Chandler, who held the post of publisher in the 1920s, served the city in a different way. According to Woody McBride, writing in the *Fedco Reporter*, during the twenties tourists came to California in the fall, winter, and spring. They stayed away in the summer, however, having picked up the idea that it was hot on the coast during summer months. To overcome that misapprehension, Chandler started the All Year Club to spread the word that most summer nights in Los Angeles called for sleeping under blankets. Club-sponsored advertisements ran in papers all over the country. By 1930, tourism had become the second largest industry in Southern California. Even though news of earthquakes would follow, nothing could stem the tide of visitors, many of whom came to stay.

At Fifth and Hope Streets stands the Los Angeles City Central Library. Designed by Bertram Goodhue and completed in 1926, it is a potpourri of Egyptian, Roman, Byzantine, and Islamic flourishes combined in one stately Beaux Arts form. In 1986 the library was twice set ablaze by arsonists. The fires destroyed 20 percent of the library's collection, although the building's magnificent rotunda and murals were saved. More than seventeen hundred volunteers turned out to rescue water-soaked books, which were freeze-dried to save them from mold. After a fund-raising drive that saw both corporations and individuals scrambling to contribute millions of dollars, the library—enlarged, restored, and upgraded—finally reopened in late 1993, more than seven years after the disastrous fires.

I-110 and CA 1
Downtown Los Angeles–
San Pedro Bay and Pacific Palisades
About 50 miles

THE WATTS TOWERS

The route now departs central Los Angeles via I-110, the aptly named Harbor Freeway, passing the University of Southern California and Exposition Park with its museums and rose garden. Exiting the freeway at Imperial Highway, it travels east to Willowbrook Avenue and then north to 107th Street, where stand the magnificent Watts Towers.

Created over a thirty-three-year period by the inspired hands of Italian immigrant Sabato Rodia, the Watts Towers have delighted thousands of admirers, narrowly escaped destruction, and been subjected to outrageous stress. In 1921, Rodia started building what he called Nuestro Pueblo, "our town," with worn-out pipes, broken dishes and tiles, seashells and bedsteads, and an unsurpassed eye for beauty. Single-handedly and in his spare time, this genius fashioned three graceful, soaring towers—one is 100 feet tall—that sparkle with 70,000 shiny fragments set into mortar covering a steel framework. Besides the incredible towers, he constructed a gazebo, a fountain, and a fish pond, and surrounded the whole with 140 feet of decorated wall. All the work was done with no scaffolding, and no welding torch or other power tools.

Today a state historic park, the structures were threatened with destruction after Rodia left, in 1954, to live with his mother in Martinez. The city declared the untended masterpieces a dangerous eyesore and ordered them torn down. In 1957 rescuers showed up in the form of Nicholas King and William Cartwright. The two men bought the property and formed a committee to restore and preserve the works of art. Today the towers are undergoing extensive restoration, work that has continued by fits and starts for almost twenty years.

BANNING'S BEAUTIFUL BAY

Continuing on the I-110 freeway, the route at last reaches the harbor, San Pedro Bay. Here, thanks to Phineas Banning, is much of what makes Los Angeles flourish: its port.

Banning came to the Los Angeles area in 1851 from Delaware to practice his trade, wagon building. He soon grew interested in public transportation and established stagecoach and railroad lines from Los Angeles to the harbor. In the 1850s Phineas Banning and Abel Stearns were the first to have the harbor dredged to create a port for landlocked Los Angeles. The much more substantial development done in the 1890s was vigorously opposed by Collis P. Huntington because he hoped to make his property in Santa Monica the port of Los Angeles.

Los Angeles Harbor in San Pedro Bay actually consists of San Pedro, Wilmington, and Terminal Island. With Long Beach, it is the busiest harbor in the United States, receiving about 20 percent of all vessels that arrive in this country. It is the second largest artificial harbor in the world. Some 20,000 persons earn their living through activities connected with the port.

Wilmington

The home where General Banning, who was also a state senator, lived until his death in 1885, stands in Wilmington, in what is now a park at 401 East M Street. Also in Wilmington is the Drum Barracks Civil War Museum at 1053 Cary Avenue. Established in 1862, the post served Southern California, Arizona, and New Mexico. It was a garrison and base for supplies as well as the terminus for camel pack trains. Units set out from here in 1862 to turn back a Confederate incursion at Tucson. Originally comprising a dozen structures, the fort today contains only the junior officers' quarters built of materials carried around the Horn. The post was abandoned in 1866.

LONG BEACH

About eight miles due east of Wilmington, at the midpoint of the crescent-shaped bay, is Long Beach, second largest city in Los Angeles County. It was incorporated in 1897 on a tidal strip of mud and sand where Indians from Santa Catalina used to meet with mainland natives for bartering.

In 1784 the king of Spain granted to Manuel Nieto a 200,000-acre tract that was divided into two ranchos, Los Alamitos and Los Cerritos. On Nieto's death, the property passed into the hands of Abel Sterns and John Temple. In 1844 Temple built, at what is now 4600 Virginia Road, an adobe that served as headquarters for his huge Los Cerritos ranch. Mildred Hoover describes it as the most magnificent adobe still existing in California. According to James Hart, the ranch was unprofitable and by 1880 had become the property of the Bixby family. Another section of that great Nieto land grant is Rancho Los Alamitos on which stands (at 6400 Bixby Road) an adobe built in 1806 once owned by José Figueroa, governor of California in 1833. The house and surrounding four-acre garden were part of a working cattle ranch until 1953. Both ranches are now the property of the City of Long Beach.

Long Beach pavillion and pier, circa 1900. Californians parked their horses and buggies right in the sand. —CHS/TICOR, USC Special Collections

249

Rancho Los Alamitos adobe in Long Beach. Built in 1806, the house was once the property of José Figueroa, governor of California in 1833. —Long Beach Convention and Visitors Council

Beautiful gardens at Rancho Los Alamitos were once part of a working cattle ranch. —Long Beach Convention and Visitors Council

For almost three-quarters of a century Long Beach was famous for its amusement park, a three-block-long area along Ocean Boulevard between Pine and Chestnut Avenues. Opened in 1902 with little more than a saltwater plunge, it grew rapidly with the addition of a dance hall and popular rides. Outstanding among the rides was the Cyclone Racer, a roller coaster, installed in 1930. It was the longest and fastest in the world and, according to many riders, also the scariest, attaining speeds up to eighty miles per hour.

The park was called "the Pike" and drew crowds as large as 50,000 on a fine day. They came to picnic on the sand, to walk the midway, and to play Lite-A-Line, a game of chance similar to bingo, but played on a pinball machine. All that remains of the Pike today is the dome-shaped Loof Building, which housed the hand-carved carousel and Lite-A-Line. The games continue to this day, at least until the city decides to raze or relocate the building.

Real Estate Schemes

Much of Long Beach's phenomenal growth in the nineteenth century is attributable to the railroads. When the transcontinental railroad reached California in 1869, residents expected settlers to rush in and fill the purse of anyone with land to sell. Arrivals were slow, however. To convince Easterners to pick up their westward pace, some of the state's biggest entrepreneurs got together in a scheme to unload their ranchos on newcomers. They created the California Immigrant Union (CIU) to lure more newcomers to the southern part of the state.

In 1880 CIU schemers convinced officials of the Bixby clan, one of the largest landholders in the state, to subdivide their Rancho Los Cerritos into the American Colony, which would sell lots for $25 an acre. When few buyers showed interest, the folks behind the plan laid out a town and in 1882 advertised an auction of city lots. A host of prospective buyers arrived at Wilmington station on auction day, but dismal sales forced the end of the American Colony. A month later those who had bought lots renamed their city Long Beach.

A few years later, when two railroads—Southern Pacific and Santa Fe—reached Los Angeles, a fare war caused a population explosion. Long Beach was one of the areas that grew in bounding leaps as a result.

But the city's location had more to do with its success than did real estate deals and slick advertising. What sets Long Beach apart from most cities is that it stands atop one of the largest oil fields in the world. Drilling that started in 1965 showed that more than a billion barrels of crude oil lie beneath Long Beach.

The casino at Avalon on Santa Catalina Island attracts hundreds of tourists each year. —Frank Pittman

Even more fortunate than Long Beach, however, is Signal Hill, once the rancho of John Temple, but now an independent city completely surrounded by Long Beach. There, on a hill rising three hundred feet above sea level, a forest of oil wells pump away, as they've been doing since 1921. Discovery of that reservoir set off one of the wildest scrambles for oil in history. The Signal Hill field is playing out, however, and experts predict that before long the town will become an exclusive residential community.

SANTA CATALINA ISLAND

Across the San Pedro Channel from Wilmington is Santa Catalina Island, one of the eight little islands that make up the Channel Islands, and the only one to be developed. The lone town on Catalina is Avalon, about one mile square, on the southeast end of the seventy-six-square-mile island.

Discovered by Cabrillo in 1542 and named San Salvador for his ship, it was renamed Santa Catalina by Vizcaíno in 1602 when he anchored there on the feast day of Saint Catherine. The Indians who were on the island to greet Vizcaíno were largely wiped out by Russians hunting sea otters. The first American visitor, according to Hart, was Capt. William Shaler in 1805.

Catalina became American property when Governor Pico granted it to Thomas Robbins, a resident of Santa Barbara, in 1846. It changed hands several times, becoming the property of James Lick, who endowed the observatory on Mount Hamilton that bears his name; the sons of Phineas Banning; and William Wrigley Jr., son of the chewing gum magnate.

Wrigley still owns all of the island except the town of Avalon. He built the elegant Inn at Mount Ida (originally his home) and the casino building, and made the island spring training grounds for his Chicago Cubs. The baseball team now works out winter's kinks in Arizona.

Back on the mainland, the route resumes on CA 1, here the Pacific Coast Highway, to cross the Palos Verdes Peninsula, a nub of mostly high-priced land that defines the northwestern end of San Pedro Bay. Next the road hugs the shore, passing some of the finest beaches in the West as it heads northward. Along the roughly thirty miles that separate L.A.'s harbor from the western end of the Santa Monica Freeway (I-10) lie Torrance, a gaggle of communities that incorporate "beach" in their names, El Segundo, Los Angeles International Airport, Venice, and Santa Monica.

The boardwalk at Venice Beach is frequently the stage for colorful street performers such as Harry Perry, roller-skating musician.
—Michelle and Tom Grimm, Los Angeles Convention and Visitors Bureau

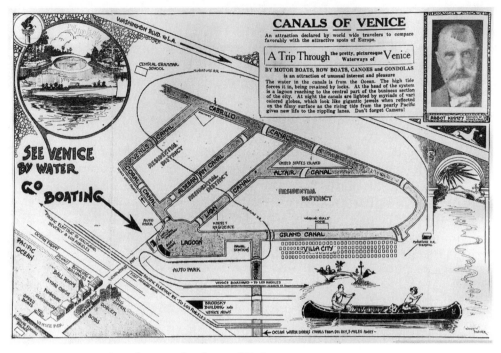

An early promotional map of Venice. —Hearst, USC Special Collections

VENICE

Venice, founded in 1904 by wheeler-dealer Abbot Kinney, was designed to look like its Italian namesake, with canals and arching bridges. In the town's heyday, gondolas plied the canals, grand hotels lined them, and symphony orchestras filled the air with great music. A plunge stood beside the boardwalk, as did an amusement pier; auction houses lined the walk cheek-by-jowl with shops dispensing tasty snacks to the hordes made hungry by the salt air. Until the late twenties Venice thrived, only to fall upon hard times just before the rest of the country went broke.

Will Rogers' Home

Just north of I-10, at 1453 Sunset Boulevard, sits Will Rogers State Historic Park, the preserved home of the great cowboy philosopher. During the twenties and thirties, the writer-actor lived here and played polo in the field across the road from the house. Rogers was just fifty-five in 1935 when he was killed in an airplane crash in Alaska, with his friend Wiley Post at the controls. His widow, Betty, left the thirty-one-room home and 186-acre ranch to the state when she died in 1944.

US 101, I-405, I-605, and CA 134
Pacific Palisades–Duarte
About 46 miles

MALIBU CREEK STATE PARK

Heading north on the San Diego Freeway (I-405), the route cuts through the Santa Monica Mountains, site of scores of movie locations. *M*A*S*H*, for example, was filmed in Malibu Creek State Park between CA 1 and the US 101 Freeway. A grass fire destroyed the army hospital setting soon after the show's final episode was completed . Only a burned-out jeep and an ambulance remain to mark the site, according to *California Parklands* magazine. Before this part of the mountains became a state park in 1975, it was called the Twentieth Century Ranch. For almost thirty years Twentieth Century Fox studios raised sets here and filmed such movies as *The Swiss Family Robinson*, *Tora Tora Tora*, and *Planet of the Apes*.

LOS ENCINOS STATE HISTORIC PARK

Approximately nine miles north of Sunset Boulevard, I-405 arrives at the junction with US 101, here known as the Ventura Freeway. A brief side trip travels west on US 101 about three miles, to 16756 Moorpark Street in Encino, Los Encinos State Historic Park. Franciscan padres first used the area as a headquarters while they searched out a site for Mission San Fernando in 1797. In 1849 it became a ranch, featuring a limestone structure that was first a blacksmith shop, then a bakery. Vincente de la Osa, owner of the property, built a nine-room adobe to serve as both home and stagecoach stop. In 1872 Basque shepherds added a stone building reminiscent of their homes in the Pyrenees. All these restored and preserved buildings sit amid pepper trees and citrus groves near a lake that dates back to 1872.

GLENDALE

The route now returns to US 101, about eight miles having been added to the distance to Duarte. Heading east, it soon becomes CA 134, while US 101 turns south as the Hollywood Freeway. CA 134 cuts across the southern end of Burbank and the northern edge of Griffith Park, one of the largest municipally owned parks in the world, to arrive at Glendale.

This mostly residential community sits on part of the former Rancho San Rafael, granted to José María Verdugo in 1784. It was one of the first grants made in Alta California. Two historic structures from

Glendale's early days are preserved within the city. Tomas Sánchez, sheriff of Los Angeles County, built the first, Casa Adobe de San Rafael, at 1330 Dorothy Drive, in 1865. The second, called the Catalina Adobe, was built for the blind daughter of José Verdugo in the 1830s. She lived in it until her death in 1861.

MOUNT WASHINGTON AND HIGHLAND PARK

Mount Washington and the area known as Highland Park are just east and south, respectively, of the junction with CA 2 (the Glendale Freeway). Highland Park blossomed into an elegant suburb at the turn of the century, but Mount Washington's steep incline discouraged development until 1909, when a hotel and incline railway came into being. A pair of canny developers built the hotel, an elaborate fifty-room affair at the top of the hill. They added the railway hoping that folks riding up the hill would be inspired to buy lots along its route. The ploy worked; everybody wanted the exclusive view lots.

The hotel became a gathering place for movie stars, but its celebrity faded when movie-making moved west. Closed as a hotel in 1916, the building served as a hospital during World War I and later as a military school. In 1925 Paramahansa Yogananda, founder of the Self-Realization Fellowship, set up the organization's headquarters in the old hotel. It stands atop the hill today, a Mount Washington landmark. The little railway is long gone.

PASADENA

Six miles farther east on CA 134 is Pasadena, home of the California Institute of Technology and the Rose Bowl and, until his death, of Thaddeus S. C. Lowe. Lowe was an inventor, balloonist, entrepreneur, and Civil War spy. At the request of President Lincoln, Lowe formed a balloon corps that was attached to the Army of the Potomac. He often sailed over enemy lines to spy on rebel forces.

After the war, Lowe moved to Pasadena, where he started the Pasadena Gas Company, lighting the streets with gas manufactured by a system he devised. He also built an inclined railway up a middling mountain in the San Gabriels just north of the city and near Mount Wilson. It was named Mount Lowe in his honor. His railway ran from 1893 to 1913, carrying passengers to a hotel he built at the top. Lowe was also one of the early supporters of Throop College of Technology, forerunner of the California Institute of Technology.

The site of Pasadena, in the foothills of the San Gabriels, was once part of the land given to Mission San Gabriel. Eventually the property fell into the hands of Benjamin D. Wilson, a Tennessee native who had

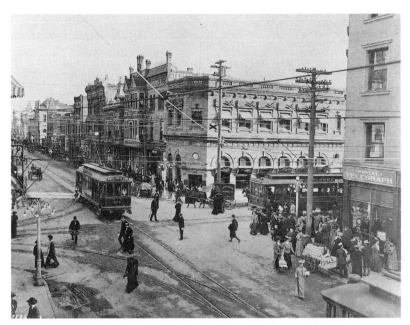

Pasadena street scene, circa 1910. —CHS/TICOR, USC Special Collections

Rounding the bend on Professor Thaddeus S. C. Lowe's Mt. Lowe Railway.
—CHS/TICOR, USC Special Collections

been a fur trapper and trader in the area of Santa Fe. He was elected mayor of Los Angeles in 1851 and held vast areas of land in California. At one time his holdings, according to Hart, included areas that are now Riverside, San Bernardino, San Pedro, Westwood, Pasadena, Alhambra, and San Gabriel. He worked with Banning to develop the harbor at Wilmington, led the battle to bring the railroad to the area, and aided in the development of San Pedro. Nearby Mount Wilson was named in his honor. Widely known for its New Year's Day parade and football game, Pasadena is also acclaimed for its Christmas Tree Lane, which is actually in neighboring Altadena. Most of the year the street is Santa Rosa Avenue, bordered by giant deodars that were planted as seedlings brought from the Himalayas in the 1890s. Each Christmas season, the trees are draped with thousands of colored lights. Visitors come from all over to drive up and down the festive street, causing monumental traffic jams.

Mission San Gabríel Arcángel

Back on the freeway, CA 134 merges with I-210 (the Foothill Freeway) to continue east. At San Gabriel Boulevard a side trip heads south to Mission Drive. About a mile west of that junction stands Mission San Gabríel Arcángel, fourth link in California's chain of missions. Founded on September 8, 1771, at a site prone to flooding, it was moved to its present site by Father Lasuén in 1775.

Completed in 1805, the church is unlike any of the others: Its distinctive facade is a side wall, not the front. The very plain entrance is at one end of the building, which has a distinctly Moorish cast with long, narrow windows and capped buttresses. The 1812 earthquakes severely damaged the monastery and felled the church tower, forcing the padres to live in the granary. In 1828 restoration was completed, with a new bell tower on the side of the building, rather than the front.

The mission flourished, producing abundant crops of corn and beans. The padres and neophytes raised great herds of cattle, too, and the mission acquired fame for its wines. It sat astride three well-traveled trails, two from Mexico to Alta California and one, at a later date, from the East Coast. Thus, it was a wayside stop for travelers of every ilk.

As a result of the secularization orders, all the mission's wealth became the property of the Mexican government. In 1843, when mission properties were returned, nothing was left at San Gabríel except ruined buildings and starving Indians. The church served as a parish church until 1908, when it became the property of the Claretian Fathers, who still protect it today.

This side trip adds about ten miles to the exploration of the Los Angeles area. The route now continues to Duarte and the junction with I-605, here called the San Gabriel Freeway, where the next adventure, Orange County, begins.

Part 8
Orange County: Orchards No More

Orange County, named by the state legislature for its famous groves, was carved out of the southeast portion of Los Angeles County in 1889. Its creation signaled an end to a battle that had seen residents of Anaheim and Santa Ana growing ever more vocal about having to travel to Los Angeles to transact all their county business. They also felt disenfranchised because Angelenos filled most county offices. Orange County is small—only 780 square miles—and extends along the ocean from Seal Beach to a little south of San Clemente. It is bordered on the west by the Pacific, on the east by San Bernardino and Riverside Counties, on the south by San Diego County, and on the north by Los Angeles County. Small though it may be, it is one of the most populous counties in California, second only to Los Angeles County.

Portolá discovered the Santa Ana River, which rises high in the mountains above San Bernardino and flows to the sea between Huntington Beach and Newport Beach, in 1769, and Padre Juan Crespí named it to honor Saint Anne. The river waters the northern portion of Orange County, creating some of the richest agricultural land in the state.

Orange County was once farmland, acre after acre of orange groves and bean fields. Strawberry beds, too, and flowers once covered the land until a pretend mouse started the tide that turned the entire area into one big tourist attraction. Walt Disney's Mickey may have plowed under the first crops, but he's had plenty of help from museums of history and dolls and wax figures, from a presidential birthplace and water parks, and from theme restaurants. Entertainment has become the force that drives the economy of Orange County.

At the seashore, recreation is the principal industry, too; fun is found on beaches and piers and boats that ply routes to here, and to there, and to no place at all. Near Huntington Beach surfers vie for the waves; near Crystal Cove State Park snorkeling and tide pooling attract visitors from all over the world. At Laguna Beach art festivals draw artists and art lovers to that Bohemian shore. There's no doubt that the county's future changed forever with the arrival of the business of having a good time.

Orange industry packing house. —CHS/TICOR, USC Special Collections

A swath of the county twenty-two miles long and about nine wide that is today known as the Irvine Ranch was once three magnificent land grants. That land and its owners have played prominent roles in the development of Orange County. The grantees in all three cases fell on hard times because of drought, other natural disasters, or bad management and sold their holdings to the likes of the McFadden brothers, James Irvine, or the Bixby family.

Like street names in other cities, those in Orange County honor their founders with such examples as McFadden Avenue, Glassell Street, Irvine Avenue and Irvine Boulevard, and Chapman Avenue. The last is named for Alfred Chapman, who, with Andrew Glassell, had a hand in founding the city of Orange.

Those who mourn the proliferation of cults in the late twentieth century may be consoled by knowing that they existed in the late nineteenth, too. In the Placentia area, for example, one George Hinde, recently from England, settled in 1876. There he built a mansion of fourteen rooms, many of which had no corners in order to discourage evil spirits that might lurk there. After Hinde had been farming for a couple of years he met Dr. Louis Schlesinger, with whom he took over leadership of a society of vegetarians. Calling themselves the Societas Fraternia, the members lived on uncooked fruits and vegetables, held property in common, and didn't believe in marriage. Intercourse between man and woman, they alleged, was encouraged solely to provide continuation of the species. They were called the Grass Eaters of Placentia, but were largely ignored until an infant member of the flock died of starvation. Hinde was charged with murdering the baby. Tried and acquitted, he continued to grow loquats, avocados, persimmons, and walnuts not far from today's centers of entertainment.

The county's course continued serenely, for the most part, and it became one of the top areas in which the upwardly mobile of Southern California chose to live. It boasted wide streets, good schools, fine homes, excellent libraries. In the waning days of 1994, however, the county treasurer revealed that he had invested the county's money unwisely, and it had shrunk by more than $2 billion, perhaps as much as 20 percent of its total value. Orange County filed for bankruptcy protection; supervisors fired the delinquent treasurer. Even Wall Street was rocked by the fiasco; the Dow Jones Industrial Average slumped more than 49 points the day of the bankruptcy filing. By year end, no one knew how much the high-living style of Orange County would be curtailed, but life in the laid-back county would undoubtedly suffer.

I-605 and I-5
Buena Park–San Clemente
About 46 miles

The first twenty-two miles or so of this new exploration travel south on I-605, from the junction with I-210, through territory that is, historically speaking, of little interest. When it reaches the junction with I-5, the route turns southeast and, nine miles from that junction, enters Buena Park in Orange County.

One of the smallest of the state's 58 counties, Orange County is easily explored via I-5 and some side trips. In the northern part of the county, cities are densely folded one against another, making it difficult to know at any given moment in exactly which one you might be. Signs along the freeway give some help.

BUENA PARK

The first city within the county's boundaries, about twenty-two miles from the junction of I-210 and I-605, is Buena Park, famous as the home of Knott's Berry Farm, which has drawn millions of visitors since 1940.

Cordelia and Walter Knott stand in front of their fruit stand in Buena Park, circa 1920. —Knott's Berry Farm

The Beach Boulevard attraction got its start in the 1920s when Cordelia and Walter Knott set up a stand beside the road to sell fresh-picked berries to passing motorists. Before long, they added Cordelia's home-made pies and jams to their wares. During the Depression they sold chicken dinners that featured feather-light biscuits and big dishes of berry preserves. After World War II, the couple expanded the attraction, adding a few rides in a western ghost-town motif. Today the park, still owned by descendants of Walter and Cordelia, covers 150 acres and welcomes millions of visitors each year.

The city of Buena Park sits on land that was part of the Los Coyotes Rancho granted to José Nieto. James A. Whitaker founded the city in 1887 near the Santa Fe line that ran from Los Angeles to Orange. Voters approved incorporation in 1953 to counter a threat of annexation by Anaheim or Fullerton.

ANAHEIM

About five miles farther along is Anaheim, the oldest incorporated and largest city in the county. Mildred Hoover calls it the pioneer town of the county and the site of one of the oldest colonial experiments in the state. Two musicians turned wine merchants, John Froehling and

264

Camp Snoopy at Knott's Berry Farm in Buena Park is a wonderland for kids and home to Snoopy and the Peanuts gang. —Knott's Berry Farm

Splashy Bigfoot Rapids at Knott's Berry Farm provide the thrills of a raging river. —Knott's Berry Farm

Charles Kohler, conceived the idea of founding a colony on the fertile banks of the Santa Ana River south of Los Angeles. Rounding up a group of interested Germans, mostly from San Francisco, they formed the Los Angeles Vineyard Society, with each member contributing $1,400. With those funds, the two men bought 1,165 acres of the Rancho San Juan Cajón de Santa Ana from Juan Pacifico Ontiveros for $2 an acre. They then enlisted the services of George Hansen, a surveyor who had arrived in Los Angeles in 1853. He had surveyed much of Los Angeles County, helping to settle land disputes.

Once the colonists were all enrolled, Hansen began to lay out a city bounded by North, South, East and West Streets. It took him three years to prepare the townsite, which included fifty farm plots and fifty lots for houses, plus a five-mile-long ditch to carry water from the river to the fields. When the colonists arrived in 1859 they christened their town Anaheim, combining *heim,* German for "home," and the name of the river. To keep cattle from trampling their vineyards they erected a fence of 40,000 poles fresh cut from willows, with gates on all four sides. In time, many of the poles took root to form a living fence around the colony. The north gate and main entrance to Anaheim was on Anaheim Boulevard at North Street. A state historical plaque marks the spot.

Pioneer Home of the Mother Colony of Anaheim today stands at 414 North West Street. —Anaheim Public Library

Even though its members weren't farmers but watchmakers and mechanics—professional types—the colony thrived. Harvests were so abundant that members had to build their own port to get products to market. The port, which they called Anaheim Landing, was on Alamitos Bay, about twelve miles away, near today's Seal Beach. Regular coastwise trade was carried on from the port for about fifteen years. A marker identifying the landing stands at the northeast corner of Seal Beach Boulevard and Electric Avenue in Seal Beach.

So profitable were all the colony's endeavors that it was expanded in 1857 and again in 1863. Much of the group's success was attributable to local Mexicans and Indians and Chinese from San Francisco who harvested the grapes. Hugh Bennett, writing in the *Fedco Reporter*, says that at its peak the colony produced a million gallons of fine wine and brandy each year. In 1884, however, vines began to die mysteriously. By 1885, 25,000 acres of vines were dead in Anaheim vineyards, attacked by some unknown disease. The culprit, according to the Department of Agriculture, was Pierce's disease, a virus spread by leafhoppers.

Pulling up the vines they had worked so hard to establish, the colonists determined to make another start. This time they planted Valencia oranges, launching a wildly successful industry that saw, for example,

Top: *Disneyland during its construction days, prior to 1950.* —Anaheim Public Library
Bottom: *Disneyland, soon after it opened in 1955, changed the face of Orange County and all of Southern California.* —Anaheim Public Library

more than ten million boxes of the golden fruit shipped from county packing houses in 1929. Orange groves grew and multiplied until after World War II, when almost half of them were uprooted to make way for housing tracts. In the late 1960s, a plague called "quick decline" began to kill off whole citrus groves. This time, however, better techniques enabled growers to fend off the disease and increase plantings so that harvests actually increased in spite of dying trees.

The first house in the colony, called the Pioneer Home of the Mother Colony, has been preserved for more than one hundred years. The original three-room structure was built by George Hansen in 1857. Twice moved from its original location at the corner of Lincoln Street and Anaheim Boulevard, it now stands at 414 North West Street.

For a time the famous Polish actress Helena Modjeska rented a house in the Anaheim colony, hoping to become a member. She and her family, however, were not farmers and grew discouraged. She returned to the stage, made a significant splash in the theatrical world, and finally retired in a remote area of Orange County.

Anaheim is known the world over as the home of Disneyland, arguably the world's first theme park. There's no dispute, however, that the famous park changed the face of Anaheim—and all of Orange County—forever. In 1950, for example, Anaheim was a center of orange production with a population of not quite 15,000. In 1960, five years after Disneyland opened, more than 100,000 persons called Anaheim home. By the time Disneyland marked its thirtieth anniversary, the city boasted more than 242,000 residents.

Orange

About five miles farther along I-5 (the Santa Ana Freeway) is the city of Orange, where Portolá camped in 1769. In 1879 a pair of attorneys from Los Angeles, Andrew Glassell and Alfred Chapman, laid out a city they called Richland and advertised as being well situated and well watered. A state historical marker designating the area as Old Santa Ana stands at the northwest corner of Lincoln Avenue and Orange Olive Road.

Church of Crystal

A brief side trip to the city of Garden Grove takes off here on the Garden Grove Freeway (CA 22). Just a few miles from I-5, on Chapman Avenue, stands the Crystal Cathedral. Made entirely of glass supported by a steel framework, the eye-catching building is the home of the Garden Grove Community Church. That church, founded in 1955 by Robert

Top: *Robert Schuller's mirror-sheathed cathedral, which opened in 1980, awes visitors to Garden Grove.* —Garden Grove Community Church

Bottom: *Interior of the Crystal Cathedral is vast and usually filled during services, even though worshippers can sit in their cars in the parking lot and hear the action.* —Garden Grove Community Church

This is the drive-in theater where Dr. Schuller started his Garden Grove Community Church. —Garden Grove Community Church

Schuller, got its start in the Orange Drive-In Theater. Preaching from the roof of the snack bar, Schuller drew increasing crowds, who liked the idea of attending church services without leaving their cars. Today's congregations can still worship in the parking lot of the Crystal Cathedral. Returning to I-5, this side trip adds five miles to the distance to San Clemente.

SANTA ANA

Continuing southeast on I-5 for four miles, the route reaches Santa Ana, seat of Orange County, about thirty-five miles from Los Angeles. It was founded in 1869 by William H. Spurgeon on land that was once part of Rancho Santiago de Santa Ana. In his book about Irvine Ranch, Robert Cleland says the site of Santa Ana was once covered with mustard plants that grew to such a height that Spurgeon had to climb a tree to see the property.

Incorporated in 1886, the town contains a downtown district of thirty-six square blocks that is listed on the National Register of Historic Places. Within that area more than thirteen major architectural styles are embodied in over one hundred buildings. They are contained by First Street, Civic Center Drive, Birch Street, and French Street. Several of these buildings were built in the 1870s, with facades added early in the twentieth century. The most recently built, the city hall, went up in 1935, replacing the one that collapsed in the 1933 earthquake.

At 211 West Santa Ana Boulevard is the old Orange County Courthouse, built in 1901, the oldest courthouse in Southern California. The most significant example in the state of the Richardson Romanesque style, it served the county continuously until 1979, when it was closed for seismic strengthening. It is in use once again as a home to county government and a museum. The historic Department One Courtroom on the third floor has been restored to its 1901 appearance.

In the summer of 1909, in an old church at Second Street and Main, a young man toiled over a secret project. Spending every cent he had and working some nights until dawn, the man finished his creation: the first airplane ever built in Orange County. The young man was Glenn Martin, who had arrived in Santa Ana that year to work in an auto business. On August 1, Martin hauled his plane to McFadden's pasture for its first real flight. He had practiced taxiing in surrounding bean fields and was confident the plane would fly. He was right.

In partnership with Donald Douglas, Martin founded an airplane company that built planes for local mail delivery and sport flying. After World War I, he moved his company to Baltimore.

The Orange County Courthouse in Santa Ana, built in 1901, is the oldest courthouse in Southern California and contains the historic Department One Courtroom on the third floor. —Anaheim Public Library

IRVINE

At Santa Ana, CA 55 (the Costa Mesa Freeway), cuts southwest toward the coast on a side trip to the sea. It passes John Wayne-Orange County Airport and the Irvine campus of the University of California.

John S. McGroarty, in his 1914 *History of Southern California*, mentioned Irvine as simply a principal railroad station of the Santa Fe line, in an area that boasted stores, churches, a school, and two large warehouses for grain and beans. Hart, in his 1987 work, defines Irvine as the largest master-planned urban community in the nation. Incorporated in 1971, the city of 75,000 acres includes the university, an industrial park, and a residential area, all carved from the original Irvine Ranch holdings. A historic area called Old Town Irvine is a renovation of warehouses, granaries, and outbuildings that were once the ranch's shipping center. It's just west of I-5 on Sand Canyon Avenue near Burt Road.

Irvine Ranch

James Irvine, founder of the great Irvine Ranch, was a Scotch-Irish immigrant who followed the lure of the gold fields. As Stephan Birmingham recounts, Irvine became disillusioned with mining when he couldn't dig up the fortune he sought, so he joined forces with a relative in San Francisco to start a grocery store. That profitable venture enabled him to start investing in real estate. Before long he formed a partnership with Benjamin and Thomas Flint and Llewellyn Bixby. That foursome acquired land in Monterey County and stocked it with sheep they drove overland from Iowa. When the Civil War created a shortage of cotton, they made a killing with their wool.

In 1864 the Flint-Bixby-Irvine combine bought up three old ranchos that totaled more than 120,000 acres and reached from the Santa Ana Mountains to the Pacific Coast, covering almost one-fifth of today's Orange County. In the 1870s Southern Pacific owners tried on Irvine Ranch a gambit that had profited them enormously in other areas. When the railroaders wanted land for right-of-way, they would simply move in and take it. Starting on a Friday, they would lay track around the clock until Monday, when courts reopened. Then corrupt judges would refuse legitimate landowners the right to tear up the newly laid track. The ploy failed on Irvine's ranch, however. When tracklayers showed up there, in 1877, James Irvine rounded up a posse and drove the crew away with shotguns and rifles.

When James Irvine became the sole owner in the 1860s, he diversified and sold land for the communities of Santa Ana and Tustin, but kept a tight hold on most of the huge ranch. It wasn't until 1965, when the University of California was established on a portion of the property, that his heirs broke it up to admit the university and city.

COSTA MESA

The side trip continues southwest to Costa Mesa, about ten miles from I-5, where the Costa Mesa Freeway (CA 55) intersects with Harbor Boulevard. At the very center of what is today a flourishing industrial and residential city, there once flowed Fairview Hot Springs. For a time a town named Fairview Springs grew up around the springs, but real prosperity eluded a succession of promoters. With the real estate bust in 1889, businesses went broke or moved away. The spa continued to operate, as did the hotel that housed its visitors. In 1903 W. S. Collins, a developer of nearby Newport Beach, renovated the old hotel, built new cottages, and added a warm-water swimming pool. In spite of his efforts the resort never took off. Changing hands several times, it continued as a marginal operation until 1918 when an earthquake shut off the flow of water. The springs disappeared forever.

In 1915 the failed community of Fairview combined with some other early settlements to form Costa Mesa. At the northwest corner of Mesa Verde Drive West and Adams Avenue stands an adobe built before 1820 as a station of Mission San Juan Capistrano. After secularization it became part of the Rancho Santiago de Santa Ana and headquarters of Diego Sepùlveda, member of a prominent California family and participant in the 1846 rebellion in Los Angeles.

At the very end of the Costa Mesa Freeway (CA 55), on Newport Bay, is one of the most exuberant resorts in the state: Newport Beach, which includes Balboa Island, Lido Isle, and the skinny Balboa Peninsula that defines Newport Bay.

With farming communities south of the Santa Ana River growing apace, it seemed to Robert and James McFadden time to open a seaport to ship products and receive supplies. The spot they chose was San Joaquin Slough, originally a hideout for smugglers, according to the Federal Writers' Project guide. On September 10, 1870, the stern-wheeler *Vaquero*, captained by Samuel S. Dunnells, had entered Newport Bay, opening it for commerce. When they took over the area in the late 1860s, the McFadden brothers and their partners, James Irvine and Benjamin Flint, dubbed it Newport. A steam schooner, the *Newport*, began in late 1875 to enter the bay every other week. Because of a dangerous shifting sandbar at the bay's entrance, the McFaddens abandoned the landing in the harbor in 1888 and built an ocean wharf. It stood nineteen feet above the water at high tide, was thirteen hundred feet long and sixty feet wide. Boats discharged lumber and building materials and loaded farm produce at the pier until 1907.

To improve business even more, the McFaddens constructed their own railroad, the Santa Ana and Newport, in 1891. It was eleven miles long and connected with the Santa Fe. In its heyday the McFaddens' transportation business had one hundred employees on their payroll and was one of the largest businesses in the county. Today a historical plaque on Dover Drive five hundred feet north of CA 1 commemorates the McFaddens' enterprise.

In 1892 the brothers acquired title to more than half of the Newport Peninsula as swamp and overflow lands. They then laid out a townsite and Newport Beach was born. Newport Pier, built in 1940 west of the intersection of Newport and Balboa Boulevards, stands on the site of McFaddens' Wharf.

Beside the pier is a segment of beach on which fishermen began in 1890 to land their dories laden with the day's catch. There the fishermen's wives would clean the fish and sell it to seafood lovers. The operation continues today and is the oldest fishing fleet in the nation. This sliver of beach was leased by the McFaddens to the fishermen; in 1967 the city of Newport Beach secured the property to assure the dory fleet its landing spot.

Home of the dory fleet beside Newport Pier. Catches of the day are sold every day. —Frances Wainwright

Southern California's famous red cars brought visitors to the Balboa Pavilion for a day's fun in the sun in 1906. —Newport Beach Conference and Visitors Bureau

The area around the landward end of Newport Pier is designated Historic Old Town, and includes eight places of historical interest, among them the site of the Newport terminus of the Pacific Electric line. When the Pacific Electric red cars reached Orange County, land sales skyrocketed, just as they had done in Los Angeles and its beach towns. The first city in the county that the line reached was Seal Beach, in 1903 called Bay City. On July 4, 1904, the first red car pulled into Huntington Beach, renamed from Pacific City to honor Henry Huntington, the moving force behind the Pacific Electric Railway Company. Amid fireworks and a free barbecue, land sales took off.

The following year the big red cars reached Newport Beach, completing what was one of the most popular day excursions of the time. The town of Balboa was laid out that same year. On July 4, 1906, the cars arrived at Balboa, after promoters of the community paid Huntington to bring the line in. Just a few weeks later three communities—Newport, Corona del Mar, and Balboa—incorporated as Newport Beach.

The Newport Bay Investment Company gave $10,000 for the construction of a pavilion on the bay that would enhance the sleepy town of Balboa. Built in 1906 as a Victorian bathhouse and terminal for the red cars, it has been the focal point of the community ever since. It has heard the music of the big bands, hosted bingo games and beauty contests, and anchored fishing tours and ferries headed for Catalina. Today it is a state historical landmark and listed in the National Register of Historic Places. Over the years it has been shored up, lighted up, reroofed,

Balboa Pavilion, built in 1906, still serves as a focal point of the community. —Newport Beach Conference and Visitors Bureau

and remodeled. Today the pavilion is authentic in both appearance and purpose. A commemorative plaque stands at 400 Main Street.

Nearby, at the southern end of Main Street near Ocean Drive, is another historical marker. This one recalls the first water-to-water flight, on May 10, 1912, of Glenn Martin's hydroplane, built in Santa Ana. The aviation pioneer flew from Newport Bay to Avalon, a distance of thirty-four miles, in thirty-seven minutes. On his return to the mainland, Martin carried the day's mail from Catalina. At that time it was the longest, fastest overwater flight ever recorded, according to the next day's edition of the *Santa Ana Register.*

Much of Balboa is of historic interest and a walking tour comprises an even ten spots worth visiting. They include the site of the Balboa Hotel, built in just ten days to be ready to welcome arrivals on the first big red cars, and the site of the Rendezvous Ballroom at Washington Street and Ocean Front.

Soto's Japanese Curio Shop used to stand at the corner of Bay Avenue and Main Street. Filled with exotic merchandise, it delighted the hearts of youngsters who pawed and purchased the strange wares for several years. Even though Soto was beloved by all, he was sent to an internment camp during World War II and never made it back.

The side trip continues along CA 1, past Corona del Mar and Laguna Beach. About seventeen miles from Laguna Beach, the route turns northeast on Crown Valley Parkway. In seven miles it intersects with the San Diego Freeway (I-5), after passing Laguna Niguel, a swank residential community. In all, this side trip adds about twenty-five miles to the distance to San Clemente.

SAN JUAN CAPISTRANO

Back on I-5 and traveling south for four miles, the route reaches San Juan Capistrano, home of the mission of the same name.

Each year on March 19—Saint Joseph's Day—tourists by the score gather in the plaza garden in front of the ruins of Mission San Juan Capistrano. They come from far and near, some even arriving at dawn, to witness the arrival of the mission's famous swallows. Some years the birds arrive on schedule, some years they don't, but visitors are never cheated, for they get to see a building unique in California.

San Juan Capistrano, officially founded on November 1, 1776, by Father Junípero Serra, had been founded more than a year before by Padre Fermín Lasuén. Father Lasuén set up a cross and dedicated the ground while a large group of Indians looked on. Natives even helped for eight days to haul timber for construction of a temporary chapel and other buildings. Work suddenly stopped, however, when the padres got news of an Indian attack at the San Diego mission. Burying the bells, the small party scurried to San Diego to take refuge in the presidio.

Ruins of Mission San Juan Capistrano display nests of swallows that are said to return each year on St. Joseph's Day, March 19. —San Juan Capistrano Chamber of Commerce

Mission San Juan Capistrano, founded by Father Junípero Serra in 1776, is home to the oldest building in California, the Serra Chapel. —San Juan Capistrano Chamber of Commerce

Once peace was assured, Father Serra identified the site by the cross that was still standing, unearthed the bells, hung them in a tree, and celebrated the first mass on the spot. Within a year the first little church was built. A modest structure that is still in use today, it is considered the oldest church in California. It is called Father Serra's Chapel because it's the only church still in existence where he is known to have said mass.

When the little church became too small for the growing congregation of neophytes, work was begun on a stone edifice. With an expert stonemason from Mexico in charge, Indians labored for endless days carrying stones from a quarry six miles away. Squeaking *carretas* (carts) hauled big boulders; the neophytes used chains to drag large stones, and carried smaller ones. Even women and children were forced to carry stones in nets on their backs. For nine years the Indians toiled to build the most magnificent church in the mission system. Its cross-shaped design featured a vaulted ceiling topped by seven domes. In all it was 180 feet long and 40 feet wide. A massive bell tower 120 feet high could be seen for miles; its four bells rang out even farther. A fiesta that lasted two days in 1806 marked the blessing of the completed church. Civil, religious, and military dignitaries from all over the state were on hand to take part in the celebration.

One December Sunday in 1812, just as mass was about to end, the earth rumbled and shook. The church's vault was rent open and its walls collapsed, dumping the massive ceiling onto the faithful below. Forty worshipers were killed, including two altar boys who had been ringing the bells. Many of the church's artifacts—statues, candlesticks, baptismal font, and the like—survived, but the padres moved back into Father Serra's church. Reconstructing such an edifice was out of the question. Slowly the business of the mission recovered. Bumper crops were harvested; thousands of cattle and sheep grazed in the fields.

Soon after secularization the mission's prosperous days came to an end. By 1844 only a handful of Indians were left and buildings had been plundered. Without tiles, adobe walls crumbled; without laborers, fields became overgrown with weeds. In 1860 restoration of the mission was attempted, but more harm than good was done. Since it had been used as a hay barn, the roof of Father Serra's church had been kept intact, assuring survival of both building and hay. In the 1890s the Landmarks Club moved to preserve the little church. What stands today, besides the ruins and Serra's adobe chapel, is all replica, rebuilt by patient hands in the 1920s.

Once a sleepy town, San Juan Capistrano is now a flourishing tourist mecca just off the freeway. The Amtrak station at 26701 Verdugo Street is a refurbished depot from the early days and has been operating since 1895. Refurbished vintage cars line its tracks.

DANA POINT

About a mile from San Juan Capistrano, north on CA 1, is the resort area of Dana Point. Hides from the mission and surrounding ranches were thrown from these bluffs to be loaded aboard ships in the harbor. Richard Henry Dana Jr. described that operation in *Two Years Before the Mast*, an account of his voyage aboard the brig *Pilgrim*. A full-size replica of that ship lies in the harbor today, welcoming visitors on Sundays. The historical marker honoring author Dana, for whom the point was named, stands at the Ken Sampson Overview at the Street of the Blue Lantern and Santa Clara Avenue.

SAN CLEMENTE

The route now returns to I-5, about two miles having been added to the trip to San Clemente. Four miles south of San Juan Capistrano is San Clemente, known as the Western White House when Richard Nixon was president. A real estate developer dreamed up the phony Spanish town in 1925.

The historical exploration of California continues in part 9, along the San Diego Freeway (I-5), heading for that city near the Mexican border.

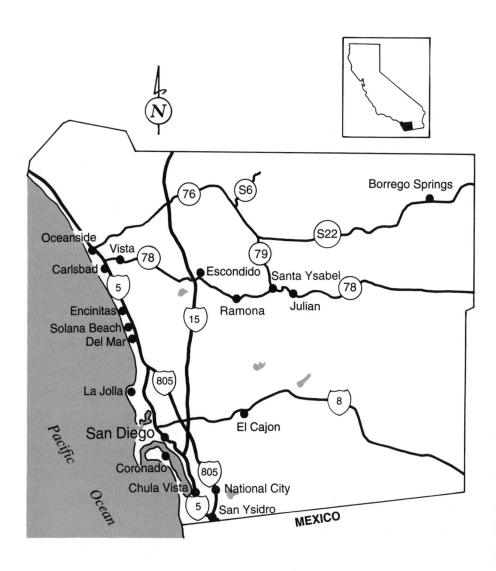

Part 9

San Diego: California's Birthplace

San Diego was one of the original twenty-seven counties of California and the city of San Diego has always been its seat. Both city and county got their names from the harbor Sebastian Vizcaíno christened in 1602. He will be remembered as the galleon commander who sailed up and down California's coast renaming bays, islands, channels, and other geographic features, despite having been strictly enjoined from doing so. Vizcaíno may have selected San Diego to create a permanent reminder of the ship he commanded: the *Saint Didacus*. Scott O'Dell writes that Vizcaíno chose that name because he anchored in the bay on the feast day of San Diego de Alcalá. Whichever reason is correct, the wonder is that his names stuck, giving us San Diego instead of Cabrillo's San Miguel and Monterey in lieu of Bay of Pines. Indeed, O'Dell points out, Vizcaíno finally got his comeuppance when he tried to rename Cabrillo's "Bay of Smoke and Fires" as Ensenada de San Andrés. The royal cartographer back in Spain noticed that Vizcaíno had reported anchoring in this bay on November 26, the feast of Saint Peter. The name of the harbor was changed to San Pedro and has remained such, in spite of attempts to call it Los Angeles Harbor.

If any single place can be accurately called the physical birthplace of California, that place has to be San Diego. If don Gaspar de Portolá's arrival at San Diego on July 1, 1769, didn't signal the birth of the great state of California, it certainly marked its conception. For with Portolá came Padre Junípero Serra, and those two men were destined to start shaping the fate of the state. Let Monterey, San Francisco, and San Jose claim what they like; the reality is that modern California began at the spot Cabrillo called San Miguel.

The first known residents of what is today San Diego County were the Kumeyaay people, who have a long history, according to Dolan Eargle, of fierce independence. When the leather jackets from Spain tried to herd them into the presidio or mission, they often resisted vigorously. Many of them fled into the desolate hills rather than be captured.

Prior to the arrival of settlers and the railroad, the hills around San Diego were covered with brush, most of it chokecherry, also called Christmas berry for its red fruit that appears in late fall. Chaparral, too, covered many of the hills—as, indeed, it still does—and dwarf oaks that produced acorns of a type the natives fancied were prevalent. Black sage abounded, too, and was popular with local bees, which produced a distinctive-tasting honey. Coronado and North Islands were almost eight feet deep in brush. Tree growth in Mission Valley below the padres' dam, on the other hand, was wiped out by early settlers.

San Diego was much slower to grow than the state's other early cities. In 1870, for example, San Diego's population numbered about twenty-three hundred; ten years later the count was scarcely more than twenty-six hundred. The first settlement outside the pueblo, according to Don M. Stewart, came into being in 1850 when William H. Davis, one of the area's early promoters, drew up a townsite on the edge of North San Diego Bay. In the area he called New Town, south of C Street and west of Front Street, Davis raised a few buildings with lumber shipped around the Horn. Most of the other structures were prefabricated and shipped from San Francisco, complete with nails, Stewart says. Davis even convinced the army to locate a post in the new addition and built a six-hundred-foot-long wharf. The settlement was slow to catch on, however, and some called it Davis's Folly. The wharf quickly fell into ruins, and the army used it for firewood.

When the Civil War ended, San Diego's time arrived, thanks to the railroad. A real estate boom made San Diego, but the railroads got that boom started. It wasn't commerce from the transcontinental railroad that stimulated the surge of land sales, but a price war between the Southern Pacific and Santa Fe Railroads. The fare from the Mississippi River to Southern California was $125 in November 1885. After fares fell to $100, then $95, Southern Pacific announced a fare of $1. As might be expected, such a bargain couldn't last, but rates stayed under $25 for a year or more. Thousands of people took advantage of the cut-rate fares to travel west.

Salesmen met trains and used brass bands, balloon ascensions, and free lunches to convince unwary purchasers to buy land sight unseen. Customers lined up for hours to bid on lots at auctions. Never mind that many of the towns being touted existed only on paper; never mind that others existed on rocky hillsides or worthless desert land. Sales soared. During this reckless period, land to the south of San Diego was developed, too, largely at the instigation of Frank Kimball.

When Alonzo E. Horton first saw San Diego, he was looking for land to develop. He had abandoned San Francisco in 1867 after hearing a lecturer sing the praises of the city to the south. While waiting for transportation to Old Town from the wharf at which he had landed, Horton strolled around what had been New San Diego, Davis's Folly. Norton met Ephraim Morse, and joined forces with that city father to buy up land on which to lay out what would be called Horton's Addition, today's central San Diego. Then he set to work to find buyers for lots in the city he would develop. He also sought to interest investors in building a railroad to San Diego. Horton tried to make a case for directing the Southern Pacific line to his city. When that tactic failed, he proceeded along other lines to develop his city.

San Diego County is bounded on the north by Orange and Riverside Counties, on the east by Imperial County, on the west by the Pacific and on the south by Mexico. At its longest point it measures about seventy miles and it varies in width from about twelve miles in the north to more than seventy at its midpoint. Three interstate highways cover most of the salient features of the county: I-5, I-15, and I-8. The last runs east and west while the first two are on a generally north-south axis. The Anza-Borrego Desert and Cleveland National Forest cover the eastern half of the county, leaving the portion closer to the sea for development.

I-5
San Clemente–San Ysidro
75 miles

SAN ONOFRE AND CAMP PENDLETON

San Clemente is the southernmost coastal town in Orange County. Just barely south of the San Diego County line is San Onofre, a nuclear generating station established in 1968 by the Pacific Gas & Electric Company. The pressurized water reactor system is designed to produce about 400,000 kilowatts of electricity. The plant is plainly visible from the interstate.

The federal land on which the reactors stand is a corner snipped from the U.S. Marine Corps training area, Camp Pendleton. Established in 1942, the camp takes up most of the vast Rancho Santa Margarita y Las Flores and extends for eighteen miles from San Clemente to Oceanside. It served as a receiving center for refugees from Vietnam in 1975.

OCEANSIDE

Just twenty-seven miles from San Juan Capistrano, at the southern edge of Camp Pendleton where the Santa Margarita River meets the sea, is Oceanside. Once a quiet beach town and "R&R" community for marines from Camp Pendleton, it is today a prosperous residential center and resort. Originally named for the nearby mission, San Luis Rey, the town's name was changed to Oceanside when the first petition for a post office was filed in 1884. It was incorporated in 1888 with a population of about one thousand. The building of Camp Pendleton in 1942 created a boom that lasted into the fifties.

MISSION SAN LUIS REY

Five miles east of Oceanside on CA 76 is Mission Luis Rey de Francia, founded in 1798 by Father Fermín Lasuén and named for Louis IX, the canonized king of France. It was eighteenth in the chain of missions as well as the ninth—and last—founded by Lasuén, who was missions president at the time. San Luis Rey was built to fill in the large gap between the missions at San Diego and San Juan Capistrano, a distance of about fifty-nine miles.

Portolá had reported some twenty years earlier that the Indians of the area were friendly, so Lasuén and his party weren't surprised when a great multitude of natives witnessed the founding ceremony. More than fifty children were baptized that day and nineteen adults sought baptism, but were told they'd need religious instruction first. For the entire life of the mission, the local population manifested such acceptance. More than two hundred neophytes joined the church during its first six months, speeding along construction of necessary adobe buildings.

Once Father Lasuén moved on, Father Peyri, senior padre at the mission, took charge. The first adobe church was completed in 1802; the present edifice was begun in 1811 and dedicated in 1815. This large building is in the shape of a cross, like the magnificent one at Capistrano, but like no others in the chain. The mission prospered from the first and came to boast an extensive water delivery system and even a sunken garden and *lavenderia* (laundry basin) in a little valley below the mission compound.

Seeing the threat of secularization looming, Father Peyri got permission to retire. When he tried to slip away unnoticed, Indians rode full tilt to San Diego to persuade him to return. They arrived at the harbor just in time to receive his blessing from the departing ship. The mission was turned over to secular authority in 1834, sold in 1846, and used by the U.S. Army for a time. It wasn't used again for religious purposes until 1893. During that long period of neglect, most of the buildings fell into ruin. Reconstruction started in 1893 and continues today.

The route returns to I-5 (the San Diego Freeway) about ten miles having been added to the distance to San Ysidro. Continuing southward, the freeway runs just inland from some of the state's finest beaches.

Carlsbad

Five miles south of Oceanside is the picturesque village of Carlsbad, founded by John Frazier. It was so named in 1866 because early settlers likened the mineral waters they discovered there to those found in Karlsbad, Bohemia. Today, a museum and gift shop called Alt Karlsbad Hanse stand on the site of Frazier's original well.

Portolá and Father Crespí took a rest stop here, on the shore of the lagoon, in 1769 while on their arduous journey to find Monterey. During that stopover they christened the lagoon Agua Hedionda.

With the arrival of the Arizona Eastern Railway in 1883, land around the lagoon was opened up to homesteaders and real estate speculators. John Frazier, founder and director of the Good Samaritan Mission in Los Angeles, was one of the former. He claimed 127 acres to the northwest of the lagoon. After tapping springs of both artesian and mineral water, he began offering sips of the water to thirsty train passengers. In time, because of the perceived healing qualities of the water, the place became known as Frazier's Station, a destination in its own right. The railroad station built in the 1880s at 400 Elm Avenue today houses the offices of the chamber of commerce.

Santa Fe Depot at Carlsbad, built in the 1880s and shown here in 1938, today houses the offices of the chamber of commerce.
—Carlsbad Chamber of Commerce

ENCINITAS

About eight miles farther along are the communities of Encinitas, Leucadia, Cardiff By The Sea, and Olivenhain, all four of which form the city of Encinitas. Even though the name means "little oak," it is called the flower capital of the world because of its commercial fields of poinsettias, gladioluses, begonias, fuchsias, and other flowers.

TORREY PINES STATE RESERVE

Approximately twenty miles south of Encinitas, a mile or so west of the freeway, the Torrey Pines State Reserve shelters half of the world's unique Torrey pines. This site is one of only two natural habitats on earth for these trees; the other is on Santa Rosa Island, almost two hundred miles to the north. Established in 1921, the reserve features hiking trails that wind through stands of trees twisted and bent by ocean winds, and scenic viewpoints on bluffs overlooking the sea. A pueblo-style building that served as a restaurant when it was built in 1923 now houses the park's visitors center.

LA JOLLA

Five miles farther along I-5 is La Jolla, famous as the site of the Scripps Institution of Oceanography, founded in 1892 by publisher E. W. Scripps and his half sister, Ellen Browning Scripps. It became a division of the University of California in 1912. The town is also the setting for the Salk Institute and an underwater park. Beaches in the area are renowned for their tide pools and caves.

At 780 Prospect Avenue stands a green cottage, built in 1904, that today houses John Coles' Book Shop. In 1905 Ellen Scripps bought the little house and remodeled it to serve as a guest house for herself and her sister. It welcomed many famous persons over the years and was even used for services by St. James Episcopal Church after a fire destroyed the church buildings. The bookstore has been in these quarters since 1966.

Traveling east of the Torrey Pines Reserve, I-5 cuts through the heart of the campus of the University of California at San Diego. Just off the freeway, at La Jolla Village Drive, stands the new Mormon temple fashioned of stone and opaque glass. The stark white, twin-spired building, with its golden statue of the angel Moroni, is only the forty-fifth temple the Church of Jesus Christ of Latter-Day Saints has commissioned in its entire 162-year history. It is one of just three in the state, serving an estimated 85,000 Mormons in San Diego and surrounding counties.

San Diego, Birthplace of the Golden State

Thirteen miles south of La Jolla is San Diego, second largest city in the state and sixth in the nation. Discovered by Cabrillo in 1542, named by Vizcaíno in 1602, it was first settled by the Sacred Expedition of Portolá and Father Serra in 1769. The expedition's primary goal was to establish a presidio at Monterey, but a base at San Diego had to be set up, too.

Mission San Diego de Alcalá

It was July 1 when all four segments of the expeditionary force finally came together, the first two from the sea and the others over land. On July 16, 1769, immediately after Portolá and his party set out to find Monterey Bay, Padre Serra founded Mission San Diego de Alcalá. He carried out the ritual in the presence of about thirty men on what came to be known as Presidio Hill, today in the center of the wishbone-shaped area south of Camino del Rio (I-8) and east of I-5.

In a procedure that would be followed more or less exactly in establishing all the other missions, Serra had a cross erected. Then, according to Helen Hunt Jackson's account as related by Mildred Hoover, a booth of branches was built. Next, he consecrated booth, cross, and ground with holy water and gave them the name of a saint. Bells hung on tree branches were rung to attract any Indians who might be within earshot; natives who showed up were given gifts of cloth or beads to win their trust. Thus was a mission founded.

Day-to-day matters at Mission San Diego were likewise typical of all the missions. Father Serra left two monks at the scene to win, convert, baptize, and teach all the Indians they could reach. A small contingent of soldiers remained, too, as guards. Several head of cattle, holy vessels, tools, and some seeds rounded out the supplies with which the newcomers were to operate the mission.

The site on the south side of the San Diego River would prove unfortunate, however, with not enough room to support the converts. In August 1774 the mission was moved upriver about six miles. Before long, buildings of logs roofed with thatch rose at the new location on today's San Diego Mission Road just east of I-15. Although that site seemed ideal, it proved to have too little water to support the field crops necessary to feed the neophytes. For that reason, the natives were permitted to stay in their villages and report to the mission to work and worship. With such a loose connection to the church, the Indians were never completely controlled by the padres.

Reconstructed Robinson-Rose house, originally built in 1853, was the commercial center of early San Diego. Today it is the visitors' center of Old Town San Diego State Historic Park.

In November 1776 a band of eight hundred Indians, fearing that the padres would eventually win over all the tribes, attacked the mission. After looting the sacristy and storerooms they set the buildings afire. Padre Luis Jayme, a blacksmith, and a carpenter were killed and two soldiers wounded. The padres fled to the presidio, where they found the garrison asleep, and remained there for some months.

Nearly eight months passed before the burned-out mission was rebuilt. When it was, it was carried out to the full quadrangle. From 1807 to 1816 the Indians toiled mightily to construct, six miles upriver, a dam and cement flumes to carry water to the mission. The route of the water passed through an almost impassable gorge, calling for herculean effort on the part of the Indians. A plaque marking the site stands on Father Junípero Serra Trail, not quite two miles north of Mission Gorge Road. At last, in 1813, the modest structure with its plain facade that is today's Mission San Diego de Alcalá was completed. It was the first link in the chain that constituted El Camino Real (the King's Highway) and extended some 650 miles to San Francisco.

Old Town

The first part of this exciting city to be explored is known as Old Town and stands near the site of the original mission. To reach it the route exits I-5 at Old Town Avenue. There, bounded on the north by Juan Street, on the south by Congress, on the east by Twiggs, and on the west by Wallace, stands Old Town San Diego State Historic Park. It is, preserved and reconstructed, the pueblo that soldiers who retired from duties at the presidio laid out in the early 1820s. In 1830 Old Town San Diego was described as a collection of brown huts with a few larger houses that were obviously the property of the upper class.

One of the earliest residents of the pueblo was Capt. José María de Estudillo, former commander of the presidio. His adobe home was built in 1827, sheltered three generations of his family, and then passed through

The Wrightington adobe in Old Town San Diego was built in the late Mexican period and a wing was added in 1852.

several owners before the Spreckels family funded its restoration in 1910. Much later they donated the home to the state. It stands on Mason Street at San Diego Avenue.

Across Calhoun Street from the Estudillo home is La Casa de Bandini, home of a son-in-law of the presidio captain. This dwelling, built in 1829, became the social center of Old Town, thanks to the popularity of its owner. When the Americans took over the city, Bandini invited Commodore Stockton to use Casa Bandini as his headquarters and gave the troops supplies and horses from his rancho. It was here that Kit Carson and Edward Beale on December 9, 1846, delivered their plea for reinforcements to rush to General Kearny at San Pasqual.

When Bandini suffered financial problems in the early 1850s, he was forced to sell his house to Albert Seeley. That gentleman added another story to the building, creating the Cosmopolitan Hotel. In later years the building was used as a store, pickle factory, and motel annex. Today it houses a restaurant.

Near the southern edge of the park stands the Mason Street School, built in 1865. It was Southern California's first publicly owned schoolhouse. Mary Chase Walker, the first teacher, recalled the area as being brown and barren, with not a tree to be seen. She called it the most dilapidated, miserable place she had ever seen. She may have disliked the setting, but she taught for almost a year before marrying the school board president, Ephraim W. Morse, one of the city's early movers and shakers. She lived in San Diego for the rest of her life.

The park abounds with colorful stories of San Diego's past; the restored and reconstructed buildings add flavor to those tales. The San Diego Union Building, for example, was prefabricated in Maine and

The two-story United States House was used as a general store as early as 1850. It later housed a butcher shop and a match factory. It is one of the earliest prefabricated buildings known.

shipped around the Horn in 1851. It has been restored to look, as much as possible, the way it did when the first edition of the daily paper came off the press in 1868. John D. Spreckels, beet sugar magnate, acquired the paper in 1888 and owned it until his death in 1926.

In the area of San Diego called Old Town, but not within the state park, are other historic sites of great interest. One of these is the Whaley House at 2482 San Diego Avenue, the first brick structure in the city. Built of bricks made in the owner's kiln, the walls were plastered with ground seashells. Another is Casa de Lopez, built about 1835 by Juan Francisco Lopez, at 3890 Twiggs Street. Called The Long House, it was one of the first substantial homes built in the pueblo.

Adjacent to the state historic park on the northeast is Presidio Park, site of the Indian village of Cosoy, which Cabrillo named San Miguel. It was here that Father Serra raised the cross to establish his first mission in California. Also in this park is Fort Stockton, which dates from about 1838 and was erected by San Diegans in anticipation of an offensive by Californios from Los Angeles. Here the Mormon Battalion on January 29, 1847, ended its march from Council Bluffs, Iowa.

At the corner of Taylor Street and Presidio Drive stands a historical marker denoting the site of the Derby Dike. George Horatio Derby, a member of the U.S. Topographical Corps, in 1853 built a dike that diverted water from the San Diego River into False Bay. A crude timber bulkhead, it was one of the first U.S. government projects in California and the first attempt to restrain the San Diego River. The dike's failure

Point Loma Lighthouse, built in 1854, overlooks the sea and the parking lot of Point Loma Preserve.

within two years was attributed to skimpy funding, not to lack of skill on Derby's part.

The Gas Lamp Quarter

South and east of Old Town is the so-called Gas Lamp Quarter, one of the largest national historic districts in the country. For a time this area was the heart of San Diego, but it fell on hard times in the 1890s, when businesses moved north of Broadway. Most of the buildings in the quarter are representations, but the Davis House at 410 Island Avenue is the real thing. Built in 1850, it was moved to this site in 1984.

On the east side of Fifth Avenue, between E and F Streets, stands a rank of Victorian buildings. Its construction is typical of commercial structures of the time. The Horton Plaza Hotel at 901 Fifth Avenue was once an office building. Built in 1913, it was converted in 1987 to its present state. The facade still boasts its original marble and gum-wood trim.

Balboa Park

In 1868 Ephraim Morse suggested that acreage should be set aside for a great city park. The city's board of trustees agreed, and appointed Morse and Thomas H. Bush, a storekeeper, to select the site. In 1870, they chose fourteen hundred hilly acres south and east of Old Town, then left them to stand barren for some years. In 1892 Kate Sessions, who operated a horticulture nursery in Coronado, asked to lease thirty

View from Point Loma overlooking San Diego Harbor, home to U.S. Navy ships on the sheltered eastern side of the peninsula.

acres of the idle parkland for another nursery. The lease required her to plant one hundred trees in the park each year and give three hundred more to the city for planting elsewhere. She complied with enthusiasm, importing tree seeds from New England, Baja California, South America, and even Australia and overseeing placement of the city trees. A plaque marks the site of her nursery at the northwest corner of Garnet Avenue and Pico Street.

In 1915 Balboa Park's acres were transformed into the site of the Panama-California International Exposition. Several structures designed by Bertram Goodhue for that event still stand in the park. In those structures Goodhue revived the extravagant style of Jose Churriguera, popular in Spain almost three hundred years earlier. For many years after the exposition, that overdone style was in great demand in California. The towers of Hearst's castle are an outstanding example.

The famous Old Globe Theatre was a souvenir of the 1935 California-Pacific International Exposition and is today the centerpiece of the Simon Edison Centre for the Performing Arts. The city's renowned zoo is also part of Balboa Park.

Point Loma

From the center of Balboa Park, Laurel Street leads directly to North Harbor Drive, from which one can turn onto Rosecrans Street, then Canon Street and Catalina Boulevard to reach Point Loma. At the very tip of the spit of land that curves around Coronado Island is Point Loma Lighthouse. Built in 1854, it was one of the first eight lights on the Pacific Coast. It was in use until 1891, when the Pelican Point Light took over. It became the site of the Cabrillo National Monument in 1913. Today it is the central feature of the Point Loma Preserve. Cabrillo's statue, a gift from his homeland of Portugal, faces northeast toward Ballast Point, his actual landing spot. According to O'Dell, Vizcaíno renamed this promontory Point of the Pebbles, but shortly after the visit of writer Richard Henry Dana aboard the *Pilgrim*, it became known as Ballast Point because ships stopped there to take on stones for ballast on their eastbound voyages. It is said that some of Boston's streets are paved with cobblestones from this California site. Several lesser historic sites are on the point and are easily reached by Cabrillo Memorial Drive, an extension of Catalina Boulevard.

Coronado Island

To visit Coronado Island (actually a peninsula at the northern end of the sliver of land called the Silver Strand) the route retraces its path to North Harbor Drive. Once again it swoops around North San Diego Bay, past downtown, then south on Harbor Drive to CA 75, and across the San Diego-Coronado toll bridge. The 2.3-mile-long span that arcs between San Diego and Coronado Island was built in 1969 and has been called one of the most beautiful bridges in the United States.

In 1885 Elisha S. Babcock and H. L. Story were wont to row across the bay to Coronado to hunt rabbits. Neither Babcock, a railroad financier from Indiana, nor Story, a piano manufacturer from Chicago, was in good health, and these outings were ostensibly to search for fresh air and sunshine. What they found, however, was more than 4,000 acres of land known as the Peninsula of San Diego, which encompasses both Coronado and North Island. With the transcontinental railroad at Barstow, only 150 miles away, they realized that San Diego's time of glory was at hand and dreamed of establishing a resort on this Coronado Island. Forming a syndicate they called the Coronado Beach Company, they bought the entire peninsula for $110,000.

The area was barren land covered with sagebrush and had to be transformed to attract investors and residents. The two men had brush cleared, trees planted, streets laid out, and a pipeline laid to bring water from the San Diego River. They developed a transportation system of ferryboats and wharves, even steam trains, to move people and materials. Even though electricity was an oddity in California, Babcock and Story built one of the state's first power plants. It furnished power not only to their hotel, but also to the entire city of Coronado until 1922.

The beautiful Hotel del Coronado, completed in 1888, is a national historic landmark. —Coronado Visitor Information Center

Launching a promotional campaign, they convinced eastern newspapers to print the pleasant daily temperatures of San Diego and persuaded Rand McNally to publish a booklet touting the advantages of life in Coronado. Isabel Babcock and Della Story regularly gave parties on a pavilion in the city. On July 4, 1886, the two men sponsored a great picnic, initiating a Coronado tradition that continues to this day. Interest in the resort grew. On November 13, 1886, the *San Diego Union* ran a column describing the ambitious resort-to-be; it inspired about 6,000 people to line up for free boat rides to the hotel site. There they were served a free picnic lunch and a pitch to invest in the new community. Story and Babcock more than recouped their original investment in that one day's sales.

In 1887, ground-breaking ceremonies were held for the Hotel del Coronado, designed by the Reid brothers, James, Merritt, and Watson. Construction began in March, employing Chinese laborers from San

Francisco and Oakland plus master craftsmen of all types. A 2,000-man crew toiled around the clock to complete the huge building in a little more than eleven months. The hotel's first guests registered on February 19, 1888. Today the elegant Victorian structure, one of the largest wooden buildings in the world, is both a national and state historic landmark.

Presidents and movie stars, royalty and illustrious commoners have stayed at the "Del." For more than a century it has tickled the imaginations of visitors, but none more than Frank L. Baum, author of *The Wizard of Oz*. It's said that Baum looked at the hotel one night after all its lights had gone on and conceived the Emerald City of Oz. True or not, the legend describes the feelings many visitors express when they first see the Hotel del Coronado.

Leaving the island, the route returns to I-5 just east of the bridge's end and continues south to National City.

NATIONAL CITY

National City lies along I-5, immediately south of San Diego's city line. It was founded by Frank and Warren Kimball, who, like Babcock and Story, sought Southern California for its healthful climate. In 1868 the brothers Kimball bought more than 26,000 acres of the Rancho de la Nación land grant. Hurriedly they threw together a hut on the property, then settled back to wait for the railroad to boost the fortunes of the community they named National City.

The California Southern Railroad arrived in San Diego in 1885, connecting that city to Santa Fe's Atlantic and Pacific line in Barstow. By 1888 thirty miles of track of the National City and Otay Railroad reached from San Diego to National City. Pulled by small engines called steam donkeys, the trains worked their way to Sweetwater Valley, east of National City. There the tracks divided, one set heading east to the La Presa resort and the other through Chula Vista to the town that is today known as San Ysidro.

Col. William G. Dickinson, a professional town planner, arrived in National City in 1886 to determine what the city needed to flourish. Besides surveying and platting, he saw, the area needed water. In the final months of 1886, he decided to build a dam on the Sweetwater River, at an upstream gorge that Frank Kimball had discovered soon after he bought his acreage. Wisely, Kimball had secured water rights for the San Diego Land and Town Company, so the damming could proceed apace. Completed on April 7, 1888, the reservoir held six billion gallons of water.

CHULA VISTA

Not only did National City prosper, but so did its neighbor to the south, Chula Vista. Land sales started in Chula Vista in 1887, when Albert Barber purchased a lot. The home Barber built for his family was typical of the day: two dormers, fish-scale shingles, and wooden gingerbread trim. Moved from its original location, the house, believed to be the oldest in Chula Vista, stands today at 151 Landis Avenue.

James Madison Johnson was another early settler. In 1888 he built a Victorian house at Fifth Avenue and F Street, started a citrus nursery on the land, and invented a lemon-washing machine in the basement. The house still exists today.

Until the late 1970s, Chula Vista was primarily an agricultural community, producing lemons and field crops. During World War I the city was the site of a kelp processing plant that produced cordite for British bombs. The plant was at that time the world's largest facility for harvesting kelp.

San Ysidro is the last town north of the Mexican border, about five miles south of Chula Vista, at Otay Mesa Road and I-805. Here the route turns north once again, to explore the inland part of the area.

I-805 and I-15
San Ysidro–Escondido
About 40 miles

Traveling north on I-805, the route now passes through the eastern edges of cities already explored: Chula Vista, National City, and San Diego. About thirteen miles north of San Ysidro, at Wabash Boulevard in San Diego, it veers northeast on CA 15, which will become I-15 as it crosses I-8. Mission San Diego stands just to the east of this point, on San Diego Mission Road.

Running just west of the Cleveland National Forest, I-15 bisects Miramar Naval Air Station, then passes through the Poway Valley, which is rich in Indian pictographs.

ESCONDIDO

Escondido got its start during the land boom that followed the completion of the transcontinental railroad. A group calling itself the Escondido Land and Town Company bought up land in the area from grape growers discouraged by the floods of 1884. The company then advertised it as a hidden garden spot. On July 4, 1888, an excursion train from Oceanside chugged into Escondido carrying potential lot buyers. The ploy was successful; land sales were remarkable and the town was incorporated two years later.

The town's library dates from 1894 and displays artifacts from the culture of the region's original residents, the Ipai or Kumeyaay. On Kalmia Avenue and Grand stands the Wardrobe, a general store that was called the Escondido Mercantile Company when H. N. Lyon opened it 1905. Even greater historic excitement, however, lies to the east.

CA 78/79/76 and I-15
Escondido–Temecula
About 100 miles

San Pasqual Battlefield State Historic Park

Eight miles southeast of Escondido on CA 78 is San Pasqual Battlefield State Historic Park, site of a brief battle of the war between the United States and Mexico. It was the turning point of the war, even though most authorities say it was a loss for the United States and the bloodiest engagement of the war in California. Mexicans and Spaniards called the place Pascual, probably after a saint, but Americans changed the spelling.

For a time the elusive goal of establishing independent Indian settlement seemed within reach at the pueblo San Pascual. After the mission at San Diego was secularized, natives formed a self-governing village here. Blending their own customs, language, and religion with those of Spain, they raised livestock and cultivated crops, along with gathering acorns and hunting game. They lived in both adobe houses and traditional brush homes. Some were Christians, but not all. The pueblo persisted for decades, before fading away, an occurrence rare in California. A census taken in 1873 shows that more than fifty men and women plus twenty-one children lived in San Pascual at the time. Their trades included, besides the mayor, cowboys, muleteers, carpenters, a blacksmith, a weaver, a charcoal maker, a miller, a farmer, a leather worker, and a maker of cheese. Today a state park visitor center sits on the site of the pueblo. The famous battle was fought on the plain across the road.

War

President James Polk declared war on Mexico on May 13, 1846. The stage was set for the battle of San Pasqual as U.S. forces, bolstered by the Bear Flaggers, took town after town. They suffered a setback in

Los Angeles when the town was retaken by residents who resented the oppressive rule of Archibald Gillespie. That revolt encouraged Californios to mobilize under Capt. José María Florés. Named acting governor and general, Florés unified the Californios, who were then ready to fight.

In June, President Polk ordered the Army of the West to march from Fort Leavenworth, in what is now Kansas, to occupy New Mexico, then continue to California. Polk expected that mission to be accomplished before winter. With Brig. Gen. Stephen W. Kearny at their head, the troops set off.

The Stars and Stripes was raised over Santa Fe on August 18 with no shots fired. Kearny lingered for a month to organize a territorial government, then set out, on September 25, for California. Expecting an easy and quick victory, Kearny downsized his forces and began what would prove to be one of the longest and most difficult marches in U.S. military history. Notwithstanding the heat and thirst that plagued him in the Colorado desert, Lt. William H. Emory, commander of the topographic engineers, kept a good record of the natural features the men encountered on the march. His work resulted in a new map of the Southwest.

Near Socorro, in Mexico, the army met American scout Kit Carson and a party of Americans and Indians. Carson reported to Kearny, incorrectly as it turned out, that U.S. forces controlled every major town in California. Because it looked as if his task was almost accomplished, Kearny sent more of his men back to Santa Fe. Then he persuaded Carson to guide the remaining one hundred troops the rest of the way.

The trek across barren desert was hard on both men and mounts, but they finally reached the town that is today called Ramona on December 5, 1846. Hungry and exhausted, they found little comfort because a cold rain was falling. Kearny soon learned that a force of Californios led by Maj. Andrés Pico had made camp at the pueblo of San Pascual. Kearny sent out a scouting patrol, only to have it spotted by Pico's men. Alerted, the Californios prepared for battle.

When dawn broke the next day, a cold rain was still falling. The spent U.S. troops rode their tired mules and horses over the eight miles of rugged hills that separated their campsite from San Pascual (changed to San Pasqual after the battle) to face the rested and superbly mounted Californios. A bloody battle ensued. The Californios' lances were overwhelming against the dragoons' short swords and rifles with damp gunpowder; eighteen Americans died on the battlefield. Four others would succumb later. Many were wounded, including Kearny. The Californios lost only one man; their wounded were never tallied. The battle's final outcome, however, is still in dispute. Both sides claimed victory, the Americans because they held the battleground, the Californios because they inflicted such damage on Kearny's troops.

After the battle, U.S. forces buried their dead and tended the wounded. The next morning they set out for San Diego, but were attacked again by the Californios five miles to the west at what is called Mule Hill. Pinned down for four days, they resorted to eating their mules to survive; hence the area's name. Kit Carson, with an Indian volunteer and navy Lt. Edward Beale crept away after nightfall on the second day, hoping to reach San Diego and convince Commodore Stockton to send reinforcements. On the night of December 10, a force of one hundred sailors and eighty marines from San Diego joined the beleaguered U.S. troops. The Californios, who had been preparing to attack, fired a single shot and fled. The battle of San Pasqual was over.

A stone marker stands on CA 78, seven miles southeast of Escondido, just across the road from the battlefield. The spot where Pico and the Californios camped the night before the battle is within a fenced area in San Pasqual State Historic Park. Another plaque, on Pomerado Road one-tenth of a mile east of I-15 and five miles southeast of Escondido, describes Mule Hill, which is now private property.

RAMONA

The exploration route continues southeast for about eleven miles to the town of Ramona in the Santa Maria Valley. The Ipai people who lived in the area called it the Valle de Pamofor. The town they called Nuevo. The name Ramona was inspired by Helen Hunt Jackson's 1884 romantic novel that bemoaned settlers' cruel treatment of the Indians. It was here that General Kearny and his dragoons camped the night before the battle at San Pasqual. The Guy B. Woodward Museum of History at 645 Main Street preserves Indian artifacts, historical exhibits, and rare documents from the past.

JULIAN, A TOWN OF HISTORY AND APPLES

Seven more miles of twisty, mountainous road leads to the gold mining town of Julian, more than 4,000 feet up in the Cuyamaca Mountains. Centuries before the actual gold strike in this area, tales of the yellow metal were bandied about—by Indians, by Vizcaíno's log-keeper, by early Mexican settlers. But it took Fred Coleman, who lived near Volcan Mountain with an Indian family, to make the first significant discovery. Late in 1869 Coleman had stopped at a stream to water his horse when he saw a yellow gleam in the streambed. Having worked in the northern

goldfields, he knew what he was seeing. Immediately he started panning with a skillet from his pack. As such news will, the story of Coleman's find soon spread throughout the county.

Into this setting, on November 1, 1869, came Drury and James Bailey and their cousins, the Julian boys, Mike and Webb. All four were from Georgia and had fought in the Civil War. All four had decided to leave the devastated South to look for a better life. Separately, they struck out for the West, only to meet up again in Nevada. Before long they found their way to Coleman Creek, which was solidly rimmed with disputing miners all looking for that yellow flash. Discouraged, they decided to move on.

Drury Bailey, however, had fallen in love with the area that is now called the Julian Valley. He declared he would settle there. After helping him build a cabin, Jim Bailey and Webb Julian went north in search of work; Drury and Mike Julian stayed behind to prospect. These two started the first quartz mine in the area and, in February 1870, formed the Julian Mining District. Soon other quartz deposits came to light and the stampede to Julian was on. With the area's population growing rapidly, Drury saw that a municipal center was needed. He hired a surveyor to plot a townsite on the part of his land closest to the mines, then named it Julian in honor of his cousin Mike.

The Julian Pioneer Museum at 2811 Washington Street houses an eclectic collection of artifacts from the town's early days, including a bathtub, wedding gowns, lace, and a pool table. The Julian Hotel at Main and B Streets is said to have been built around 1887 by a former slave. Today the community is known as a tourist center and a producer of excellent apples.

A MISSION OUTPOST

The route now retraces itself for seven miles from Julian to Santa Ysabel, site of an *asistencia* (mission outpost). The first mass was celebrated here on September 20, 1818, according to a marker that stands on CA 79, 1.4 miles north of the town. Even though more than 450 neophytes became attached to the *asistencia*, priestly visits became rare after secularization and the buildings fell into ruins. The chapel that stands today was built in 1924, with funds from Father Edmond La Pointe, a Canadian-born missionary. He is buried beside the church he served for twenty-nine years.

LAKE HENSHAW

Leaving Santa Ysabel the route takes off to the northeast on CA 79 toward Morettis Corner, seven miles away. There CA 79 branches off to the east, while CA 76 heads west. Near this junction is the southern tip of Lake Henshaw, a reservoir in the San Diego water system. Eargle tells us the creation of that body flooded lush marshes that once sustained the native residents of ten villages that flourished in the valley called Valle de San José by the padres.

WARNER SPRINGS

A side trip eight miles to the northeast on CA 79 reaches Warner Springs, a small community on the edge of the Los Coyotes Indian Reservation. The springs and surrounding rich land were once the center of Cupeño life, as evidenced by petroglyphs to be found in the area, but the San Luis Rey and San Diego Missions appropriated both springs and land. After secularization, Jonathan Trumbull Warner, a Connecticut-born trapper and trader who came to California in 1831, took over the property. Like so many others, he took Mexican citizenship in order to receive an extensive land grant in 1844.

Warner's Ranch

As the first bit of civilization west of the Colorado Desert, Warner's ranch became a famous way station for all who entered the state over the emigrant trail from Yuma. In 1846 Kearny and his dragoons sought refuge there on a night before the battle at San Pasqual. The next year Warner provided a stopover point for the Mormon Battalion on their march from Santa Fe to San Diego. Later still, the ranch became a stop on the Butterfield stage route, with the first coach arriving on October 6, 1858. It had traveled from Tipton, Missouri en route to San Francisco, a distance of twenty-six hundred miles. The house that sheltered so many weary travelers stands about four miles southeast of Warner Springs on County Road S2, just under a mile from CA 79.

Warner allowed the Indians to continue to live on what was now his property. Indeed, he put some of them to work on the ranch and paid them three dollars a month, the going rate for Indian labor at the time. He lashed them from time to time, too, also a custom of the times. In 1851 an Indian uprising inspired Warner to move back to Los Angeles.

The Indians Revolt

The so-called Garra Revolt occurred when Antonio Garra, chief of the Cupeñas, tried to form a great union of local tribes to drive the Americans out of Southern California. He managed to recruit help to plunder several ranchos and kill some Americans, but a pro-American chief of the Cahuillas betrayed him. Garra and several other Indians were executed for their part in the matter, as was William Marshall, a former seaman from New England. Hubert Bancroft says Marshall had jumped ship in San Diego in 1845, then hired on as manager of Warner's rancho in 1846. He was on hand, according to Bancroft, when Kearny and his troops arrived in December. Accused of being the instigator of the Indian uprising, Marshall was charged with high treason and hanged in 1851. In retaliation for the revolt, according to Eargle, the army destroyed local Indian food supplies and burned Garra's village.

By 1880 Warner Ranch property had fallen into the hands of John G. Downey, governor of California in 1861 and 1862. It was then that the Indians' right to live on what had been their land was disputed. After a suit heard by the U.S. Supreme Court, the right of the Indians to occupy the land was denied.

In 1903 Downey's heirs refused to sell the land around the hot springs to the federal government for an Indian home place. Richard F. Pourade says the Indians pleaded eloquently to be allowed to stay where they had always lived, but the Downey family was adamant. Finally the natives

Mount Palomar Observatory features what was once the world's largest telescope.
—Mount Palomar/Caltech

were ordered to move to Pala, some forty-five miles away. That journey has been represented as a western version of the Trail of Tears.

The route returns now to the junction of CA 79 and CA 76, at Moretti's Corner, about fourteen miles having been added to the distance to Temecula. CA 76 skirts the southwestern edge of Lake Henshaw to arrive at County Road S6, fifteen miles from Moretti's Corner. This twisty, mountainous road amid chaparral and rocks leads to Palomar Observatory, some eleven miles north of CA 76.

PALOMAR OBSERVATORY

The dream of creating a 200-inch reflecting telescope, larger than anything existing at the time, was launched in 1928 when the International Education Board gave $6 million for the construction of such an instrument and the buildings to house it. In 1948 the Rockefeller Foundation added another half-million dollars to the fund. The site atop Mount Palomar was chosen for its sixty-one-hundred-foot elevation above coastal fog and its clear skies.

Corning Glass Works in New York cast the Pyrex disk for the big telescope's mirror in 1935. The disk remained in the oven for almost two years and was then shipped to Pasadena. It arrived by rail at the California Institute of Technology on April 10, 1936. Grinding was done by the Institute's optical shops. Meanwhile the dome and housing for the telescope were completed in 1938. The onset of World War II in 1941 interrupted the mirror's polishing, which was put on hold. At last, on November 19, 1947, the finished mirror left Pasadena by truck, and the big telescope's first photographic observation was recorded on January 26, 1949. It was a fifteen-minute exposure of a galactic nebula. In recent years the telescope has been surpassed in size by others and hampered by light pollution from San Diego.

PALA

The route to Temecula has been lengthened by about twenty-two miles when the side trip returns to CA 76. It continues through the Pauma Valley to the intersection with County Road S16 and the community of Pala. Here is Mission San Antonio de Pala, the only unit of the California mission system to survive in its original purpose: to serve the Indians.

Founded in 1816 by Father Antonio Peyri, Mission San Antonio de Pala was an *asistencia* to the larger Mission San Luis Rey. The outpost thrived. In the 1830s, Father Peyri reported that it had about thirteen hundred Indians, a church and dwellings, and granaries. They grew a variety of field crops and grains as well as grapes and fruits. The remote location of the church helped to save it from the worst depredations that befell so many missions after secularization. Consequently, the chapel and the west wing of the church, partially restored by the Landmark Club in 1903, stand as they have for well over 150 years.

Restoration of the rest of the buildings was begun in 1954 and completed five years later. Today the restored outpost includes a school with more than one hundred students, most of whom are Indians from the many reservations in the area. A museum and gift shop housed in the church's original west wing contains a rich display of artifacts, statues, and important relics.

Six miles west on CA 76, the route rejoins I-15 to cover the last twelve miles to Temecula, a city that will be explored in part 10, "The Varied Inland Empire."

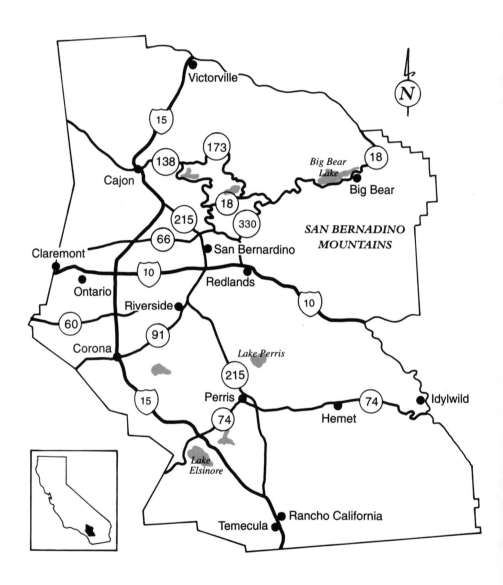

Part 10
The Varied Inland Empire

Probably no other portion of the state echoes California's diversity as well as the Inland Empire—Riverside and San Bernardino Counties. Bordered on the north by the San Bernardino Mountains and National Forest, the area nestles between the high and low deserts, taking traits from both. It encompasses two large cities that make up one of the largest marketing areas in the country. But it also contains—besides the ubiquitous citrus groves—apple and cherry orchards, mountain lakes, ski areas, vineyards, wineries, and a world-famous natural amphitheater. It's replete with historic sites, not as well known, perhaps, as a Hearst Castle or an Old Town, but with fascinating tales to tell.

One of those stories recalls an early attempt to turn this arid, near-desert landscape into a booming agricultural region. Louis Prévost, a French botanist, in 1854 introduced the idea of producing silk in the region then known as Jurupa. The scheme caught the fancy of farmers and promoters, who rushed to join his California Silk Center Association of Los Angeles. That group bought part of the Juan Bandini Rancho, some acres in the Hartshorn Trust, and acreage in the Jurupa Rancho on the east side of the Santa Ana River. Most of this land was to be planted with mulberry trees on which to feed silkworms.

In 1866 the California legislature, sold on the promise of silk, enacted legislation that would pay bonuses for participation in the silk industry. A bounty of $250 went to anyone who planted five thousand mulberry trees and kept them thriving for two years. One hundred thousand salable silkworm cocoons garnered a bonus of $300. Magazines and newspapers were filled with articles on the care and feeding of silkworms. Within three years an enormous number of mulberry trees covered the area; the movement became more obsession than business venture. Prévost established a mulberry nursery and a cocoonery where silkworms would be raised, hoping to outstrip even France and Japan in the production of fine silk.

Scott O'Dell comments that the silk production movement was unprecedented, even in a locale noted for zany promotions. The venture smacked of a grand chain-letter scheme wherein money was made by raising silkworm eggs, selling them to investors who would raise more silkworm eggs, and so on. Charles Nordhoff writes that, although California's climate and soil are both right for silk production, a great deal of money was wasted in the attempt. He reported that mulberry trees were planted in the wrong places and too close together. Some farmers even planted the wrong variety—trees that silkworms wouldn't eat. Very little fiber was produced and the only thing ever fashioned from California silk was a flag for the Capitol dome in Washington, D.C.

It's not surprising, then, that the craze dwindled away after Prévost's death in 1869. All wasn't in vain, however. The Southern California Colony Association, headed by John North, bought the Silk Center's land for $3.50 an acre and created a town they called Jurupa. The name was later changed to Riverside.

The San Bernardino National Forest, which separates the Inland Empire from the Mojave Desert, contains Big Bear Lake, a reservoir named after the natural lake that once sparkled nearby. A single-arch granite dam built in 1884 by one Frank Brown to provide water for the city of Redlands created the present-day lake. A plaque on the western edge of the lake, at the intersection of CA 18 and CA 38, tells how engineers vowed the dam wouldn't hold and proclaimed a miracle when it did. The national forest also encloses Lake Arrowhead, planned, according to O'Dell, as an irrigation project, but now just a reservoir for mountain runoff. It is today a recreational attraction of great renown, the largest mountain lake in Southern California.

I-15
Temecula–CA 60 Junction
50 miles

TEMECULA

Saying of itself, "Kit Carson passed this way . . . twice," the town of Temecula reveals its pride in the past. Local Native Americans called it "Where the Sun Shines through the Mist" or "Rising Sun." In 1797 Padre Juan Roberto de Santiago became the first white man to encounter those locals, the Temeculas (possibly a subgroup of the Cahuilla people). When Santiago reported that meeting to the king of Spain, Charles IV established the area as one of several land grants, including the one to Mission San Luis Rey. About 1820 a chapel and granary were built here by the padres of that mission.

The town's first site was about a mile south, where the Temecula River meets Murrieta Creek to become the Santa Margarita River. Temecula's second location was about three miles to the south, where it served as a relay station on the Butterfield stage route from 1858 until 1861, when the route was shifted because of the Civil War. The town then became an important layover spot for travelers on the Southern Immigrant Trail. When newly laid railroad tracks missed Temecula by three miles, the town simply moved once again, to its present location. In 1964, the Kaiser-Aetna organization took over the entire Vail Ranch, the land grant made after secularization, and renamed it Rancho California—all but Temecula.

Temecula is believed, according to Tom Hudson, to be the oldest town in California still known by its aboriginal name. It's certain that it's the site of the first inland Southern California post office, established in 1859.

Front Street, from Third to Sixth, is lined with buildings of historic significance. Among them is a private residence built in 1882 that once was the Welty Hotel. It's on Main Street, a little north of Front. Across the street is the Temecula Mercantile, which served as a terminal for jerk line freighters (freight wagons drawn by many pairs of animals controlled by a long line) that delivered goods to isolated ranches in the area.

LAKE ELSINORE

A little more than nineteen miles northeast of Temecula is the community of Lake Elsinore. Called Little Sea by the Indians, this shallow body of water for which the town is named sits at the edge of the Cleveland National Forest, about two miles off I-15. It lies in a trough at the base of the Santa Ana Mountains, rising and falling with seasonal rainfall. It has been known to vanish in dry years.

Before Franklin Heald discovered Lake Elsinore, it had been known as Laguna Grande, and Agustin Machado owned much of the land around it. Machado bought the property from Abel Stearns in 1858 and held it until 1873, when both land and lake became the property of developers and the land was renamed Lake Elsinore Valley. When Stearns and Machado owned it, the lake offered a place of rest and refreshment to travelers such as Kit Carson, John Trumbull Warner, and John C. Frémont. It served as a way station for the Butterfield stages, too, where weary travelers were offered refreshment in Machado's little adobe. Most of those who passed through commented on the barrenness of the countryside, which was home only to Indians and cottonwoods, plus deer and antelope that grazed on the sparse grass.

In 1873 Charles A. Sumner bought the property from Machado and started making changes. Noticing the steam that rose from the tules at the lake's edge, he began to fence in the noxious water from which the vapor rose. The Indians stopped him, pointing out that ailing cattle drank that water and it cured their illness. Water samples Sumner sent to Los Angeles for analysis confirmed the Indians' assessment. The report came back saying the water contained valuable minerals, so Sumner left the fence unbuilt.

If a monument were needed to remind folks in the valley of Sumner's stewardship, the eucalyptus trees would serve nicely. According to Hudson, in 1874 or 1875 O. W. Childs of Los Angeles gave Sumner some seeds from trees that grew in Australia. After planting them in a bed near his house, Sumner pronounced the summers too hot and winters too cold for the trees to do well. He was wrong. The trees flourished to provide seeds for most of the blue gum groves in Southern California. James Hart reports, on the other hand, that William C. Walker's Golden Gate Nursery in San Francisco advertised blue gum seedlings as early as 1856. Some historians say William Wolfskill was the first Southern Californian to cultivate eucalyptus, in the 1860s. Whoever really introduced the weepy, fragrant trees to California, they are now part of the state's scenery, as commonplace as oaks.

In downtown Lake Elsinore there stands an 1887 Victorian structure replete with gingerbread and a wooden veranda. Today an antique shop called the Chimes, it was originally the Crescent Bath House, built on an artesian well from which gushed hot mineral water. According to Kathy Strong, original Roman-style bathtubs and massage areas are still intact in the historic landmark. It was this spa that stimulated the growth of the community.

Precious Coal

Also contributing to the growth and continuing health of Lake Elsinore Valley was a discovery made by Madison Chaney, a former stagecoach driver, and his wife, Esther. All during the summer of 1883 the pair toiled, he digging while she pushed a wheelbarrow filled with dirt, to expose a sizable vein of coal in the hills northwest of Elsinore. One year later, according to Eloise Elkins, writing in the *Fedco Reporter*, William Collier, one of the founders of the town, pitched in with financial backing. Chaney's single tunnel became seven, miners were hired, and rails were laid into the mine. Mules pulled filled cars to wagons waiting

Depot at Orange Empire Railway Museum in Perris. The park features a collection of railcars used all over the world. —Sheldon Liss, Orange Empire Railway Museum

to haul the coal to the railroad. In a single year, more than 7,000 tons were shipped to Redlands, Anaheim, San Diego, and Los Angeles.

Ten years later, Chaney sold his interest in the coal mine to James Hill and C. H. Albers, who called the mine Alberhill Coal and Clay Company. While continuing to mine coal, they developed clay deposits, which were more profitable. By the early twentieth century, mining of the low-grade fuel ceased, but not of clay. About five miles north of the community of Lake Elsinore lies the town of Alberhill, locale of the Pacific Clay Products Company.

PERRIS

Before proceeding to Alberhill, the route takes a short side trip into the San Jacinto Basin. That term is used to designate the lowland area of Riverside County that lies between the San Jacinto Mountains on the east and the Santa Anas on the west. Ten miles from Lake Elsinore, east along CA 74, in this basin is the town of Perris, once known as Pinacate, Spanish for "stink bug."

*Passengers wait to board the Inland Empire's famous yellow
cars that now operate at the Orange Empire Railway Museum.*
—Sheldon Liss, Orange Empire Railway Museum

The town came into being shortly before the arrival of the California Southern Railroad in 1882. That same year, Pinacate was designated as a station on that line and subsequently on the Santa Fe, when it arrived in 1885. In 1886 a dispute over land titles resulted in the town's moving about a mile and a half north to the site of today's Perris.

The town is home to the Orange Empire Railway Museum, a collection of railcars used all over the world in earlier days. Founded in 1956, the outdoor museum covers twelve acres and contains one of the largest collections of its kind in the world: 150 vehicles, at last count. It is at 2201 South A Street.

The rock dwelling in the Pinacate picnic area of the Railway Museum is believed to be the oldest building in the region. Built as a store by L. D. Reynolds, postmaster of Pinacate, around 1882, it also served as a stage stop on the route to San Jacinto. Other buildings related to railroading have been moved from distant sites. One example is the Oil Junction Station at the northeastern end of the park. It is from the joint Southern Pacific and Santa Fe Oil City branch north of Bakersfield.

HEMET

The side trip continues southeast three miles on Matthews Road, then due east along CA 74 fourteen miles farther to Hemet, home of the Ramona Pageant. Founded in 1898, Hemet sits in a farming region liberally sprinkled with Indian petroglyphs and homes for retired persons. It is famous, however, for its natural amphitheater called the Ramona Bowl. There each spring since 1923 the town's residents have staged a production of Helen Hunt Jackson's 1884 novel of life in early California. The novel was so widely popular that many people believe its characters to be real, with legends persisting about the so-called Ramona Country. Just to the north of Perris is a tiny town named Alessandro, after the novel's ill-fated Indian hero, and an Alessandro Boulevard runs through eastern Riverside.

Also in Hemet, on California Avenue, is Maze Stone County Park, which features a collection of Native American rock art. The park is named for one rock that is covered with what William Logan and Susan Ochshorn call "a mysterious labyrinthine pattern." Also, at the southern end of Santa Fe Street, at the foot of a hill, is a boulder pitted with pictographs.

The route returns now to I-15 having added about fifty-four miles to the distance to the junction with CA 60. Twenty-one miles from CA 74, I-15, now labeled the Corona Freeway, crosses CA 91 (the Riverside Freeway). Travelers willing to bypass many colorful towns of the Inland

Alessandro gallops through the Ramona Bowl at Hemet during one of the area's annual productions of Helen Hunt Jackson's Ramona.
—The Ramona Pageant

Vicente Lugo ranch house, circa 1892. —CHS/TICOR, USC Special Collections

Empire may want to detour northeast sixteen miles to reach Riverside directly. The historic route, however, continues along the eastern edge of the Cleveland National Forest, past the towns of Alberhill and El Cerrito to Corona. Taking a more northerly turn, it continues through Norco and Mira Loma, to the junction with CA 60. To the west lie Chino, Pomona, Ontario, Claremont, and Upland, all largely residential communities.

CHINO

Chino is an orchard and sugar beet–growing area on CA 83, near its junction with CA 60. The town got its start around 1841 when Isaac Williams built a large adobe home on today's Eucalyptus Avenue, about a block west of CA 71 and Pipeline Avenue. The land was part of the great Rancho Santa Ana del Chino, given to Williams by his father-in-law Antonio María Lugo. It became famous as a pleasant stopover for travelers on the Southern Emigrant Trail and later a station on the Butterfield stage route.

The battle of Chino took place at Williams' adobe in 1846 when a group of Americans, including Benjamin D. Wilson, took refuge there.

When the house was surrounded by Californios, a skirmish followed that saw one of the attackers killed and several defenders wounded. Williams eventually surrendered to protect his small children, and about twenty-four Americans were taken captive. Their victory in this battle encouraged the Californios to take on Gillespie at Los Angeles a few days later. A plaque at Chino Fire Station Number Two marks the site of the adobe, now vanished. Wilson went on to become a conciliator during the Mexican War and, in 1851, mayor of Los Angeles. He also worked with Phineas Banning to develop the harbor at Wilmington. Mount Wilson is named for him.

POMONA AND ONTARIO

West of Chino, on CA 60, is Pomona, site of the annual Los Angeles County Fair. North of Chino on CA 83 is Ontario, founded in 1882 by George Chaffey. He planned the community to be a model one, with an agricultural base supported by irrigation and hydroelectric systems owned jointly with its neighbor Etiwanda. It was in the Imperial Valley, however, that Chaffey really made his mark.

Inside a citrus packing house in Ontario, circa 1905. —CHS/TICOR, USC Special Collections

315

Top: *Sumner Hall in Claremont, soon after its construction in the early 1880s as the Claremont Hotel. It never served as a hotel.* —Pomona College

Bottom: *Sumner Hall after it was given to Pomona College. Classes began in January 1888.* —Pomona College

A Central Pacific Railroad emigrant train of 1883. Emigrant trains at that time included passenger cars for families moving west, freight cars for household goods, and livestock cars for animals. Low fares enticed families to move to the area. —Southern Pacific Railroad

CLAREMONT

Claremont, about three miles west of CA 83 and a little north of I-10, is home to the Claremont Colleges. That group comprises six separate schools, all offering different programs, but sharing a library and other facilities. The original school was Pomona College, founded in 1887 by Congregationalists. It was followed by Scripps, Harvey Mudd, Pitzer, Claremont Men's College, and Claremont Graduate School.

In her book about Claremont, Judy Wright says that Indian Hill, a mesa a few hundred yards northeast of the intersection of Foothill and Indian Hill Boulevards, offers substantial evidence that Serranos lived in the area as recently as the middle of the eighteenth century. The land was well watered by San Antonio Creek and artesian springs, and the food supply was bountiful, with ample oak trees and plentiful small game. When Mission San Gabriel was founded, the Claremont area became grazing grounds for the padres' sheep and cattle. Smallpox

Santa Fe Railroad tracks run along historic Route 66 over Cajon Pass in the Inland Empire. —Bob Lundy, Route 66 Museum

outbreaks in 1862 and 1873 took a heavy toll on the natives and by 1883 few of them remained. The handful who did manage to remain alive went to live on the Morongo Indian Reservation, where they intermarried with Cahuillas. There are no pure Serranos alive today.

Another Land Boom

The Pacific Land and Improvement Company, a Boston firm, founded Claremont in 1887. To lend an appearance of vitality, the company had brush cleared from the townsite, and built a few houses, a land office, and the Claremont Hotel. The Santa Fe Railroad added a depot south of the hotel. Advertisements distributed far and wide proclaimed the virtues of "Claremont the Beautiful." Land sales began on April 7, 1887, stimulated by some of the most flowery language boomtown promotion has ever produced. The usual brass bands and picnic lunches contributed to the $20 million in sales racked up in the town's first year. The land boom lasted only about a year, but it had a significant effect on the entire area. It eliminated the pastoral economy of the Spanish and Mexicans that had characterized California history since 1769. The gold rush shaped the character of Northern California; the land rush did the same for Southern California.

ROUTE 66

A short side trip to the east along Foothill Boulevard to Rancho Cucamonga brings the history buff to the legendary Route 66. At 8916-C Foothill Boulevard, long the name of the fabled route in these parts, stands California's oldest winery, Thomas Brothers. It was originally part of a land grant to Tiburicio Tapia, who planted grapes on the land in 1839. When Route 66 reached California, it cut a swath right through the ancient vineyards. Today one of the winery's buildings is a Route 66 museum and visitors center. Here are mementoes of that twenty-four-hundred-mile road that ran from Santa Monica to Chicago. Established in 1926, it was decertified in 1985, but the segment from San Bernardino to San Dimas, about twenty miles, is still officially named Route 66. Returning south on I-15, this side trip adds fourteen miles to the distance to the junction of I-15 and CA 60.

CA 60/91 and I-10
Junction I-15/CA 60–Redlands
About 30 miles

RIVERSIDE

Twelve miles east of I-15 stands the city of Riverside, seat of the county of the same name. Earliest residents of the area left their mark, literally, in pictographs that can be seen on rocks scattered throughout the surrounding area. According to Irving Stone, Riverside, besides being the home of the navel orange and the oldest air force base on the West Coast (March Field), was also the first community in the country to stage an outdoor Easter sunrise service and to have an electrically lighted outdoor Christmas tree.

In 1774 Capt. Juan de Anza, making his way from Arizona to Monterey, became the first white man to pass through the area. In passing, he constructed a bridge across the Santa Ana River on what was the land grant of don Juan Bandini. The don gave part of the grant to his daughter Arcadia and her husband Abel Stearns. The rest went to Louis Rubidoux, member of a well-known family of fur trappers. Rubidoux, one of the first settlers in the region, stayed in the area to become a judge, supervisor, and supporter of education. More than one hundred years after de Anza's visit, the town was founded by the Southern California Colony Association (under the leadership of John North), which had bought the land from silkworm raisers. Riverside was incor-

A fruit-packing shed in Riverside, circa 1930. —Riverside Visitor and Convention Bureau

porated in 1883. The county was created in 1893 by carving away and combining portions of San Bernardino and San Diego Counties.

Tasty Gold

The citrus industry in California began with the arrival of the padres, who planted oranges and lemons at the missions. San Gabriel led the missions in plantings, with about four hundred trees on six acres, but the products bore little resemblance to the fruit we know today. The fruit was small, bitter, and difficult to peel. In 1834 Jean Louis Vignes set out the first commercial orange grove in Los Angeles, even though his first love was wine grapes.

Another early citrus grower was William Wolfskill, a one-time fur trapper who came to California in 1831. In 1841 he planted a commercial orange grove in the vicinity of Los Angeles and soon became the largest producer in the southern part of the state.

But it remained for a homemaker in Riverside to put the industry on the way to becoming the gold mine that it is today. In 1870 Eliza Tibbets and her husband, Luther, an alfalfa farmer, moved to Riverside from Washington, D.C. Their neighbor in Washington had been William O. Saunders, superintendent of horticulture in the Bureau of Agriculture. When the bureau received a dozen newly budded navel orange trees from Brazil in 1870, Saunders wrote his friends the Tibbets about the unusual fruit bursting with sweet flavor, with no seeds and an easy-to-peel skin. Eliza asked him to send her a couple of offspring of those trees, should he succeed in propagating them.

In 1873, Saunders shipped two trees to his friends in California. Eliza planted them on the couple's eighty-acre homestead, where they flourished to form the parent stock for the entire navel orange industry in California. One of the parent trees still thrives today at Magnolia and Arlington Avenues; the other died after being moved to the courtyard of the Mission Inn.

By 1895 those trees had made Riverside the nation's richest city per capita, according to Vince Moses, Curator of History at the Riverside Municipal Museum. The marvelous golden fruit sparked a second gold rush that endured far longer than the first.

Citrus State Historic Park, opened in the summer of 1993, was created to tell the colorful story of this industry that plays such an important role in California's economy. It is also planned to preserve the vanishing landscape of citrus groves, packing houses, wind machines, smudge pots, and all the rest. The entrance to the park, at Van Buren and Dufferin, is marked by a giant orange like the ones that used to dot roadsides all over the state, where all the fresh-squeezed orange juice you could drink was to be had for as little as twenty-five cents.

The Gage Canal

That the Riverside area became the ideal place to grow the so-called Washington navel orange was due in no small part to Matthew Gage and his canal, a portion of which is preserved within Citrus Park. About 1885 Gage claimed some 640 acres of land under the Desert Lands Act, according to Ron Schafer, chief ranger at the park in 1992. That law, passed in 1877, provided 640 arid acres at $1.25 per acre, to anyone willing to reclaim the land by irrigation, although they did not necessarily have to live on it. Gage had only three years in which to bring water to the land in order to validate his claim. Building all sorts of tunnels and wooden flumes, he managed to get water from the Santa Ana River near Loma Linda as close as an arroyo just south of Riverside's original square-mile plot. Deeply in debt, he bought more land and extended the canal to a total length of a little more than twenty miles, still short of his claim.

Tiled roofs and towers of Mission Inn Hotel in Riverside. The elaborate establishment, which never served as a mission, was started by Frank Miller in 1875. —Riverside Visitor and Convention Bureau

In 1888, owing well over a million dollars and unable to borrow more locally, Gage turned for help to a wealthy Briton, William Crewdson. Forming the Riverside Trust Company, that financier took over all of Gage's land and water rights, as well as the uncompleted canal. The company assumed all of his debts, too, and named him manager of the Gage Canal Company. The canal was finished, crossing Mockingbird Canyon (just to the south of today's Citrus Park) first via a flume, but eventually with a dam, locks, and a spillway that created Mockingbird Canyon Lake. The final length of the canal was twenty-three miles; the area it watered blossomed and became famous as Arlington Heights, the best place in the world to grow oranges.

Never a Real Mission

Arguably even more famous than the navel orange is Riverside's pride: the Mission Inn. In 1873 Christopher Columbus Miller, a newly hired engineer of the fledgling city, built an adobe cottage for his family at Seventh and Main Streets. Mildred Hoover says it was the first solid-walled house in the city. In 1875 the family decided to host paying guests in the home they called Glenwood Cottage. Over the years it gained a reputation for pleasant hospitality, creating a need for wings and additions to the original building.

Actually in charge of the entire operation was C. C. Miller's son Frank, who in 1902 bought out his family and turned the hotel into a showcase for treasures gathered during his world travels. Today the hotel is a blend of many architectural styles: Mission Revival, Spanish, and Mediterranean, with influences from Europe, Asia, and Central America. It is a national, state, and city historic monument, reopened in 1993 after extensive renovation.

A city that's proud of its history, Riverside claims more than eighty other historic sites worthy of attention. One of the better known is Heritage House, built in 1891 at Magnolia near Adams. The Queen Anne Victorian home was built for Catherine Bettner, the widow of a New York attorney and president of the Riverside Fruit Company. Complete with domed tower and elaborate fretwork, the mansion is listed in the National Register of Historic Places. At 3525 Orange Street stands the Universalist-Unitarian Church built of Arizona sandstone in 1891. Architect A. C. Willard designed the building to recall a medieval English parish church.

The Heritage House in Riverside was built in 1891 at Magnolia near Adams for the widow of the president of the Riverside Fruit Company.
—Riverside Visitor and Convention Bureau

San Bernardino

Leaving Riverside, the route travels northeast along CA 91 for about ten miles to reach San Bernardino, seat of that county.

San Bernardino County, organized in 1853, was created from parts of Los Angeles and San Diego Counties and is the largest county in the state. The name derives from the Spanish for Saint Bernard. To the north and east of its most populated area lie the San Bernardino National Forest and Mountains. In those mountains are Lake Arrowhead and Big Bear Lake. Beyond both forest and mountains are the great deserts of California.

California's Mormon City

The city of San Bernardino had its beginning in 1810 as an *asistencia* of Mission San Gabriel, which was destroyed several times by unhappy Paiutes. Its true founders, however, were Mormons, some of them former members of the Mormon Battalion and some pilgrims from Brigham Young's flock in Utah.

Scott O'Dell, in *Country of the Sun*, says that in 1851 the attractions of California impressed even the Mormons in Utah. In March of that year a train of 150 wagons carrying almost five hundred men, women, and children set out for the Golden State without Brigham Young's blessing. Fearing that these emigrants were seeking physical, not spiritual, gold, Young tried to dissuade them, but failed.

The hardships along the trail pioneered by Jed Smith were severe and many wished they had heeded Young's advice. Indians stole their horses and mules, two snowstorms impeded their progress, mountain passes were steeper than they had foreseen, and food for both animals and humans grew scarce. Stalwart they were, however, and June found the first of the band arriving at the agreed-upon marshalling place, a mile or so from today's Devore railroad station. By mid-July the entire party had rendezvoused in a sycamore grove in Cajon Canyon. Today a plaque marks the site of that camp in Glen Helen Regional Park at 2555 Devore Road, just under a mile west of Devore. Another monument stands beside CA 138, not quite four miles west of I-15, some twenty miles north of San Bernardino. This one marks the pass by which the Mormons entered the San Bernardino Valley in 1851.

At the camp, the group drew up rules for the conduct of their affairs and started a day school, while two apostles set out to find financing for the purchase of Rancho San Bernardino, which they had selected as the site of the city they would establish. They raised the money by the simple expedient of asking all Mormons working in the goldfields around San Francisco to contribute their tithe for the purpose. They gathered a down payment of $8,000 fairly quickly and, on September 22, reached an agreement with the Lugo brothers to purchase the land for a total of $77,500.

Thinking they had bought some 100,000 acres, the saints (Mormons) planned to sell some acreage to pay off the mortgage rapidly in order to avoid prolonged payment of 30 percent annual interest. They found, however, that their new holdings were only about 40,000 acres. From that spread they chose the most favorable square mile and laid out a town they called San Bernardino. They started at once to build homes for themselves, only to be interrupted by the so-called Garra Revolt.

Quickly, the Mormons turned their attention to building a stockade that would shelter the entire community. Working day and night, they fashioned an enclosure of logs 700 feet by 300 feet on what is now the courthouse grounds. Even though the revolt was short-lived, the Mormons remained inside the stockade for more than a year. A historical marker at the corner of Arrowhead Avenue and Court Street marks the site of that stockade.

Once peace seemed assured, the saints planted grapes and fruit trees and constructed a grist mill. Sawmills powered by swift-flowing mountain streams provided lumber for their homes. Stores opened; streets were laid out. The city blossomed under the cooperative efforts that characterize Mormon undertakings.

Brigham Young, however, wasn't appeased. He hadn't changed his mind about a settlement in California and, in 1857, recalled the apostles who had been at the head of the movement. About half of those who lived in San Bernardino returned to Salt Lake City; half didn't. The loss of so many of their fellows slowed the growth of their beautiful community.

The Mysterious Arrow

One final historic spot in the area remains to be examined. A plaque stands in Wildwood Park, at the intersection of Waterman Avenue (CA 18) and 40th Street. Pedro Fages first remarked on the spot described on the plaque when he explored the San Bernardino Valley; Jedediah Smith saw it too, when he shaped the trail through Cajon Pass. It is visible for miles around.

An Indian legend says the Creator placed this noted landmark high on a mountain slope above the valley to guide the Cahuillas when they were driven from their homes. It is a huge arrowhead composed of outcroppings of quartz and gray granite, pointing straight at the fertile valley and healing mineral springs. Another old tale claims Brigham Young saw the arrow in his dreams and ordered a colony established in its vicinity. That story, however, isn't credible, since Young so staunchly opposed the westward travel of members of his flock. It's possible that Elders Amasa M. Lyman and Charles C. Rich, who headed the group that laid out San Bernardino, interpreted the arrowhead as a favorable sign.

REDLANDS

Leaving San Bernardino, the historical route continues eastward along I-10 toward Redlands, whose name derives from the color of the soil on which it stands. In the beginning, Redlands was part of Rancho San Bernardino, José del Carmen Lugo's land grant. During the 1840s Lugo used the outpost mission's buildings here. When Mormons bought the land in 1851, they razed the buildings and planted an orange grove; however, oranges never did well in this spot, which, legend has it, was cursed by an Indian medicine man. The mission buildings were restored in the late 1930s by the Works Progress Administration with the advice of the San Bernardino County Historical Society. Today the chapel stands at 26930 Barton Road, east of Nevada Street.

In Sylvan Park on University Street stands another historical plaque. This one marks the Zanja, or ditch, that the Franciscan fathers designed and Indians dug to carry water to the mission's fields. Constructed in 1819 and 1820, it was the first irrigation system in the valley and served the rancho after secularization, then carried water to settlers' fields and farms. Finally it delivered water to the Redlands domestic water supply.

YUCAIPA

Most of the rest of San Bernardino County lies in the Mojave Desert, which you will read about in the next section of this book. One exception stands about fourteen miles southeast of Redlands, just off I-10: Yucaipa. This area supported a large number of Serranos, who called it Yucaipat, "wet lands," and lived at this site most of the year. At 32183 Kentucky Street stands the Sepulveda Adobe, which dates from 1842 and is said to be the oldest residence in the county.

This side trip adds a final twenty-five miles or so to the exploration of the Inland Empire. The route now plunges into the once-feared Mojave Desert.

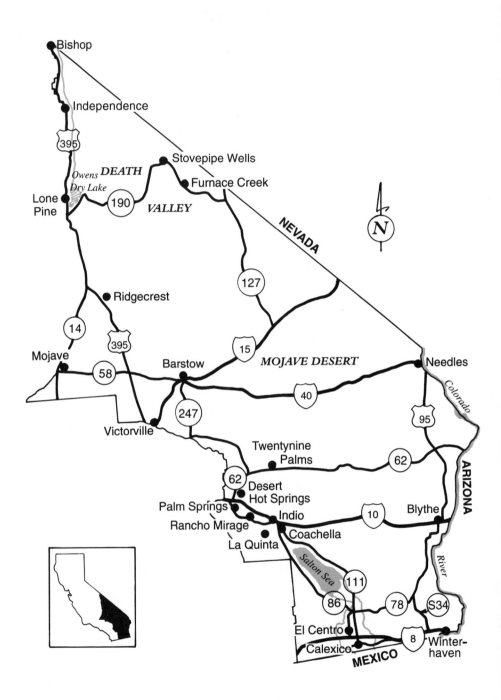

Part 11
The Majestic Deserts

California's deserts are not only huge, accounting for almost one-quarter of all land in the state, they are also misunderstood. Even today few appreciate the beauty and fertility of those great expanses. And few save "desert rats" afford these arid expanses the respect that is their due. Many who visit the Colorado and Mojave Deserts regard their landscapes with distaste, if not horror. Yet thousands make their homes and livelihoods there, in the low desert and the high, where such cities such as Palm Springs and Lancaster flourish. Recreation areas grow apace, too. Golf courses, water parks, and historical landmarks lure all but the most timid to explore the creosote-studded sandy hills, and fields that blaze with wildflowers during springs that follow wet winters.

The deserts are fragile, as well, easily destroyed by such human playthings as automobiles and motorcycles. Tender plants trampled by a careless footstep may never spring back to life; gentle animals like the tortoise and horned toad will soon be found only in zoos, their kind obliterated in the wild by heedless off-road vehicles and careless humans. The comic roadrunner may soon perform its antics only on movie screens. All are threatened: the desert hare, the tiny chipmunks that scurry across back roads just one leap ahead of speeding cars, lizards that do push-ups on sunny rocks. Only the coyote thrives to howl at full moons and even its habitat grows smaller each year.

The Colorado Desert covers about 4,000 square miles and encompasses the Coachella and Imperial Valleys and the Salton Sea. It's also known as the southern or low desert and is actually part of the Sonoran Desert that extends into Arizona and Mexico.

The Colorado River might be said to have been to the Imperial Valley what Marshall's gold discovery was to the Mother Lode country. Water from that mighty river transformed what was wasteland into productive and profitable fields. Rising west of the Continental Divide, the Colorado flows southwest through Colorado, Utah, and Arizona before reaching Mexico. It enters Baja California at Yuma, Arizona, and rushes down to empty into the northernmost tip of the Gulf of California. With its tributaries it drains parts of seven states.

At 1,450 miles, the Colorado is the longest river west of the Rockies. It proved to be a formidable foe of early explorers who tried to sail up the mighty watercourse. According to the Federal Writers' Project guide, Hernando de Alarcón discovered the river in August 1540, when his party sailed up it in small boats, possibly as far as Alta California. However, many other would-be travelers on the Colorado were turned away by its tidal bore, which is, according to Scott O'Dell, second only to the Hangchow Bore in China. As recently as 1922, O'Dell says, a shipload of workers heading for the Imperial Valley was swamped by the great tidal flow and eighty-six persons were washed to their death. Taming the river and putting its water to work made life in the Imperial Valley possible.

Before the introduction of water for irrigation, this great area was an immense wasteland. Those who had the foresight, courage, and persistence to find ways to water the desert should be honored as heroes, particularly by those who enjoy grapefruit, tomatoes, grapes, dates, and other riches from the fertile desert.

The Mojave Desert spreads over some 15,000 square miles south of the Sierra Nevada and north of the San Bernardino, San Gabriel, and Chocolate Mountains. It's called the northern or high (because of its altitude) desert. To the east lie Nevada and Arizona; to the northeast is Death Valley, dramatically different.

On the southern edge of the Mojave is Joshua Tree National Monument. The area within the monument is one of transition, changing from low desert to high, from Colorado to Mojave. According to *The California Missions*, the delineation is clear between the scrub vegetation and delicate wildflowers of the low desert and the more flamboyant plants of the high. As interesting and beautiful as it may be, little of the area's history remains within the national monument.

Joshua trees, the plants for which the area is named, are actually giant yuccas, members of the lily family. One popular legend has it that Mormons named them, likening their shape to that of a praying prophet Joshua. The plants grow mostly at 3,000–5,000 feet elevation and are found scattered throughout Utah, Nevada, and Arizona, as well as Southern California. The eastern part of the park is marked by creosote bush, spindly ocotillo, and cholla cactus.

The infamous Owens Valley is geographically part of the eastern Sierra Nevada, but it is more like the desert than the mountains since its water was stolen to slake the thirst of Los Angeles and its land speculators. It will be explored in this section.

Besides being beautiful and fertile, the California deserts are deceptive and dangerous. The wise history buff will stay on marked roads when exploring and will heed warnings about flash floods. A brilliant day with only white clouds scudding around in the piercing blue sky can become a day of tragedy in, well, a flash. Water falling during rainstorms in the mountains rushes down hillsides to wash over low-lying roads. Arroyos (dry washes) are particularly treacherous spots, but the most dangerous are usually marked.

"The Desert Queen" sailing on Rosamond Dry Lake, Mojave Desert, 1905. Miners built and used this unique vehicle to cross the three-mile lake bed. —CHS/TICOR, USC Special Collections

I-10, CA 111, and CA 86
Redlands–El Centro
145 miles

BEAUMONT AND BANNING

Exploration of this vast area starts at the edge of the Inland Empire, on I-10, heading east. Fifteen miles from Redlands the route reaches Beaumont, on a plain atop San Gorgonio Pass that cuts between San Jacinto and San Gorgonio Peaks, both of which are often topped with snow. J. Smeaton Chase says the pass "forms the dividing line between California barren and California fertile." According to Mildred Hoover, Beaumont was once a stopping point on the upper branch of the old emigrant trail from Warner's Ranch.

The Federal Writers' Project guide says the region was opened up in 1853 by Dr. I. W. Smith, a Mormon, in hot pursuit of a straying herd of cattle. Doctor Smith trailed the animals all the way from San Bernardino, finally corralling them just north of where Beaumont is today. Impressed by the region, he settled there almost immediately, living a lonely existence until a stage station was established, and a hotel in 1884.

According to Strong, that hotel, the San Gorgonio Inn, was actually in Banning, six miles to the east. Constructed in 1884 as the Bryant House, it was partially destroyed by fire in 1930. One of the artifacts snatched from that fire was a register of guests that included President and Mrs. Grover Cleveland who stayed there on December 30, 1884. The hotel, which has been remodeled several times since the fire, stands at 150 East Ramsey Street in Banning.

CABAZON

Six miles farther east is Cabazon, home of the tiny Morongo reservation for the Cahuilla. Over the years the tribe has gained notoriety for aggressively pursuing its right to conduct huge bingo games to raise money for reservation upkeep. Long freight trains are often seen inching their way over San Gorgonio Pass, propelled by extra engines from a Southern Pacific roundhouse in Cabazon. Tracks were first laid in 1875, after the railroad secured the cooperation of the sometimes unfriendly natives by promising them free rides.

PALM SPRINGS

A little more than six miles east of Cabazon the route crosses CA 111, the road to Palm Springs, since the 1920s the retreat of presidents

Palm Springs takes advantage of the area's clean air, blue skies, and spectacular mountain views to promote tourism. —Palm Springs Desert Resorts Convention and Visitors Bureau

and movie stars. That city is just eleven miles southeast of I-10. Originally the home of the Cahuilla, Palm Springs was discovered by de Anza in 1774 and named Agua Caliente, for its mineral springs. Today's town was born in 1876, when Southern Pacific laid tracks through the Coachella Valley. The city is named for the native Washington palm trees that abound in the area, some of which are estimated to be more than fifteen hundred years old. Particularly fine stands grow on the Agua Caliente Indian Reservation just to the south. Clusters of berries produced by these trees were a dietary staple of the Cahuilla.

The reservation holds most of the tales of the area's past, in a scenic section called "Indian Canyons." Listed in the National Register of Historic Places, Palm, Andreas, and Murray Canyons are accessible, mostly on foot or horseback, only in late fall and winter months. According to Strong, rock art, house pits and foundations, dams, and the remains of food processing areas make visiting the canyons worthwhile, if taxing. The entrance to this historic area is via a toll road just off Palm Canyon Drive.

Within the city are the Cornelia White House, at 221 South Palm Canyon Drive, and the McCallum Adobe. The White House was built of railroad ties in 1893 to serve as a guest house for the town's first hotel. The neighboring adobe dates back to 1884 and illustrates desert life before resort days.

Palm Springs is famous for its aerial tramway that carries tourists over Chino Canyon to the top of 8,000-foot Mt. San Jacinto.
—Palm Springs Desert Resorts Convention and Visitors Bureau

Leaving Palm Springs, the route continues for twenty-four miles on CA 111 along the edge of a state game refuge. It passes the resort towns of Cathedral City, Rancho Mirage, and Palm Desert before reaching CA 86 at Indio.

INDIO

Today a resort, Indio got its start in 1876 as a construction camp for Southern Pacific builders. It calls itself the Date Capital of the World, even though it produces raisins and citrus fruit, too, and is a distribution center for the fruits of the entire Coachella Valley.

Such prodigious fruit raising in a desert was made possible by irrigation. Since 1941 water from the Colorado River has been carried west from Parker Dam, the source of Lake Havasu, via the Colorado River Aqueduct. In 1948 the Coachella Canal began directing water northward from the All American Canal near the international border.

THE SALTON SEA

Leaving Indio, CA 86 turns due south to travel through thirty-five miles of desert just west of the Salton Sea. It passes Oasis, 149 feet below sea level, Coolidge Spring, and Salton City, at an elevation of minus 87 feet.

The unprepossessing body of water to the east lies in what is called the Salton Sink, a depression that covers more than 2,000 square miles and stretches from San Gorgonio Pass to the Gulf of California. According to Lynne Foster, this basin is the largest area of dry land below sea level in the Western Hemisphere and contains the Coachella, Imperial, and Mexicali Valleys. Scientists say it was created by earth movements along the San Andreas Fault.

During the last couple of million years, the Colorado River has periodically filled lakes in this great basin. The Salton Sea is only the most recent and by far the smallest, at thirty-eight miles long and from nine to fifteen miles wide. Still, it is the largest lake in California. It came into being after canals were built near Yuma to divert water from the Colorado River to irrigate the Imperial Valley.

Irrigation Genius

Well over a hundred years ago, Oliver M. Wozencraft, having completed stints as a delegate to the first state constitutional convention and a federal Indian agent, turned his attention to the Imperial Valley. One of three men who strove to make the southern desert blossom, Wozencraft is known as the Father of the Imperial Valley. It was he who first perceived that what covers the area isn't simply useless desert sand, but alluvial soil deposited by centuries of floodwater from the Colorado. With water it would bloom.

After conceiving the idea of watering the vast desert, Wozencraft sought help from the state legislature. In 1859 that body granted him all state rights in the Salton Sink. His next step was to seek a patent from the federal government. That he never acquired because the attention of Congress was focused on the Civil War and the problems of Reconstruction. Attempts to interest investors in the project failed, too, and Wozencraft died in 1887, his dream of transporting Colorado River water across the desert unfulfilled. He never knew that his appeals had caught the attention of George Chaffey, Charles R. Rockwood, and Anthony H. Heber. They picked up where Wozencraft left off. Overcoming legal, financial, and engineering obstacles, the trio diverted a portion of the Colorado's flow and began irrigating the desert.

The work was accomplished by an organization named the California Development Company, which was put together mainly by Heber and Rockwood in 1896. They hired Chaffey to run it. Before meeting up with this pair, Chaffey had created the communities of Etiwanda and Ontario in the 1880s. He had developed the idea of mutual water companies and built the first hydroelectric plant in California.

George Chaffey,
the genius who
caused the desert
to bloom.
—The Bancroft Library

In Australia he had successfully colonized arid regions by providing water for irrigation.

An extensive boom resulted from the successful irrigation of this area, too. Walton Bean says Chaffey's inspired name, Imperial Valley, changed the image of the region from that of arid wasteland to flourishing agricultural empire. Towns such as Imperial, Calexico, Holtville, and El Centro sprang up. In 1901 the first Colorado River water flowed from a point near Yuma, into Mexico, and north to the Imperial Valley. By the end of 1904, well over 100,000 acres of land had been reclaimed. Before that dream was accomplished, Chaffey had parted company with Heber and Rockwood.

Soon after Chaffey's departure, and following a series of financial and political crises, Rockwood grew impatient with the rate of water flow through the canal Chaffey had engineered. The Colorado was low, thanks to meager winter snows, and the canal was silting up; the situation called for action. Rockwood ordered a canal cut to bypass the gate that controlled the rate of flow from the main aqueduct. According to Robert Cleland, in *California in Our Time*, Mexico was slow to approve the construction of a similar gate on the diversionary channel. Early in 1905, the first of five floods surged down the Colorado. Attempts to close the new canal proved futile and by the end of June water was coursing up an old wash called the New River at the rate of 14,000 cubic feet per second. The water naturally settled into the below-sea-level center of the Salton Sink. Because the break was in Mexico, the U.S. government refused to intervene and the flow continued for two years. Finally, to save its tracks, Southern Pacific took matters into its own hands, dumping thousands of railcars of rock, clay, and gravel into the rushing waters. By the time the flow was halted, the Salton Sea had been formed.

Fed by runoff waters from agriculture, the sea's depth remains fairly constant, rising and falling with wet years and dry, although its salinity, at 30 percent and rising, is greater than that of the ocean. It's full of chemicals, too, from fertilizers, and sewage from Mexico. Its water is chocolate color, its odor awful. Fishermen are advised to eat sparingly of their catches. An article published in the *Los Angeles Times* during the summer of 1993 reported that the first small steps are being taken to reclaim the lake. Progress will be slow because of the state's poor financial condition, but those who love the Salton Sea are optimistic.

ANZA-BORREGO DESERT STATE PARK

Thirty-three miles from Coachella the route crosses County Road S22, called the Borrego Salton Seaway, which heads west. A significant side trip travels this road. For twenty-one miles it passes through twisted layers of sedimentary rock, called by Irving Stone a miniature Grand Canyon of pale rainbow-colored hills. County Road S22 then enters Anza-Borrego Desert State Park, named for the Spanish explorer who crossed the desert in 1774 and the bighorn sheep that populate it. Covering 600,000 acres, the park is the largest in the contiguous forty-eight states, extending over about one-third of San Diego County, as well as parts of Imperial and Riverside Counties. All the other parks in California's extensive system would fit nicely into Anza-Borrego. It's home to 600 species of plants and 350 kinds of animals, birds, and reptiles and contains badlands, natural springs, and waterfalls plus wildflowers in spring.

PEGLEG SMITH'S MINE

About thirty miles from CA 86 the route enters the little town of Borrego Springs, which is completely surrounded by the park. The road turns sharply south to become Pegleg Road. On Henderson Canyon Road, which continues west, about a thousand feet from the junction with Pegleg Road, stands historical marker 750. It honors Thomas L. "Pegleg" Smith, fur trapper and mountain man, whom Chase calls the patron saint of prospectors. Chase also claims Pegleg was Jedediah Smith's brother, but no other evidence of that relationship exists.

Legend has it that Smith found a gold mine near the spot where the marker stands. Camping in the area one night in 1829, Smith picked up some interesting black rocks—gold nuggets—coated by a dark desert varnish. Jean E. Andrew, writing in the *Fedco Reporter*, says Smith carried them with him as curios, perhaps even aware they were gold. In 1850 he returned to the desert, but could never again find the butte where he had picked up those nuggets. Until he died in 1866, he told and retold the story of his gold find. The legend says scores of prospectors have died in fruitless searches for Pegleg's lost lode. Jerry Schad says that in the 1960s the editors of *Desert Magazine* received a sample of genuine black-coated gold nuggets from an anonymous man. He claimed to have discovered the lost mine, but the whereabouts of the mine or, indeed, the man's identity were never revealed. Today, each searcher adds ten stones for luck to the big rock pile beside the marker before setting out to look for the mine.

Many Routes

About three miles to the southeast of this point stands another state historical plaque, number 673. It marks the general area where, in 1775, the Anza expedition camped. Called the Borrego Sink, the earth here yielded up enough water to satisfy the needs of 240 humans and 800 head of stock from wells dug deeper than the height of a man. These thirsty campers were the *pobladores* (populators) that Anza herded through the desert to reach Mission San Gabriel in January 1776.

The route continues on County Road S22 for about eighteen miles until it reaches a junction with County S2, which turns southeast into an area called Great Earthquake Valley. Not quite twelve miles after making that turn, and just north of the intersection with CA 78, the historical route reaches the site of the San Felipe station of the Butterfield Overland Mail, which operated from 1858 to 1861. CA 78 approximates an ancient trade route used by natives.

Farther along, less than six miles south of the intersection of CA 78 and County Road S2, and a half mile to the east, stands a marker identifying this portion of the road as the Butterfield Overland Mail Route. The Mormon Battalion, Kearny's one hundred dragoons behind Kit Carson, and scores of emigrants who eventually settled the West traveled this route. Just to the left of the marker can be seen a scar inflicted by heavy Butterfield stages. Cartographers of the day labeled this route the Southern Emigrant Trail, but those who trod it called it the Journey of Death, marked by the bleached bones of cattle, horses, and humans.

A couple of miles farther along on County Road S2, a historical marker denotes Box Canyon, an important part of the route of the Mormon Battalion. On January 19, 1847, that staunch group, led by Col. Philip St. George Cooke, using only hand tools, hewed through the rocky walls of the narrow gorge. They thereby opened up the first road into Southern California.

Vallecito Stage Coach Station County Park

About five miles northwest of Agua Caliente is the entrance to Vallecito Stage Coach Station County Park. The park, which Strong describes as being in "a green valley with beautiful springs," features a restored stagecoach station at which Butterfield stages used to stop in the mid-1800s.

Ghosts are to be seen in the area, too. According to a local legend, four bandits robbed a coach along this route, somewhere between the Carrizo and Vallecito stations. The stage driver and two of the bandits were killed, but a ghost stage continued on, and visitors sometimes hear its clatter today. The surviving bandits buried their $65,000 loot before they quarreled over its distribution and shot each other to death. Legend

Vallecito Stage Coach Station as it appeared in the 1920s. Today it is restored and stands in a county park. —Anaheim Public Library

has it that the money is still buried in the area, guarded by the ghost of the dead leader's horse, which rears up and effaces all traces of the treasure when any human gets close to it.

One hundred four miles after departing from CA 86, the side trip reaches Ocotillo, at the conjunction of I-8 with County Roads S2 and S80, thirty-one miles west of El Centro. The side trip has added one hundred thirty-five miles, and a significant amount of history, to the distance to El Centro.

The Desert Tower

A side trip of about twelve miles to the southwest along old CA 80 (marked S80) arrives at a more recent historical marker, but one that is indeed worth the added distance. One mile north of the I-8 and In-Ko-Pah Park interchange stands the Desert Tower. Built in 1922 and 1923 by Bert Vaughn of Jacumba, it honors the pioneers and road builders who opened up the area. In the 1930s W. T. Ratcliffe carved the stone animals that hide in rocks around the tower.

Painted Gorge

Retracing the distance to County Road S2, the route makes one final detour, on County Road S80, for about four miles to the east. It reaches Painted Gorge Road, a dirt road on the north side of the highway. The average car can proceed a fair way up this road; the rest of the trip is best accomplished on foot. The walls of the gorge are bright red and mustard color, thanks to copper, sulfur, and iron deposits in the rocks. At the upper end of the gorge marine fossils are found, including coral, mussels, and worms, evidence that in prehistoric times the sea covered the area. These two side trips add about thirty miles to the distance to El Centro.

El Centro–Winterhaven
55 miles

EL CENTRO

El Centro, the seat of Imperial County, was named and laid out in 1905 by W. F. Holt, reputed to be the first developer in the valley. Also responsible for the town of Holtville, Holt bought up large blocks of stock in the Imperial Water Companies from the California Development Company. He had a hand, too, in developing the hydroelectric plant that takes advantage of a nearby drop in the Alamo River.

James Hart says El Centro is known as the largest city below sea level in the Western Hemisphere, at minus forty-five feet. It is also one of the chief shipping and storage areas of the Imperial Valley.

The fifty-five miles that separate El Centro from Winterhaven are generally barren, both physically and historically, with a couple of exceptions. For most of its length the route runs along the All American Canal, one facet of the Hoover Dam complex. The All American, whose entire length is within the United States, was built to replace Chaffey's seventy-mile-long Imperial Canal, some fifty miles of which cut through Mexico.

HILLS OF SAND

Another area of historic interest is the Imperial or Algodones Sand Dunes that lie east of the Coachella Canal, thirty-three miles east of El Centro and north of I-8. These hills of sand, the most widespread dune field in California, have long been an obstacle to travelers moving east and west in the southern end of the valley. Juan de Anza and other early explorers were forced to take long detours around the impassable system of dunes. Schad writes that some of Anza's party became hopelessly lost in the dunes and were forced to retreat to a watering hole for several weeks. They finally looped well to the south to bypass the treacherous hills of sand.

While a small number of pioneers did manage to cross them with horse and mule pack trains, the dunes hindered the state's commerce until the first road across the dunes was built in 1911. It was laid by volunteers from Yuma, the Imperial Valley, and San Diego, and it was known as the auto railroad. Parallel rails consisting of two-by-twelve-inch planks were laid end to end and bound with two-by-six-inch cross ties. Great driving skill and concentration were required to keep a car's wheels on the planks.

The plank road on the Algondones Sand Dunes was built in 1916 to make travel over the sand possible. —Bob Pittman

The plank road—one somewhat easier to drive—has been preserved and is commemorated by historical marker 845. The seven-mile-long road was built in 1916 of four-inch-thick planks spiked together and bound with steel in eight-by-twelve-foot sections. Although it provided for passing areas, disputes often arose over which car could continue forward and which had to back up to the nearest turnout. When shifting sands covered portions of the road, its sections could be moved with a team of horses. The plank road lasted until 1926, when a two-lane asphalt highway replaced it. The marker stands on the south side of I-8, fifteen miles east of Holtville.

The Southern Pacific Railroad was built along the eastern edge of the dunes in the late 1800s. Company towns such as Glamis, Amos, and Ogilby grew up around railroad sidings. Only Glamis survives today because it serves as a staging area for off-road vehicle riders.

From 1951 until 1964 the navy used parts of the dunes as an impact range. Although the area has been searched for unexploded ordnance, it's possible that shifting sands will reveal an occasional shell or rocket. The U.S. Navy requests that visitors to the dunes leave untouched any ordnance found.

WINTERHAVEN

Eighteen miles farther along I-8 is Winterhaven, across the Colorado River from Yuma, Arizona. Here, where ferries used to ply, a great multilane bridge now spans the river. Yuma's old Fourth Avenue bridge, made of steel girders, remains in place, even though it is no longer in use.

At 350 Picacho Road (County Road S24) in Winterhaven stands a marker that calls to mind the days of Fort Yuma. In the 1780s, before the coming of U.S. troops, Dolan Eargle writes, the Spanish maintained a mission and fort here. In 1781 the Quechans attacked that post and freed themselves of the Spanish yoke. In July of that year they destroyed Mission La Purísima Concepción about a mile to the south. They also destroyed another mission, San Pedro Y San Pablo de Bicuner, to the north of Winterhaven. The marker memorializing the site of that mission stands on County Road S24, a little more than four miles northeast of Bard. The natives were able to maintain their independence until 1849, when the Americans invaded and opened Fort Yuma, called Camp Calhoun until 1855. After many set-tos between the Americans and the Quechans, a reservation was finally established in 1884 at the site of the old mission. Today, the former officers' mess is a Quechan museum.

Bridges across the Colorado River tie Winterhaven, California, to Yuma, Arizona, at California's southernmost point. —Bob Pittman

343

PICACHO

A little more than eighteen miles north of Winterhaven on Picacho Road, on the bank of the Colorado River where it momentarily flows from east to west, is the site of Picacho, an early gold-mining community. Remi Nadeau writes that Mexicans located the first placers in this area in 1862 and a pueblo grew, complete with bullfights and fiestas. Around the turn of the century the town took on a more American flavor when it became a hard-rock mining center. With the opening of the mines near Picacho Peak, big stamp mills were built, one of them linked by a short-line railroad to Picacho Mine. Little remains of the town today, except an abandoned rock house and some mill ruins. A marker stands just over eighteen miles north of Winterhaven on Picacho Road. The route returns to I-8.

St. Thomas Church at the site of Mission La Purísima Concepción, near Winterhaven, destroyed by the Quechans in 1781. —Bob Pittman

I-8, County Road S34, CA 78, and US 95
Winterhaven–Needles
167 miles

Distances are vast in the Mojave and exploring this portion of it proves that point. Much of the territory to be covered will be of small interest, historical or otherwise. But the significance of what is there is too great to bypass.

THE CARGO MUCHACHO MOUNTAINS

Leaving Winterhaven, the route retraces itself for twelve miles on I-8 to County Road S34, entry to the Cargo Muchacho Mountains and the Gold Rock Mining District. Four miles from the interstate is Ogilby Station, once a prosperous town on the Southern Pacific Railroad. Little is left of it today, but in the cemetery some of the old headstones can still be read. According to Foster, sometime in the 1820s several Spanish prospectors were pursuing their fortune in the mountains just to the east, which were then without a name. Two of those gold seekers returned to camp one day with pockets filled with nuggets. Hence the name Cargo Muchacho, "loaded boy."

TUMCO

More than twenty years passed, however, before Pete Walters of Ogilby discovered the first vein at Gold Rock, the southernmost goldfield in the state and one of the richest. The plaque that tells the tale of Tumco, the boomtown that came to be known as Hedges, stands on Gold Rock Ranch Road one mile east of County Road S34 and nine miles north of I-8. Once a town with a population of 2,500, all that now remain are a few crumbling walls and a cyanide vat.

BLYTHE

Twenty-four miles from I-8 the route reaches CA 78 to head for Blythe, forty-five miles to the northeast. Here called Ben Hulse Highway, the road cuts across a barren landscape, truly the low desert, with most elevations being around sea level and even mountaintops rising to only about 2,000 feet. The Chocolate Mountains lie to the northwest, the Barren Mountains to the west.

When Coronado came to this part of California, natives had been living here for centuries, perhaps as long as ten thousand years. Ancient trails can still be seen crossing the forbidding landscape. A marker denoting one of these trails stands two miles west of CA 78's intersection with County Road S34.

The route soon passes through the Palo Verde Valley that runs along the Colorado River and arrives at Blythe, named for its developer, Thomas Blythe, an Englishman and irrigation promoter. According to the Federal Writers' Project guide, Blythe filed claims on 40,000 acres under the Swamp and Overflow Act, believing he could turn the area into another Nile River Valley. He succumbed to a stroke without realizing that dream, leaving his claims to be taken over by the syndicate that laid out the town in 1910. The area around Blythe was once planted in cotton but is now a source of lettuce, melons, alfalfa, and barley.

THE INDIAN LORE MONUMENT

The route continues along US 95, traveling north beside the Colorado River for some distance. Joshua Tree National Monument lies sixty-seven miles to the west, just north of I-10, past the McCoy and Palen Mountains, a couple of dry lakes, and little else.

About fifteen miles north of Blythe and just off US 95 to the west stands what Logan and Ochshorn call "one of the most mysterious monuments in California." It is the Indian Lore Monument: three sets of giant intaglios, men and animals carved into the rock mesa at least five thousand years ago by unknown people. The largest man is 167 feet long, with an arm spread of 164 feet. The human figures, according to the Federal Writers' Project guide, are well proportioned, and the animals resemble horses, antelopes, or deer, except that they boast long buffalo tails. Because of their size, the figures weren't recognized until 1932, when they were first photographed from the air.

In the ninety-two miles that separate Blythe from Needles, little except the intaglios will excite history lovers. Forty miles north of Blythe, at Vidal Junction, US 95 crosses the Colorado Aqueduct and continues. It passes what Foster calls the Rice Valley Sand Dunes on the west and the Whipple Mountains on the east. Almost forty-eight miles from Vidal Junction is Needles, named for the sharp peaks that rise to the east in Arizona.

NEEDLES

Established in 1869 as a steamboat landing and supply station on the old emigrant trail, in 1883 Needles became a rail center for the Santa Fe Railroad. The train depot and a Harvey House hotel have been carefully preserved.

At the Colorado River bridge on K Street stands historical marker number 781. It identifies a portion of an old Indian trail, still visible in spots, that ran roughly parallel to the Colorado on the California side. This is the trail that Garces and his Mojave guides followed in 1776 and Jedediah Smith used in 1826.

I-40 and CA 58
Needles–Mojave
210 miles

Leaving Needles, the route picks up I-40, once the path of the famous Route 66, to travel across what the Federal Writers' Project guide describes as a bleak plateau baking in fierce sunlight. Creosote and tumbleweeds stud the pale soil; the road shimmers with mirages. To the north lies the East Mojave National Scenic Area, roughly 1.5 million acres of desert land set aside for preservation in 1980 by the Bureau of Land Management. It stretches from Barstow to Needles between the two major highways, I-40 and I-15. The region includes the Providence Mountains and the state recreation area named for them.

ANCIENT CAVERNS

The most isolated unit in the state park system, Providence Mountains State Recreation Area is reached via Essex Road, a little more than forty-five miles west of Needles. Fifteen miles north of the interstate the side trip reaches the visitors center, which offers directions for exploring Mitchell Caverns National Preserve. For centuries these caves provided shelter for Indians roaming the Mojave; archaeologists have found food caches, fire pits, and tools in them. In 1929 prospector Jack Mitchell discovered them as he searched for silver. Staking a claim on the caverns, he named them Tecopa and El Pakiva, built a road, and opened them to the public in 1932. In 1956 Mitchell sold the property to the California Department of Parks and Recreation.

The caves were sculpted over the last twelve million years by rainwater seeping through the soft limestone bedrock. Stalactites hang from the ceiling; stalagmites rise from the floor. Ribbons, draperies, and shields decorate the walls. Only about one cave in forty thousand exhibit, as these do, all three types of cave formations: dripstone, flowstone, and erratics. Today the caves are dry and cool, usually around 65 degrees Fahrenheit.

Returning to I-40, this side trip has added about twenty-four miles to the trip to Mojave.

OLD NATIONAL TRAIL HIGHWAY

The route backtracks on a northeasterly heading, past the Granite and Old Dad Mountains. To the north are the Kelso Dunes, highest in the state and said to be composed of sand that sings, or at least hums, when it shifts.

Thirty-six miles west of Needles the Old National Trail Highway, retracing a part of the route traveled by Father Garces and Jedediah Smith, swings to the south of I-40. Traveling some of the most desolate territory in the west, it cuts through the Fenner Valley. Passing the parched desert towns of Essex, Cadiz Summit, and Chambliss, it reaches Amboy, about forty miles after leaving I-40. This tiny desert town stands at the northern edge of Bristol Dry Lake, creator of spectacular mirages.

Twenty-five miles farther along, the road, which also duplicates old Route 66, reaches Ludlow and rejoins I-40, after passing through Bagdad. According to the Federal Writers' Project guide, Bagdad was once a rip-roaring mining camp, home of the War Eagle and Orange Blossom gold mines. It is one of the driest spots in or near the Mojave Desert, with an annual mean rainfall of only about two inches. This detour adds eight miles or less to the distance to Mojave.

Continuing to the west, I-40 passes between the Cady Mountains to the north and the Newberries to the south in an area labeled the Mojave Valley. Little is written of the Mojave River because it is largely invisible, often flowing below the surface of the land. Sally Bowman, however, writing in the *Fedco Reporter*, says it rises in the San Gabriel Mountains, then flows northeast for about a hundred miles through Victorville and Barstow before losing itself in the sand. Lines of mesquite growth are tip-offs to the underground course of this mysterious river, which finally dies in its sink, Soda Lake, to the east of the Cronise Mountains.

DAGGETT

Continuing westward for almost fifty miles, the route reaches Daggett, just three miles east of Barstow. It got its start as a railroad camp, a busy depot for the Calico Mine. According to Nadeau, its residents bragged that it was the worst place between Mojave and New York. Today it is the site of a U.S. Marine Corps installation. Strong says several historic buildings still stand along the streets of the town that once was a way station on the San Bernardino–Daggett–Post Office Springs freight line. The route continues westward.

BARSTOW

In spite of sitting in the midst of a formidable desert, Barstow has always had a lot going for it. When gold was discovered in the nearby Calico Mountains in the 1890s, Barstow became a supply center. It was, as well, a junction for overland and Death Valley expeditions. Once called Fishpond, its name was changed to Waterman Junction to honor the governor, who owned a local silver mine. When it became a division point for the Santa Fe Railroad in 1886, the name was changed once more to honor William Barstow Strong, president of the railroad. It is today the diesel headquarters for the Achison, Topeka & Santa Fe Railroad and stands at the junction of I-40, I-15, and CA58.

Evidence of Barstow's importance in the history of railroading is obvious in the Harvey House, one of many restaurants built by Fred Harvey to serve train passengers, that stands at First Avenue and Riverside Drive. Originally built in 1885, the restaurant burned in 1908. The present building, designed by architect Mary E. J. Coulter, was constructed in 1910–13. Originally called Casa del Desierto, it is one of the best examples in the state of depot-hotels from the turn of the century. When Harvey died in 1901, according to Shefrah Ann Rozenstain writing in the *Fedco Reporter*, he left his sons a chain of forty-seven restaurants and fifteen hotels. The fabled organization with its Harvey Girl waitresses all got started because Fred Harvey didn't like the food he was served while traveling as a freight agent for the Burlington Railroad.

CALICO

Before continuing westward toward Mojave, a side trip must be undertaken to the northeast. Roughly eight miles along I-15 is the Ghost Town Road exit. Four miles north on that road is the town of Calico, whose mines yielded up between $13 and $20 million in silver and almost $10 million in borates between 1881 and 1907. The largest mine in the district, the Silver King, was staked out in 1881.

In spite of that productivity, Nadeau says Calico is more lucrative as a ghost town than it was as a mining center. The owners of Knott's Berry Farm bought the remains of Calico in 1950 and began a restoration project that has resulted in an authentic, if touristy, mining town. Stores, saloons, and even a house made of bottles, stand above ground, and part of an old mine shaft has been shored up and made safe for visitors.

In its heyday 2,000 miners lived in this town in the Calico Mountains, named for their rock formations in shades of green and rose. The town's newspaper, founded by San Diegan John Overshiner, was named the *Calico Print*. Vying for fame with the cleverly titled newspaper was Dorsey, the town's canine mail carrier. A black-and-white shepherd, Nadeau relates, Dorsey for three years carried the U.S. mail from Calico to nearby Bismarck mines.

349

Top: *Hank's Hotel is a restored version of the hostelry that used to shelter miners during Calico's heyday.* —Calico Ghost Town

Bottom: *Visitors clamber over the rocks in Calico Ghost Town, an authentic restoration of a real mining community of the 1880s.* —Calico Ghost Town

THE CALICO EARLY MAN SITE

Continuing along Calico Road for about three miles, the route regains I-15 at the Yermo exit. Seven miles farther east at Minneola Road is the Calico Early Man Site, site of what are possibly the oldest human relics to have been found in North America. Some scientists suggest that some of the stone tools found on the site are at least 200,000 years old. More than 6,000 artifacts have been found in the dig, which was begun in 1942 when an amateur archaeologist discovered ancient stone tools at this spot. In 1962 Dr. Louis S. B. Leakey convinced the National Geographic Society to fund further excavations.

The side trip now returns to I-15 and retraces the route to Barstow. About thirty-five miles have been added to the distance to Mojave.

BORON

Leaving Barstow, the route travels west along CA 58, a two-lane road that undulates across thirty-five miles of desert to the San Bernardino County line, just east of Boron. There it becomes a freeway.

Boron's only claim to fame is the presence of the world's largest open-pit borax mine just five miles north of the freeway. Here is the source of most of the Western Hemisphere's borates, chemicals that are used in soap, cosmetics, fertilizers, fiberglass, insecticides, enamel, and the heat-shielding tiles that protect spacecraft. The firm that owns the mine, U.S. Borax Inc., is a direct-line descendant of the company that operated the Harmony Works in Death Valley and the 20-mule team wagons. A viewpoint that overlooks the huge mine features one of the original borax wagons, complete with its water caisson.

Continuing westward for twelve miles, the route reaches the northern gate of Edwards Air Force Base. A dry lake here received the first space shuttles to touch down on land. Some space missions still return to earth here.

MOJAVE, END OF THE 20-MULE TEAM LINE

The route continues on CA 58 for seventeen miles to reach Mojave, for five years the terminus for the historic wagons that hauled borax from Death Valley to the railroad. A marker on Sierra Highway in the center of town points out that the Death Valley–Mojave trail ended just one-half mile west of here. J. W. S. Perry, a superintendent at the mine in Death Valley, 165 miles away, built the first of those famous wagons here.

To the west lie the Tehachapi Mountains, the official western edge of the desert. The search for the history of California's Mojave Desert continues on a northerly heading.

The Space Shuttle Endeavour *lands at Edwards Air Force Base after a nine-day mission in Earth orbit.* —NASA

CA 14, US 395, and CA 190
Mojave–Stovepipe Wells
About 185 miles

THE RAND DISTRICT

For the next one hundred miles or so, the route, CA 14, travels northeast, paralleling the Los Angeles Aqueduct, and is marked as a scenic route on most maps. Twenty-one miles from Mojave is Cantil, an all-but-abandoned town that marks the start of a side trip to the colorful Rand District, the site of a major gold discovery in 1895. At the village of Cantil, Redrock-Randsburg Road takes off to the northeast.

At the southeast corner of Pappas Ranch on Pappas Road, one-half mile south of Valley Road in Cantil, stands a historical monument. It marks the site of a spring that refreshed horse thieves and emigrants alike in the nineteenth century. The legend on the plaque says the Manly-Jayhawk Death Valley party was revived here after slogging from Indian Wells through the desolate area that is now China Lake Naval Weapons

Center. The site was also a station on the Nadeau Borax Freight Road. Remi Nadeau was a French-Canadian who arrived in Los Angeles in 1861. He became the leader in the freighting business by establishing lines that served most of the isolated area of the region.

The desert had seemed to be played out in the mid-1890s; the country was in the midst of a depression and the price of silver had plummeted. All these woes were, at least temporarily, forgotten in the Mojave with the discovery of gold. The first strike, according to Nadeau's great-grandson of the same name who published a history on the subject in 1992, was made at Goler, between Red Rock Canyon and Randsburg.

Thirteen miles from the turnoff at Cantil the side trip reaches the site of the town of Garlock where, in 1896, Eugene Garlock built a stamp mill to crush ore from the Yellow Aster Mine on Rand Mountain. The side trip continues for seven more miles to Randsburg on US 395.

A trio of prospectors—Singleton, Burcham, and Mooers—discovered the Yellow Aster (or Rand) Mine here in April 1895. In 1907 tungsten was found at Atolia, a few miles to the southeast, and in 1919 another pair of prospectors found the famous California Rand Silver

The Elite Theater provided entertainment to miners in Randsburg, Kern County, circa 1900. —CHS/TICOR, USC Special Collections

Mine at Red Mountain. Even today, solitary prospectors can be seen at work in the hills around the area and some mines still operate. The history of the Rand District is well told at the Kern County Desert Museum on Butte Avenue in Randsburg.

The side trip now returns to CA 14, some fifty miles having been added to the distance to Stovepipe Wells.

RED ROCK CANYON AND FREEMAN JUNCTION

About four miles north on CA14 is Red Rock Canyon. For thousands of years these splendid rocks were on the trade route of Native Americans, and later a landmark for emigrants, including the ill-fated Manly-Jayhawk party in 1850.

At Freeman Junction on CA 178, just two-tenths of a mile west of CA 14, stands a marker that commemorates the passing this way of Joseph Walker in 1834, just after he crossed the 5,245-foot Walker Pass. Fifty miles from Mojave, CA 14 merges with US 395, which continues northward. The naval weapons center lies to the east and national forests to the west.

THE STORY OF OWENS LAKE

After another sixty-five miles the route reaches Olancha and the junction with CA 190 at the southernmost tip of Owens Lake. Now just a soggy bed of chemicals, Owens Lake was once a true body of water, one on which at least one steamer sailed. According to Foster, when Walker passed this way in 1834 the lake was as much as thirty feet deep and covered one hundred square miles. Today, however, winds blow ghostly clouds off the edges of the lake, which has been systemically drained by the Los Angeles Aqueduct as the thirsty city to the south squeezes the last drop of moisture out of the Owens Valley. Recent court decisions have reduced the amount of water pumped, but for most of the Owens Valley relief has come too late.

Something has to be done, however, about those clouds of dust, for they are hazardous to humans. According to an article in the *Los Angeles Times*, the Environmental Protection Agency required the Great Basin Unified Air Pollution Control District to find a solution. The little agency with only fifteen employees, which didn't cause the problem, has until 2001 to cure the problem. The obvious remedy, refilling the lake, won't work; that would require all the water now flowing to faucets in Los Angeles. Some think restoring part of the water, creating a new wetlands, might be successful. It remains to be seen.

The Owens River Valley was a prosperous place at the turn of the century. Some of the mines had played out, it's true, but the commerce and population they inspired had given agriculture in the area quite a boost. Water flowed down the eastern slopes of the Sierra; the land was fertile. Farms and ranches produced alfalfa, corn, apples, grapes, and wheat. By 1883 the railroad had reached the valley and its 4,000-plus residents anticipated a prosperous future.

In 1904 William Mulholland, chief engineer of Los Angeles' water department, arrived with his plan to pipe the valley's water to his city more than two hundred miles away. Without revealing his intent to valley residents, he made plans for the aqueduct that would irrigate the San Fernando Valley while leaving the Owens Valley quite literally high and dry. The dry Owens Riverbed, dusty Owens Lake, withered orchards, and sere fields testify to the results.

CARTAGO

Before heading northeast on CA 190, a short side trip beckons. Three miles north of Olancha stands all that's left of Cartago, in its heyday a bustling landing where the *Bessie Brady* docked after crossing the lake. A miniature side-wheeler with a twenty-ton capacity, she regularly plied a route from Swansea on the east side to the dock on the west. There Remi Nadeau's twenty-mule freight wagons, as many as eighty each day, loaded on silver ingots for transport through Los Angeles to San Pedro. At the port the ingots were loaded onto another boat and shipped up to San Francisco for refining. On the return trip, wagons were crammed with hay, wine, potatoes, and chickens—all destined for the settlers and miners of the valley. This commerce has been credited with contributing heavily to the surge of growth that Los Angeles experienced in the late 1860s and 1870s, after the land boom died out.

CERRO GORDO

Seven miles farther north and one mile east of US 395 stands a marker noting the site of Col. Sherman Stevens' charcoal kilns. In June 1873, Stevens built just west of this spot a sawmill and flume that connected with the bullion road to Los Angeles. Lumber and charcoal were loaded on the *Bessie Brady* to cross the lake and were then hauled up the steep hill to Cerro Gordo Mine. Since all the wood around Cerro Gordo had already been burned, charcoal had to be imported to keep the smelters running.

Retracing the ten miles to Olancha, the side trip swings around the southern end of Owens Lake on CA 190 for fifteen miles. At the junction with CA 136, another side trip starts. This one heads northeast for three miles to the village of Keeler. Eight miles east of the town and almost straight up, at 9,000 feet, is the Cerro Gordo Mine, often called California's Comstock. The road is steep and winding although it has been recently improved, according to historian Nadeau. The remains of Victor Beaudry's smelter can still be seen, as can the American Hotel and other buildings. Visitors are discouraged, Nadeau says, because mining is still going on in the hills.

Discovered in 1856 by Pablo Flores, Cerro Gordo, "Fat Hill," was worked only sporadically until Mortimer Belshaw arrived in the spring of 1868. Belshaw was a mining engineer who came bearing promises of backing from San Francisco investors and knowledge of new smelting technology. Victor Beaudry, who joined forces with Belshaw, had run a general store in Independence for some years and had opened another near the mines in 1866. Quick to loan money to prospectors down on their luck, he soon acquired shares of a variety of claims.

These two men united to form the Union Mining Company, which, before long, controlled most of Cerro Gordo's ore processing, as well as some silver mining. Belshaw even built a toll road from the shore of Owens Lake to the mining camp high on a ledge in the Inyo Mountains. He thereby controlled supplies of everything needed to keep the mine and smelter running: charcoal, water, food, and so on. In 1869 the pair put up the money to get Remi Nadeau started with his freight company.

Other mines and other smelters were opened on the mountain and beside the lake. Competition wasn't always gentlemanly, and fighting—both physical and legal—erupted often. Even so, it was estimated that by 1880, when the field played out, $17 million had been removed from the mountainside.

SWANSEA

The side trip now descends the mountain and goes a short distance north on CA 136 to the site of Swansea. All that remains to be seen where the headquarters of the Owens Lake Company, Belshaw's rival, once stood are two buildings dating from the 1870s, one brick and one adobe, and the crumbled remains of the smelter.

Returning to CA 190, the main route continues, with the side trip having added about thirty miles to the distance to Stovepipe Wells.

DEATH VALLEY

Both Death Valley, the destination of this leg of historical exploration, and the Cerro Gordo are within Inyo County. It was incorporated in 1866 from territory in Mono and Tulare Counties. Lying between the Sierra Nevada on the west and the state of Nevada on the east, the county contains both the highest and lowest points in the lower forty-eight states:

Mount Whitney and Death Valley. In the White Mountains at the northern end of the county grows a bristlecone pine tree that is forty-six hundred years old, the oldest living thing in the nation.

CA 190 squiggles and climbs its way eastward through the Panamint Valley, over the Panamint Range, up and down Towne Pass. Seventy miles from its junction with CA 136, CA 190 reaches Stovepipe Wells in the heart of Death Valley National Monument, established in 1933 to preserve a spot unique in the nation. About 140 miles long, from 6 to 15 miles wide, all but one corner of the park is in California's Inyo County, and that corner lies in Nevada. The actual Death Valley is much smaller than the national monument. The Panamint Range defines its western edge, while the Grapevine, Funeral, and Amargosa Mountains delineate the eastern. Indians called the place Tomesha, "ground afire."

The 3,000-square-mile chasm—not truly a valley since it wasn't carved by rivers—was created over thousands of years by upheaval of the earth's crust resulting in mountains as high as 11,049-foot Telescope Peak. The collapse of a portion of that same crust has left the area called Badwater 282 feet below sea level, the lowest point in the United States. W. A. Chalfant points out, however, that a great deal of this area is much like any other desert, with the same average supply of watering places. Fewer than forty miles separate its western rim from the nearest point in Owens Valley, but those miles are what make Death Valley the formidable arena that it is.

For more than 9,000 years humans inhabited the valley. During the Ice Age, the climate was much milder than it is today, but even as the climate turned hostile, new groups of natives moved in. Shoshonis, who arrived about a thousand years ago, wintered in the valley.

Exploration of the 3,231 square miles of the valley, which should be undertaken only in the cool months, can consume days. Several spots, however, reveal an exceptional amount of history and are not to be missed.

Six miles east of the village of Stovepipe Wells and not quite three miles north on an unpaved road is the water hole for which the village is named. Near the sand dunes and at the junction of two Indian trails, it was discovered by a prospector digging for water in the area. He marked the well by driving a stovepipe into the sand beside it.

Farther north, about thirty miles, is a tourist trap of the first, ahem, water: Scotty's Castle. Death Valley Scotty, Walter Scott, a one-time trick rider with Buffalo Bill's Wild West Show, came to California in the 1880s, seeking a fortune, but perhaps not one to be had by digging in the earth. Claiming to have worked as a water boy for a surveying party, driven a borax wagon, and, finally, found a mine in Death Valley, he gained

Death Valley Scotty's original home in the desert.
—Cecil W. Stoughton, National Park Service

The castle home in Death Valley of Walter Scott, who found there's more than one way to dig up wealth in the desert —Cecil W. Stoughton, National Park Service

the patronage of Chicagoan Albert Johnson. With Johnson's money, Scotty built his castle and regaled all who would listen with tales of his rich strike. Actually, the riches he found were in Chicago and belonged to a quiet, practical businessman who succumbed to Scotty's blandishments. The National Park Service bought the castle in 1970.

There's Borax in Them Thar Hills

A genuine source of historic riches is to be seen on CA 190 about fifteen miles south of Stovepipe Wells, not quite two miles south of Furnace Creek. Here are old adobe buildings and the remnants of a borax processing plant, the famous Harmony Borax Works, built in 1882.

In the deserts of California, more money has been made from borax than from gold; huge sums are still being realized each day from that great excavation near Boron. In 1880 Aaron Winters, a poverty-stricken prospector, staked a large claim on land that would become the Harmony works. Needing money, he soon sold the claim to William T. Coleman, of San Francisco, for $20,000. This is the same Coleman who was a member of the Committee of Vigilance of 1851 and a foe of labor organizer Denis Kearney.

With the help of plentiful water from springs in Furnace Creek Wash and cheap Chinese labor, Coleman developed the Harmony Borax Works. At first the mineral didn't have to be mined but simply scooped up; it lay on top of the ground in white clumps called cottonballs. The only processing needed was to dissolve the clumps, then allow the solution to cool, forming crystals of borax.

Between 1883 and 1889, the famous 20-mule team wagons hauled thirty tons of borax crystals at a time from this spot deep in Death Valley. Over the rugged mountains they went and across the desolate desert to the railhead at Mojave, 165 miles each way. Each team was actually composed of eighteen mules and two horses. Because of their greater strength and obedience, the horses were always in the wheel position, often with the driver astride the near (left) wheelhorse. The animals were controlled by a single jerk line fixed to the bit of the near lead mule, always the smartest animal in the group. That line ran for more than one hundred feet through rings on all near mules' harnesses to the driver's hand. O'Dell says the driver's main means of control—other than the jerk line—was a whip with a twenty-two-foot lash. To chide an animal beyond the reach of the lash, the driver used pebbles he pegged at the recalcitrant mule's rump.

Coleman had a hard time making a go of the borax works and, in 1888, was forced to sell it to F. M. "Borax" Smith. Smith managed to

The Harmony Borax Works at Death Valley, circa 1888.
—U.S. Borax Inc.

A 20-mule team sets off across the high desert, bound for the Mojave railhead where its cargo of borax will be loaded onto railcars. —U.S. Borax Inc.

buy up several marginal borax claims in the area and founded the Pacific Coast Borax Company. Borax continued to be a profitable mining venture in Death Valley until 1928 when that vast deposit near Boron was discovered.

Adventures of the Jayhawkers

As the exploration of Death Valley turns north again, it's time to learn how the place got its name. In September of 1849 a group of more than a hundred wagons assembled at Salt Lake City, proposing to travel to the goldfields of California. A short distance out of Salt Lake the party met a pack train leader who told them of an old Indian route that would shorten their trip by five hundred miles. Soon after the encounter, the party broke up, with most of the wagons opting for the shorter route. It wasn't long, however, before many of the shortcut seekers realized the new route was too difficult, too unproven. They hurried to rejoin the emigrants who had stayed on the original trail, leaving just a few dozen wagons still pursuing the shortcut.

Part of this crew was a group of young bachelors who called themselves the Jayhawkers. Others in the party were a varied assortment: old and young, families and singles, strangers. On Christmas Day this assortment of souls struggled through what is today called Furnace Creek Wash (roughly the route of CA 190 from Death Valley Junction) to find themselves in a formidable salty sink that had once been a freshwater lake. A state historic monument standing beside CA 190, a little more than one mile southeast of Furnace Creek, marks this entrance.

Suffering from thirst and hunger, and unable to reach a consensus about how to escape this latest hazard, the party decided to split up again. This time several wagons went southwest while the Jayhawkers headed northwest, up the valley. About twenty-five miles north and west along CA 190, another monument stands about one hundred feet south of the roadway at Stovepipe Wells. This one marks the spot at which the northbound party burned their wagons, dried the meat of some of their oxen, and struggled westward on foot over Towne Pass.

The so-called Bennett-Arcane contingent of the party fared even worse. Reaching Tule Spring, a spot seventeen miles south of Furnace Creek to the west of the road to Badwater, the group could go no farther. Here they were stranded and nearly perished from starvation. William Lewis Manley and John Rogers, young single members of the party, struck out on foot to seek help. At last they reached San Fernando. Returning with supplies after nearly a month, they led the party to San Francisquito Rancho near today's Newhall. A historical marker beside unpaved West

Charcoal kilns at Wildrose in Death Valley.
—E. Mang Jr., National Park Service

Side Road notes the site of this camp. According to legend, it is this party that gave the valley its name. Leaving the valley after the ordeal, one of them turned back to survey the scene of their great hardship and said, "Goodbye, Death Valley." The truth is, of course, that most members of all the parties survived the harsh experience, undoubtedly because it was winter. Had they attempted the valley crossing in summer, it's likely none of them would have lived to tell the story. A tale with contrary results—of families perishing because they found themselves traveling in winter—is told in the exploration of the High Sierra.

The route heads northwest to Furnace Creek, Stovepipe Wells, and on over Towne Pass, leaving Death Valley behind.

CA 190, CA 136, and US 395
Death Valley–Bishop
142 miles

LONE PINE

The seventy-one miles that separate Stovepipe Wells from US 395 are mostly retraced miles. The route once again climbs Towne Pass, continues to Panamint Springs, and returns to Keeler with its access to Cerro Gordo. Two miles after gaining US 395, the route arrives at Lone Pine, gateway to the Owens Valley. It's rugged country, bleak to the east and soaring to the west, sparsely populated in both directions. Many early movies were shot on Movie Flat Road, west and northwest of Lone Pine. Thirteen miles to the west is the start of Whitney Portal Trail, a steep path to the top of Mount Whitney, the highest peak in the lower forty-eight states. Hoover says the first cabin in Lone Pine was built in 1861, followed by enough others that a "fine settlement" was reported two years later. It is now an outfitting station for those who would climb the great mountain to the west.

On March 26, 1872, a severe earthquake, probably of magnitude eight or greater, rent the Owens Valley, opening a great fault paralleling US 395. Along this crevice land dropped from four to twelve feet. Twenty-nine persons perished during the dreadful shaking, crushed by adobe buildings that collapsed on them. Many of them—experts estimate from fourteen to twenty-one—are buried in a common grave that lies two hundred feet west of the roadway just under a mile north of town. Since the area was so sparsely settled at the time, the number killed represented a large percentage of the town's population.

Most experts agree that the Alabama Hills fault was responsible for the that temblor. One visible reminder of that quake is Diaz Lake on the west side of US 395 on the south end of town. Technically, it is a sag pond, cupped by two fault scarps (ridges) created by the quake. The land between them sank, allowing the lake to form.

A TIME OF INFAMY

Not quite ten miles north of Lone Pine is the area the Spanish christened Manzanar, for "apple." At the turn of the century it was a fertile garden spot, with bountiful orchards, which had to be abandoned when the area degenerated into a desert after Los Angeles appropriated its water. So the land stood barren until an even more nefarious act populated it once again.

In the spring of 1942 a full-grown city of more than 10,000 residents, mostly from California, sprang up here. Half of the population was women, one-quarter school-age children. They lived here for three and one-half years, imprisoned even though none had been charged with any crime and none would ever be so charged. The government called them evacuees, but what they were was prisoners.

Just two hundred feet west of US 395, near Reward Road, stands a marker that identifies the euphemistically named Manzanar Relocation Center, an American concentration camp. It's one of two that were set up in the state; the other was at Tule Lake in the Shasta-Cascade region.

On February 19, 1942, President Franklin D. Roosevelt signed Executive Order 9066, which directed all U.S. residents of Japanese ancestry—native-born citizens, naturalized citizens, legal alien residents—to be confined as potential enemies of the United States. No German Americans or Italian Americans were similarly confined, only those of Japanese background.

On March 31, 1942, notices were posted in certain communities on the West Coast alerting all residents of Japanese descent that they were going to have to leave their homes. Families were registered and each assigned an identity number. Both baggage and people were hung with tags bearing those numbers, not quite tattoos, perhaps, but personality destroyers, nonetheless. These loyal, industrious citizens were given as little as three or four days to dispose of their personal property and real estate. Cars, houses, plots of land—all were sold for tiny fractions of their values. One woman, given only three days to put her affairs in order, sold a twenty-room hotel for $500. One grower asked to be allowed a few extra days to harvest his crop of strawberries. Denied permission, he plowed the berries under, only to have the FBI charge him with sabotage and put him in jail. Thousands of similar tales of injustice have been told by those evacuees over the years, tales of deprivation that cover the United States with shame.

Arriving at the camp, a bleak place surrounded by barbed wire and gun towers, the new residents found 504 barracks equipped with steel army cots and straw mattresses, electricity and laundry facilities, plus communal mess halls. A family of four was allotted living space measuring twenty feet by twenty-five feet. Their only comforts came from the two suitcases apiece they had been allowed to carry on the buses or trucks that herded them to Manzanar. Conditions were harsh: Temperatures soared to well over one hundred in the summer and fell to near zero on winter nights. In spite of the climate and the shortage of water that had created the desert, camp residents were required to grow their own food.

All that's left as reminders of that horrible era are some ornamental gateposts, a large garage—formerly the camp auditorium—and a shockingly beautiful monument in the cemetery.

INDEPENDENCE

The route continues north along US 395 for six miles to Independence, seat of Inyo County. In the town is a museum that chronicles, through artifacts, photographs, and eyewitness accounts, the days of Manzanar. Maintained by a former resident of the prison camp, the museum is at 155 Grant Street. At the museum is an old number eighteen narrow-gauge locomotive that once pulled cars on the Carson & Colorado Railroad. Preserved here also, at 303 North Edwards Street, is the Commander's House, built in 1872 for the commander of Camp Independence. The Victorian wood-frame house is believed to be the oldest in the valley.

Another, slightly newer house stands in Independence. Still a private residence on Market Street is the former home of Mary Austin, who wrote *The Land of Little Rain*, a collection of essays about the region.

BISHOP

Fifty-six miles separate Independence from Bishop. In that distance US 395 passes between the Inyo National Forest to the east and Sequoia National Forest and Park and Kings Canyon National Park on the west. Always traveling beside the Los Angeles Aqueduct, it passes Big Pine, near the bristlecone pine forest, where the oldest living things in the country grow. Fifteen miles from Big Pine is Bishop.

LAWS

Two side trips finish off the exploration of California's magnificent deserts. The first heads northeast on US 6. Four miles from Bishop is the old town of Laws where, Aubrey Drury says, the first cabin in the Owens Valley, a structure of sod and stone, was built in 1861. A historic monument marks the site at the intersection of US 6 and Silver Canyon Road.

Nearby is a marker denoting the site of Camp Independence, established July 4, 1862. Col. George Evans led a military expedition here after settlers complained of troubles with the natives. When hostilities ceased, the camp closed; in 1865 war broke out again and the camp was reoccupied as Fort Independence until it was abandoned in 1877.

Laws is also the site of historical marker number 953, the station and yard of the Carson & Colorado Railroad. The C&C was a narrow-gauge line that ran from Mound House, Nevada, near Carson City, through Laws, to Keeler, a distance of about three hundred miles. Between 1883 and about 1915 this line provided the only reliable means of transportation in and out of Owens Valley. Service ended on April 30, 1960, for the last narrow-gauge public carrier operating west of the Rockies. Also to be seen are the agent's house, the post office, and the Wells, Fargo building.

WHAT CAUSED THE BATTLE?

The side trip returns to Bishop and continues southwest along Bishop Creek on CA 168. A little more than five miles from town is the site of the Bishop Creek battleground. According to the plaque, on April 6, 1862, a battle took place on this spot between newly arrived settlers and Paiutes and Shoshonis, original inhabitants of the land. Ingenuously, the plaque says, "The reason for this battle is lost but brave men on both sides died here for a cause which they held inviolate." Dolan Eargle points out that 65,000 acres of ancestral lands were taken from these natives with the coming of the settlers. It would be hard not to fight for tribal homelands, hunting grounds, and sacred burial grounds.

The route returns to Bishop, with a little less than twenty miles added to our exploration.

Bishop is an arbitrary stopping point, for the terrain doesn't change dramatically at this point from barren to majestic. Indeed, most experts define the Owens Valley as continuing northward for a few more miles. But change has been taking place; towering peaks now cast long shadows across the roadway. Forests draw close and this point of demarcation is as good as any other. The final region of California to be combed for history is at hand: the High Sierra.

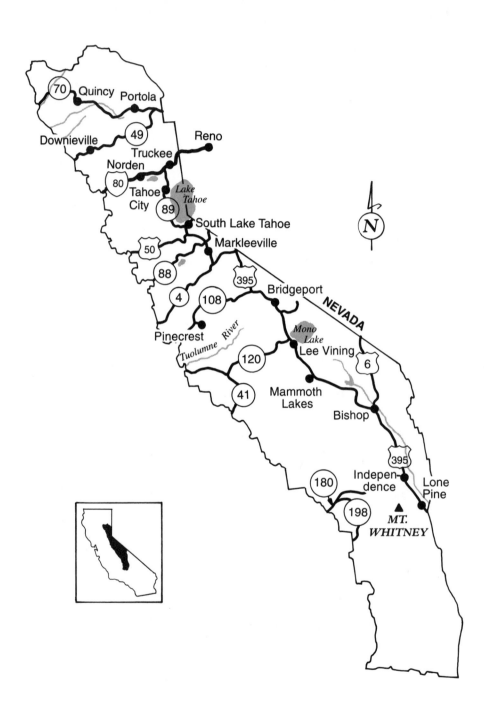

Part 12
The Magnificent Sierra Nevada

The Sierra Nevada, Spanish for "snowy mountains," is a huge range, more than four hundred miles long and from sixty to eighty miles wide. All but a corner of it lies in California; the exception pokes into Nevada along the eastern shore of Lake Tahoe.

The Sierra defines the eastern edge of the great Central Valley and the western limit of the Owens Valley. The northernmost point of the range stands just a few miles south of Mount Lassen, the southernmost peak of the Cascades, but it's hard to tell where one of those mountain ranges leaves off and the other begins. The Sierra runs southeasterly from Lake Almanor, its beginning, for about three hundred fifty miles, then turns due south for about eighty miles to Tehachapi Pass, its southern end.

No one knows exactly how long humans have lived in the Sierra Nevada, but evidence is plentiful that early peoples had summer camps in the range. Arrowheads, obsidian chips, and other artifacts reveal human presence as much as a thousand years ago. The Yokuts, Miwok, and Maidu lived on the western side of these mountains, the Washo and Monos on the eastern. Francis Farquhar points out that even though these tribes weren't from the same stock, they had similar lifestyles. They developed no organized civilization, no cultivated fields, no permanent buildings, and little government. Residents of the dry area east of the mountains were more mobile than their western counterparts. Each group had its own territory and hunting grounds, although some overlapped.

The Yokuts were the first Indians of the Sierra to have contact with Spanish missionaries and explorers in the 1770s. The first whites to see the great range were Capt. Pedro Fages and Father Juan Crespí in 1772. Jedediah Smith was the first white person to cross it in an easterly direction, in 1827; the first group to make a westward crossing included Joseph Walker and Zenas Leonard in 1833–34. Joseph B. Chiles, a Kentuckian, crossed the Sierra first with the Bidwell-Bartleson party in 1841, again in 1843, and one more time in 1848, when he escorted John Frémont's children on a transcontinental trek to join their father.

The Sierra Nevada constituted a barrier to Spanish exploration and occupation. The formidable mountains barred the Russians, too, from moving eastward from their settlements at Bodega Bay and Fort Ross. In 1819 Lt. José María Estudillo sketched his perception of the great mountains, and pretty accurate it was, showing forests and rivers in their proper places and high peaks covered with snow. The Spanish, however, never took advantage of that information, but left it for other Europeans to first test themselves against the great snowy mountains.

The California State Geological Survey carried out the first organized exploration of the Sierra Nevada. Led by Josiah Whitney, that group of seven mapped much of the central and southern portions of the range, until that time largely unknown. Named state geologist in 1860, Whitney that year headed up a team that included Chester Averell, William More Gabb, William Ashburer, Charles F. Hoffmann, Clarence King, and William H. Brewer. For fourteen years they surveyed the state, trying to collect samples of all its resources. Long before the task was completed their funds ran out, but the group did get the High Sierra mapped. When the survey's funding expired, the group continued for a time on its own resources; the Yosemite guidebook it published was printed at Whitney's expense. His reward was having the state's highest peak named for him.

The western slopes of the Sierra Nevada are home to the world's largest life form: *Sequoia gigantea*, "big trees." They are found along a 250-mile range in these mountains and the first white person to see them was probably Joseph Walker, during his 1833 Sierra crossing. Sequoias didn't, however, come to the attention of the public at large until 1852 when a hunter named A. T. Dowd discovered the Calaveras Grove in the gold country.

California does not divide neatly into discrete sections. Most of the foothills of the Sierra Nevada have been explored in part 3, "Gold Country." Southern portions of the eastern slopes have been visited in part 11 as part of the great desert, which they strongly resemble. What's left, however, enshrines a great deal of California's early and dramatic history.

Much of this history has been preserved through the auspices of a society that got its start in Sierra City, the last town of consequence on the golden thread that is CA 49. The Ancient Order of E Clampus Vitus was organized in 1857 as a burlesque of fraternal societies. Its head is the Noble Grand Humbug; members are called Clampers. Although it started out as a hoaxing group, local chapters in the various Sierra towns engaged in some charitable activities. In 1931 Carl Wheat and other members of the California Historical Society revived the group, whose purpose today is to authenticate gold rush lore and to place plaques at historical sites, as well as to have fun.

US 395
Bishop–Nevada Border
131 miles

Following US 395, the route meanders north, climbing steeply along the eastern slopes of the Sierra Nevada. It passes Round Valley to the east, attains the Sherwin summit, almost 7,000 feet above sea level, then drops down slightly to pass Crowley Lake, one of the reservoirs of the Owens Valley water delivery system. It's a spot popular with fishermen because the Department of Fish and Game keeps it well stocked.

CONVICT LAKE

Twenty-seven miles northwest of Bishop and just west of the highway is Convict Lake, scene of a bloody battle. In 1871 twenty-nine convicts—murderers, robbers, and horse thieves—broke out of prison at Carson City, Nevada. Six of them headed south, encountering mail carrier William Poor, whom they robbed and killed. Indignation over this outrage was so great that a posse quickly formed at Benton, just a few miles from the state boundary. Trailing the criminals into southern Mono County, the posse sighted them going up Monte Diablo Creek, ever after called Convict Creek. On the morning of September 24 the posse caught up with three of the convicts beside the lake at the head of the creek. There the two sides shot it out, and Robert Morrison, a Benton merchant, was fatally wounded. The desperadoes fled toward Round Valley, where they were later captured. Taken to Bishop, two of them were hanged, and a third returned to prison.

ONE MORE LOST MINE

The road continues northward, passing Mammoth Mountain, one of the largest ski areas in the country. This popular tourist attraction was originally discovered because of still another lost mine legend. This one has it that three German brothers struggling to reach California's goldfields in the early 1850s finally got to the headwaters of the Owens River. While camping someplace between Mammoth Peak and Mono Lake, Mildred Hoover writes, one of the brothers picked up a chunk of granite in which were embedded bits of gold, like blueberries in a muffin. Since winter was drawing near, the brothers had to hurry out of the Sierra; only one of them survived to reach the Mother Lode country. Delirious when he finally reached shelter, he was still clutching pieces of that rich rock, but could only vaguely describe where he found it. This legend set off a search for the lost granite mine that continues today. Even though gold was never found, the beauties of the area were: Gem Lake, June Lake, Shadow Creek, Rainbow Falls, even Deadman Creek, named, the story goes, in honor of those who searched for the lost mine.

About twenty-four miles north of the Mammoth Lakes area, over Deadman Summit with its elevation of more than 8,000 feet, the route reaches a junction with CA 120 and the start of a side trip whose destination is seventy miles to the west.

YOSEMITE, A HELL OF A PLACE

CA 120 takes off from US 395 in a twisting, up-and-down fashion, heading west through Tuolumne Meadows, where the river valley broadens to almost a mile, and over Tioga Pass, nearly 10,000 feet high. The meadow in summer is green and grassy, surrounded by alpine scenery of breathtaking beauty. The destination of this road, which is closed in winter months, is Yosemite National Park, jewel of the Sierra Nevada.

Indians of the Miwok tribe entered the Yosemite Valley region as early as 100 B.C. They were known as Ahwahneeche, and their region, Ahwahnee. They lived simply, using nature's bounty only as required for survival.

In 1833, William Jones says, Joseph Walker and his party of trappers actually discovered the Yosemite Valley, even though they didn't enter it. Blind to the beauties they saw from the valley's rim—thundering waterfalls, rock formations, and scenic vistas unsurpassed in the entire world, Walker viewed the valley as a disappointment because he found no beavers in the area. The first whites to enter the valley, in 1849, were W. P. Abrams and U. N. Reamer, in the vanguard of the gold rush. They noted it in a diary, but hurried on to join the search for gold. The natives observed all these outsiders, but allowed them to come and go in peace because they didn't seem to threaten the Indians' way of life.

Matters changed, however, when Kit Carson discovered the first lode gold mine near Mariposa, just west of Yosemite. Prospectors swarmed into the area to go down in history as forty-niners. Towns sprang up all through the hills, boomed for a time, and died when the gold played out. One of the principal players in this drama was James Savage, owner of trading posts in the foothills, whose business boomed with the influx of miners.

Aerial view of Yosemite Valley. —Richard Frear, National Park Service

Clouds shroud snowcapped Half Dome in Yosemite National Park. Half Dome rises almost 5,000 feet above Yosemite Valley and the Merced River.
—National Park Service

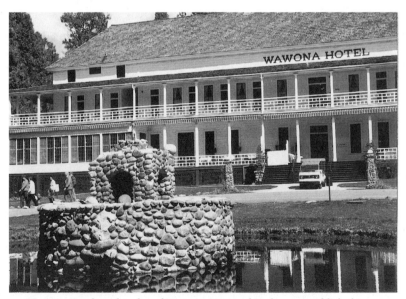

Wawona Hotel, at the edge of Yosemite National Park, was established in 1856 and is one of California's oldest classic hotels. —Frank Pittman

Yosemite Falls, highest in the nation, thunders to the valley floor in the spring when rivers are full.
—Frank Pittman

The Indians were apprehensive as they watched ever-increasing numbers of settlers flooding into their homeland. Again and again they were driven from territory they had inhabited for centuries; careless miners destroyed their food sources. Fearful for their own survival, they tried to drive out the unwelcome settlers by burning trading posts and killing their residents. Miners, of course, retaliated, determined to drive the Indians from the mountains. The first of the Indians' attacks was against Savage's station on the Merced River not far below Yosemite Valley. Thus began what has been called the Mariposa Indian War.

Governor John McDougal soon deputized a posse called the Mariposa Battalion to hunt down the offenders, 350 Miwok, Yokuts, and Chowchilla led by Chief Tenaya. James Savage, commissioned a major in the state militia, led the posse with Lafayette H. Bunnell at his side. They plunged into the mountains from which the attackers had come, hot on the trail of the miscreants. With the river high, the temperature low, and the snow deep, Savage wasn't impressed with the area in which

375

Merced River at springtime flood courses through the Yosemite Valley. —Frank Pittman

he found himself. In fact, according to Jones, Savage's only comment was, "It's a hell of a place." Bunnell, on the other hand, was so enthusiastic about the valley that he proposed christening it Yosemite, the name the settlers applied to the very people they were trying to destroy.

Word of the valley's splendor spread slowly, however, for no adequate description of it reached outside settlements. When it finally did, writers, artists, and photographers came to reproduce what they saw and show it to the world. Little thought was given, at the time, to preserving the assets of the valley, but it caught the attention of Frederick Law Olmsted, the landscape architect who had designed New York's Central Park. A conservationist as well as a designer, Olmsted sized up the situation when he arrived in 1863 and threw his not-inconsiderable weight behind the drive to make a park of the Yosemite Valley. Congress moved swiftly and on June 30, 1864, Abraham Lincoln signed the Yosemite Grant into law. The area became a state park that year and a national park in 1905.

Today's park covers almost 1,200 square miles and contains three great groves of sequoias: the Merced, Tuolumne, and Mariposa. Yosemite Falls is the highest in the nation; El Capitan is the world's largest granite monolith at 3,000 feet. The Wawona Hotel near the south entrance to the park was established in 1856 and is one of the state's oldest classic hotels.

Near the visitors center on the valley floor is a complete Indian village, the National Park Service's interpretation of Miwok culture twenty years after initial contact with non-Indians. Here the daily life of the natives is well drawn. The Ahwahneeche continued to use native plants such as acorns for food; their method of preparation is demonstrated. The village contains a *u-mu-cha* (bark dwelling house), *chuckah* (structures for storing acorns), and a *hangi* (roundhouse).

The side trip returns to US 395, a total of nearly 140 miles of extraordinary beauty having been added to the distance to the Nevada state line.

LEE VINING

About half a mile farther along, the route reaches the town of Lee Vining. It was named for the man who in 1852 led a party of prospectors to the first gold strike in the area. According to Hoover, Lt. Tredwell Moore and second infantry troops trying to round up Chief Tenaya and the last of the Indians from Yosemite Valley discovered that gold. Moore failed to catch up with the natives, but, Farquhar says, he discovered gold-bearing quartz and other minerals near Mono Lake. In returning to Camp Miller on the San Joaquin, Moore traveled to the east and south of Yosemite, breaking a new trail, later known as the Sunrise, over the Sierra.

Tenaya had escaped to the east, to the territory of the Monos, with whom he lived for about a year. Then, with a few of his retainers, he tried to return to his old home in Yosemite. Some of those traveling with Tenaya stole horses from the Monos, calling down their wrath on the head of their one-time friend. The Monos found the old chief and stoned him to death, thereby putting an end to hostilities in Yosemite.

The Tufa Towers of Mono Lake

Lee Vining, twenty-six miles north of Mammoth, sits at the edge of a great alkaline lake, sixty square miles flanked by towering snow-covered peaks on the west, and volcanic craters on the east. Once a great inland sea that covered the Mono Basin, Mono Lake is judged to be 700,000 years old, the oldest lake in North America. Desolate and barren as it may seem, the lake is an important breeding ground for sea gulls.

Its salty water cannot support fish, but brine shrimp and brine flies thrive in it. Indeed, *mono* is a Yokuts word meaning "flies." Monos who lived in the area used to collect brine fly grubs that hatch around the edge of the lake to trade to the Yokuts for acorns. The grubs were an important protein source for both Monos and Yokuts.

When the lake begins to warm up in the spring, the hard cysts that have encased brine shrimp eggs during the winter break open, releasing the tiny shrimp. Both shrimp and flies are important sources of food for nearly three hundred species of birds that inhabit the Mono basin. As many as 50,000 gulls breed here in a single season and some 90,000 Wilson's phalaropes at a time may lay over at the lake on their migration from Canada to South America. Eared grebes feed here, too, along with scores of other birds.

The most unusual aspect of Mono Lake is its tufa towers, limestone spires, that rise in ghostly array from several parts of the lake. Since 1941, when Los Angeles started diverting the streams that once fed the lake, its water level has dropped significantly. Thus, the water no longer covers tufa formations, created when calcium from submerged hot springs mixes with the carbonates in the salty water. Once exposed, the formations start to crumble to dust. A naturalist is on hand at the South Tufa Area to explain the phenomenon.

BAD, BAD BODIE

Leaving the Mono Lake Tufa State Reserve, the route continues for seventeen miles, over Conway Summit, to a junction with CA 270 and another side trip. This one, a twenty-eight-mile round-trip that plunges once again into desert and includes a three-mile stretch of dirt road, explores Bodie State Historic Park. Probably one of the most famous ghost towns in the West, Bodie sits on a windswept prairie in a state of arrested decay.

It was remote; it was rich; it was bad. Murders, robberies, and fistfights were as common as tumbleweeds. In 1879 six men were shot in a single week; undertaking was one of the more prosperous businesses in Bodie. A park brochure quotes the Reverend F. M. Warrington denouncing the town as "a sea of sin lashed by tempests of lust and passion." It's hard to say what made the place so bad, unless the locale and climate demanded toughness of character.

Founded in the late 1850s, Bodie was named in honor of Waterman S. Body—also known as William Bodey—who discovered a piddling little bit of gold in the windswept hills just north of Mono Lake. The little town didn't amount to much until 1877, when the Standard Company hit pay dirt and a giant gold rush transformed Bodie. From a hamlet of twenty residents it grew to a boomtown of several thousand with a red light district, a Chinatown, stores, hotels, and all the rest. Twenty-mule freight wagons came from as far away as Mojave; stagecoaches from Carson City, Sonora, and the Owens Valley daily brought new prospectors. The thirty or so mines that tunneled below the town yielded a total of $25 million in gold and silver, Remi Nadeau reports. Fortunes were won and lost at gaming tables, too.

By 1882 Bodie's decline had begun. In 1887 the Standard Mine merged with the Bodie, but the area's underground treasure was exhausted, hauled away during the twenty or so years of the town's existence. Jim Cain, one of the town's first arrivals, refused to accept the passing of his town. Gradually he bought up mines and buildings until he owned most of the town. Living there with his family, he opened the bank each day at 10 A.M., even though there were no customers. When the automobile and surfaced roads brought Bodie within reach of tourists in the 1920s, Cain showed off his town to awed travelers, insisting that it would come back.

In 1932, a fire swept away two-thirds of what had been the best-preserved wooden ghost town in the West. Some of its structures were rebuilt, some saved. Still to be seen are the Odd Fellows Hall and Miners Union Hall; the firehouse stands on Main Street. On Green Street are the Boone Store, the Wheaton and Holis Hotels, the land office, and the schoolhouse. Today Bodie is a state historic park, with cobwebs in the windows and tumbleweeds in the streets. Coyotes trot through the dust and howl from the hills.

Dogtown and Bridgeport

Back on US 395, the route continues toward the Nevada border. Just a mile or so north of the turnoff to CA 270, near the cliff along Dogtown Creek, are the ruins of Dogtown, site of the first gold rush on the east side of the Sierra. According to William Logan and Susan Ochshorn, the name derives from miners' slang for a place of shoddy, temporary construction.

Bridgeport, just another mile farther along, has been the seat of Mono County since 1864. Its courthouse, built in 1880, is one of the best examples of the Italianate style in California. Despite being made entirely of wood, the building is remarkably well preserved. The Mono County Historical Museum on School Street displays a good collection of artifacts from Bodie and the towns of Masonic and Boulder Flat.

SONORA

Leaving Bridgeport, the road travels northwest for about twelve miles to climb Devil's Gate Summit, named for a mass of cracked green rock that rises above both sides of the highway. Four miles farther along it reaches a junction with CA 108, Sonora Junction.

Jedediah Smith is said to have been the first non-Indian to cross the Sierra in 1827 near what is now called Sonora Pass. That almost 10,000-foot grade rises nearly ten miles west of the junction on a road that leads to the town of Sonora on the Sierra's western slopes. A marker honoring Smith's effort and the completion of the Mono-Sonora Road stands fourteen miles east of Sonora.

Wagons carrying supplies to mines east of the Sierra used this road from 1864 onward. It was also the route of a weekly stage that ran from Sonora to Bodie. Today's CA 108 winds through the Stanislaus Forest, roughly duplicating the old road, remnants of which can be seen here and there.

Leaving the junction, US 395 takes a sharp turn northward to follow along the West Walker River, the route Jedediah Smith took in 1827 on his way to Salt Lake City. Joseph Walker followed this river to its source in 1833–34 in his passage to central California. In 1841 the Bidwell-Bartleson party traveled this way, as well. In the eighteen miles or so that separate Sonora Junction from the state line, the road passes Walker, Coleville, and Topaz. Just short of the state line, this exploration section ends.

CA 89
California Border–Truckee
95 miles

CA 89 travels west from US 395, climbing Monitor Pass and leaving Mono County as it descends. Alpine County, which the road enters, straddles the crest and eastern slopes of the Sierra. Its eastern boundary coincides with that of the state. Indeed, prior to 1864 it was considered part of Nevada. Alpine County is one of the most sparsely settled of California's counties, with a population density of about two persons per square mile.

LOOPE

Eleven miles from its junction with US 395, CA 89 passes a tiny hamlet called Loope. Nadeau says this village is the site of the old mining town of Monitor. In the 1860s and 1870s the town flourished, even supporting a newspaper, but almost nothing is left of it today. Mines in this district produced silver and copper along with some gold.

THE EMIGRANT TRAIL

Seventeen miles from its junction with US 395, CA 89 meets CA 4, a poor road subject to winter closures. Weather permitting, a short side trip begins here. Twelve miles to the west it reaches Ebbetts Pass, named for Maj. John Ebbetts who discovered this trail. Called the Emigrant Trail, the route was opened up in the early 1850s. No wagons traveled it, however, until 1864 when a toll road named Carson Valley and Big Tree Road was completed to provide access to the Comstock Lode in Nevada. The side trip returns to CA 89, having added twenty-four miles to the distance to Truckee.

MARKLEEVILLE AND WOODFORDS

Six miles northeast of CA 89 is the town of Markleeville, seat of Alpine County. Jacob J. Marklee filed a claim on one hundred sixty acres in Douglas County, Nevada, on June 23, 1862. After the boundary survey, it was determined that his land was in California. During the rush to the Comstock Lode, the town was built on his land. The county courthouse now stands on the site of his cabin.

CA 89 reaches Woodfords seven miles north of Markleeville, at the junction with CA 88. A remount station of the Pony Express was established here on April 4, 1860, when Warren Upson scaled the mountains during a blinding snowstorm to make his way down the eastern slope of the Sierra en route to Carson City. Five weeks later, however, the Pony Express was rerouted by way of Echo Summit and Luther Pass.

ODD FELLOWS, A SCOUT, AND EMIGRANTS

Before heading north on CA 89, a side trip to the southwest takes off along CA 88 to visit three historical spots. The first is a memorial to pioneer Odd Fellows, a little more than fourteen miles west of Woodfords. Here on some large rocks near Carson Pass a group of pioneers inscribed their names and the emblem of the Independent Order of Odd Fellows.

At the summit of the pass named for him stands a marker honoring Kit Carson. It was here that the scout carved his name on a tree when he guided John C. Frémont over the Sierra Nevada on a government exploration. The original inscription was cut from the tree and is now at Sutter's Fort in Sacramento.

Not quite three miles farther along, a marker identifies the spot, beneath Caples Lake, where the Old Emigrant Road of 1848 used to cross a meadow. From this 9,460-foot summit that trail descended to Placerville. That difficult route became obsolete when a better one was created in 1863.

The Mail Had to Go Through

While these routes were being debated and shaped, there was mail to be delivered. By the summer of 1858 Jared B. Crandall, of the Pioneer Stage Company, operated a stage over an unfinished road east from Placerville to Carson Valley. Going was rough in all weather, however, and winter snows put an end to mail delivery for the season. Sometimes pack mules and horses got the job done. When animals couldn't make it through the snow, a most remarkable man took over.

In January 1856, a man called Snowshoe Thompson, on skis he fashioned after ones he remembered from his boyhood in Norway, glided over the snow to deliver the mail. During the next twenty-six years he made trip after trip through the snow, carrying fifty to eighty pounds of mail and supplies on his back. Wearing no heavy overcoat and carrying no blankets, Farquhar writes, Thompson made the eastward journey from Placerville to Carson Valley in three days; the return trip he often accomplished in two. This stalwart's grave is in Genoa, Nevada.

Returning to CA 89, the side trip has added thirty-four miles to the distance to Truckee. In the next fifteen miles, the route climbs Luther Pass and continues about eleven miles to the town of Echo Lake and the junction with US 50. A side trip to the west takes off here.

Strawberry Flat and Kyburz

Eleven miles along US 50 stands Strawberry Flat, a popular place for stopovers in the rush to harvest Nevada's silver. Nadeau says among the worst hazards those travelers faced during their journey over the Sierra were the wayside taverns. One of the best, however, was known as Berry's Station at Strawberry Flat. Hundreds congregated there each night demanding plates of pork and beans and floor space on which to sleep. The next morning they'd douse their heads in the horse trough and set off again in search of the wealth to the east.

A historical marker standing on US 50, a little less than nine miles east of Kyburz, remembers the resort established by Swift and Watson in 1856 that became a remount station for the Pony Express. On April 4, 1860, Division Superintendent Bolivar Roberts waited there with a

This archival photo of Lake Tahoe belies the incredible beauty of the largest Alpine lake in North America. —Anaheim Public Library

string of mules to help Warren Upson through the blizzard raging at Echo Summit.

MEYERS

Back at Echo Lake, about twenty-three miles having been added to the distance to Truckee, the route swings northeast through Meyers, site of another spot of historical interest. In the Yank's Station shopping center on US 50 and Apache Avenue a marker denotes the location of the easternmost remount station in California of the Central Overland Pony Express. Here a trading post established in 1851 became a popular hostelry and stage stop operated by Ephraim "Yank" Clement. Used as a remount stop until 1861, this is the station at which Warren Upson changed ponies on April 28, 1860, before riding on to Friday's in Nevada, the end of his stint.

LAKE TAHOE

Seven miles from Echo Lake, CA 89 turns to the northwest and, about eight miles later, reaches Emerald Bay on the south shore of Lake Tahoe. Of glacial origin, Lake Tahoe sits at an elevation of more than 6,000 feet, partly in California's Placer and El Dorado Counties and partly in Nevada. It is almost twenty-two miles long and twelve wide, with a surface area of 193 miles—the largest Alpine lake in North America. Mark Twain wrote that he thought it must present the fairest picture the entire world could afford.

The first non-Indians to report seeing the lake were Frémont and his cartographer, Charles Preuss, in 1844. James Hart says Frémont at first simply referred to it as a lake entirely surrounded by mountains, then christened it Lake Bonpland, to honor a French botanist. Politics being what they are, the lovely lake was officially named Lake Bigler in 1854 in honor of John Bigler, third governor of California. Bigler was so outspoken about his secessionist views, however, that he lost favor in the state and a move was started to name the lake for its Indians. But it wasn't until 1945 that the legislature got around to formally declaring the name to be Tahoe, from the Washo word meaning "water" or "lake."

A Taste of the Fjords

Soon after the turn of the century wealthy Californians came to regard Tahoe as the ideal place to spend their summers. Accordingly, they built what they considered rustic retreats: several thousand square feet of living space on many acres of land next to the water.

Emerald Bay is a large cove on the southwest side of Lake Tahoe. Often called a lake within a lake, it is probably the single most photographed part of the lake. It so reminded Mrs. Lora J. Knight of a Norwegian fjord that she decided to build her summer home there in an appropriate style. What that decision yielded is Vikingsholm, called Tahoe's hidden castle, one of the finest examples of Scandinavian architecture in the United States. Looking for all the world like a Norse fortress, Vikingsholm was built in the summer of 1929 by two hundred skilled workers. Great stone walls rise to meet wooden roofs; sunlight sparkles through leaded windows. Every room boasts hand-wrought light fixtures and door latches. The grand furnishings clearly indicate that Mrs. Knight spared no expense in creating her hideaway. Employing a staff of fifteen, she regularly entertained six to ten guests. Usually those guests weren't famous personalities, but Will Rogers and Charles Lindbergh are both reported to have visited her. She spent sixteen summers there until her death in 1945 at the age of eighty-two. The castle was sold. In 1953 the unusual mansion was donated to the state by its owner, Harvey West. As a state park it is today accessible from the lakeside by boat or from CA 89 by foot.

Members of the National Park Service refer to Lake Tahoe as "the park that got away." Too late, they have realized that it should have been preserved, every mile of it. Instead developers have cluttered most of the Nevada shore with taco stands and casinos, while too many visitors have polluted the once crystalline waters. The California side is somewhat better, comprising as it does five state parks, wilderness trails, and abundant wildlife.

TRUCKEE

The route continues along CA 89 for a little more than thirty-five miles, skirting Lake Tahoe and passing the entrance to Squaw Valley, California's premier ski area and site of the winter Olympic Games of

1960. Just south of I-80 it crosses the Placer-Nevada County line and reaches the town of Truckee, named for the river on which it stands. The river, in turn, was named by the Elisha Stevens party to honor the Paiute who directed them to it in 1844.

Tales of Donner Pass

Stevens (spelled Stephens by some authorities, including Farquhar) was a trapper and frontiersman who led a large party overland to California in 1844. That group of emigrants, called the Murphy-Townsend-Stevens party, takes a place on the pages of history as the first to take wagons across the Sierra and the group to discover what was later named Donner Pass. They also gained fame because somewhere on the upper Yuba River the women of the party survived a winter in the Sierra. All but two of the men continued on foot to seek help at Sutter's Fort. One of the men who stayed behind was in reality a teen-ager, Moses Schallenberger, who lived alone in a cabin near where the Donner memorial stands today. Mike Hayden says Schallenberger survived his ordeal because he trapped foxes for food and read books while waiting for relief. Years later Schallenberger would write a detailed account of that winter.

Meanwhile, in a cabin on the banks of the Yuba, Mrs. Martin Murphy gave birth to a baby daughter whom she named Elizabeth Yuba. She was the first child to be born in the Sierra. The men of the party soon returned and by March the entire party had reached safe harbor.

The Paiute guide who had pointed the way for them was the grandfather of Sarah Winnemucca, who grew up to be educated at Saint Mary's convent at San Jose. After suffering brutal treatment at the hands of Indian agents on an Indian reservation at Pyramid Lake in Nevada, she lectured at San Francisco and elsewhere on the plight of the Indian. She wrote *Life among the Paiutes* in 1883 and conducted a school for Paiute children in Lovelock, Nevada, on land donated by Leland Stanford.

In Truckee stands a historical marker at the Southern Pacific station at 70 Donner Pass Road. Its plaque tells how advance forces of the railroad's construction crew built forty miles of track east and west of town, moving supplies by wagon and sled, while the railroad's progress awaited completion of tunnels through the Sierra. Miles of roadbed were blasted from the sides of cliffs by charges placed by Chinese miners who were lowered headfirst on ropes, according to Hayden. The explosions set off huge snowslides that caused many casualties. Summit Tunnel opened in December 1867, and the line reached Truckee on April 3, 1868. The Sierra had been conquered.

Just three miles to the west of Truckee the final tale of California's turbulent history is told. It's an often-told story and a tragic one, but nonetheless one that proves how persistent and indomitable the human spirit can be. A historical marker commemorating the events that took place here stands on Old Highway 40 at I-80 and the Truckee exit. Surrounding the marker, at the eastern end of Donner Lake, is Donner Memorial State Park, a 353-acre park with a museum enshrining artifacts that illustrate the events of the winter of 1846.

Led by George and Jacob Donner and James Reed, the group that would forever be known as the Donner party set out from Illinois in April of 1846. At Fort Bridger, Wyoming, on the Continental Divide, they decided to break off from the main body of their party and travel by a shorter route described in an open letter from Lansford W. Hastings.

Driven by political ambition, Hastings had in 1845 written a book, *The Emigrants' Guide*, describing a route to California that Frémont had revealed to him. Unfortunately, Hastings related this route to anyone who would hear him, although he had not tried it out. The so-called Hastings Cutoff went southwest from Fort Bridger, along the south side of the Salt Lake, to Pilot Knob, then below the Ruby Mountains and on to the Humboldt River near today's Elko. It was this dreadful route through the desert that slowed the passage of the Donner party and led to their ultimate tragedy.

Twenty-three wagons carrying twenty-seven men, seventeen women, and forty-three children reached the approach to Donner Pass late in October. Traveling in three groups, the last containing the Donner family, they began the ascent. On Halloween the advance group camped not far from Schallenberger's cabin. An inch of snow lay on the ground and a storm was approaching. Looking ahead, those in the vanguard could see snow piled high in the pass. The next day they pressed on, only to find snow so deep they couldn't keep to the trail; they had no choice but to turn back. They camped at the cabin once again. The next day, November 2, a heavy rain fell, leading the emigrants to hope it would wash the snow away. They didn't realize that what was rain at this lower elevation was more snow higher up.

The second section of the wagon train arrived and most of the party decided to press on the following day. Realizing they could never get wagons through the snow, they started out—some on foot, others riding horses or mules. Almost every traveler carried a child. In his diary Patrick Breen, a member of the party, wrote that they made another attempt with the wagons on the same day. In any event, they had almost made it to the top of the pass when darkness fell. Exhausted, they camped that night in the snow, only to be covered by another foot of it during the night. At daybreak they struggled back to the cabin. The Breen family arrived at last and established themselves in the abandoned cabin. The emigrants built two others, named for the Murphy and Graves families, who made up the largest part of their residents.

Rain and slushy snow fell, day after day. The travelers built cabins with tents, wagon canvases, and hides of slaughtered oxen for roofs. They would be warm enough, but food grew ever more scarce while snow on the pass piled up, deeper and deeper. It soon became apparent that even killing all their cattle and mules wouldn't provide enough food to get them through the winter. One hunter killed a bear; others shot a coyote, an owl, and a couple of ducks. The situation was perilous. On Friday, November 20, 1846, Breen's diary entry read, in part: "We now have killed most part of our cattle having to stay here untill next spring & and live on poor beef without bread or salt."

The party had divided into two groups, one camping at Donner Lake, where the memorial stands, and the other in cabins on Alder Creek. Breen noted in his diary that snow fell for days on end; the few clear days brought little relief because the cold intensified when snow wasn't falling. A party of twenty-two set out on November 21 to try to bring help. They made it over the pass and camped one night on the other side but grew discouraged and turned back.

One storm followed another and on December 13 Breen noted that the snow was now eight feet deep. On the sixteenth the weather cleared and another group assayed an assault on the pass. Seventeen persons set off, but two gave up early on. The ten men and five women who persisted became known as the Forlorn Hope. Carrying only six days' rations, they made slow progress, taking two days to get to the top of the pass. They forged on, since turning back meant certain death. One of them, Charles F. Stanton, gave up on the sixth morning out and remained sitting by the paltry fire when his companions set out again.

This group got lost in the snow. For days they floundered; some died and their starving companions promptly ate them. At last they reached foothills where snow lay only in patches. There they were lucky enough to find a deer that fed them temporarily. Others died. At last the handful of survivors straggled into an Indian village and were led to the Johnson Ranch in Wheatland. Two men and all five women outlived the ordeal of thirty-three days of cold and starvation and exhaustion.

About the time the seven were reaching warmth and food, Breen was noting in his diary, "tough times, but not discouraged our hopes are in God. Amen." His fellow emigrants were dying off, however. Mrs.

Reed, after killing the family dog and living off its body for almost a week, set off with her twelve-year-old daughter and two adults to escape. After four nights in the snow they turned back, just before another storm hit that brought the level of snow to thirteen feet.

On the last day of January a heroic rescue party struck out from the Sacramento Valley. When their number had dwindled down to seven, they cached some of the supplies they carried and struggled on through a raging storm. On February 18, just before sunset, they reached the cabins. They distributed food sparingly and prepared to leave. Three of the rescuers went on to the Donner tents and returned with two adults and four of the older children. On February 11 the seven valiant rescuers set out, shepherding three men, four women, and fifteen children, one as young as three. They expected to live on the cached food. Unfortunately, animals had plundered those caches. A man and a child died before the group met up with a second relief party heading for the camp.

The second relief party was led by James Reed, whose wife and two older children were with the rescued group. Two more of his children remained at the lake, however, so Reed hurried on, carrying food for all the emigrants. Arriving at the camp on March 1, he found much evidence of cannibalism. On March 3 he began his return journey with one man, two women, and fourteen children, including three from the Donner cabin.

The return trip was almost as difficult as the winter had been: They were caught by a severe storm and couldn't proceed until March 8. By that time, many in the group were too weak to continue, so Reed's relief party pressed on with just three children. The other emigrants were finally found by a third rescue party. By that time only eleven were still alive; they also had resorted to cannibalism.

Part of this third relief group took the eleven survivors down the mountains; the rest continued to the camp. They brought out the three young daughters of George and Tamsen Donner and a young man, leaving behind Mrs. Donner and her dying husband, whom she refused to abandon. Mrs. Graves and German-born Louis Keseberg remained at the camp, too. Only Keseberg was alive, hale and hearty, when a final rescue party arrived in the spring.

Of the eighty-seven who had started out on the journey, only forty-seven lived to tell the tale, to profit from the mistakes that caused the tragedy. Setting out on an unknown path at Hastings' suggestion was a mistake; so was choosing to rest for a few days near Truckee before trying to crest the formidable pass. Most folks agree, however, that keeping themselves alive by eating their companions' bodies was not a mistake. The argument over that position rages on today and will, no doubt, never be finally settled.

The historical exploration of California is now complete. A drive of less than one hundred miles down I-80 ends in Sacramento, seat of government of the most perplexing, most frustrating, most exciting state in the Union.

Bibliography

Allen, Robert L. *The Port Chicago Mutiny*. New York: Warner Books, 1989.

Armor, John, and Peter Wright. *Manzanar*. Photos by Ansel Adams. Commentary by John Hersey. New York: Times Books, 1988.

Bachelis, Faren Maree. *The Pelican Guide to Sacramento and the Gold Country*. Gretna, LA: Pelican Publishing Company, 1987.

Bancroft, Hubert Howe. *Register of Pioneer Inhabitants of California, 1542 to 1848, and Index to Information Concerning Them in Bancroft's History of California Volumes 1–5*. Reprint, Los Angeles: Dawson's Book Shop, 1964.

Bean, Walton. *California: An Interpretive History*. New York: McGraw-Hill Book Company, 1978.

Beck, Warren A., and Ynez D. Haase. *Historical Atlas of California*. Norman: University of Oklahoma Press, 1974.

Beck, Warren A., and David A. Williams. *California: A History of the Golden State*. New York: Doubleday and Company, 1972.

Bing, Leon. *To Do or Die*. New York: Harper Collins Publishers, 1991.

Birmingham, Stephan. *California Rich*. New York: Simon and Schuster, 1980.

Botts, Myrtle, et al. *The History of Julian*. Julian, Calif.: Julian Historical Society, 1969.

Bowen, Ezra, et al. *The High Sierra*. New York: Time-Life Books, 1972.

California Historical Landmarks. Sacramento: California Department of Parks and Recreation, 1982.

Chalfant, W. A. *Death Valley: The Facts*. Stanford: Stanford University Press, 1936.

Chapman, John L. *Incredible Los Angeles*. New York: Harper and Row, 1967.

Chase, J. Smeaton. *California Desert Trails*. Boston and New York: Houghton Mifflin Company, 1919.

Clappe, Louise A. K. S. *The Shirley Letters*. San Francisco: Thomas Russell, 1922.

Cleland, Robert Glass. *California in Our Time, 1900–1940*. New York: Alfred A. Knopf, 1947.

———. *From Wilderness to Empire: A History of California*. Edited by Glenn S. Dumke. New York: Alfred A. Knopf, 1969.

———. *The Irvine Ranch*, 3rd ed. San Marino, Calif.: The Huntington Library, 1962.

Cramer, Esther R. *La Habra: The Pass Through the Hills*. Fullerton, Calif.: Sultana Press, 1969.

Decker, Barbara, and Robert Decker. *Road Guide to Death Valley*. Mariposa, Calif.: Double Decker Press, 1989.

Discover the Californias. Official California Travel Guide. San Francisco: California Tourism Corporation, in association with *Golden State Magazine* and the California Department of Commerce, Office of Tourism, 1992.

Drury, Aubrey. *California: An Intimate Guide*. New York: Harper and Brothers, 1947.

Eargle, Dolan H., Jr. *The Earth Is Our Mother: A Guide to the Indians of California, Their Locales and Historic Sites*. San Francisco: Trees Company Press, 1986.

Ellsberg, Helen. *Mines of Julian*. Glendale, Calif.: La Siesta Press, 1972.

Engbeck, Joseph H., Jr. *La Purisima Mission*. Sacramento: California Department of Parks and Recreation, 1979.

Farquhar, Francis P. *History of the Sierra Nevada*. Berkeley: University of California Press, 1965.

Farrell, Harry. *Swift Justice: Murder and Vengeance in a California Town*. New York: St. Martin's Press, 1992.

Faulk, Odie B. *U.S. Camel Corps: An Army Experiment*. New York: Oxford University Press, 1976.

Fay, James S., and Stephanie W. Fay, eds. *California Almanac*. 4th ed. Santa Barbara: Pacific Data Resources, 1990.

Federal Writers' Project Staff. *California: A Guide to the Golden State*. Reprint, New York: Hastings House, 1967.

———. *San Francisco: The Bay and Its Cities*. New York: Hastings House, 1940.

Foster, Lynne. *Adventuring in the California Desert: The Sierra Club Travel Guide to the Great Basin, Mojave, and Colorado Desert Regions of California*. San Francisco: Sierra Club Books, 1987.

Fisher, Anne B. *The Salinas: Upside-down River*. New York: Farrar and Rinehart, 1945.

Fowler, Harlen D. *Camels to California*. Stanford: Stanford University Press, 1950.

Fox, Maude A. *Both Sides of the Mountain*. Palm Desert: Desert Magazine Press, 1954.

Glasscock, C. B. *Here's Death Valley*. New York: The Bobbs-Merrill Company, 1940.

Hallan-Gibson, Pamela. *The Golden Promise: An Illustrated History of Orange County*. Northridge, Calif.: Windsor Publications, 1986.

Hart, James, D. *A Companion to California*. Berkeley: University of California Press, 1987.

Hayden, Mike. *Guidebook to the Lake Tahoe Country*. Vol. 2, *Alpine County, Donner-Truckee, and the Nevada Shore*. Los Angeles: Ward Ritchie Press, 1971.

Hogan, William, and William German, eds. *The "San Francisco Chronicle" Reader*. New York: McGraw-Hill Book Company, 1962.

Holliday, J. S. *The World Rushed In: The California Gold Rush Experience*. New York: Simon and Schuster, 1982.

Hoover, Mildred Brooke, H. E. Rensch, and E. G. Rensch. *Historic Spots in California*. Stanford: Stanford University Press.

Houk, Walter, Sue Irwin, and Richard A. Lovett. *A Visitor's Guide to California State Parks*. Sacramento: California Department of Parks and Recreation, 1990.

Houston, James D. *Californians Searching for the Golden State*. Berkeley: Creative Arts Book Company, 1985.

Hoyle, Millard F., Sr., ed. *Crimes and Career of Tiburcio Vasquez*. Hollister, Calif.: San Benito County Historical Society, 1927.

Hudson, Tom. *Lake Elsinore Valley: Its Story 1776–1977*. Lake Elsinore, Calif.: Laguna House, 1978.

Hundley, Norris, Jr. *The Great Thirst: Californians and Water, 1770s–1990s*. Berkeley: University of California Press, 1992.

Jones, William R. *Yosemite: The Story Behind the Scenery*. Las Vegas: KC Publications, 1989.

Klotz, Esther. *Riverside and the Day the Bank Broke: A Chronicle of the City*. Riverside, Calif.: Rubidoux Press, 1972.

Krell, Dorothy, ed. *The California Missions: A Pictorial History*. Menlo Park, Calif.: Lane Publishing Company, 1979.

Lee, W. Storrs, ed. *California: A Literary Chronicle*. New York: Funk and Wagnalls, 1968.

Levy, JoAnn. *They Saw the Elephant: Women in the California Gold Rush*. Norman: University of Oklahoma Press, 1992.

Lewis, Donovan. *The Sawmill of Destiny: 1847–1852 Coloma,Calif*. Placerville, Calif.: Donella Enterprises, 1982.

Logan, William Bryant, and Susan Ochshorn. *The Smithsonian Guide to Historic America: The Pacific States*. New York: Stewart, Tabori and Chang, 1989.

Long, Margaret. *The Shadow of the Arrow*. Caldwell, Idaho: The Caxton Printers, 1941.

Lussier, Tomi Kay. *Big Sur: A Complete History and Guide*. Monterey: Big Sur Publications, 1988.

Mauldin, Henry K. *History of Lake County*. Vol.1, *Clear Lake and Mt. Konocti*. San Francisco: East Wind Printers, 1960.

McCall, Lynne, and Rosalind Perry. *California's Chumash Indians*. A Project of the Santa Barbara Museum of Natural History Education Center. San Luis Obispo: E-Z Nature Books, 1986.

McDonald, Douglas, and Gina McDonald. *The History of the Weaverville Joss House and the Chinese of Trinity County, California*. Medford, Ore.: McDonald Publishing, 1986.

McGroarty, John Steven. *A History of Southern California*. 1914. Reprint, Fresno: California History Books, 1975.

McWilliams, Carey. *Southern California Country*. New York: Duell, Sloan and Pierce, 1946.

Miller, Bruce W. *Chumash: A Picture of Their World*. Los Osos, Calif.: Sand River Press, 1988.

Nadeau, Remi. *Ghost Towns and Mining Camps of California: A History and Guide*. Santa Barbara: Crest Publishers, 1992.

———. "The Saga of Nadeau's Teams." *Westways* (July, 1957): 10.

Neihardt, John G. *The Song of Jed Smith*. New York: The Macmillan Company, 1941.

Newmark, Harris. *Sixty Years in California: 1853–1913*. 3rd ed. Cambridge, Mass.: The Riverside Press, 1930.

Nordhoff, Charles. *California: For Health, Pleasure, and Residence: A Book for Travellers and Settlers*. 1872. Reprint, Berkeley: Ten Speed Press, 1973.

O'Dell, Scott. *Country of the Sun: Southern California, An Informal History and Guide*. New York: Thomas Y. Crowell Company, 1957.

Outland, Charles F. *Man-Made Disaster: The Story of St. Francis Dam*. Glendale, Calif.: The Arthur H. Clark Company, 1963.

Pourade, Richard F. *The Glory Years*. San Diego: Union-Tribune Publishing Company, 1964.

Price, Peter. *The Battle at San Pasqual, December 6, 1846, and the Struggle for California*. San Diego: Pembroke Publishers, 1990.

Pumphrey, Margaret B. *Under Three Flags*. Caldwell, Idaho: The Caxton Printers, 1939.

Sangwan, Baljeet, ed. *The Complete Lake Tahoe Guidebook*. Tahoe City, Calif.: Indian Chief Publishing House, 1987.

Schad, Jerry. *Afoot and Afield in Orange County*. Berkeley: Wilderness Press, 1988.

———. *California Deserts*. Helena and Billings, Mont.: Falcon Press Publishing Company, 1988.

Schwartz, Henry. *Tales of Old Town*. San Diego: San Miguel Press, 1980.

Spaulding, Edward Selden, ed. *Adobe Days Along the Channel*. Santa Barbara: The Schauer Printing Studio, 1957.

Spencer-Hancock, Diane. *Fort Ross*. Jenner, Calif.: Fort Ross Interpretive Association, 1980.

Starr, Kevin. *Americans and the California Dream, 1850–1915*. New York: Oxford University Press, 1973.

Stewart, Don M. *Frontier Port: A Chapter in San Diego's History*. Los Angeles: The Ward Ritchie Press, 1965.

Stewart, George R. *Donner Pass and Those Who Crossed It*. San Francisco: California Historical Society, 1960.

Stone, Irving. *Men to Match My Mountains: The Opening of the Far West*. Garden City, NY: Doubleday and Company, 1956.

Teggart, Frederick J., ed. *Diary of Patrick Breen: One of the Donner Party*. Golden, Colo.: Outbooks, 1986.

Thompson, R. A. *The Russian Settlement in California: Fort Ross*. Jenner, Calif.: Fort Ross Interpretive Association, 1982.

Tweed, William C. *Sequoia-Kings Canyon: The Story Behind the Scenery*. Las Vegas: KC Publications, 1980.

Vaeth, Gordon. "USS *Macon*: Lost and Found." *National Geographic* (January 1992): 117.

Verardo, Denzil, and Jennie Verardo. *The Bale Grist Mill: Symbol of Pioneer Times in Napa Valley*. Oakland: California State Parks Foundation, 1984.

Walton, John. *Western Times and Water Wars: State, Culture, and Rebellion in California*. Berkeley: University of California Press, 1992.

Whitney, Stephen. *A Sierra Club Naturalist's Guide to the Sierra Nevada*. San Francisco: Sierra Club Books, 1979.

Winnett, Thomas, and Jason Winnett. *Sierra South: One Hundred Back-Country Trips in California's Sierra*. Berkeley: Wilderness Press, 1980.

Wright, Judy. *Claremont: A Pictorial History*. Claremont, Calif.: Claremont Historic Resources Center, 1980.

Zauner, Phyllis. *Sacramento: A Mini-History*. Tahoe Paradise, Calif.: Zanel Publications, 1979.

Newspapers, newsletters, etc.

Anaheim Museum Press, vol. 3, no. 9.

California Parklands: The State Parks Magazine (Spring 1988–Fall 1990).

Fedco Reporter (1991–1993).

Glendale News Press (1991–1993).

League of Women Voters of Anaheim, California. "Know Your City," 1984.

Los Angeles Times.

Orange County Historical Commission. *Federation Newsletter*, vol. 8, no. 3 (1989).

Index

400

Gualala, 62
Gualala Point, 62
Guerra, Maria Teresa de
la, 198
Gulf of California, 335
Gum Shun (Gold Mountain), 40
Gunther's Island, 56
Guy B. Woodward
Museum, 299

Half Moon Bay, 187
Hallidie, Andrew S., 17,
173
Hamilton Air Force Base, 66
Hamilton, Sam, 96
Hampton, 239
Hanford, 129
Hanford, James, 129
Hanford, R. G., 166
Hangtown, 96
Hanover, Rita, 43
Hansen, George, 265, 268
Haraszthy, Agoston, 16, 70
Harding, President Warren
G., 176
Hardwick, 129
Harmony Borax Works,
351, 359
Harnischfeger, Tony, 233
Harriman, E. H., 231
Hart Department Store,
157
Hart Memorial Park, 131
Hart, Mills D., 130
Harte, Bret, 56, 57, 90
Hartnell, William Edward
Petty, 198, 219
Hartshorn Trust, 307
Harvey, Fred, 349
Harvey House, 346
Hastings, Judge Serranus
Clinton, 167
Hastings, Lansford W., 386
Hastings Cutoff, 386
Hatfield, Charles, 18, 227
Hayward, Alvinza, 95
Hayward fault, 154, 197
Heald, Franklin, 309
Hearst, Millicent, 208
Hearst, William Randolph,
164, 207
Hearst Castle, 207, 292,
307
Hearst Foundation, 201
Heber, Anthony H., 335

Hecker Pass, 161, 193
Hedges, 345
Hemet, 312
Heney, Francis J., 147
Herald-Express
(newspaper), 208
Heritage House, 323
Herrold, Charles, 156
Herrold, Sybil, 156
Hetch Hetchy Valley, 1, 147
Higuera, María Josefa, 153
Hildreth, Thaddeus, 89
Hill, James, 311
Hinde, George, 262
Hock Farm, 114
Hoffmann, Charles F., 370
Hollister, 192, 195, 196, 197
Hollister, William, 197
Hollywood, 19, 225
Hollywood Bowl, 239, 241
Holt, W. F., 341
Holtville, 336, 341
Honey Lake Valley, 33
honey industry, 159
Honeydew, 60
Hood, William, 132
Hooker Jim, 35
Hoopa Valley, 58
Hoopa Valley Indian
Reservation, 55
Hoover, Herbert, 163
Hoover Dam, 341
Hope, Bob, 241
Hopkins, Mark, 118, 119
Hornitos, 85
Horton, Alonzo E., 283
Horton Plaza Hotel, 291
Horton's Addition, 283
Hospital Cove, 181
Hot Creeks, 35
Hotel del Coronado, 294
House of Happy Walls, 71
Hovden Cannery, 203
Hudson's Bay Company, 64
Humboldt Bay, 51
Humboldt County, 55
Humboldt Redwood State
Park, 60
Humboldt State University,
56
Humbug Creek, 103
Hundley, Norris, Jr., 109
Hunter Liggett Military
Reservation, 200
Huntington and Hopkins
Hardware, 124

Huntington Beach, 261, 275
Huntington, Collis P., 17,
118, 130
Huntington, Henry, 17,
231, 275
Hupa, 51
Hyde Street Pier, 178
hydraulic mining, 80, 104,
112

Ide, William B., 11, 47
Imperial, 336
Imperial Canal, 341
Imperial County, 283, 341
Imperial Valley, 16, 315,
329, 335
Imperial Water Companies,
341
Ince, Thomas, 19
Independence, 365
Independent Order of Odd
Fellows, 381
Indian Bar, 81
Indian Canyons, 333
Indian Grinding Rock State
Historic Park, 94
Indian Hill, 317
Indian Island, 56
Indian Lore Monument,
346
Indian rebellion at Santa
Ines, 217
Indian Wells, 352
Indio, 334
Industrial Workers of the
World, 113
Infernal Caverns, 32
Inland Empire, 308
International Education
Board, 303
International Foursquare
Gospel Church, 241
International
Longshoremen's
Association, 21
Inyo County, 356, 365
Inyo Mountains, 356
Inyo National Forest, 365
Ipai Indians, 297, 299
Irvine Avenue, 262
Irvine Boulevard, 262
Irvine Ranch, 262, 270, 272
Irvine, James, 262, 272, 273
Isaac Todd, 193
Ishi, 112

About the Author

Ruth Pittman, a veteran writer, researcher, and journalist, grew especially interested in California history while writing four metro-guide books on Bakersfield, Palmdale, Lancaster, and Hawthorne. Prior to that she worked as managing editor for the weekly *Boron Enterprise* in southern California and as advertising manager for the *Hollister Evening Freelance* in northern California. In more recent times she has led seminars and workshops on nonfiction writing all over southern California and has addressed numerous writers' gatherings as a guest speaker. She is a member of the National Writers Club and the American Society of Journalists and Authors.

Although her interest in California history remains strong, in 1994 she moved to Milford, Ohio, to be near her daughter in Cincinnati. Always eager to learn more about her surroundings and to share with others how history plays a role in everyday events, she immediately undertook to write *Roadside History of Ohio*.